Innovation Economics, Engineering and Management Handbook 1

Innovation Economics, Engineering and Management Handbook 1

Main Themes

Edited by

Dimitri Uzunidis
Fedoua Kasmi
Laurent Adatto

iSTE

WILEY

First published 2021 in Great Britain and the United States by ISTE Ltd and John Wiley & Sons, Inc.

ISTE Ltd
27-37 St George's Road
London SW19 4EU
UK

www.iste.co.uk

John Wiley & Sons, Inc.
111 River Street
Hoboken, NJ 07030
USA

www.wiley.com

Library of Congress Control Number: 2021932077

British Library Cataloguing-in-Publication Data
A CIP record for this book is available from the British Library
ISBN 978-1-78630-456-8

MIX
Paper from responsible sources
FSC® C013604

Contents

Introduction

General Presentation

> *"Innovation is everything in the economy that is either not being done, or not being done again."*
> - Dimitri UZUNIDIS

Agility, flexibility and rapid adaptation to change are becoming the key words for growth and development in our society. Finding new ways of doing things and creating something new out of what already exists remains essential when facing crises (economic, social and environmental). The ability to innovate is therefore the main condition for maintaining the competitiveness and performance of companies, regions and territories in a changing context. Innovative activity has long been considered a driving force for "progress", but its impact on the transformation of socio-economic systems is greater when a succession of profound changes are introduced on broader scales (organizational, social, environmental, political, behavioral, etc.). Achieving these transformations requires the mobilization of resources, information, knowledge and networks of specific actors in order to guide innovation efforts to respond to more global challenges such as reducing environmental impacts, building resilience, and improving health, safety and people's well-being. Through what mechanisms and under what conditions does innovation enable more radical changes that progressively and sustainably reorient our modes of development? This is the overall question that this two-volume encyclopedic book answers, by mobilizing a set of interdisciplinary theories and concepts devoted to the study of innovation.

Innovation, in fact, consists of the design and marketing of new goods and technologies, the application of new working methods or the conquest of new markets. Today's knowledge-based economy implies that innovation is the result of greater interaction between businesses, universities, public institutions, consumers

---

Introduction written by Dimitri UZUNIDIS and Fedoua KASMI.

and citizens. Innovation networks create new knowledge and contribute to the diffusion of new socio-economic and technological models, through new modes of production and distribution. Innovation results from technological, organizational and commercial changes.

How do organizations design and manage innovation processes? What strategies and management tools do they apply for the concrete implementation of innovation processes? What role do innovation policies play in driving these processes? How does innovation impact competitiveness and performance? This involves analyzing companies' technological opportunities, organizational strategies and the integrated management of research and development, marketing and financial projects, etc.

This book is dedicated to the study of innovation. Theoretical reminders are associated with the discussion of concepts. Written in a didactic way, the reader will easily be able to situate the current debates around the need for technological and social innovation and the imperative of creating a climate conducive to the launch of large-scale innovation processes, because the current socio-economic stakes are as important as they are global. The book consists of two volumes. The first one is devoted to the presentation of the basic concepts. Its aim is to provide a broad and precise overview of the fundamental issues addressed by economists, historians and engineers specializing in innovation. The second volume contains a set of studies of current concepts and opens the debate on the evolution of the concept of innovation in the years to come.

The innovation process has a causal relationship with a problem – technological, economic, social – posed to the market economy and identified consciously or unconsciously by its actors (companies, entrepreneurs, consumers, etc.). Innovation is thus linked to the search for the optimal solution to the problem posed. This presupposes the use of knowledge and information from practice, experience and scientific activity. Innovation is itself a cumulative and historical process defined by six major characteristics highlighted in this book: (a) the impacts of innovation are difficult to predict; (b) the scale of diffusion of innovation is difficult to calculate; (c) innovative activities are asymmetric and staggered in time; (d) the time of learning, execution and diffusion plays a crucial role in the act of innovating; (e) the business environment conditions the time, scale, nature and impacts of innovation; and (f) innovations are interdependent.

In new approaches to innovation, the entrepreneur and the company are studied through their skills and their function of resource creation. Gradual or radical innovation thus becomes endogenous and is integrated into a complex process characterized by a lot of feedback and interactions in production and marketing networks: clusters, sectors and territorial or national innovation systems. The innovative organization is presented as a dynamic system composed of specific and diversified skills. Through the acquisition, combination and mobilization of these competencies, the innovator (entrepreneur or organization) can create technological resources and evolve the relationships it maintains with its environment. This explains the importance of design, application and development management in the implementation of an innovation process. An innovation system (sectoral, territorial or national) mobilizes a set of knowledge and skills resulting from learning processes and integrated into its memory. This knowledge must be enriched in order to be valorized by technological, organizational and commercial innovation. The survival of the system depends on its capacity to innovate, which enables it to face external aggressions, to transform and endure. External stimuli (competition, product substitutability, innovation policies, etc.) are generated by the economic context and affect the means of selection of entrepreneurs, companies and other public or private institutions. Selection procedures are shaped by the business climate: the nature of the product market, the availability of capital and labor, the pace of innovation, the effects of public policies, etc. They can, therefore, create alternatives to the mode of operation, management and production of a given firm (of an organization or, more generally, of a particular innovation system). It is thus clear that the effectiveness of innovation management is highly dependent on the internal capacity to seize external opportunities. The authors of this book repeatedly stress that innovation is part of the dynamic growth model based on uncertainty, risk and profit. The "flaws" that characterize an economic system are, however, important sources of opportunities for investment, production and the diffusion of innovations.

The richness of this book is the result of the reflections developed within the Research Network on Innovation (RNI) and carefully selected to take into account current and historical analyses, the relationship between technological mutations and social change, and the presentation and perspective of management, strategies and innovation policies. The authors are among the most eminent specialists of the Network, whose main objectives are the study of innovation processes in today's information and knowledge society, the analysis of the intensification of links between the worlds of research and business, and the examination of the modes of appropriation and management of innovation by companies from a global as well as local or sectoral perspective. The Network has more than 1,500 researchers in 36 countries specializing in the multidisciplinary study of innovation: economics, management, engineering, sociology, history, law, epistemology, anthropology and psychology of the innovator.

The guiding principle of the studies presented in the two volumes allows us to understand the systemic nature of innovations and to reflect on their potential for dissemination and application, to study how innovations question our categories of thought and challenge the traditional mapping of knowledge… to think about the meaning of innovation.

This book is the continuation of a set of books dedicated to the study of innovation in the "Innovation in Engineering and Technology" Set published by ISTE and Wiley:

– *Innovation Engines: Entrepreneurs and Enterprises in a Turbulent World* (2017).

– *Science, Technology and Innovation Culture* (2018);

– *Collective Innovation Processes: Principles and Practices* (2018);

Divided across two volumes, it is composed of four long chapters on epistemology, economics, management and engineering that trace the contours of the holistic conception of innovation and continues with 81 shorter chapters that present and discuss, according to the sensitivity of their authors, the key notions associated with the studies of innovation. Note that the last chapter of Volume 1 on "X-Innovation" is devoted to highlighting the complexity of the concept in order to open perspectives for future research on innovation.

We would like to thank our colleagues Sophie Boutillier (University of the Littoral Opal Coast), Thierry Burger-Helmchen (University of Strasbourg), Vanessa Casadella (University of Picardie), Joëlle Forest (National Institution of Applied Sciences, Lyon), Michaël Laviolette (University of Lyon), Laure Morel (University of Lorraine), Francesco Schiavone (Parthenope University of Naples), Bérangère Szostak (University of Lorraine) and Corinne Tanguy (AgroSup-Dijon) for their contribution to the conception of this book.

We express our gratitude to our colleague Laurent Adatto for his contribution to the finalization of this important project.

Finally, it is important to mention the contribution of our colleague Blandine Laperche, President of the Research Network on Innovation, to the realization of this project. We express our gratitude and best wishes to her.

1

Economy – Innovation Economics and the Dynamics of Interactions

1.1. Introduction

Capitalism cannot and will never be stationary, Schumpeter once said. In a process of "creative destruction", the technologies of the present become obsolete, while innovations emerge and feed new economic cycles. Economic history (Braudel 1979) clearly shows new combinations of production factors: products, production processes, sources of raw materials and semi-finished products, organization of work and markets. In short, innovations have fueled economic growth. Since the 18th century, a number of economists, such as A. Smith, J.B. Say, D. Ricardo, T.R. Malthus, K. Marx, etc., have provided the conceptual bases on which the economic theories of innovation have been developed.

Innovation economics was born in the wake of the industrial economy, in the aftermath of World War II. The neoclassical approach first considered technical progress as an exogenous phenomenon, a residue of the production function in models of economic growth (Solow 1956, 1957), and the economists were mainly interested in its effects on the economy, especially on employment. But the recognition of its role in economic growth and evolution, in the wake of the work of J.A. Schumpeter, led them to study in greater detail the mechanisms of its genesis, at the micro, meso and macro levels.

The evolutionary theories initiated by R. Nelson and S. Winter (1982) focus on the genesis of innovation within organizations. They see it as a systemic phenomenon,

Chapter written by Sophie BOUTILLIER, Vanessa CASADELLA and Blandine LAPERCHE.

resulting from the interaction between actors within organizations (giving rise, through learning, to organizational routines, a source of change and inertia), as well as resulting from fruitful interactions between organizations and institutions (analyses in terms of innovation systems at different scales: local, regional, national, sectoral). A country, like a company, is situated, in its development, on a technological trajectory that largely conditions its capacity to assimilate new technologies.

For their part, endogenous growth theories (Romer 1994) study technical progress as the result of private and public investment in the sphere of the economy, particularly in knowledge, infrastructure and human capital. Private investments are made by individuals motivated by profit. Economic growth is then determined by the behavior of economic agents and macroeconomic factors. The field of public policy then becomes paramount, and theoretical work calls for the replacement of big scientific and technical programs that marked the post-war period by more indirect modes of intervention. They are based, on the one hand, on the framework conditions for innovation (by strengthening the components and interactions within innovation systems), and, on the other hand, on incentives to invest and innovate, particularly for firms. This results in positive externalities, which can be seen as the basis for justifying government intervention.

This contribution looks back at some of the evolutions of the major issues of innovation economics. In the first part of the chapter, we attempt to define and develop the meaning of the word innovation, with a particular interest in the work of J.A. Schumpeter. Then, in the second part, we look at the difficult issue of measuring innovation, in particular because of its multifaceted nature. The identification of the key actors of innovation (entrepreneurs, large companies, as well as universities, so-called third places) is the subject of the third part. It reveals their diversity and the need for their interaction to ensure both the production and the diffusion of innovation. The fourth part of this chapter is devoted to the question of these systemic relationships and to the evolution of policies dedicated to strengthening them.

1.2. The definition of innovation and the primacy of J.A. Schumpeter's work

While the concept of innovation is omnipresent today and symbolizes the latest form of modernity, it is nevertheless very old and has not always been associated with progress and growth. According to B. Godin (2014), this concept dates back to Antiquity and was used by Greek philosophers in their political theories. This political meaning remained dominant until the 19th century. Until then, innovation evoked a "change in the established order" in politics and religion. Innovation was thus subject to prohibitions (e.g. by King Edward VI of England in 1548), and religious or political innovators (such as the French revolutionaries of the

18th century and the reformers of the 19th century) faced charges, imprisonment or worse. It was not until the 20th century that the meaning of the word "innovation" changed and became associated with progress, creativity and economic growth. From that century on, "there is no longer any doubt that innovation has become a virtue, not a vice" (Godin 2014, p. 33). Innovation then clearly became associated with technology.

J. A. Schumpeter is considered the first economist to use and construct an economic theory of innovation. Yet, before him, classical economists were largely interested in the changes brought about by technical progress, a term found in the writings of A. Smith, D. Ricardo, J.B. Say and K. Marx, to name but a few. At the beginning of the 19th century, Saint-Simonism (H. de Saint-Simon, 1760–1825) widely popularized the idea that technical progress (via "industrialism") was the necessary condition for improving the well-being of humanity. Moreover, as pointed out by B. Godin (2014), the sociologist G. Tarde (1843–1904) is often mentioned as the first to have devoted theoretical writings to innovation at the end of the 19th century. In *The Theory of Economic Development* (1981), Schumpeter considers that evolution results from the implementation of new combinations of means of production: the manufacture of a new good, the introduction of a new production method, the opening of a new outlet, the conquest of a new source of raw materials or of semi-finished products, the realization of a new organization, such as the creation of a monopoly situation. The importance of this definition and, more generally, of the Schumpeterian analysis of innovation can be explained by several arguments, which we present below:

First of all, this definition is important because, for the first time, it distinguished the various forms that innovation can take, without reducing it to technology. This variety is central to the contemporary definition proposed by the OECD in the *Oslo Manual* (OECD 2005), which distinguishes the product, process, new business method and new organizational method (OECD 2005). The most recent definition (OECD 2018) focuses on the enterprise and simplifies this definition by distinguishing product and business process innovation (OECD 2019). The notion of "business" processes refers to the traditional functions of the enterprise. It brings together process, and the organizational and marketing innovations defined in previous versions of the manual.

However, in the Schumpeterian analysis of long-term economic cycles (business cycles), the so-called Kondratieff cycles or waves, technology plays a major role. In *Business Cycles* (1939), Schumpeter in fact links the three Kondratieff movements from 1750 to 1940 and the three waves of fundamental innovations, which essentially concern technology: textiles, iron and steel, steam at the end of the 18th century, railways in the mid-19th century; and electricity, automobiles, chemicals at the beginning of the 20th century. The role of technological innovation was then crucial in explaining economic cycles (Uzunidis 1996). These innovations lead to an increase in supply capacity (increased demand for production goods, lower production costs, increased quantities of new products on offer) and a revival of demand (new consumption needs, credit). We also find this primacy of technology in the analysis in terms of the techno-economic paradigm proposed by C. Freeman and C. Perez (Freeman 2008; Perez 2010). This is defined as the set of most successful or profitable practices, in terms of the choice of inputs, methods and technologies, and organizational structures, business models and strategy. The paradigm forms a kind of common sense that facilitates technology diffusion.

In Schumpeter's analysis, innovation is therefore associated with evolution and change. This is the second essential point. It is new combinations that cause the hurricane of "creative destruction" (2008), continuously destroying old elements and creating new ones. Thus, the changes brought about by innovation also have negative consequences. Going back to the analysis of long waves, over-investment in the growth phase is punished by losses, layoffs and bankruptcies, creating a "vacuum cleaning" effect that can unleash the entrepreneurial spirit again.

This central role of technology, and therefore the potential for change it offers, is still a subject of debate today. For R. Gordon (2016), for example, information and communication technologies affect a smaller number of activities compared to the key technologies of the second industrial revolution (electricity, automobiles and aviation), which hampers the recovery of activity. Other authors, however, believe that current technologies bring many opportunities, jobs and growth, but that the economic and social system does not sufficiently promote their exploitation and diffusion. According to D. Archibugi (2016), for example, massive public investments, in science and technology, as well as in infrastructure, should be made to help companies develop marketable products and services. The current context of the strong financialization of the economy, which makes stock market investments more remunerative and more risky than productive ones, also plays a key role in the absence of the long-awaited recovery of a new long-term cycle (Uzunidis 2003). The orientation of science and technical progress towards short-term profitability objectives and the insufficient consideration of major challenges (such as climate change, population aging, pandemics) are also obstacles to the emergence of a new cycle.

Admittedly, and this is the third argument justifying the importance of Schumpeter's contribution, not all innovations have the same effects. New combinations may result from continuous and small-scale transformations – minor or incremental innovations – and their effect on economic structure is therefore limited. New combinations that appear discontinuously are similar to radical innovation. These are innovations that have a significant impact on the market and the activity of firms. This impact may concern the modification of market structure, the creation of new markets or the rendering of existing products obsolete. In reality, however, in Schumpeter's analysis of cycles, new combinations appear in clusters, thus combining major and minor innovations. Radical innovations initiated by entrepreneurs begin the cycle. The creation of profit opportunities attracts mimicking entrepreneurs who propose minor innovations and thus extend the growth trajectory at a slower pace until the cycle turns around. Researchers today refer to a third category, "disruptive" innovation (Christensen 1997, 2003). Its characteristic is to introduce new performance criteria by targeting different users. It is opposed to continuous innovation and favors new entrants who adopt a different business model. Thus, the notions of disruptive and radical innovation are close, but radical innovation is more associated with new technologies, stemming from scientific and technical progress, while disruptive innovation can also be associated with non-technological changes. Products may be simpler or offer new features that will appeal to new consumers.

The fourth argument is that innovation corresponds to an "economic function" embodied by certain individuals. For Schumpeter, these are the "entrepreneurs", whose function is to execute new combinations (Schumpeter 1981). We will return to its characteristics later. By emphasizing this function of commercialization or introduction into production, Schumpeter highlights the essential difference between novelty or invention (in the technical field) and innovation. If the invention is defined as a technical solution to a technical problem, innovation consists of productive and commercial exploitation, with the aim of making a profit. The characteristic that distinguishes a mere novelty from an innovation is that the latter involves implementation, whether it is a market launch for a product or service or a productive use for process, marketing or organizational innovations. The objectives of innovation are always economic: to increase sales, to open new markets, to reduce the costs of production, of internal organization, or of internal and external transactions, and to increase labor productivity.

However, the creative power of entrepreneurship and the arrival of the "troop" of entrepreneurs, at the heart of his analysis in *The Theory of Economic Development* (Schumpeter 1981), depersonalizes itself in the course of his work, showing Schumpeter's awareness of the nature and scope of the transformations that took place in the structure of capitalism since the beginning of the 20th century. The observation of the existence of what he calls "trustified capitalism" in *Business Cycles* (1939) will receive increasing attention to the point of becoming the essential cause of the historically determined character of capitalism in *Capitalism, Socialism and Democracy* (2008). The planning of technical progress by large companies and the development of private research laboratories with the aim of strengthening the potential for innovation mark the "bureaucratization" of technical progress. Technical progress is becoming depersonalized and automated (Schumpeter 2008). This bureaucratization, which is necessary to face competition, is a sign of the strengthening of monopolistic structures, which will, according to him, overwhelm both entrepreneurial spirit and capitalism (see section 13.4). Contemporary economists, especially neo-Schumpeterians, refer to this evolution by evoking a "Schumpeter Mark I" in which it is small firms that innovate, and a "Schumpeter Mark II" in which it is large firms that play this role (Malerba and Orsenigo 1995). In fact, as we show below, systemic relationships unite actors within innovation systems.

1.3. How can we measure innovation, in all its forms?

Innovation is a multifaceted phenomenon and is not easily confined to a typical indicator. This is also the case for the measurement of economic growth, which is expressed, despite the limitations of this indicator, by the evolution of gross domestic product (GDP). Research & Development (R&D) and patents have long been considered as key indicators of innovation, the former measuring the resources allocated to innovation and the latter evaluating the results of the activity.

The measurement of R&D is based on data collected from companies and research organizations, according to the codification carried out by the *Frascati Manual*, the seventh edition of which was published in 2015. Gross domestic expenditure on R&D (GERD) refers to the total expenditure on R&D performed by businesses, the government, higher education and the private non-profit sector at the heart of the economy. These expenditures include R&D financed from abroad, but exclude the financing of the R&D activities of foreign businesses. R&D intensity is established by the ratio of R&D expenditure to GDP for a country or the ratio of R&D expenditure to turnover for companies.

Global R&D capacity, as measured by public and private investment, has doubled since the mid-1990s. This increase in global R&D capacity is due in particular to the growth in corporate spending, which accounts for about 70% of total R&D spending. While the financial crises that marked the period (the crisis in emerging countries in the early 1990s, the crisis of new economy start-ups in 2001, the financial crisis of 2008) have led to cyclical reductions in R&D investment, companies are also relying on innovation to boost the growth of their activities. This can also be explained by the strong increase in spending as a percentage of GDP in emerging countries (China, Korea and Israel), compared with slower growth in the EU-28, the United States or Japan.

One of the major limitations of this indicator is that R&D appears to be mainly focused on science and technology and has difficulty capturing the expenditure incurred to bring about other forms of innovation, whether organizational or commercial. The services that make up an important part of the new solutions offered by companies are better evaluated by marketing expenses, which are not included in the R&D measurement. As a result, the expenditures made by small firms (which rarely employ researchers) to innovate organizationally or commercially are poorly understood and, therefore, not considered as being very innovative.

A patent is an industrial property title granted to an inventor for a period of 20 years, often used as an indicator of results and innovation performance. It has the advantage of being an available and reliable indicator, whose databases are public. Worldwide patent registration statistics show a strong growth in patent registrations from the 1970s onwards. Innovators around the world filed some 3.3 million patent applications in 2018, an increase of 5.2% for the ninth consecutive year of growth. At that time, approximately 14 million patents were in force worldwide. The largest numbers of patents in force were registered in the United States (3.1 million), China (2.4 million) and Japan (2.1 million) (WIPO 2019).

However, as an indicator of innovation, the patent also suffers from many limitations. On the one hand, it only measures registered "inventions", thus leaving aside all other possible forms of innovation. On the other hand, many inventions are not patented, especially if they do not meet the criteria of novelty, inventive step and industrial application. An invention that is useful, but not innovative (so if it is already part of the state of the art, in other words everything that has been made public at the filing date), will not normally be able to pass the stage of the research report carried out by the industrial property institute. A registered patent does not always result in an innovation, i.e. a new product launched on the market or a new process integrated into the production process. Many patented inventions remain unexploited, often for strategic reasons. For example, some patents are intended to deceive competitors about the technological trajectories followed. Sleeping patents are also very common. In this case, they are not exploited because the profit prospects are lower than the costs of bringing them to market. The company holding the patent may not have the resources necessary to exploit the invention or may prefer to wait for the previous invention to become fully profitable before launching a new one (in this case, one can speak of "technological Malthusianism").

However, criticisms have been made about the quality of patents, particularly those granted in the United States in the years 1990–2000, given the favorable attitude of this country towards inventors. In reality, the criteria for patentability have, in many cases, been little respected, leading to the multiplication of low-quality patents and numerous challenges and lawsuits. The statistics would thus be distorted by the multiplication of these "rotten" patents. Another difficulty related to the measurement of patents lies in the fact that they are national titles valid in the countries where protection has been claimed (apart from the unitary patent in Europe, the use of which still depends on the ratification of certain agreements between signatory countries). In order to avoid counting them several times, statisticians have defined an indicator called a "patent family" which designates a set of patents filed in several countries to protect the same invention. We distinguish, for example, triadic "patent families", which are a set of patents filed with three of the main offices, namely the European Patent Office (EPO), the Japanese Patent Office (JPO) and the United States Patent and Trademark Office (USPTO).

Innovation indicators are not limited to these two; they also include the number of researchers, scientific publications, amounts devoted to financing innovative firms (venture capital), registrations of other intellectual property titles (trademarks, designs), revenue generated by innovative firms, diffusion of key technologies, etc. A better understanding of the innovation process leads not to limiting research to traditional indicators but to refining the evaluation of innovation efforts and performance by using other indicators. For example, at the firm level, statisticians (see OECD 2019) seek to better measure intangible investments that are not R&D (such as software and databases), or the interactions that firms develop with other firms or institutions. At the country level, indicator scoreboard and summary indicators are being developed to quantify innovation.

In Europe, the European Union Innovation Scoreboard (created in 2001) provides a synthetic indicator for ranking countries according to their innovation performance. Four categories of countries are defined: modest innovators, moderate innovators, notable innovators and innovation champions. The results for 2019 were as follows.

Sweden, Finland, Denmark and the Netherlands appeared to be the leaders in innovation, positioning themselves well above the European average. Notable innovators included the following countries: Luxembourg, Belgium, the United Kingdom, Germany, Austria, Ireland, France and Estonia. Their results were slightly above (or close to) the European average. The performance of moderate innovators was between 50% and 90% of the European average. This category included many countries in Eastern and Southern Europe, such as Portugal, Czech Republic, Slovenia, Cyprus, Malta, Italy, Spain, Greece, Lithuania, Slovakia, Hungary, Latvia, Poland and Croatia. Finally, the modest innovators, Romania and Bulgaria, had a performance below 50% of the European average.

This synthetic indicator – the Summary Innovation Index – is based on four broad categories of indicators and 10 dimensions of innovation. The "framework conditions" take into account the essential factors of innovation performance, and this category includes human resources, the attractiveness of the research system and the environment conducive to innovation. "Investments" measures public and private investment in innovation. "Innovation activities" seeks to measure the efforts made by firms, distinguishing between the characteristics of innovators, networks and intellectual assets. Finally, the "Impacts" category considers impacts on employment and sales. In total, the composite indicator is constructed from 27 indicators.

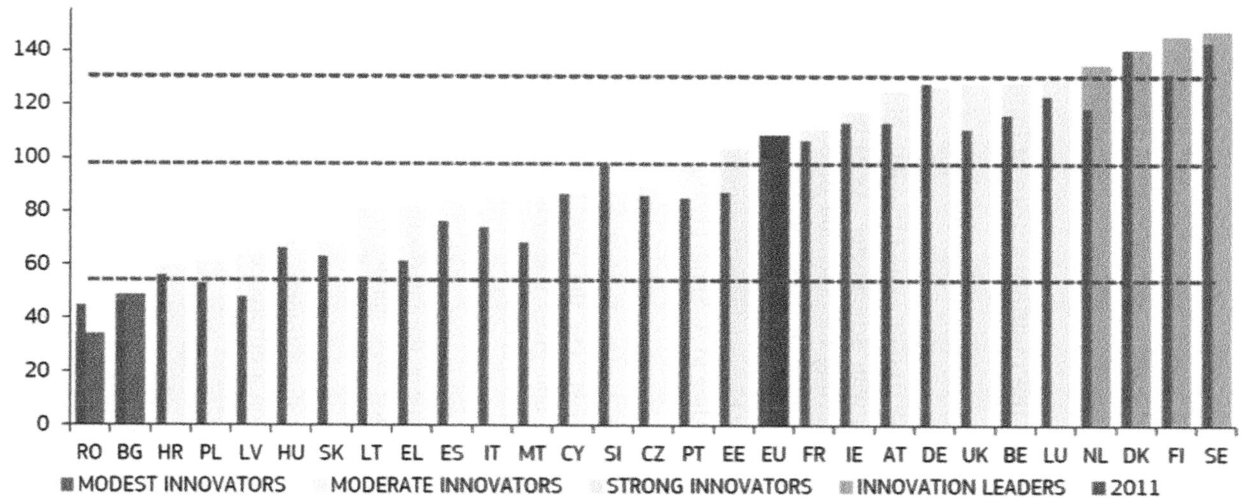

Colored columns show Member States' performance in 2018, using the most recent data for 27 indicators, relative to that of the EU in 2011. Gray columns show Member States' performance in 2011 relative to that of the EU in 2011. For all years, the same measurement methodology has been used. The dashed lines show the threshold values between the performances groups in 2018, comparing Member States' performance in 2018 relative to that of the EU in 2018.

Figure 1.1. *Member countries' innovation performance (source: European Innovation Scoreboard 2019). For a color version of this figure, see www.iste.co.uk/uzunidis/innovation1.zip*

Such an indicator makes it possible to monitor the performance of the European Union and of each country over time, as well as serves as a guide for the definition of public policies adapted to the specific problems encountered in each country. One notable result is that the countries that champion innovation show similar performance in each dimension of innovation measured. This leads to a view that the overall strength of the national innovation system plays a key role in innovation performance (see section 1.5).

1.4. From the entrepreneur to the multiple actors of innovation

While Schumpeter was the first economist to develop an innovation theory, he also designated the entrepreneur as the economic agent who achieves "new combinations of production factors" (Boutillier and Uzunidis 2016). Entrepreneurial economics certainly did not begin with Schumpeter. As early as the 18th century, the entrepreneur was already attracting the attention of economists, but more to emphasize their ability to take commercial risks (the merchant) than to design and manufacture new products (the industrialist) (Cantillon 1755). The figure of the "projector" was generally devalued because his extravagant projects ran the risk of a general crisis, harmful to all, according to A. Smith (1759, 1776).

As pointed out above, technical progress did not appear in the 18th century. It is a permanent feature of human societies. During the 18th century, however, a twofold evolution can be observed. On the one hand, technical progress is intrinsically linked to the market and gives rise either to the production of new consumer goods intended for the final consumer or to the production of machines for companies that automate production processes. On the other hand, there is a separation between science and technology. This evolution is evident in Say's (1803) definition of the entrepreneur as the intermediary between the scientist who produces knowledge and the worker who applies it to industry. The entrepreneur thus creates markets, wealth and jobs.

Whereas until the 18th century, the entrepreneur was essentially a merchant and, in this sense, could be dependent on a difference between sale and purchase prices (Landes *et al.* 2010). In the 19th century, the entrepreneur became an industrialist. Until this period, the field of technology was rather that of the craftsman (Zilsel 1942). This evolution did not take place without resistance nor social and political conflicts; machines were then qualified as job killers (Jarrige 2009). However, while many craftsmen disappeared, caught up in the big businesses that reduced them to the precarious condition of factory workers, others became entrepreneurs and created industrial empires, via the development of new technologies (electricity, mechanics, automobiles, telecommunications, aviation, etc.) (Perrin 2017).

The managerial company model (separation between ownership and management of capital) became a norm by the end of the 19th century, mainly in the United States and then in Western Europe. Schumpeter (2008), an attentive reader of Marx, detected in this evolution a major change in capitalism, which was becoming bureaucratized (see section 13.2). This observed disappearance of the entrepreneur marks the continuation of a process of division of labor between the manager (who manages the firm) and the shareholder (who finances it through the shares they buy). The entrepreneur, the driving force of the first Industrial Revolution, disappears to the benefit of a new institution, the managerial company.

In the years following the end of World War II, during the period of reconstruction, the economies of industrialized countries underwent an unprecedented transformation (Dockès 2020), taking advantage of new technologies and heavy investments developed during the war (automobiles, aviation, chemicals, nuclear, digital, IT, etc.). The entrepreneur was then seen as an endangered species, with the future belonging to the "technostructure" (Galbraith 1967) thanks to the "visible hand of managers" (Chandler 1977). This period of strong growth was based on the partnership between the large company and the labor society. The State then played a central role in financing scientific research and planning the economy, contributing to the development of managerial firms in highly capital-intensive sectors (steel, telecommunications, transport, energy, petrochemicals, etc.) (see section 13.5). The time had come for mass production and consumption. Gradually, this model was seized, leading to the "great turnaround" of the 1970s (Dockès 2020).

Big corporations entered a crisis period; the markets created by the innovations of the post-World War II period were saturated. Unemployment was rising sharply in the industrial countries. Large companies no longer generated enough jobs, and even drastically reduced their workforce in order to reduce their costs. From the end of the 1970s onwards, the creation of companies appeared as a means of public policy to reduce unemployment whatever the job seeker's profile (women, young people, elderly people, immigrants, non-qualified people, etc.). The creation of a company then became a kind of injunction to designate this process of socio-economic transformation. Bringing the Schumpeterian entrepreneurial theory up to date, the injunction is not only about job creation (and first and foremost that of the entrepreneur), but also about innovation, which is more than ever necessary to strengthen the competitiveness of economies. The new entrepreneur must be an innovator like their peers and is an integral part of the national innovation system in a knowledge-based economy (see section 1.4). The entrepreneurial society (Audretsch 2007) gradually began taking over from the labor society.

The entrepreneur, who had been sidelined by the managerial company, then made a big comeback by developing new innovations. They act in the sense in which Say understood it, i.e. as an intermediary between the scientist and the worker. The scientist was no longer isolated in an obscure laboratory, as was imagined in the 18th and 19th centuries, but was part of the great scientific laboratories financed by States, often by the army (Isaacson 2015). Young entrepreneurs, poorly endowed with capital, but very imaginative and with a keen sense of business, created industrial empires, giving rise, for example, to what we now refer to as GAFAM (Google, Apple, Facebook, Amazon, Microsoft). The large firm did not disappear, therefore, but took on a new form, favoring subcontracting and cooperative relationships via open innovation (Chesbrough 2003), rather than the model of vertical integration which the managerial firm of the 1950s–1970s was based on, inspired by the legacy of the first Industrial Revolution. The firm has taken the form of a network firm, combining classical integration with multiple cooperative relationships with universities, other competing firms (coopetition), complementary firms (customers and suppliers), start-ups, communities and crowdsourcing (Laperche and Uzunidis 2019). The constitution and development of its knowledge capital (i.e. all the information and knowledge produced, accumulated and systematized by the company with the aim of innovating) is carried out collectively (Laperche 2017). The principle of open innovation offers innovative entrepreneurs, who have become start-uppers, the opportunity to develop cooperative relationships with large companies, as well as with research centers and universities (Audretsch and Link 2017), as put forward with the concept of the "triple helix" (Etzkowitz 2003).

How companies manage their innovation process is a key theme in innovation management. The work of Nonaka and his co-authors, for example, focuses on the genesis and circulation of knowledge in the organization. This is the SECI (socialization, externalization, combination, internalization) model (Nonaka and Takeushi 1995), where innovation in the organization emerges from the interaction between explicit and tacit knowledge, associated with a circulation of knowledge from the individual to the inter-organizational level. Similarly, the C-K theory (which stands for concept and knowledge) focuses on issues of creativity within design and provides further developments on the genesis of knowledge within organizations (Hatchuel and Weil 2009; Le Masson and Macmahon 2016).

This work on the production and dissemination of knowledge within organizations is part of resource theory. The authors place particular emphasis on the role of competencies (especially key competencies (Prahalad and Hamel 1990)) and capabilities in explaining the competitive advantage of firms. Capabilities develop new specific assets gathered in organizational routines, which are called "dynamic capabilities" by Teece *et al.* (1997). They refer to the "firm's ability to integrate, build and reconfigure internal and external competencies to respond quickly to changes in the environment". Among these dynamic capacities, the absorption capacity is central to the analysis of firms' knowledge capital formation. Absorptive capacity was first defined by Cohen and Levinthal (1990) as the firm's ability to recognize the value of new information, transform it into knowledge, assimilate it and apply it for business purposes. The firm is then open to its environment, and the management of multiple cooperative relationships is considered a "managerial innovation" (Mignon *et al.* 2020).

Universities have also transformed themselves to become entrepreneurial and play a more active role in innovation. The economic context, marked by a decline in public funding for research, is contributing to a radical metamorphosis in the work of the researcher who also becomes an entrepreneur, by creating a spin-off, or by filing patents, etc., responding to the injunctions of all up-and-coming entrepreneurs (Lanciano-Morandat 2019). It is also in universities, primarily in the United States, that major transformations are taking place. In the laboratories of the Massachusetts Institute of Technology (MIT), hackers and makers are appearing who will also contribute to transforming production methods, with an entrepreneurial and creative approach.

The first hackers formed a closed club: they are distinguished by their technical prowess. Unlike the Fordist company, which was then dominant, they worked in a collaborative and horizontal way. Each could take the ideas of the other and improve them (Capdevila 2015). This principle was also developed with fablabs at the end of the 1990s, again at MIT (Morel and Le Roux 2016). The objective is to be able to "create anything and everything". The experiment is bearing fruit. Students do not hesitate to hijack the machines to satisfy their needs. The principle of "Do It Yourself" then takes on its full meaning, even if some people date it back to the end of the 18th century (Berrebi-Hoffmann *et al.* 2018). The word "hacker" appeared in the mid-2000s (Anderson 2012), to designate a reality that had, in fact, emerged in the United States in the 1960s and 1970s. The phenomenon of hackerspaces became global in the 1980s, and was not limited to developed countries.

In this same trajectory, another phenomenon appeared at the beginning of the 2000s in California, participating in the development of the entrepreneurial society, that of coworking, which is also referred to as the "third place" (Oldenburg 1989). Coworking or collaborative workspace has its origins both in the recent evolution of digital technologies (Lallement 2015; Berrebi-Hoffman *et al.* 2018) and in the desire of many employees to escape the interventionism of the managerial enterprise with its oppressive rules. The aim is to help "coworkers" develop their creativity and imagination in the absence of any authoritative or hierarchical relationships. Although these coworking spaces bring together a wide variety of people in different situations, they generally aim to offer good working conditions in terms of autonomy of organization, and even conviviality. Coworkers are not subject to working hours. They are not salaried employees but entrepreneurs (or even self-employed), masters of their working hours, but rarely of their income, as many of them work under precarious conditions (Hill 2015). The entrepreneur is plural, competition is severe: many are called, but few are chosen (Aldrich 2011).

The genesis of innovation is thus both a multiple phenomenon and the result of the involvement of a growing number of organizations and economic agents, and not only the expression of a heroic entrepreneur. The recognition of this collective nature of innovation has a strong impact on innovation policies, which increasingly target the functioning of innovation systems at different scales.

1.5. Innovation policies and the innovation system

The term "innovation policy" is relatively new. Initiated in the 1960s by the SPRU (Science Policy Research Unit), it was quickly reappropriated by international organizations in the 1990s (Fagerberg *et al.* 2011). This evolution is part of a process of major economic transformations that occurred after the end of World War II and accompanied the development of the managerial enterprise. It is linked to the understanding of the innovation phenomena. Indeed, if science policies have been oriented towards the creation of academic knowledge, the training of scientists and fundamental research, technology policies are more related to the commercialization or non-academic valorization of scientific knowledge. In this context, innovation policies have often been reduced to activities related to R&D and scientific activity. However, public innovation management policy is compartmentalized into three broad categories (Sharif 2006):

– Science policy, inherent in the promotion and production of scientific knowledge, representing the allocation of resources between different scientific activities.

– Technology policy, which is based more on technologies used, developed and which are strategic within the economy.

– Finally, innovation policy, which is similar to innovation processes as a whole, based not only on the content of scientific and technical innovations but also on the institutional structure of the economy.

The role of the State in the management of an innovation policy is indeed to design institutional arrangements that allow support for innovation activities and the application of basic research. However, this must be done without compromising the selection of projects or the evaluation of research work (Metcalfe 1994). In the end, innovation policies are differentiated according to the very conceptualization of innovation: broad or narrow (Edquist 2004). It is interpreted as "narrow" when it is strictly related to science and technology and as "broad" when it encompasses all forms of ancillary policies (educational, social) that indirectly affect innovation processes.

Public institutions and organizations play a key role in generating and promoting innovation. In particular, they strengthen the competitive environment for firms on the international market (Dogson 2009). The development of an innovation policy involves taking into account the evolutionary, dynamic and interactive nature of innovation processes (Leitner *et al.* 2010). This nature, characterized by the diversity of interactions and collaborations and their intensity, is primarily a result of the conditions of policy definition, but above all of their implementation and evaluation. Secondly, it is a result of the social coordination of various institutions.

The "broad" definition of innovation policy is necessary to better integrate innovation dynamics. Beyond the conception of innovation by its purely technological appearance, the set of policy instruments that influences innovation in one way or another is considered. An innovation policy requires the capacity to coordinate policy choices between different territorial scales (the relative importance of these scales is contingent on the characteristics of economies and their political regimes) in specific areas or sectors. The objective of an innovation policy is to facilitate interactions between technology users, creating different learning situations that massify the mechanisms for imitating and disseminating technologies. The tool for implementing these innovation policies is the innovation system. Concept, approach, work, notion, instrument, object; the innovation system has been discussed both in academic and institutional circles since the late 1980s and as an economic policy instrument for comparing national technological performances (OECD 2002). But whatever the debates in this case, marking the flexibility of the concept according to the empirical field visited, the authors unanimously agree on the theoretical footprints on which the system is based. These are the evolutionary and institutionalist theories, the latter two references being complementary, within an economy based on understanding, learning and knowledge (Freeman 1988; Lundvall 1992; Nelson 1993). Evolutionary theory is based on the reasoning that innovation processes are dynamic, sequential, cumulative and irreversible (Dosi *et al.* 1988). Therefore, an innovation system never reaches an optimal stage and equilibrium, because learning processes are subject to continuous change, are undetermined and dependent on developmental pathways. Institutionalist theory, inspired by North (1990), shows the importance of institutions as benchmarks or guides for the functioning of these systems. The institutional structure of the economy creates a model of constraints and incentives that shape and channel the behavior of actors. In other words, institutions are the rules of the game of an innovation system.

As with public policy, innovation in the innovation system approach has been rapidly segmented, first of all by its geographical dimension. Indeed, the approach to innovation systems is broad and there are alternative frameworks (Gregersen and Johnson 1997):

– sectoral systems relating to a specific sector or technology (Malerba 2004);

– localized systems, built on spatial proximity and identifiable on several geographical levels, on a local, regional, national or global scale (Lundvall 1992).

For example, the local approach has been adopted in order to identify and understand the different forms of territorialized productive organizations (Courlet 2001). The national approach is based more on socio-economic, cultural and historical elements than the local approach (Chaminade *et al.* 2018). The processes of creating, disseminating and/or absorbing knowledge from locally produced or imported technologies depend on the institutions, organizations and actors that influence the learning capacity. These actors create a permanent climate of evaluation and criticism of existing processes, making the territory in which they operate more effective. This is the challenge of innovation ecosystems, including processes of learning and routines (Adner 2006; Boutillier *et al.* 2016; Laperche *et al.* 2019). These innovation platforms and ecosystems represent a lever for the development of new markets and a new semantic grid of innovation networks.

Usually, it is the field of empirical analysis that defines the boundaries of the system at the conceptual level. In other words, the innovation system is given a specific name appropriate to the objective and context analyzed (Edquist 1997). The national framework is a natural delimitation of innovation systems, although their international dimension has been recognized for many years (Lundvall 1988) and a number of works in innovation economics analyze the way national actors use and absorb knowledge from outside (Casadella and Uzunidis 2017). The segmentation of the approach also aims at conceptualizing innovation in a broad and a narrow approach (Mytelka and Smith 2001). The main strength of a "narrow" national innovation system (NIS) lies in the analysis of the impact of national technology policies on the innovative behavior of firms. This NIS includes only those organizations and institutions necessary for research and exploration activities, such as R&D departments, technological institutes and universities. The broad definition includes, by indexing the components of the narrow NIS, all the political, social, economic and cultural institutions affecting learning, research and exploration activities: the financial system, monetary policies, the internal organization of private firms, the primary and secondary education system, the labor market, etc. At a more microeconomic level, the strength of the NIS lies more in the efficiency of business networks (large and small), in the various interactive learning practices within purchasing, production and sales activities, than in actual R&D activities.

Today, NISs are maintaining increasingly complex collaborative relationships across national boundaries and are more adaptive and scalable (Binz and Truffer 2017). Similarly, they are more inclusive systems where frugal innovation and local knowledge play a key role. The effect of inclusiveness at the heart of NIS is an emerging field of research that comes into its full legitimacy with an understanding of bottom-up dynamics, particularly in developing or transition countries (Chaminade *et al.* 2018).

Choosing the best tools to implement innovation policies requires an understanding of innovation financing. This financing is problematic, complex and must be understood as the right balance between relevant levers and regulated, controlled spending. Governments therefore have a role to play in proposing coherent and appropriate tools.

Many tools have been implemented to attract innovators to the desired territories. For example, in France, two main types of support have been developed: direct support, in the form of subsidies or national programs, and indirect support, in the form of incentives (particularly tax incentives). In the 1990s, the R&D subsidy policy was oriented towards "Major Programs" dominated by large companies, towards research sectors such as aeronautics, aerospace, nuclear energy and NICTs, as well as, in a more original way, towards support for R&D networks using national or international tools. Gradually, indirect R&D support has taken precedence over direct intervention. They include all those that do not give rise to direct payments to firms from public bodies, but which modify their environment and investment opportunities (Lhuillery *et al.* 2003). In France, the *Crédit d'impôt recherche* (CIR – Research Tax Credit) is the major innovation support mechanism (Liu 2013). It is an incentive measure allowing a tax reduction calculated on the basis of R&D expenses incurred by companies. With its last major reform, in 2008, this measure, which is very popular with businesses, became the main tax expenditure of the Ministry of Higher Education, Research and Innovation with a cost of 6.2 billion euros for 2019 (Sénat 2019).

The French system seems to be a judicious one (France Stratégie 2016) and other countries have also followed this path. Canada, for example, proposes a fairly similar program through the SR&ED (Scientific Research and Experimental Development) tax credit. It is a federal tax incentive program designed to encourage Canadian companies to carry out R&D in this country. It is the same with the United Kingdom and its "R&D tax relief". Spain also uses similar designations: its R&D and Innovation Tax Credit, with the parallel implementation of national and international subsidies for R&D, reductions in social security contributions for R&D personnel or patent boxes for reduced costs related to intellectual property, also applied in the United Kingdom.

Overall, tax credit is strictly controlled within the European Union and there is a risk of a race for tax optimization, particularly with regard to the transfer of intellectual property rights in low-tax countries (OECD 2010). But in the end, it is still difficult to assess the effectiveness of this support, which may, depending on the case, result in total substitution or significant knock-on effects, by way of a whole range of intermediate effects. Public funding is necessary. However, care must be taken with regard to the institutional and regulatory details of the allocation of this support (Kessler 2008). To this end, the interest is not in enabling firms to reach out to the state for tax credits or subsidies, but rather in creating an overall environment that is conducive to innovation through the development of innovative firms, in the current context of the entrepreneurial society.

1.6. Conclusion

The recognition of the role played by innovation in economic growth has led to the proliferation of academic work and public policy tools on how to stimulate, generate, disseminate and measure innovation at the level of individuals (entrepreneurs, employees, managers, researchers, workers) and of collectives, as well as of the organizations and institutions that support them. Initially considered as the engine of innovation, the role of the entrepreneur was reduced during the years of strong growth, to the benefit of large companies, and has come back to the forefront since the end of the 20th century, but taking place in the meanders of the network company. Innovation systems are evolving. They are being configured and revisited from the structuring of an international scale to a more local scale. They are also sustainable, inclusive and able to play an active role in economic development. Innovation is, by definition, where it is not expected, in new paths and trajectories.

Economists have very quickly turned their attention to the double face of innovation, the one that initiates, generates and the one – the same one – that destroys. In both cases, the management of innovation and progress seemed to be in the hands of our societies, holding real power but marked by flagrant asymmetries. Controlling progress for (endogenous) growth requires substantial public investment to solidify the education, transport and health infrastructures that will be the basis of future growth. Yet public investment is often the first to be reduced as a result of austerity policies. The fragility of industrial society sometimes shatters, and the efforts made to control evolution and transform the pitfalls into progress seem to be reduced to nothing. Perhaps then, it is the definition of progress that is an issue, based for decades less on improving the living conditions of the greatest number of people than on the quest for short-term profit. Innovation, but to what end? Economists' thinking should certainly be oriented towards this path, to better master the future.

1.7. References

Adner, R. (2006). Match your innovation strategy to your innovation ecosystem. *Harvard Business Review*, 84(4), 98.

Aldrich, H. (2011). *An Evolutionary Approach to Entrepreneurship*. E. Elgar, Cheltenham.

Anderson, C. (2012). *Makers. The New Industrial Revolution*. Randoms House Business, New York.

Archibugi, D. (2016). "Blade runner economics: Will innovation lead the economic recovery?" *Research Policy*, 46, 535–543.

Audretsch, D. (2007). *The Entrepreneurial Society*. E. Elgar, Cheltenham.

Audretsch, D. and Link, A. (2017). *Universities and the Entrepreneurial Ecosystem*. E. Elgar, Cheltenham.

Berrebi-Hoffmann, I., Bureau, M.-C., Lallement, M. (2018). *Makers. Enquête sur les laboratoires du changement social*. Le Seuil, Paris.

Binz, C. and Truffer, B. (2017). Global innovation systems – A conceptual framework for innovation dynamics in transnational contexts. *Research Policy*, 46, 1284–1298.

Boutillier, S. and Uzunidis, D. (2016). *The Entrepreneur: The Economic Function of Free Enterprise*. ISTE Ltd, London and John Wiley & Sons, New York.

Boutillier, S., Carré, D., Levratto, N. (2016). *Entrepreneurial Ecosystems*. ISTE Ltd, London and John Wiley & Sons, New York.

Braudel, F. (1979). *Civilisation matérielle, économie et capitalisme, XVe–XVIIIe*. Armand Colin, Paris.

Capdevila, I. (2015). Les différentes approches entrepreneuriales dans les espaces ouverts d'innovation. *Innovations, revue d'économie et de management de l'innovation*, 48, 87–105.

Casadella, V., Liu, Z., Uzunidis, D. (2015). *Innovation Capabilities and Economic Development in Open Economies*. ISTE Ltd, London and John Wiley & Sons, New York.

Chaminade, C., Lundvall, B.A., Haneef, S. (2018). *Advanced Introduction to National Innovation Systems*. E. Elgar, Cheltenham.

Chandler, A. (1977). *The Visible Hand. The Managerial Revolution in American Business*. Harvard Business Press, Brighton, MA.

Courlet, C. (2001). *Territoire et régions, les grands oubliés du développement économique*. L'Harmattan, Paris.

Cohen, W.M. and Levinthal, D.A. (1990). Absorptive capacity: A new perspective on learning and innovation. *Administrative Science Quarterly*, 35(1), 128–152.

Chesbrough, H. (2003). *Open Innovation. The New Imperative for Creating and Profiting from Technology*. Harvard Business Press, Brighton, MA.

Christensen, C.M. (1997). *The Innovator's Dilemma: When New Technologies Cause Great Firms to Fail*. Harvard Business School Press, Brighton, MA.

Christensen, C.M. (2003). *The Innovator's Solution: Creating and Sustaining Successful Growth*. Harvard Business School Press, Brighton, MA.

Dockès, P. (2020). *Le capitalisme et ses rythmes, quatre siècles en perspective*. Classiques Garnier, Paris.

Dogson, M. (2009). Asia's national innovation systems: Institutional adaptability and rigidity in the face of global innovation challenges. *Asia Pacific Journal of Management*, 26(3), 589–609.

Dosi, G., Freeman, C., Nelson, R.R., Silverberg, G., Soete, L. (1988). *Technical Change and Economic Theory*. Pinter, London.

Edquist, C. (1997). *Systems of Innovation, Technologies, Institutions and Organizations*. Pinter, London.

Edquist, C. (2004). Reflections on the systems of innovation approach. *Science and Public Policy*, 31(6), 485–489.

Etzkowitz, H. (2003). Innovation in innovation: The triple helix of university-industry-government relations. *Social Science Information*, 42, 293–337.

European Commission (2016). *European Innovation Scoreboard*.

Fagerberg, J., Fosaas, M., Bell, M., Martin, B.R. (2011). Christopher freeman: Social science entrepreneur. *Research Policy*, 40, 897–916.

Freeman, C. (1988). Japan: A new national system of innovation? In *Technical Change and Economic*, Dosi, G., Freeman, C., Nelson, R.R., Silverberg, G., Soete, L. (eds). Pinter, London.

Freeman, C. (2008). *Systems of Innovation: Selected Essays in Evolutionary Economics*. E. Elgar, Cheltenham.

Galbraith, J.K. (1967). *The New Industrial State*. Princeton University Press, Princeton.

Godin, B. (2014). Une histoire intellectuelle de l'innovation. De l'interdit politique à la politique publique. In *Principes d'économie de l'innovation, Business and Innovation*, Boutillier, S., Forest, J., Gallaud, D., Laperche, B., Tanguy, C., Temri, L. (eds). Peter Lang, Brussels.

Gordon, R.J. (2016). *The Rise and Fall of American Growth, the US Standard of Living Since the Civil War*. Princeton University Press, Princeton.

Gregersen, B. and Johnson, B. (1997). Learning economies, innovation systems and European integration. *Regional Studies*, 31, 5.

Hatchuel, A. and Weil, B. (2009). C-K design theory: An advanced formulation. *Research in Engineering Design*, 19(4), 181–192.

Hill, S. (2015). *Raw Deal: How the "Uber Economy" and Runaway Capitalism are Screwing American Workers*. ST Martin's Press, New York.

Isaacson, W. (2014). *The Innovators, How a Group of Hackers, Geniuses and Geeks Created the Digital Revolution*. Simon & Schuster, New York.

Jarrige, F. (2009). *Au temps des "tueuses de bras" : les bris de machines à l'aube de l'ère industrielle (1780–1860)*. PUR, Rennes.

Kessler, M. (2008). Comment financer l'innovation ? *Regards croisés sur l'économie*, 3(1), 173–176.

Lallement, M. (2015). *L'âge du faire*. Le Seuil, Paris.

Lanciano-Morandat, C. (2019). *Le travail de la recherche. Production de savoirs et pratiques scientifiques et techniques*. CNRS Editions, Paris.

Landes, D.S., Mokyr, J., Baumol, W. (2010). *The Invention of Enterprise*. Princeton University Press, Princeton.

Laperche, B. (2017). *Enterprise Knowledge Capital*. ISTE Ltd, London and John Wiley & Sons, New York.

Laperche, B. and Uzunidis, D. (2019). The knowledge capital of the network firm: Socialization versus business appropriation of scientific work. In *The Future of Education and Labor*, Blast, G., Carayannis, E., Campbell, D.J. (eds). Springer, Cham.

Laperche, B., Lima, E., Seuillet, E., Trousse, B. (2019). *Ecosystèmes d'innovation. Regards croisés des acteurs clés*. L'esprit économique, L'Harmattan, Paris.

Le Masson, P. and McMahon, C. (2016). Armand Hatchuel et Benoit Weil: la théorie C-K, un fondement formel aux théories de l'innovation. *Les grands auteurs du management de l'innovation et de la créativité*. EMS Editions Management et Société, Paris.

Leitner, A., Wehrmeyer, W., France, C. (2010). The impact of regulation and policy on radical eco-innovation. The need for a new understanding. *Management Research Review*, 33(11), 1022–1041.

Lhuillery, S., Marino, M., Parrotta, P. (2014). Evaluation de l'impact des aides directes et indirectes à la R&D en France. Report, French Ministry of Higher Education and Research, Paris.

Liu, Z. (2013). The research tax credit in the policy mix for innovation: The French case, *Journal of Innovation Economics & Management*, 12(2), 199–223.

Lundvall, B.A. (1988). Innovation as an interactive process: Form user-producer interaction to the national system of innovation. In *Technical Change and Economic Theory*, Dosi, G., Freeman, C., Nelson, R.R., Silverberg, G., Soete, L. (eds). Pinter, London.

Lundvall, B.A. (1992). *National Innovation System, Toward a Theory of Innovation and Interactive Learning*. Pinter Publishers, London.

Malerba, F. (2004). *Sectoral Systems of Innovation: Concepts, Issues and Analyses in Six Major Sectors in Europe*. Cambridge University Press, Cambridge.

Malerba, F. and Orsenigo, L. (1995). Schumpeterian patterns of innovation. *Cambridge Journal of Economics*, 19, 47–65.

Metcalfe, J.S. (1994). Evolutionary economics and technology policy. *The Economic Journal*, 104(425), 931–944.

Mignon, S., Ayerbe, C., Dubouloz, S., Robert, M., West, J. (2020). Managerial innovation and management of open innovation. *Journal of Innovation Economics & Management*, 32(2), 3–12.

Morel, L. and Le Roux, S. (2016). *Fab Labs: Innovative User*. ISTE Ltd, London and John Wiley & Sons, New York.

Mytelka, L. and Smith, K. (2001). *Innovation Theory and Innovation Policy: Bridging the Gap, DRUID Conference*. Aalborg School, Denmark.

Nelson, R.R. (1988). Institutions supporting technical change in the United States. In *Technical Change and Economic Theory*, Dosi, G., Freeman, C., Nelson, R.R., Silverberg, G., Soete, L. (eds). Pinter, London.

Nelson, R.R. and Winter, S.G. (1982). *An Evolutionary Theory of Economic Change*. The Belknap of Harvard University Press, Cambridge Press, Cambridge, MA.

Nonaka, I. and Takeuchi, H. (1995). *The Knowledge Creating Company*. Oxford University Press, New York.

North, D. (1990). *Institutions, Institutional Change and Economic Performance*, Cambridge University Press, Cambridge.

OECD (2002). *Dynamising National Innovation Systems*. OECD Editions, Paris.

OECD (2005). *Oslo Manual. Guidelines for Collecting and Reporting Data on Research and Experimental Development*, 3rd edition. OECD Editions, Paris.

OECD (2010). *Taxation, Innovation and the Environment*. OECD Editions, Paris.

OECD (2015). *Frascati Manual. Guidelines for Collecting and Reporting Data on Research and Experimental Development*, 7th edition. OECD Editions, Paris.

OECD (2018). *Oslo Manual*, 4th edition. OECD Editions, Paris.

OECD (2019). *Oslo Manual. Guidelines for Collecting and Reporting Data on Research and Experimental Development*, 4th edition. OECD Editions, Paris.

Oldenburg, R. (1989). *The Great Good Place*. Da Capo Press, Boston, MA.

Perez, C. (2010). Technological revolution and techno-economic paradigms. *Cambridge Journal of Economics*, 34, 185–202.

Perrin, C. (2017). Petites entreprises dans l'histoire industrielle. *Marché & Organisations*, 30.

Prahalad, C.K. and Hamel, G. (1990). The core competence of the corporation. *Harvard Business Review*, 68(3), 79–92.

Schumpeter, J.A. (1939). *Business Cycles. A Theoretical, Historical and Statistical Analysis of the Capitalist Process*. McGraw-Hill Book Company, New York.

Schumpeter, J.A. (1981). *The Theory of Economic Development*. Routledge, Abingdon.

Schumpeter, J.A. (2008). *Capitalism, Socialism and Democracy*. Routledge, Abingdon.

Sénat (2019). Rubrique économie, finances et fiscalité. Report [Online]. Available at: http://www.senat.fr/rap/l18-147-323/l18-147-32318.html.

Sharif, N. (2006). Emergence and development of the national innovation systems concept. *Research Policy*, 35, 745–766.

Teece, D.J., Pisano, G., Shuen, A. (1997). Dynamic capabilities and strategic management. *Strategic Management Journal*, 18(7), 509–533.

Uzunidis, D. (1996). Schumpeter et mouvements longs de l'économie : aspects critiques de l'actualité économique. *Innovations, cahiers d'économie de l'innovation*, 4, 119–140.

Uzunidis, D. (2003). Les facteurs actuels qui font de la science une force productive au service du capital. *Innovations, cahiers d'économie de l'innovation*, 17, 51–78.

Westmore, B. (2013). R&D, patenting and growth: The role of public policy. OECD Economics Department Working Papers, 1047, OECD Editions, Paris.

Zilsel, E. (1942). The sociological roots of science. *The American Journal of Sociology*, 47, 544–562.

2

Management – Managing Innovation According to Space, Time and Matter

2.1. Introduction

Managing innovation can be summed up by two famous phrases. The first is attributed to the scientist Archimedes: "Eureka, I have found it". It applies to the individual; it is a cognitive and emotional phenomenon that leads them to feel a certain wonder and the pleasant sensation of having found a solution to a problem (Lubart *et al.* 2015). In management, this discovery or "revelation" focuses on a management situation (Amabile 1988; Carrier and Gélinas 2011) such as, with reference to Olso's Manual, the design of a new product or service, a new organization or commercialization or a new business model (Lubart *et al.* 2015). Coming from the mind of an individual, this creative idea arises *a priori* spontaneously from the reorganization of information, facts, knowledge and experiences that they have accumulated during formal or informal research, alone or with other individuals in the organization or not, such as consumers. Therefore, this idea does not come alone. It is nurtured by an enabling context and interpersonal relationships that enable such discovery.

However, this idea may prove to be a failure, hence the second phrase put forward by Winston Churchill: "Shoot for the moon, and if you miss you'll land among the stars". Even if the idea is original, new and promising, it is possible that it will never be applied in the organization, for economic, financial, technological or marketing reasons (St-Pierre *et al.* 2017). Furthermore, if it is implemented, studies

---

Chapter written by Bérangère L. SZOSTAK, Michael E. LAVIOLETTE and Thierry BURGER-HELMCHEN.

indicate that the failure rate of innovations that are brought to market is around 85%. Indeed, innovation is only effective from the moment the novelty is introduced, as the etymology of the term indicates. Regardless of how enthusiastic they may be, the bearer of the idea will struggle to convince and interest enough people around them, hence the risk of a lack of ownership of the idea within the organization (Royer 2002). Kotter (2016, p. 12) explains, "The deeper you get into it, the more obvious it becomes that convincing others to 'buy' your ideas is both a human issue and a vital skill". In fact, innovation implies an exploratory approach where the individual interacts both to enhance the value of his idea and to revise it according to the feedback from his interlocutors. Beyond technical knowledge or know-how, social skills – such as empathy, listening, persuasive communication and networking – are just as important.

If we agree that innovation is experimenting and testing, we must admit that trial, error and failure will be a part of the experiment as well. The Wright brothers spent three years trying different glider prototypes with multiple failures before they achieved their first successful motor-powered and controlled flight in an aircraft. The failures were a source of learning, allowing the two brothers to improve their idea into an innovation. In the corporate world, innovation also goes through many failures in the form of unfinished, unvalidated, or overly expensive ideas, etc. Even if it does not lead to innovations, this knowledge is very useful and feeds the organization's creative slack, i.e. a pool of ideas that the organization can draw from to innovate again (Cohendet and Simon 2015; Gay and Szostak 2019). This consolidates its capacity to innovate, or propensity to realize, innovations (Hadjimanolis 2000; Wang and Ahmed 2004; Kmieciak *et al.* 2012). It took Nestlé more than 15 years to find the right commercial and strategic formula to sell espresso to a mass market. Several times, the project was almost abandoned after several failures in the market.

The brief discussion of these famous formulas applied to the world of organizations leads us to underline how difficult it is to manage innovation: it involves individuals, the organization, their capacities and resources; it requires a variably long time frame due, among other things, to potential failures; it meshes the internal space of the organization, and also the external space. However, innovation is essential to exist in a competitive market, to differentiate oneself from one's competitors, or to create a new activity, or even a new market, in a disruptive manner (Porter 1996; Kim and Mauborgne 2005; Christensen *et al.* 2015). The question that many managers then ask themselves is: how to manage innovation? In other words, how do we find the ideas that give rise to innovations, select them and share them within the organization and with other stakeholders?

The purpose of this chapter is to propose the elements of response according to three complementary dimensions, summarized in a symbolic way under the three notions: "space, time and matter".

– The first is particularly concerned with space, as seen from the perspective of organizational boundaries. The objective is to understand their roles in innovation, the actors involved, and the challenges posed for organizations in terms of innovation management.

– The second dimension focuses on presenting the emblematic processes of innovation, in particular the stage gate from the idea to the implementation of the innovation.

– The third dimension refers to the material, sensitive version of innovation, i.e. the product, the service, a new organization, etc., and returns to its appropriation by individuals and the challenges faced by managers.

2.2. Managing innovation: a question of space

If innovation is born somewhere, in the form of an idea, its development requires a favorable environment, so that it can be nourished by knowledge and exchanges between people who are relatively close, in order to trust and understand each other. Indeed, proximity is required, especially a certain cognitive proximity, in other words, individuals with the same knowledge and skills base who can learn from one another (Boschma 2004). It is for this reason that it is accepted that innovation initially requires a delimited space, a place composed of experts, such as researchers or designers, and also with technical tools, such as scientific apparatus or creative methods. In fact, the work of innovation takes place within a given perimeter with a degree of specialization of activities in research and development units, design centers, laboratories, etc. Beyond this specialization, these spaces are mainly made up of social and material interactions (Hall 1966; Massey 2005). Thus, contextualized practices develop, with a certain degree of confidentiality and even clandestinity (Guérard and Seidl 2013; Grenier and Denis 2017).

This delimitation and specialization of innovation has been contested by a double movement. On one hand, innovation has become an imperative for all companies subject to ambiguous, uncertain, complex and volatile environments (Bennis and Nanus 1985). These conditions imply greater organizational flexibility, with faster rhythms in developing products for the markets. On the other hand, innovation has been progressively democratized (von Hippel 2005) with the idea that innovation is no longer the producer's activity of creation and also that of users with the simpler and more accessible use of information technology, and more recently, of the 3D printer. This openness to innovation is defended by the proponents of open innovation (Chesbrough 2003, 2006; von Hippel 2005). They point to a paradigm shift in innovation management from a rather closed mode to a more open mode, at both organizational and individual levels. This approach calls the more internalized model of innovation into question, where spaces are more closed and specific to the organization, through a more externalized model with more open spaces, less centered around an organization linked to communities or collaborative movements (Bohas *et al.* 2017).

This greater porosity still raises questions about how to manage innovation spaces. While innovation has never been a closed phenomenon, these contemporary models refer to a less linear, more dynamic or even more turbulent approach. In this context, how should the organization manage these spaces? Is it necessary to delimit or widen the spaces for innovation? What about the configuration of these spaces?

2.2.1. *Delimiting and/or expanding organizational spaces*

A first "centripetal" perspective is that of a delimitation of innovation spaces. Whether it is a simple idea or an invention as a starting point, its development presupposes knowledge between actors who can engage in rich and rapid exchanges, connections that make it possible to develop expert knowledge, whose cross-fertilization would promote in-depth learning (Camagni 1991; Maskell and Mamberg 1999). As proximity theorists defend (Torre and Gilly 2000), proximities (physical, social, cognitive, etc.) favor these types of virtuous interactions, which explain the existence of innovation departments, learning communities, innovation networks, clusters or innovation ecosystems where strong links are crucial. Of course, these networks where expert knowledge circulates are not completely closed, as it is absolutely essential that they are constantly irrigated with new knowledge to give rise to new ideas and creativity (Cohendet and Llerena 1997). Nevertheless, the underlying assumption is that innovation in these spaces is related to absorptive capacity (Cohen and Levinthal 1990) – an ability of the organization to identify the value of new information, to assimilate it and apply it for commercial purposes. This capacity depends on knowledge and skills already acquired by the firm's actors in their past exploration and exploitation of technologies and markets. In fact, there is a form of path dependency (Antonelli 1997; Belussi and Sedita 2009) guiding new explorations of new ideas to extend existing knowledge bases, in order to develop innovation. These pathways allow for faster progress in the learning process to innovate.

A second "centrifugal" perspective is that of widening the space for innovation by opening up organizational boundaries. Organizational boundaries tend to lock individuals and groups into cognitions that are too similar, and this is reinforced by social reproduction mechanisms (Bourdieu and Passeron 1970), which can induce, at a more macro level, paradigms that lock the organization into a dominant logic that can restrict its capacity to innovate (Prahalad and Bettis 1995; Kor and Mesko 2013). This lack of openness would explain the inability of certain large firms (such as Kodak, Ericsson and Motorola) to innovate when they had all the knowledge and human capital necessary to do so. Consequently, this perspective underscores the importance of de-embedding relationships and interactions for the contribution of new ideas and knowledge, particularly through the strength of weak ties (Granovetter 1985). The hypothesis here is that innovation depends on a combined capacity to identify, capture and integrate knowledge or resources for innovation into the established organization (Teece *et al.* 1997). In contrast to the absorptive capacity approach, it is less the stock than the flow which guides innovation paths.

However, too much openness can be counterproductive for two reasons. On one hand, firms run the risk of rapid imitation by competitors, hence the importance of forms of protection for their intellectual property. On the other hand, a multiplication of interaction spaces can end up generating too much noise, too much information that is difficult to combine, leading to misunderstanding and dispersion in the end. In fact, openness does not need to be complete for an organization. It is more a question of creating porosity through specific connections from internal space to external space, by leveraging technologies in the form of licensing or spin-offs, and also from external space to internal space by including new technologies from other networks (Chesbrough 2012).

However, these two perspectives are not incompatible. A balanced approach allows us to understand that innovation needs both centripetal and centrifugal movements to advance more quickly and efficiently. In the beginning, innovation may need some form of protection, even though this incubation does not take place in a vacuum. The metaphor of the baby as a fetus can be enlightening here. The fragility of the fetus presupposes its protection in the womb. Although isolated and nourished in the amniotic fluid, the baby remains in contact with the world. After birth, interaction and openness become more fundamental. Innovation needs porosity and connectivity in a balanced way at different times and in different contexts. Moreover, business incubators have two functions of protection and intermediation, as Amezcua *et al.* (2013) have pointed out. Beyond the spaces dedicated to innovation, this duality is inherent to any organization, which like a living organism, contracts and expands, explores and exploits, opens and closes, specializes and diversifies, etc. Thinking of innovation as any complex phenomenon implies not opposing opposites but thinking of them in a complementary relationship (Morin 2005).

Thus, rather than two opposing movements, they are two complementary movements: (1) a protective delimitation movement to concentrate resources, develop expertise and make sense (Weick *et al.* 2005) in a given space to allow innovation to emerge and (2) a reticular enlargement movement to develop resources, nourish expertise and make sense (Gioia and Chittipeddi 1991) to allow innovation to unfold. These movements can be understood as forms of coupling (Weick 1976) inherent in organizations and systems. Sometimes, an organization decouples itself from its environment in order to constitute and preserve a form of integrity. Sometimes, it couples with its environment to develop and assert a form of legitimacy (Pache and Santos 2013). This complementarity argues for a conception of change and innovation as permanent organizational processes (Tsoukas and Chia 2002), a continuous process of perpetual organizational emergence.

2.2.2. *Developing links within and outside the spaces*

The classic players in innovation are the designated specialists: R&D engineers, designers, product developers, actors of change in production processes, etc. By broadening the perimeter or space for innovation, the innovation players are also multiplied. Thus, anyone involved in the design of new products and processes becomes an innovator (Dyer *et al.* 2009), as well as anyone who transforms them into opportunities (Shane and Venkataraman 2000) in organized forms (Gartner 2017). In recent years, we have observed a democratization of these two roles that were previously specialized and reserved for a minority (Audretsch 2007). This democratization goes hand in hand with the idea that innovation is a permanent process of an organization's evolution, which is circumscribed in time and delimited within certain organizational boundaries. It seems to accelerate with the possibility of everyone participating and contributing systematically to innovation in the firm, thanks to the potential of information and communication technologies, opening up a networked society (Castells 2000).

Taking this democratization of innovation one step further, every employee is now a potential innovator: they are encouraged to propose ideas and formalize them in a system that allows them to be selected and developed with the support of the company. Thus, companies have set up innovation systems that allow all employees to participate in the innovation effort. A variety of systems to support the genesis of novelty under various names have therefore emerged: organizational creativity, participative innovation, etc. These approaches make it possible to increase the level of knowledge (Cohen and Levinthal 1990). Through new combinations, this improves the absorption capacity of the company, by seeking new ideas and knowledge in close connection with established knowledge. These approaches are useful because they increase the internal knowledge base and allow it to be renewed by adding new knowledge, circulated by internal, rather than external actors (Laviolette *et al.* 2016). They are also interesting because they allow the actors of the firm to free themselves from the organizational routines of innovation creation, particularly in the delimited spaces of R&D, where innovation is legitimate, to experiment and test in the margins of the organization, other forms of innovation, making it possible to multiply the dynamic capacity of the firm 10-fold. These devices promote and support already existing forms of innovation operating in interstices, which have sometimes been difficult to recognize or have even been rejected by the dominant currents in the firm. The emblematic examples of the post-it or *Nespresso*, or even microcomputing explain that innovation, especially radical innovation, often takes place in the margins because it breaks away from the dominant models (Christensen *et al.* 2015).

The identification of these emerging ideas and the recognition of their bearers are the first steps for their development within the organization. However, the company should not stop there. Once the "good ideas" have been selected, the support and development of these ideas involves obtaining resources and, above all, putting them in contact with other knowledgeable players, in order to turn the idea into an opportunity for the company internally or externally. It is at this level that incubation facilities can play a crucial role as dedicated spaces for transforming ideas into opportunities, whether they be products for a new market or processes to improve the organization itself. We find here, the importance of this phase, or centrifugal movement, to protect the development of the innovation idea through selected resources and links. However, even though the development of new knowledge is often protected, innovation spaces do not operate in a vacuum. They are connected to knowledge and information networks on technologies, markets and society as a whole. At the scale of a city, Simon (2009) demonstrates the importance of innovation communities operating in different social groups with different roles and activities. For a company located in this city that wants to benefit from this new knowledge, it is important to establish varied relationships with the actors in the different areas of innovation where the standards are not the same.

Thus. if intra-organizational links are important for the company, it is crucial to develop inter-organizational links to support and develop innovation. This stratification of the space of relationships can be done according to the classical logic of upstream and downstream, if we refer to the value chain (Porter 1990). A firm can then characterize the first circle of partners upstream of the innovation, be they design firms, component and material suppliers, research laboratories, etc. (Porter 1990). There are specific partners that contribute to the design activity of the innovation. These actors sometimes become assimilated to internal actors because the collaborations are so strong and recurrent. A second circle of partners upstream of the innovation is more related to the activities of diffusion, or even the marketing of the innovation. This stage involves players such as innovation intermediaries in charge of commercialization; they are accelerants or service providers for the commercialization of the innovation, leading users or other groups of community players more sensitive to certain uses, and potentially promoters of the innovation.

However, this distinction between exploration and exploitation actors is not enough. Innovation is deployed through the permanent circulation of these different actors, who are fairly hybrid between several networks, which are referred to as innovation intermediaries (Howells 2006). Their intermediation activities consist of finding new partners, organizing transactions between two or more parties, mediating collaborations and advising on finding financing. Their hybrid identity seems to be a key aspect in enabling these actors to promote the circulation of knowledge and resources between innovation spaces with often-conflicting labor standards (Boltanski and Thevenot 1991).

Ultimately, innovation management according to space is particularly fruitful if we consider space as an organized arrangement of expertise, relationships and interests deliberately constructed to foster the emergence of ideas, or even support their development and diffusion to other geographical and political scales (Westley *et al.* 2014; Grenier and Denis 2017). In fact, innovation management implies a spatial strategy aimed at (1) designing and shaping spaces according to two joint movements of delimitation and enlargement and (2) configuring them by developing links inside and outside of these spaces, with particular care for intersections where key actors such as intermediaries operate. More than a geographical or physical delimitation, it is its relational nature that stands out, but it also has a material and temporal dimension. The innovation space can be defined as spatiotemporal events where actors gather at a given point to make sense and give meaning, with an aspiration to develop new ideas and practices (Massey 2005; Sergot and Saives 2016). Thus, there is a circumstantial aspect of innovation that can be theorized, certainly with space, and also with time and matter.

2.3. Managing innovation: a matter of time

An innovation process can easily be represented as a sequence of steps, each with its own duration and rhythm. Innovation management seeks to reduce this time, while reducing costs and improving the chances of success. We talk about time-to-market or innovation races. As a result, management practices for R&D teams and project management have been developed to accelerate the production of innovation, such as open innovation, concurrent engineering or Scrum practices (Burger-Helmchen and Raedersdorf 2018). It is also the time of the decision that forces the standardization of points of view in companies.

2.3.1. *The innovation process, a long-term process*

There are many representations of the innovation process in literature. One of the simplest visually, and yet one of the richest in terms of interactions and representation of time, is that proposed by Cohendet and Simon (2015). Their work has been widely used in literature on creativity and innovation (Bathelt *et al.* 2017). It is a holistic model that brings creativity, knowledge and innovation into interaction and can easily be described in four main steps encompassing the views and discourses of all managers. Figure 26.1 is a reproduction of this model.

The process from idea to product is long, complex and highly strategic (Birkinshaw *et al.* 2012). Once ideas are generated, companies must convert them, which takes time, financial resources and skills. During the process, different points of view, storytelling techniques and worldviews collide. The classic representation of the innovation process is mostly in the form of a *stage-gate* (Pahl *et al.* 2006), which is shown in the lower part of Figure 26.1.

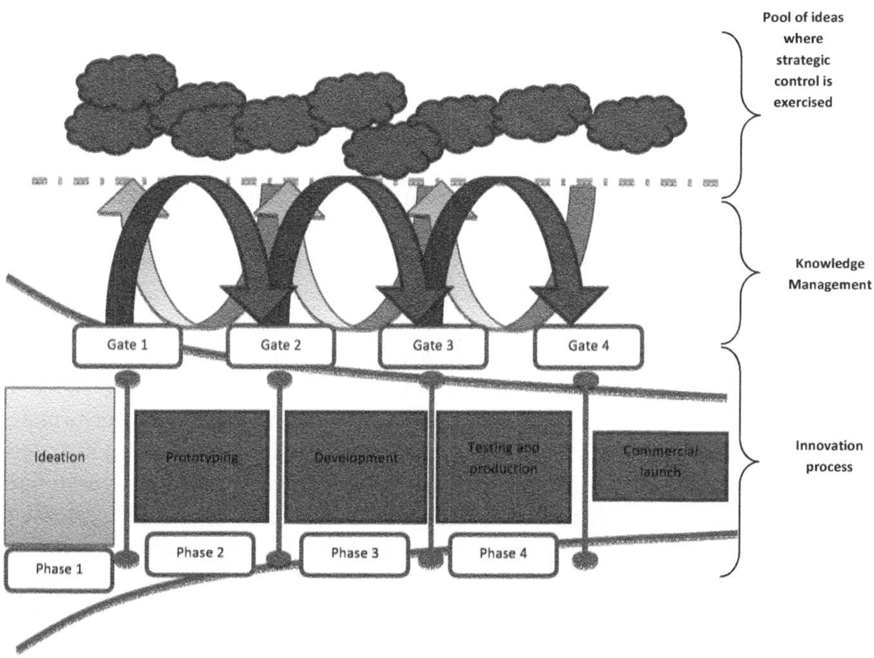

Figure 2.1. *An innovation process (source: Cohendet and Simon 2015). For a color version of this figure, see www.iste.co.uk/uzunidis/innovation1.zip*

The first step is the ideation. Innovation management is interested in techniques to generate a large number and variety of ideas (Agogué 2016). During this stage, the selection of ideas is not final; the least promising ones are not entirely discarded.

In this representation, non-validated ideas are put into organizational memory for later use. It is a "stock" with special characteristics.

David (2018) shows that each step of the process requires knowledge management based on human interaction or relying on an information system. The main challenge of knowledge management is the pooling of knowledge from the different phases of the stage-gate and its reuse in other projects, leading to its improvement or the creation of new knowledge (Hussler and Burger-Helmchen 2019). A fundamental element of the process is the "pool" or repertoire of ideas. This pool of ideas not only contains possibilities to be explored, but above all contributes to the selection process. This creative pool, whose characteristics are shaped by the culture and history of the company, has strategic implications throughout the innovation process. Thus, creativity – non operationalized – will not disappear during the other phases of the process: it feeds the pool of ideas, shapes and co-creates the decision-making process for future decisions.

2.3.2. *Managing innovation means managing the time for decisions*

It is recognized that the different actors involved in this process have different views on opportunities and on what ideas are worth developing (Boisot and Macmillan 2004). In order to make sense of innovation processes, researchers and practitioners work to use representations of reality. These simplifications are not the same in all organizations. They depend on the culture of the organization and the knowledge and skills of the person designing the model. Depending on the knowledge of each manager, the model will focus on certain types of elements. Finance managers will focus on costs, financial risks and other key performance indicators (KPIs). Figure 26.2 emphasizes that each decision-maker has a manifesto (a theoretical representation that corresponds to their own values and worldview). These worldviews are implemented in codebooks that are functional, sectoral or hierarchical. Each activity will have a specific set of key performance indicators (KPIs), ultimately leading to a decision at the end of the process. Such an approach, originally designed for business models, can easily translate into process innovations that can rationally explain why different people within a company have radically different views on innovations and ideas.

These decisions are sometimes imposed by the market or by the internal rules of the organization, and at other times are left without clearly established limits. In all these circumstances, the objective of the decisions is to improve the position of the company, to produce innovation, and also to capture value, to appropriate it.

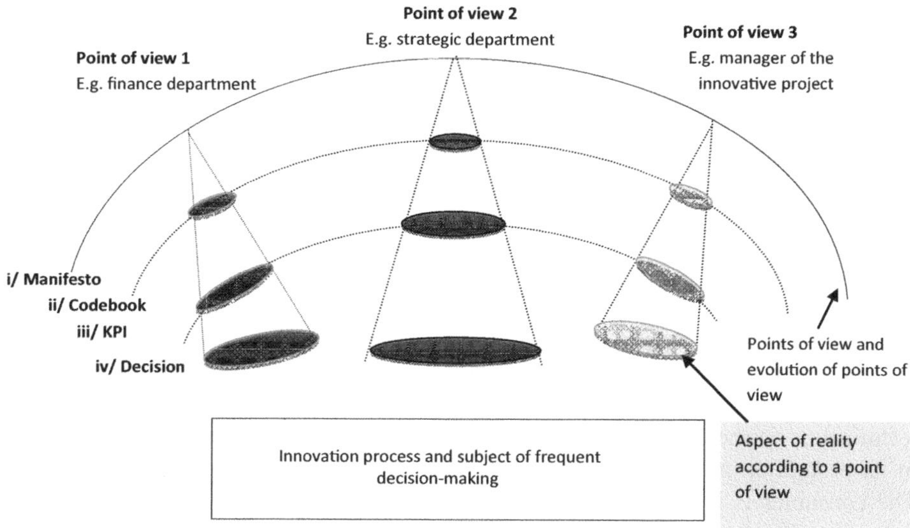

Figure 2.2. *The meeting of viewpoints during the innovation process (source: Bollinger 2020). For a color version of this figure, see www.iste.co.uk/uzunidis/innovation1.zip*

2.4. Managing innovation: a question of matter

Once the idea has been developed, improved and transformed, in a particular time and space, into an innovation (product, service, organizational, business model, etc.), the question of its appropriation arises. Appropriation can be understood as "the action of adapting something to a given use", and also as "appropriating something, making it one's own". More graphically, it is also "the natural action by which food enters the body" (https://www.cnrtl.fr). In the case of innovation management, this leads us, on one hand, to question what it means to adapt an innovation and make it one's own, and, on the other, to understand the modalities for implementing such an action. We propose to answer these questions according to the type of "organism", or actor in the organization. We have chosen three emblematic ones: (1) consumers, (2) members of the organization and (3) shareholders.

2.4.1. *The appropriation of innovation by consumers*

According to Schumpeter, innovation is the first commercial transaction of an invention. In other words, a customer is willing to invest resources in the invention. Essentially, this means that this client identifies the value of this invention in relation to a use that is specific to them. Then, the organization has to propose an attractive value for the client. Up until the mid-2000s, the consumer remained “at the end of the chain”; this meant that this value had to be anticipated and identified at the beginning of the innovation process, with a high risk of going wrong. Since then, the consumer’s position has evolved, and they are now involved in the co-creation of the product, participating in its promotion and dissemination (Cova and Cova 2009). In this sense, marketing research emphasizes how essential it is to integrate the consumer from the beginning of the process, which facilitates the identification and proposal of a particular value.

This is referred to as “consumer empowerment” (Fayn *et al.* 2019). This “delegation of power to the consumer” can be initiated by the organization itself in a “top-down” movement. In this case, it leaves the consumer free to choose certain technical or aesthetic characteristics, it includes them in the creation of the product, in its promotion and distribution (Cova and Cova 2009; Piligrimiene *et al.* 2015). The consumer is in a partnership relationship with the company. By contrast, this delegation of power can be more of a “power grab” by the consumer, who, for example, via comments on social networks, can direct consumption. It is more of a liberation according to a “bottom-up” movement, which can express an assertion of counter-power on the part of consumers in the face of traditional consumption, or even a civic commitment to more sustainable and democratic structures (Papaoikonomou and Alarcón 2015).

According to the two movements mentioned, consumer empowerment does not imply exactly the same notions in marketing (Fayn *et al.* 2019), which consequently influences work in innovation management. In the case of the “top-down” movement, it is a question of relational marketing (establishment of lasting relationships with the consumer) or *marketing knowledge* (mobilization and development of customer skills), whereas in the case of the “bottom-up” movement, it is more the notions of consumerism (or consumer resistance) or engagement (involvement of the customer beyond the transaction). However, the notion of brand community (a group of customers attached to the same brand values) is present in both, knowing that the “bottom-up” movement is favored by information and communication technologies, and, more broadly, by digital technology. Indeed, social media, evaluation platforms and online petitions reinforce the power of the consumer in the face of the organization (Fleck and Ambroise 2019). Ignoring this becomes impossible and, above all, a strategic error with serious consequences.

One of the challenges facing contemporary organizations concerns the ways in which innovation is appropriated by these creative, committed, even critical consumers, in the face of consumer society, by these consumers capable of expressing a counter-power without the limits of time and space via digital technology. It is true that organizations have always benefited from consumers’ good ideas, and research has already explored many ways of doing so, such as listening to customers via Web 2.0. (Viot 2010), design thinking approaches (Brown 2009) or crowdsourcing (Pénin and Burger-Helmchen 2012). However, given the intensity of these issues and the growing power of consumer criticism of the capitalist economy, it is essential to pursue these investigations in innovation management and reflect on the most relevant modalities, according to the type of consumer empowerment, in particular. This therefore questions the appropriation of innovation by the members of the organization.

2.4.2. *Appropriation of innovation by the members of the organization*

A major obstacle in innovation within organizations is often the organization itself, especially its members. Indeed, as Kotter (2016) makes explicit, when faced with novelty, these members express fears and may not adhere to it, not because of the poor quality of the innovation itself, but because of power games, the refusal to have their routines disrupted or to lose their resources, etc. Royer (2002) shows that this phenomenon is all the more important when we are at the beginning of the innovation process, at the time of the idea, when decision-making is essentially socio-political. Indeed, tangible and measurable results are hardly conceivable, hence the significance of fears and doubts. Little by little, the decision becomes rational, because the innovation achieves its material dimension: the actors can experiment, test, discuss and measure it more. Although this state of affairs has been investigated by major authors such as Akrich *et al.* (1988a, 1988b) or Burgelman (1983), it is still relevant today. Indeed, the subject is not exhausted insofar as contemporary organizations are confronted with major changes, be they economic, social or environmental (Gay and Szostak 2019), as well as health crises. We note that all of this calls the classic status of the innovation champion, leader or manager as the bearer of innovation into question. For example, in some organizations, they are becoming collective and protean.

This is particularly the case in co-operatives defined as "mutual aid enterprises that are democratically owned and controlled by the people who use its services" (Briscoe and Ward 2000). These organizations of the Social and Solidarity Economy are, in fact, atypical, since, by construction, the "leader" is collective and is a consumer-owner. We can consider it as *de facto* "empowered"[1]. In France, they include agricultural cooperatives, merchant cooperatives, SCOPs[2], SCICs[3], certain banks and mutual insurance companies. The impact of these characteristics on

1 Neologism in French.

2 SCOP: *Sociétés Coopératives Participatives,* employee-owned companies.

3 SCIC: *Sociétés Coopératives d'Intérêt Collectif,* stakeholder-owned companies (employees, clients, suppliers, local institutions, funders, etc.).

innovation management is significant. In their study, Capelli *et al.* (2016) show, among other things, that consumer-members propose more new ideas, which are, moreover, more feasible, than non-member consumers. Moreover, the ideas of the first group are considered more innovative and of a higher quality than those of the second group. Although this work deserves to be continued, we can highlight two conclusions. First, new statuses of idea bearers are emerging: it is no longer just a question of internal members, a manager or a leader, it can occupy several statuses simultaneously, which, in the classic format of the organization, are not compatible (owner and consumer). Second, their involvement seems more significant, potentially resulting in less reluctance in the face of novelty and easier appropriation, even though the facts show that there is very often an ideology (organic vs. traditional food; local vs. non-local), which may also explain why certain ideas echoing this ideology are more easily appropriated.

That said, they remain men and women, subject to questioning in the face of change. And the appropriation of innovation can be difficult, to the point of making it impossible. It is also important to think about how this appropriation will take place. For example, making the innovation one's own may involve discursive strategies (convincing through rhetorical arguments) (Suddaby and Greenwood 2005) or mobilizing employees themselves in the decision-making process (Defélix *et al.* 2015). Another modality consists of integrating it into already existing practices, in order to limit the effect of novelty (Gay and Szostak 2019). This is how companies develop design thinking, not only to develop innovations, but also to engage the members of the organization in the search for insights and the collection and selection of new ideas. Others exploit prototyping practices to materialize ideas and make them tangible to facilitate discussions. In the end, ownership of innovation by members of the organization is a *sine qua non* for innovation, echoing Churchill, to reach for the moon. Another condition to consider concerns a final actor: the owners of the innovation, who have allocated resources to the development of the innovation.

2.4.3. *Capturing the value of innovation*

While in the previous subsections more emphasis has been placed on the social and societal dimensions of the issue of appropriation of innovation, it should be recalled that this phenomenon also refers to the capture of the economic value of innovation. Indeed, organizations innovate to generate a difference from their competitors; they seek to increase the number of customers, revenues and economic results. This is how intellectual property comes into play in the subject at hand.

From a legal standpoint, there are several ownership regimes that should not be confused (Binctin 2018). Literary and artistic property (copyright, neighboring rights) exists because of the birth of creation, while industrial property (patents, trademarks and designs) requires formalism. For example, the patent is filed with a recognized institution, such as the INPI in France, the European Patent Office in Europe or the World Intellectual Property Organization (WIPO). The function of these regimes is to protect actors who have invested different resources (financial, material, etc.) in the development of innovation. From this perspective, organizations today no longer focus on a single regime, but combine them (Granstrand 1999; Reitzig 2004). Thus, the ability to combine intellectual property rights becomes an issue for them, whether large or small (Le Bas and Szostak 2016). When opportunities arise without the legislator having been able to regulate the terms, organizations exploit contract laws. This is notably the case to circumscribe the intellectual property rights of different contributors who have committed themselves to a collective project for the development of an innovation.

While these appropriation modalities primarily aim at the full capture of economic value, other modalities develop the idea that property rights are not a monolithic whole, but a bundle of rights. According to Schlager and Ostrom (1992), there is the right of access, the right to harvest, the right of management, the right to exclude and the right to alienate. This is the current of "creative commons", which is similar to the culture of the "free" (Broca and Coriat 2015). Thus, the different rights may be held by different actors, which leads innovation management, to consider the question of appropriating the value of innovation from a different, but complementary, angle. Indeed, free movement does not question intellectual property, since it uses its foundations (Binctin 2015). On the contrary, it poses new challenges for organizations, and also for the regulator, notably on the question of the distribution of rights between actors and on the rules to be retained in this perspective. It could encourage better recognition of the contributions of employees, among others.

In conclusion, the appropriation of innovation remains a subject to be questioned because of the evolution of society from the point of view of the consumer, who is now more creative and has more power over the organization, of the members of the organization whose status is more protean than before, and also of the question of the ownership of this innovation.

2.5. Conclusion

This chapter showed that innovation management is a discipline in constant development, at least according to the three dimensions chosen here, namely, space, time and matter. Inspired by technological and social developments, practitioners and researchers are therefore redoubling their creativity to invent new tools and practices likely to improve the course of the innovation process, hoping for "Eureka" by aiming for the moon.

It should be remembered that there are many key points to understanding innovation management (Fagerberg *et al.* 2006; Shane 2009; Burger-Helmchen *et al.* 2016; Shalley *et al.* 2016; Paulus and Nijstad 2019). Each provides subtle insights into a particular aspect of the complex process of innovation. However, they all share the belief that innovation needs the individual, the team, the organization and the markets to succeed and spread, which is why it is important to continue to consider this in future research on innovation management.

2.6. References

Agogué, M. (2016). Alex F. Osborn : le brainstorming, premier outil de support à la pensée créative. In *Les grands auteurs en management de l'innovation et de la créativité*, 1st edition, Burger-Helmchen, T., Hussler, C., Cohendet, P. (eds). Editions EMS, Paris.

Akrich, M., Callon, M., Latour, B. (1988a). A quoi tient le succès des innovations ? *Gérer et comprendre. Annales des mines, les annales des mines*, 4–17.

Akrich, M., Callon, M., Latour, B. (1988b). L'art de l'intéressement : le choix des porte-parole. *Gérer et comprendre. Annales des mines, les annales des mines*, 14–29.

Amabile, T. (1988). A model of creativity and innovation in organizations. *Research in Organizational Behavior*, 10(2), 123–167.

Amezcua, A., Grimes, M., Bradley, S., Wiklund, J. (2013). Organizational sponsorship and founding environments: A contingency view on the survival of business-incubated firms, 1994–2007. *Academy of Management Journal*, 56(6), 1628–1654.

Antonelli, C. (1997). The economics of path-dependence in industrial organization. *International Journal of Industrial Organization*, 15(6), 643–675.

Audretsch, D. (2007). *The Entrepreneurial Society*. Oxford University Press, Oxford.

Bathelt, H., Cohendet, P., Henn, S., Simon, L. (2017). *The Elgar Companion to Innovation and Knowledge Creation*. Edward Elgar Publishing Ltd, Northampton, MA.

Belussi, F. and Sedita, S. (2009). Life cycle vs. multiple path dependency in industrial districts. *European Planning Studies*, 17(4), 505–528.

Bennis, W. and Nanus, B. (1985). *Leaders: The Strategies for Taking Charge*. Harper & Row, New York.

Binctin, N. (2015). *Stratégie d'entreprise et propriété intellectuelle*. LGDJ, Paris.

Birkinshaw, J., Bouquet, C., Barsoux, J.-L. (2012). The 5 myths of innovation. *MIT Sloan Management Review*, 52(2), 43–50.

Bohas, A., Faure, S., De Vaujany, F.-X. (2017). Tiers-lieux & espaces collaboratifs : laboratoires et révélateurs des nouvelles pratiques de travail. Paper, RGCS (Research Group on Collaborative Spaces).

Boisot, M. and Macmillan, I.C. (2004). Crossing epistemological boundaries: Managerial and entrepreneurial approaches to knowledge management. *Long Range Planning*, 37(6), 505–524.

Bollinger, S.R. (2020). Creativity and forms of managerial control in innovation processes: Tools, viewpoints and practices. *European Journal of Innovation Management*, 23(2), 214–229.

Boltanski, L. and Thévenot, L. (1991). *De la justification : les économies de grandeur*. Éditions Gallimard, Paris.

Boschma, R. (2004). Proximité et innovation. *Économie rurale*, 280(1), 8–24.

Bourdieu, P. and Passeron, J.-C. (1970). *Éléments pour une théorie du système d'enseignement*. Editions de minuit, Paris.

Briscoe, R. and Ward, M. (2000). *The Competitive Advantages of Co-Operatives*. Centre for Cooperative Studies, National University of Ireland, Cork.

Broca, S. and Coriat, B. (2015). Le logiciel libre et les communs : deux formes de résistance et d'alternative à l'exclusivisme propriétaire. *Revue internationale de droit économique*, 29(3), 265–284.

Brown, T. (2009). *Change by Design. How Design Thinking Transforms Organizations and Inspires Innovation*. HarperCollins, New York.

Burgelman, R. (1993). A process model of internal corporate venturing in the diversified major firm. *Administrative Science Quarterly*, 28, 223–244.

Burger-Helmchen, T. and Raedersdorf, S. (2018). *Pro En Management*. Vuibert, Paris.

Burger-Helmchen, T., Hussler, C., Cohendet, P. (2016). *Les grands auteurs en management de l'innovation et de la créativité*, 1st edition. Editions EMS, Paris.

Camagni, R. (1991). Local "milieu", uncertainty and innovation networks: Towards a new dynamic theory of economic space. In *Innovation Networks: Spatial Perspectives*, Camagni, R. (ed.). Belhaven Press, London.

Capelli, S., Falchi, A., Hussler, C., Sabadie, W. (2016). Co-innover avec ses consommateurs : oui, mais lesquels ? De l'intérêt d'impliquer les consommateurs-membres dans le processus d'innovation des entreprises coopératives. *Gestion 2000*, 33(4), 117–141.

Carrier, C. and Gélinas, S. (2011). Quelles pratiques les pme peuvent-elles utiliser pour favoriser l'intrapreneuriat ? *Gestion*, 36(4), 22–33.

Castells, M. (2000). *The Rise of the Network Society*. Blackwell, Cambridge.

Chesbrough, H. (2003). *Open Innovation: The New Imperative for Creating and Profiting from Technology*. Harvard Business Press, Boston, MA.

Chesbrough, H. (2006). *Open Business Models: How to Thrive in the New Innovation Landscape*. Harvard Business Press, Boston, MA.

Chesbrough, H. (2012). Open innovation: Where we've been and where we're going. *Research-Technology Management*, 55(4), 20–27.

Christensen, C.M., Raynor, M.E., McDonald, R. (2015). What is disruptive innovation? *Harvard Business Review*, 93(12), 44–53.

Cohen, W. and Levinthal, D. (1990). Absorptive capacity: A new perspective on learning and innovation. *Administrative Science Quarterly*, 35(1), 128–152.

Cohendet, P. and Llerena, P. (1997). Learning, technical change and public policy: How to create and exploit diversity. In *Systems of Innovation*, Edquist C. (eds). Pinter, London.

Cohendet, P. and Simon, L. (2015). Introduction to the special issue on creativity in innovation. *Technology Innovation Management Review*, 5(7), 5–13.

Cova, B. and Cova, V. (2009). Les figures du nouveau consommateur : une genèse de la gouvernementalité du consommateur. *Recherche et applications en marketing*, 24(3), 81–100.

David, A. (2018). Understanding the invention phase of management innovation: A design theory perspective. *European Management Review*, 16(2), 383–398.

Defelix, C., Mazzilli, I., Gosselin, A. (2015). Articuler les politiques de GRH et les stratégies d'innovation : des modèles à l'épreuve des faits. *Revue de gestion des ressources humaines*, 2(96), 60–72.

Dyer, J., Gregersen, H., Christensen, C. (2009). The innovator's DNA. *Harvard Business Review*, 87.

Fagerberg, J., Mowery, D.C., Nelson, R.R. (2006). *The Oxford Handbook of Innovation*, 1st edition. Oxford University Press, Oxford.

Fleck, N. and Ambroise, L. (2019). Brand practices faced with augmented consumers. In *Augmented Customer Strategy: CRM in the Digital Age*, N'Goala, G., Pez-Pérard, V., Prim-Allaz, I. (eds). ISTE Ltd, London and John Wiley & Sons, New York.

Gartner, W. (2017). *Entrepreneurship as Organizing*. Edward Elgar Publishing, Cheltenham.

Gay, C. and Szostak, B. (2019). *Innovation and Creativity in SMEs*. ISTE Ltd, London and John Wiley & Sons, New York.

Gilly, J.-P. and Torre, A. (2000). *Dynamiques de proximité*. Editions l'Harmattan, Paris.

Gioia, D. and Chittipeddi, K. (1991). Sensemaking and sensegiving in strategic change initiation. *Strategic Management Journal*, 12(6), 433–448.

Granovetter, M. (1985). Economic action and social structure: The problem of embeddedness. *American Journal of Sociology*, 91(3), 481–510.

Granstrand, O. (1999). *The Economics and Management of Intellectual Property: Towards Intellectual Capitalism*. Edward Elgar Publishing, Cheltenham.

Guerard, S. and Seidl, D. (2013). Spaces of institutional work: A wonder drug and the single technology appraisal procedure in UK. *Academy of Management Proceedings*, 15952.

Hadjimanolis, A. (2000). An investigation of innovation antecedents in small firms in the context of a small developing country. *R&D Management*, 30, 235–245

Hall, E. (1966). *The Hidden Dimension.* Garden City, New York.

Howells, J. (2006). Intermediation and the role of intermediaries in innovation. *Research Policy*, 35(5), 715–728.

von Hippel, E. (2005). Democratizing innovation: The evolving phenomenon of user innovation. *Journal für betriebswirtschaft*, 55(1), 63–78.

Hussler, C. and Burger-Helmchen, T. (2019). La connaissance : l'atome de la stratégie. In *Les grands courants en management stratégique*, Liarte, S. (ed.). EMS, Caen.

Kim, C. and Mauborgne, R. (2005). *Blue Ocean Strategy*. Harvard Business School Press, Cambridge, MA.

Kmieciak, R., Michna, A., Meczynska, A. (2012). Innovativeness, empowerment and IT capability: Evidence from SME. *Industrial Management & Data Systems*, 112(5), 707–728.

Kor, Y. and Mesko, A. (2013). Dynamic managerial capabilities: Configuration and orchestration of top executives' capabilities and the firm's dominant logic. *Strategic Management Journal*, 34(2), 233–244.

Kotter, J. (2016). Des méthodes pour sauver les bonnes idées. *Harvard Business Review*, 11–15.

Laviolette, E.-M., Redien-Collot, R., Teglborg, A.-C. (2016). Open innovation from the inside: Employee-driven innovation in support of absorptive capacity for inbound open innovation. *The International Journal of Entrepreneurship and Innovation*, 17(4), 228–239.

Le Bas, C. and Szostak, B. (2016). Appropriation de l'innovation, multiprotection et actifs complémentaires : le cas d'une pme de télémédecine à l'ère numérique. *Revue française de gestion*, 42(254), 129–145.

Lubart, T., Mouchiroud, C., Tordjman, S., Zenasni, F., (2015). *Psychologie de la créativité*. (ed). Armand Colin, Paris.

Maskell, P. and Malmberg, A. (1999). Localised learning and industrial competitiveness. *Cambridge Journal of Economics*, 23, 167–185.

Massey, D. (2005). *For Space*. Sage Publications, London.

Morin, E. (2005). *Introduction a la pensée complexe*. College essays, Points, Seuil.

Pache, A. and Santos, F. (2013). Inside the hybrid organization: Selective coupling as a response to competing institutional logics. *Academy of Management Journal*, 56(4), 972–1001.

Pahl, G., Beitz, W., Feldhusen, J., Grote, K.-H., Wallace, K., Blessing, L.T.M. (2006). *Engineering Design: A Systematic Approach*, 3rd edition. Springer London Ltd, London.

Papaoikonomou, E. and Alarcón, A. (2015). Revisiting consumer empowerment: An exploration of ethical consumption communities. *Journal of Macromarketing*, 37(1), 40–56.

Paulus, P.B. and Nijstad, B.A. (2019). *The Oxford Handbook of Group Creativity and Innovation*. Oxford University Press, New York.

Piligrimiene, Z., Dovaliene, A., Virvilaite, R. (2015). Consumer engagement in value co-creation: What kind of value it creates for company?. *Engineering Economics*, 26(4), 452–460.

Porter, M. (1996). What is strategy? *Harvard Business Review*, 74(6), 61–78.

Prahalad, C.K. and Bettis, R. (1995). The dominant logic: Retrospective and extension. *Strategic Management Journal*, 16(1), 5–14.

Reitzig, M. (2004). Strategic management of intellectual property. *MIT Sloan Management Review*, 45(3), 35–40.

Royer, I. (2002). Les procédures décisionnelles et le développement de nouveaux produits. *Revue française de gestion*, 3(139), 7–25.

Schlager, E. and Ostrom, E. (1992). Property-rights regimes and natural resources: A conceptual analysis. *Land Economics*, 68, 249–269.

Sergot, B. and Saives, A.-L. (2016). Relating place and organization: A situated tribute to Doreen Massey. *M@n@gement*, 19(4), 335–352.

Shalley, C., Hitt, M.A., Zhou, J. (2016). *The Oxford Handbook of Creativity, Innovation, and Entrepreneurship*, Reprint. OUP USA, Oxford, New York.

Shane, S. (2009). *The Handbook of Technology and Innovation Management*. Wiley-Blackwell Chichester.

Shane, S. and Venkataraman, S. (2000). The promise of entrepreneurship as a field of research. *Academy of Management Review*, 25(1), 217–226.

Simon, L. (2009). Underground, upperground et middle-ground : les collectifs créatifs et la capacité créative de la ville. *Management International/Gestiòn Internacional/ International Management*, 13, 37–51.

St-pierre, J., Bertrand, J., Uwizeyemungu, S. (2017). Accroître la performance en innovation des pme grâce à la gestion des risques : étude exploratoire sur des pme manufacturières. *Gestion 2000*, 34(5), 315–336.

Suddaby, R. and Greenwood, R. (2005). Rhetorical strategies of legitimacy. *Administrative Science Quarterly*, 50(1), 35–67.

Teece, D., Pisano, G., Shuen, A. (1997). Dynamic capabilities and strategic management. *Strategic Management Journal*, 18(7), 509–533.

Tödtling, F. and Trippl, M. (2005). One size fits all? Towards a differentiated regional innovation policy approach. *Research Policy*, 34, 1203–1219.

Tsoukas, H. and Chia, R. (2002). On organizational becoming: Rethinking organizational change. *Organization Science*, 13(5), 567–582.

Viot, C. (2010). "Toi aussi, deviens mon ami" : intégrer le web 2.0 dans sa stratégie de communication. *Décisions marketing*, 58, 77–82.

Wang, C.-L. and Ahmed, P.-K. (2004). The development and validation of the organisational innovativeness construct using confirmatory factor analysis. *European Journal of Innovation Management*, 7(4), 303–313.

Weick, K. (1976). Educational organizations as loosely coupled systems. *Administrative Science Quarterly*, 21(1), 1–19.

Weick, K., Sutcliffe, K., Obstfeld, D. (2005). Organizing and the process of sensemaking. *Organization Science*, 16(4), 409–421.

Westley, F., Antadze, N., Riddelli, D., Robinson, K., Geobey, S. (2014). Five configurations for scaling up social innovation: Case examples of nonprofit organizations from Canada. *The Journal of Applied Behavioral Science*, 50(3), 234–260.

3

Agriculture – Agricultural and Food Innovations and Agro-ecological Transition

3.1. Introduction

Three main periods in the history of the use of the concept of innovation in agriculture can be distinguished (Temple *et al.* 2019). The first period, which does not explicitly discuss the notion of innovation, but the question of technical progress, is affirmed by agricultural scientists, covers the two centuries preceding World War II. The second period covers the 30–40 years following World War II, during which the notion of innovation, posited by Schumpeter (1935), was deployed in all sectors. The third period, starting in the 1980s, is marked by a concomitance between the questioning of the previous development model and a renewal of the concept of innovation that diversifies its use in agriculture. Through the prism of these three periods, we will successively examine how the scientific communities have dealt with agricultural innovation, in order to explore the specificities of agricultural and food activities that make these activities interact with the use or conceptualization of innovation.

3.2. Two centuries of agricultural revolution without "innovation"

In the context of the famines between the 18th and 19th centuries, agriculture was called upon to respond to food demands, as well as to an industrialization that reduced the relative number of farmers and necessitated an increase in productivity. Technical changes (cultivation practices, tools) triggered a slow agricultural revolution, differentiated according to territories and sectors, closely linked to the

---

Chapter written by Ludovic TEMPLE.

development of industry and trade. All these changes benefited from the progress of knowledge on plant functioning and soil fertility. They were also linked to the institutionalization of agronomic research, carried out by the experiments of agricultural notables and then by public action (Jas 2005). These two centuries of agricultural transformation were observed by the first economists and sometimes inspired their vision of technical progress. This was the case, in the 18th century, of physiocrats (such as Quesnay) who argued that the investment of rich farmers, enlightened by new methods, would improve the efficiency of agriculture. Classical economists (Smith, Ricardo, Mill, Say, etc.) then turned their attention to technical change, based, above all, on observations of the infant industry. For Smith, the introduction of new machines and the division of labor were the result of initiatives by economic actors (in particular, craftsmen), and also implied profound institutional and contractual changes, to which technical innovations were therefore subordinate (Labini 2007). In agriculture, for example, he suggested the introduction of long-term rental contracts to encourage investment. For his part, Ricardo (1817) identified two forms of improvement in agriculture, namely "[...] those that increase the productive capacity of the land [...]" (new rotations, fertilizers, etc.) and "[...] those that, through improved machinery, make it possible to obtain the same product with less work [...]". Say associated the image of the farmer, already dear to physiocrats, with an entrepreneur in the agricultural industry and insisted on the links between technical changes in agriculture and those in industry. Marx, whose work in agriculture put technical progress into a historical perspective that would lead to an *appropriation of living labor by capital*, a kind of a violation for workers and peasants, also saw that it was necessary for the progress of humanity.

While the question of technical change in agriculture was largely ignored by the academic economists of the 19th century, it was, on the other hand, very present among the first chemists, agronomists, rural economists and agricultural historians. The analysis of technical change was also the subject of work in rural sociology at the beginning of the 20th century, which analyzed the social and political conditions that governed the technical transformations in European agriculture.

3.3. The green revolutions driven by linear and technological innovation design

The post-war historical and macroeconomic contexts generated an institutional environment that placed the State at the center of productive investment in the sector of food and agriculture. In this context, the models developed in the industry in terms of research specialization, economies of scale, competitiveness and the dissemination of technical artifacts were applied to innovation in agriculture. A consumer society structured by an agro-industrial and agri-food sector (cereals, oilseeds, meat) became globalized. Innovation became the driving force of competition. The objective of international agronomic research was then focused on increasing global food production through new technologies, known as the green revolution.

During this period, the social sciences studied and supported technical changes in agriculture using the notion of innovation conceived as the process of farmers adopting new technical objects (seeds, fertilizers, pesticides, machines, etc.) that have been developed by research and industry. Rural sociology, with Rogers' work in the United States, thus, for over 30 years, provided analytical methods for the diffusion of new technologies, studying the obstacles to their adoption according to typologies of adopters. Other work analyzes societal resistance to agricultural modernization (Mendras 1970). A Marxist-inspired school of thought also criticized agricultural innovation as a means of extending capitalism in order to integrate agriculture into industrial sectors.

3.4. The notion of innovation in the face of agricultural and food transitions

The succession of crises in the economic growth model that is based on industrialization, by renewing the role of agriculture and food in development mechanisms, calls into question the very nature and conceptualization of innovation in order to respond to global challenges. The work of development economists in this case highlights how pressure on resources structures the innovation capacities of agrarian societies, which enhance the productive potential of ecosystems (Boserup 1981). The notion of innovation focused by a technological definition becomes more complex as it broadens to include the institutional organizational dimensions that structure the conditions of change. In this renewal, the diffusionist paradigm of innovation in agricultural research becomes fragmented, and new approaches and new uses of innovation in agriculture emerge. There are at least three categories of uses that can be highlighted (Touzard *et al.* 2014).

Agriculture and agribusiness can, first of all, be simply considered as empirical fields among others, into which we can import the academic frameworks of innovation analysis (evolutionism, neo-institutionalist, regulation); hence the work related to the development of national innovation strategies (Faure *et al.* 2019). Secondly, in political economy on the changes in the sector and its relationships with society.

Finally, it is necessary to underline the existence of analyses, often linked to development actions in agriculture. Innovations are then associated with the particular functioning of farms, the management of externalities and local resources (land, water, landscapes, etc.), and concern products whose quality is linked to their origin, which calls for specific approaches to localized agri-food systems. The analysis of sectoral conditions of innovation leads to the use of specific concepts, such as Agricultural Innovation Systems (Klerkx *et al.* 2010), calling for a reform of the organization of research or public policies for innovation in agriculture.

In sociology, several research communities are documenting these evolutions of the notion of innovation. The work of Chambers *et al.* (1989) and Darré *et al.* (1989), in particular, paves the way to research that restructures local empirical knowledge and endogenous innovation. They shift the analysis from categories (researchers, farmers, etc.) to local networks of actors structuring collective innovation capacities. Other research brings a consideration of the history and the institutional context that determine technical and organizational changes into the analysis (Chauveau *et al.* 1999).

This emergence contributes to the development of a new approach to producing knowledge and innovation on living organisms, with a view to promoting varietal innovation, which has been disrupted by societal controversies on genetically modified organisms. At another level, analysis of the role played by the evolution of technical systems, such as agro-ecology and social structures, according to organizational scales, questions the theoretical frameworks for analyzing transitions.

The analysis of innovation in, or related to, the agricultural sector thus prompts new disciplinary collaborations in order to integrate the role of institutions, networks or knowledge. These collaborations underline the importance of local context for social innovations: sustainable nutrition and/or territorial development thus contribute to the renewal of work on innovative environments and local productive systems.

3.5. Sector specificities of innovation in agriculture and food

The meaning given to innovation in the field of agriculture therefore takes into account, in part, the specificities of agricultural activity itself: geographical diversity, diversity of sectors, diversity of types of farming: family, entrepreneurial, organizational (cooperatives), etc. Innovation refers to different forms of processes that structure the implementation of technical, institutional and organizational changes and their systemic interactions. Using the term "agricultural innovation" questions whether agriculture as an activity of exploitation of natural ecosystems specifies innovation processes or whether it doesn't. Therefore, we can propose three axes of differentiation of these specificities, in biophysical, socio-economic or organizational dimensions.

The biophysical dimension concerns the dependence of innovation processes (conditions of emergence, adoption and deployment) on the increasing instability of climatic variables affecting the activity. It also relates to the biological and therefore living dimension of agricultural products. These two attributes determine the instability variables of technical processes (production, conservation) that generate risks and, therefore, collective strategies (coordination, contracts) to regulate these risks. However, in the economic sense, the introduction of this risk factor is an intrinsic reality of innovation.

The second dimension refers to the specificities of the agricultural production function linked to the weakness of economies of scale in agriculture. It is partly explained by a lower rate of return on capital investment than in other sectors. It refers to social structures of production that are still predominantly based on fragmented modes of production using family labor, even if certain forms of agro-industrialization are necessary in certain sectors governed by industrial processing activities such as ripening facilities and the food processing industry.

This limited profitability, due to the structuring of agricultural activity, leads the public authorities to compensate for its shortcomings through public investment in agronomic research, which creates a dynamic dedicated to the governance of innovation that is exogenous to agrarian societies. Thus, even if they do not oppose each other, innovations of an endogenous (induced by farmers and actors themselves) and exogenous (driven by public authorities and other institutions) nature have specific proportions in agriculture. Finally, some cross-cutting innovations (technological, genetic, digital) are the result of inter-organizational and supranational collaborations and require long cycles of diffusion and appropriation.

Finally, agricultural innovation is specific because of the multifunctional nature of the resources it uses, mainly land and water, which have non-market identity heritage functions. These territorially anchored production "factors" make certain agricultural innovations difficult to generalize or transpose from one territory to another.

3.6. Conclusion

In economics and sociology, the analysis of change in agriculture, including food, is part of the shifting history of technical progress towards different forms and meanings of innovation. The territorial anchoring of innovation highlights the importance of debates and controversies concerning the modification of living things, food security and agro-ecological transition. Innovation becomes an intermediate object that allows the construction of interdisciplinarity between economics and sociology by associating management, geography and agronomy.

The three dimensions that specify innovation processes in agriculture and food explain the dedicated needs for the coordination of economic agents and, therefore, the forms of professional organizations and regulatory institutions (biosafety standards, quality labels) that structure sectoral policies. Recently, agricultural innovation has been doubly challenged by the convergence of two issues: that of ecological transitions allowing for the management of the renewal conditions of ecological resources that determine the equilibrium of ecosystems and, thus, of biological and human life in an inclusive manner, and that of the acceleration of sciatic and technical progress in biotechnologies and digital technologies, which structure both the technological promises and the societal risks associated with their conditions of realization.

3.7. References

Boserup, E. (1981). *Population and Technological Change: A Study of Long-Term Trends*. The University of Chicago Press, Chicago.

Chambers, R., Pacey, A., Thrupp, L.A. (1989). *Farmer First: Farmer Innovation and Agricultural Research*. The Bootstrap Press, New York.

Chauveau, J.-P., Cormier-Salem, M.-C., Mollard, E. (1999). *L'innovation en agriculture, questions de méthodes et terrains d'observation*. IRD Éditions, Paris.

Chiffoleau, Y. and Touzard, J.-M. (2014). Understanding local agri-food systems through advice network analysis. *Agriculture and Human Values*, 31(1), 19–32.

Darré, J.-P., Le Guen, R., Lémery, B. (1989). Changement technique et structure professionnelle locale en agriculture. *Économie rurale*, 192–193, 115–122.

Faure, G., Toillier, A., Mathé, S., Triomphe, B., Temple, L. (2019). Evaluación de los sistemas de innovación agropecuaria para el diseño de políticas públicas: una revisión de la literatura. In *Sistemas y políticas de innovación para el sector agropecuario en América Latina*, Goulet, F., Le Coq, J.-F., Sotomayor, O. (eds). E-papers, Rio de Janeiro.

Jas, N. (2005). Déqualifier le paysan, introniser l'agronome, France 1840–1914. *Écologie & politique*, 2(31), 45–55.

Joly, P.B. (2001). Les OGM entre la science et le public ? Quatre modèles pour la gouvernance de l'innovation et des risques. *Économie rurale*, 266(1), 11–29.

Klerkx, L., Aarts, N., Leeuwis, C. (2010). Adaptive management in agricultural innovation systems: The interactions between innovation networks and their environment. *Agricultural Systems*, 103(6), 390–400.

Labini, P. (2007). Développements scientifiques, innovations technologiques, croissance et productivité. *Revue d'économie industrielle*, 118, 79–90.

Mendras, H. (1970). *La fin des paysans. Innovations et changement dans l'agriculture française*. Armand Colin, Paris.

Ricardo, D. (1817). *On the Principles of Political Economy and Taxation*. John Murray, London.

Temple, L., Chiffoleau, Y., Touzard, J.M. (2018). Une histoire de l'innovation et de ses usages dans l'agriculture. In *Innovation et développement dans les systèmes agricoles et alimentaires*, Faure, G., Chiffoleau, Y., Goulet, F., Temple, L., Touzard, J.M. (eds). Éditions Quæ, Versailles.

Touzard, J.M., Temple, L., Faure, G., Triomphe, B. (2014). Systèmes d'innovation et communautés de connaissances dans le secteur agricole et agroalimentaire. *Innovations*, 43, 13–38.

Vanloqueren, G. and Baret, P.V. (2009). How agricultural research systems shape a technological regime that develops genetic engineering but locks out agroecological innovations. *Research Policy*, 38(6), 971–983.

4

Anthropology – Anthropological Aspects of Innovation: Defining Benchmarks

4.1. Introduction

In purely academic terms, which is only one criterion among others, innovation is not an anthropological theme. And yet, through the observation of techniques and material culture, anthropology deals with the question of innovations, as authors such as Robert Creswell, Bruno Latour, Pierre Lemonnier, André Leroy-Gourhan, Daniel Miller, Marcel Mauss, François Sigaut or Jean Pierre Warnier have shown. Through the explanations it provides on the problematic links between objects, tools, know-how, humans and their imagination, it produces the intellectual tools that will allow us to understand how new technologies are transforming all societies, whether they are "archaic" or "modern".

In 1914, Bronislaw Malinowski, a Polish anthropologist exiled in England, was sent by his university to New Guinea. Because of the advent of World War I, he became stranded in the Trobriand archipelago, in the Pacific Ocean, where he unexpectedly set up an investigation. The location of the investigation was chosen according to the opportunities and constraints of access to the field. Improvising a survey in the face of the emergence of an unexpected change or innovation represented the first and foremost skill of the anthropology of innovation. Its objective is to understand the social logic of both the production of innovations and of their dissemination using a specifically anthropological method.

In 1922, Malinowski published his famous work, *Argonauts of the Western Pacific*, which describes the *kula*, a system of gifts and counter-gifts, based on shells, both utilitarian and symbolic, which circulate within the Trobriand society.

Chapter written by Dominique DESJEUX.

Thanks to this field research, he introduced a methodological innovation whose effects were felt all the way up to "design thinking", one of the approaches that is used today by designers to understand the processes of innovation, focusing on the experience of populations, on their daily lives, on their practices. At the starting point, the researcher masters nothing. They start without any preconceived ideas, i.e. without any hypothesis on the substance of the innovation or change they are going to investigate. In the course of the fieldwork, depending on the evolution of the phenomenon, they will be able to change the angle of observation, in contrast to, say, quantitative surveys by questionnaire, where it is not possible to change the questions during the course of the survey. It is a situation that we find when approaching an "exotic" country with an unknown culture, a new situation such as that of the lockdown linked to COVID-19, or when we have to talk about the future, i.e. an uncertain and unpredictable and somehow exotic world.

Malinowski's investigation can be considered as one of the first to use an inductive method, i.e. an *in vivo* method, anchored in real life where nothing is under control, in contrast to *in vitro* laboratory investigations, where everything is under control in order to search for an independent causal variable. In anthropological investigations, the universes observed are made of stability and instability. The second characteristic of the anthropology of innovation is to know how to create reference points in an unknown and shifting world, thanks to the observation and description of what emerges, without knowing where it will lead the researcher.

4.2. Innovation, a total social phenomenon, between invention, diffusion and reception

Induction does not mean that the survey is methodless. Anthropology approaches the question of novelty as a "total social fact", which includes the utilitarian and the imaginary, to use the expression of the anthropologist Marcel Mauss in *The Gift* (1925). This means that anthropology is not limited to the technical dimension of innovation. It shows that technical rationality is not sufficient to explain the social circulation of an innovation, be it to accept or oppose it.

Its diffusion depends on the power relations in which it is involved, on who will gain or lose from the implementation of the change, or on the different meanings given to it by the actors. The anthropology of innovation does not postulate technical determinism. On the contrary, it shows that every innovation is embedded in a triple material, social and symbolic dimension. What can vary is the weight that each approach will give to one or other of these dimensions to explain the "success" or "failure" of an innovation.

At the heart of theoretical discussion, there remains one open question, that of knowing whether objects are actors (as in the "actor-network" by Madeleine Akrich, Michel Callon and Bruno Latour), whether they participate in societal action as systems of concrete objects that organize the constrained play of social actors (as in the anthropology of material culture), or whether they produce a technical determinism that constitutes a constraining force for social actors (as in the vision of a part of the world of "sciences and techniques"). At the very least, it is necessary to distinguish between active objects such as viruses that act without the help of men, and passive objects such as a pen that depend on human beings to act.

Another debate is whether an innovation occurs incrementally or by breakthrough, following the work of Christensen (2002). Very often, we find that a disruptive innovation does not exist, as such, but is the result of a whole aggregation of incremental innovations.

Very often, the term innovation is associated with invention. It is understood as a moment of creativity, the production of a new idea, a new technology or a new service, individual or collective, as in the departments for "innovation and development" (or marketing), in companies. Conversely, the anthropology of innovation chooses another division of reality, another scale of observation, which shows that innovation is a collective process over time that takes place in a nonlinear and non-mechanical way.

This is why anthropological and sociological qualitative surveys, such as that of Norbert Alter, will formally distinguish three stages: that of invention, the moment of creation of something new, such as a new molecule in the pharmaceutical field, a new digital technology, a new agricultural technique, a new distribution system, a new model of management; that of innovation, which is the social process by which an invention is diffused through digital and "pre-digital" social networks that are supportive to the interplay of actors in favor or against this or that change; and that of reception, which is the moment when the invention is transformed into an object or a service that must correspond to a use, to a material or symbolic utility, and therefore to a problem to be solved, in a professional or domestic space.

Throughout the process, "invention" is often transformed. The transformation, reinterpretation or translation, depending on the theoretical approaches, of the invention conditions its progress through a company, an administration or an NGO. It is even very often observed that one of the conditions of success of an invention is it has been reinterpreted throughout this itinerary up to its arrival at the final user's home, whether this be a company or a consumer. Innovation in anthropology is part of a collective process of change made up of the interplay of actors, in which relations of power and cooperation, energy, logistics and the magico-religious intertwine.

4.3. The force of constraints or innovation as a process of insertion in a field of contradictory forces

The anthropology of innovation is a strategic approach that shows that actors act under constraint, either to trigger change or, conversely, to slow it down. The empirical observation, linked to the realization of numerous qualitative field surveys, is that there is no change, and therefore no innovation, without the existence of constraints prior to the interplay of actors. The lockdown linked to COVID-19 is an exceptional example of this, since it has blocked almost all population mobility in a very large number of countries. The containment constraint makes it possible to understand what emerges, what is maintained or what disappears. It is an "upstream" constraint that corresponds to what is also called the forces that govern us, whether these forces are the "invisible hand of the market", God, multinational corporations, fate, the fatum of the Romans or the ananké (Ἀνάγκη) of the Greeks, predestination, determinism, nature, the Shì 势, the course of events in Chinese thought, or habitus in the social sciences.

At the same time, once the innovation process has been triggered, it appears that the actors are confronted with a whole series of material, social and symbolic constraints that make it possible to understand the human dimension of the diffusion of an innovation. We can identify 11 of these, but of course there may be fewer or more. The important thing to remember is that these constraints rationally explain why some actors favor, prevent or allow change to take place.

Let us take the very general question of frugal consumption. If we try to get French consumers to buy French products, which is a new practice from the consumers' point of view, and that these products are more expensive than Spanish or Dutch products, depending on the season, we understand that the constraint of purchasing power limits French purchases. The constraint explains the discrepancy between the positive or negative representations associated with innovation and actual practices.

This means that there is not only an economic, technical or scientific rationality, but that there exists visible or subterranean social logic. Anthropology seeks to understand the logic of what appears irrational to an economist, a doctor or an engineer. These are the forces that organize the interplay of actors throughout the process of production of innovation up until its reception. To understand constraints is to understand the underground rationalities, the social logic that explain the unfolding of innovation processes.

The first five constraints that "delay" innovation processes are material: the time constraint, the space constraint, the budget or the purchasing power constraint.

A more anthropological constraint is that of the system of concrete objects that will or will not allow the use of the invention. The last material constraint is that of available human energy. This is particularly important in innovations that affect the domestic space and thus the traditional division of tasks between men and women.

The three social constraints relate to learning, for example, the learning of a new digital technology, which, if it is too complex, will slow down its adoption; the importance of pre-digital or digital social networks that will play the role of prescriber or opponent of innovation; and the nature of group norms that often implicitly define what is prescribed, allowed or forbidden socially. The three symbolic and psychosocial constraints relate to mental load, i.e. the stress that can result from the adoption of an innovation; personal or professional identity, depending on whether or not it is questioned by the innovation; and perceived risks in relation to the novelty, whether it is a danger or a security measure.

The anthropology of innovation allows us to show that a technology does not exist in itself, but that it is the result of a whole process of social construction in terms of its emergence. External constraints play a triggering role in this process, and this can be found throughout its diffusion, with constraints acting as filters either in favor or against this novelty.

4.4. Conclusion

The anthropology of innovation clearly shows the complexity of the process of change, which requires simultaneous shifting through geographical mobility, through mobility over time with history, and through mobile knowledge depending on the scale of observation (Desjeux 2018). To innovate is to transgress, to take risks, either to be dismissed or marginalized depending on the situation. This shows that innovation is not given and therefore explains the importance of constraints as drivers of innovation.

Today, with global warming, the risk of pandemics or war, the question of innovation is being reversed. Since the 18th century, i.e. since the beginning of the coal age, the industrial revolution and consumer society, most innovations have been organized around five objectives: simplifying uses through industry, chemistry and fossil energy; saving time; spending less human energy by using industrial energy; increasing productivity and thus the quantity of goods consumed; and finally paying less by lowering the costs and prices of goods consumed.

With the new constraint of sustainable consumption, innovation must help to limit the quantity of goods consumed and increase their durability, which often increases costs and prices, which thus contradicts innovation processes that have been going on for more than two centuries. Some innovations, such as cooking more from fresh products, increase the mental burden of some social actors, mainly women at home. Some of these innovations contradict the purchasing power constraints of the lower middle classes, even if none of this is automatic. Innovating today requires changing the reasoning and methods of the innovation processes that have been organizing our societies for 250 years.

4.5. References

Akrich, M., Latour, B., Callon, M. (2006). *Sociologie de la traduction : textes fondateurs.* Presses des Mines, Paris.

Alter, N. (2000). *Innovation Ordinaire*. PUF, Paris.

Christensen, C. (2002). *The Innovator's Dilemma.* Harper Business Essentials, New York.

Creswell, R. (1975). *Éléments d'ethnologie*. Armand Colin, Paris.

Desjeux, D. (2018). *The Anthropological Perspective of the World.* The Inductive Method Illustrated, Peter Lang, Brussels.

Leroi-Gourhan, A. (1964). *Le geste et la parole II*, Albin Michel, Paris.

Malinowski, B. (2002). Argonauts of the Western Pacific. Routledge, London.

Mauss, M. (1923). *Sociologie et anthropologie*. PUF, Paris.

Sigaut, F. (1975). *L'Agriculture et le feu.* Mouton, Berlin.

Warnier J.-P. (1999). *Construire la culture matérielle : l'homme qui pensait avec ses doigts.* PUF, Paris.

5

Business – Business Creation and Innovative Entrepreneurial Ecosystems

While the objective of economic theory is to explain the mechanisms of wealth creation, economists have only very recently raised the question of the location of companies and its impact on their development and *vice versa*. Moreover, although the entrepreneur was identified very early on as a major economic actor, the modalities of their capacity to innovate as an actor are still debated (Boutillier and Tiran 2016; Boutillier and Uzunidis 2016).

Since the beginning of the 20th century, many theories have been developed to formulate explanations to understand the economic dynamics of territories and the role of entrepreneurs. The business ecosystem (BE) (Moore 1993, 1996) is one of the most recent concepts in this field, broadly defined as a set of interactions between firms belonging to different fields of activity sharing a common strategic vision around a pivotal firm that imposes its technology. Moore gives the latter an important power to organize markets and industries. The ecosystem provides a relevant reading grid for understanding the strategies of firms in a given context, which is not reduced to territorial parameters alone, but includes a wide variety of stakeholders, who, in different ways, maintain exchange relationships, in a process of co-evolution.

The use of the ecosystem in the human and social sciences has grown considerably since the 1990s. It is easily used to explain many complex phenomena: entrepreneurship, innovation, business relations, etc. (Scaringella and Radziwon 2018). The BE and the entrepreneurial ecosystem (EE) have attributes in common, including the existence of synergistic relationships between various stakeholders. The BE and EE do not offer the same reading grid (Stam 2015; Brown and Mason 2017). The EE includes a territorial dimension that is not favored in the BE, as well

Chapter written by Sophie BOUTILLIER.

as a public policy and entrepreneurship support dimension (Boutillier *et al.* 2016). However, although this borrowing from biology is widely criticized (Fréry *et al.* 2012), the ecosystem remains no less relevant in explaining economic dynamics, primarily entrepreneurial ones concerning innovation in the broad sense of the term (product, process, organization), which should prompt us to take this metaphor seriously (Kuckertz 2019). This reference to biology is indeed rich in lessons (selection, adaptation, competition, cooperation).

5.1. The company, the territory and the ecosystem

Marshall (1885) is the essential reference in terms of territorial economy. "Industrial districts" and "industrial atmosphere" have long been part of the vocabulary of economists. But beyond a kind of alchemy supposed to operate between the territory (having a set of resources) and the entrepreneurs (with other stakeholders, such as the State, consumers, workers), the question arises of the nature of these synergistic relations and the modalities of their realization. These synergistic relations are materialized by exchanges of goods and services, raw materials, semi-finished products, technologies, knowledge, workers, etc. by a common vision that is shared by all, orchestrated by a pivotal firm. This territorial space is also homogeneous by virtue of the economic activities that develop there. In the same vein, Perroux (1950) distinguishes between commonplace and economic spaces. The "banal space" is defined in the geographical sense of the term; the economic space is defined at the level of the firm (generally large) that organizes and structures it. It also acts as a sort of force field between different actors. Under these conditions, Perroux breaks with the model of pure and perfect competition by developing the principle of a hierarchical market organization. Moreover, the exceptional success of certain sites, such as Silicon Valley, has also raised questions for researchers. Porter's (1990) answer is that of the "cluster", which has since been widely adopted by the scientific community, which he defines summarily as a group of firms and associated institutions linked by common elements and complementarities.

The BE (Moore 1993, 1996) forms a part of this trajectory of thought by sketching a new conception of competition: the (pivotal) firm organizes and structures the market in which it is positioned. In biology, the ecosystem is in fact a group formed by a community of living beings interacting with its environment. Its components develop a dense network of dependencies, exchanges, energy, information and various materials that enable life to be maintained and developed. The major interest of the ecosystem is to build a bridge between the micro and the macro (Roundy *et al.* 2018). Indeed, systemic analysis allows us to dissect the different components of a complex problem by highlighting nonlinear relationships. In spite of the criticisms made, the biological metaphor is not superficial; it cannot be reduced, as is often the case, to the image of a self-regulating system. Whether it is a biological or an entrepreneurial ecosystem, in both cases, it is necessary for an external actor to intervene to support this process of self-regulation, through appropriate public policy measures (Kuckertz 2019). For Moore (1993, 1996), the analogy with biology and the theory of evolution is obvious. It mobilizes all the tools of biological analysis. He even goes so far as to formulate the idea of an "ecology of competition" to explain that the survival of a firm depends on its capacity to evolve in its ecosystem, questioning itself in view of the transformation of its environment. A BE, like a biological ecosystem, is born, develops and transforms itself by adapting to new contingencies. Moore questions the nature of the relationship between the market and the firm by including a wide variety of actors, such as companies, the State, consumers and trade unions. The BE is an economic community supported by the interaction between a pivotal firm and different stakeholders. This community produces goods and services by bringing value to consumers. Over time, the skills and roles of the different stakeholders co-evolve and align their behavior with the pivotal firm (or several pivotal firms). The idea of co-evolution among BE stakeholders is widely favored. These companies will have a leadership role that can evolve over time. The function of the ecosystem leader is to bring value to the community, as they will engage stakeholders to act with a shared vision to adapt their investments and find mutually supportive roles. Moore thus favors cooperative relationships over competitive ones. The BE-based analysis shows that companies are not isolated entities, but develop their own strategies based on relationships of complementarity, cooperation and competition. These interactions, in turn, foster the creation and development of common skills and resources, sources of sustainable competitive advantages. A BE does not necessarily take place in a given geographical space; the stakeholders that make it up may be geographically close or distant.

5.2. From the business ecosystem to the entrepreneurial ecosystem: polymorphous innovation dynamics?

Although close, BE and EE reading grids are different, although, in essence, they both defend the idea of an innovation dynamic that is born from the interactive relationships between firms, entrepreneurs and institutions. The EE includes a territorial dimension, which is not favored in the BE. But this is not the only difference. The BE is said to have been born in 1995 (Roundy *et al.* 2018) following a study of Silicon Valley. Since then, it has been adopted by many researchers. A wide variety of definitions of the BE can be identified. These definitions focus on various aspects, depending on the researcher's objectives. Interaction relationships between interdependent actors are frequently favored (Stam 2015). In addition to companies, other actors are involved, first and foremost institutions participating in the development of a "local entrepreneurial environment" (Masson and Brown 2014). The EE is also known for its capacity to support the creation of start-ups through open innovation strategies (Pustovrh *et al.* 2020). In this sense, an EE is not closed, while being marked by strong geographical and socio-cultural characteristics. The entrepreneur plays an important role. Roundy *et al.* (2018) emphasize the intentionality and adaptive tensions of entrepreneurs (existence of key agents that influence cognitive relationships and entrepreneurial behavior) and the coherence of entrepreneurial activities (many entrepreneurs share the same intentions and values that help shape the structures of the EE through a "business friendly community"). Cognitive relationships between entrepreneurs are privileged (Nambisan and Baron 2013). Moreover, although the EE is characterized by a strong internal coherence due to the above-mentioned elements, it is also an open system. The EE is permeable to the entry of new resources thanks to investors who share the same values.

The EE also includes a public policy dimension (Isenberg 2010) aimed precisely at supporting entrepreneurial activity and innovation in a given territorial space. The EE is also seen as a powerful tool for fighting poverty by enhancing individual initiative (Prahalat 2005). In this sense, the EE is not the result of an individual decision (public or private), but of a set of interactions that emerge in the absence of a "global controller" (Roundy *et al.* 2018). The BE also includes a set of interrelationships between different stakeholders, which may include not only other businesses, consumers, etc., but also universities or non-profit organizations. Autio *et al.* (2014) criticize the theories of entrepreneurship that essentially focus on the individual dimension of the entrepreneur while neglecting the contextual aspects (industrial, technological, organizational, institutional, social, temporal and spatial). Cultural dimensions are largely emphasized to characterize an EE through the sharing of common values. Venture capitalists also present on the territory support the creation of start-ups there because they are convinced of their chances of success. Regional or local public authorities organize events to support entrepreneurial activity at the territorial level (Scaringella and Radziwon 2018). By emphasizing the role of the entrepreneur, the EE also includes the idea of bottom-up development, generally by poorer populations who find in entrepreneurship an opportunity to create their own jobs. In this context, we will speak of an agile innovation that comes from the combination of reduced resources. The institutional changes that emerged from the 1990s with the end of the Cold War and the planned economy are widely discussed. The market and the creation of companies within the framework of these changes have been singled out as powerful tools to fight poverty (Prahalat 2005).

Criticizing the use of the term ecosystem, which is used excessively in their opinion (BE, EE, innovation, etc.), Scaringella and Radziwon (2018) constructed a reading grid to identify the invariants of the ecosystem approach. We will use it to distinguish the BE from the EE, highlighting invariants and characteristics. The invariants are the following: 1) territory 2) values; 3) stakeholders; 4) economic theories; 5) social policy; 6) knowledge and 7) results obtained by the BE or EE (see Table 3.1).

Invariants	Description	
	Business ecosystem	**Entrepreneurial ecosystem**
Territory	**Close relationships between stakeholders**	**Preferred geographical dimension (region, country)**
Values: trust, sense of community, mutual understanding, reduced uncertainty, culture, history, routines	Trusting relationships between stakeholders forming a community involved in a co-creation process	Sharing of common values uniting stakeholders with a shared vision of entrepreneurship
Stakeholders: firms, inter-firm networks, other stakeholders	A network of interacting inter-company relations facilitating the dynamics of learning processes between stakeholders who develop complementary activities Apart from firms, other stakeholders play a major role: consumers, suppliers, subcontracting firms, manufacturers of related products and services	Network of inter-firm relations and support institutions for business creation (e.g. incubator) Importance of the role of the public authority in supporting local development through business creation and innovation.
Economic theories	Economics of localization, spin-offs, industrial economy (economies of scale)	
Social: cooperative/competitive relationships between stakeholders, job creation, human resources	Cooperative and/or competitive relationships within the framework of a co-opetitive relationship Symbiosis between stakeholders Importance of job creation	Stimulation of technical progress, socio-economic interactions between private companies in symbiotic relationships and the production of new knowledge through interactions
Knowledge: different types, dynamics of creation, synergistic relationships	Protection of knowledge (patent) Knowledge mobility and synergistic relationships between innovation resources	Production of new knowledge through interaction relationships Creation of start-ups
Outcome: innovation and entrepreneurship development	Value creation Innovations to improve performance Competitive advantage through collaboration in a network of value creation in a process of adaptation/evolution	GDP growth Radical innovations A process of co-creation and evolution encouraged by public policies

Table 5.1. *Business and entrepreneurial ecosystems, invariants and own characteristics (source: Scaringella and Radziwon (2018))*

There are subtle differences between the BE and EE. The dominant idea is the creation of an economic community whose members maintain synergistic and co-creative relationships to encourage innovation. The territorial dimension is diminished in the BE as opposed to the EE, which also emphasizes coherence, which is reinforced by appropriate public policy measures. The BE is part of a reflection that favors individual initiative. Poorer populations are thus accorded a route out of poverty by innovating. Emphasis is placed on the coherence of the ecosystem and on the sharing of common values and objectives among stakeholders. The role of innovation support institutions (e.g. incubators) is frequently emphasized in the BE. On the other hand, in the BE, it is the pivotal firm that is designated as a driver for innovation.

5.3. References

Boutillier, S. and Tiran, A. (2016). La théorie de l'entrepreneur, son évolution et sa contextualisation. *Innovations. Revue d'économie et de management de l'innovation*, 50, 211–234.

Boutillier, S. and Uzunidis, D. (2016). *The Entrepreneur: The Economic Function of Free Enterprise*. ISTE Ltd, London and John Wiley & Sons, New York.

Boutillier, S., Carré, D., Levratto, N. (2016). *Entrepreneurial Ecosystems*. ISTE Ltd, London and John Wiley & Sons, New York.

Brown, R. and Mason, C. (2017). Looking inside the spiky bits: A critical review and conceptualisation of entrepreneurial ecosystems. *Small Business Economics*, 49, 11–30.

Fréry, F., Gratacap, A., Isckia, T. (2012). Les écosystèmes d'affaires, par-delà la métaphore. *Revue française de gestion*, 222, 69–75.

Kuckertz, A. (2019). Let's take the entrepreneurial ecosystem metaphor seriously! *Journal of Business Venturing Insights*, 11 [Online]. Available at: https://www.sciencedirect.com/science/article/pii/S2352673419300095.

Marshall, A. (1885). *Economics of Industry*. Macmillan, London.

Moore, J. (1993). Predators and prey: A new ecology of competition. *Harvard Business Review*, 71(3), 75–86.

Moore, J. (1996). *The Death of Competition: Leadership and Strategy in the Age of Business Ecosystems*. Harper Business, New York.

Perroux, F. (1950). Les espaces économiques. *Economie appliquée*. Archives de l'ISEA, 1, 225–244.

Porter, M. (1990). *The Competitive Avantage of Nations*. The Free Press, New York.

Pustovrh, A., Rangus, K., Drnovsek, M. (2020). The role of open innovation in developing an entrepreneurial support ecosystem. *Technological Forecasting & Social Change*, 152 [Online]. Available at: https://www.sciencedirect.com/science/article/pii/S0040162518315488.

Roundy, P.T. (2019). Back from the brink: The revitalization of inactive entrepreneurial ecosystem. *Journal of Business Venturing Insights*, 12 [Online]. Available at: https://reader.elsevier.com/reader/sd/pii/S2352673419300885?token=5DCCDEE880F1008A05D70B924F4E1651AD4630A54C6293C87B58677B28B78F76031179525377DF3733E0F504B9F69B7A.

Roundy, P.T., Bradshaw, M., Brockman, B.K. (2018). The emergence of entrepreneurial ecosystems: A complex adaptative system approach. *Journal of Business Research*, 86, 1–10.

Scaringella, L. and Radziwon, A. (2018). Innovation, entrepreneurial, knowledge, and business ecosystems: Old wine in new bottles? *Technological Forecasting & Social Change*, 136, 59–87.

Stam, E. (2015). Entrepreneurial ecosystems and regional policy: A sympathetic critique. *European Planning Studies*, 23(9), 1759–1769.

6

Capacity – Innovation Capacities and Learning Dynamics

6.1. Introduction

The term "innovation" has given way to "capacity" in work relating to innovation systems over the last twenty years and, more particularly, in the context of developing countries, where the diffusion and absorption of foreign knowledge is positioned upstream of its constitution (Casadella and Uzunidis 2018).

Originally, innovation capacities proved to be relevant in the literature on technology transfer. Transfer is defined by UN regulations (1971) as the transfer of knowledge for the manufacture of a product or the provision of a service. It is a transfer of knowledge between firms belonging to different countries, an exchange of equipment or techniques from one country to another. Technology transfer can take place from one company to another, from one foreign country to another, from a research laboratory to a newly created or existing company. Part of the innovation process comes from this technology transfer. Technology transfer refers to the diffusion and the opportunity for actors and territories to reappropriate foreign technology (Casadella *et al.* 2015). Obviously, technology transfer alone is not enough to create dynamic innovation. It is the entire meso-, micro- and macroeconomic environment that must be considered, hence the importance of systemic interactions between productive and academic spheres and, above all, of the so-called "capacity" for innovation.

Chapter written by Vanessa CASADELLA.

We first present the link between innovation capacities and learning dynamics, before looking at the diversity of these capacities and deducing the value of building skills within innovation systems.

6.2. Learning and innovation capacities

Neoclassical economists have been interested in allocation problems within a general equilibrium context. Individual agents, by virtue of their preferences and information (notably technical knowledge), must make rational choices among the various alternatives proposed. From this perspective, conclusions on the organization of the economic system are known: allocating resources to achieve objectives. As these resources are always limited, choices have to be made. This being the case, this vision cannot correspond to an understanding of current economic development phenomena. Indeed, if firms or states intensify their efforts to allocate existing resources (capital, labor), and if each separate unit produces the same product with the same technique, they become much less competitive because of the repercussions on demand (consumers). Innovation therefore goes beyond the principle of allocating resources, in a context where the speed of technical change is constantly accelerating. It is less a question of knowing how to distribute resources related to labor and capital factors, than of creating and using diverse knowledge through learning processes. In addition, the information and specific knowledge that agents have is less important than their ability to make, have made or to use knowledge. The latter includes the ability to do new things, to cope with new situations and to gain access to new information. In short, companies must constantly look for new knowledge to use in production, such as new products or processes. To do this, they must be part of a Learning Economy (Lundvall and Borras 1999), which means that the current change does not lie in the intensive use of knowledge, but rather in the acceleration of the speed of change, which leads to a very rapid depreciation and obsolescence of skills and knowledge. Consequently, the essential factor in the competitiveness of firms lies more in the capacity to acquire new skills rather than in the possession of a certain stock of knowledge or access to information.

6.3. The diversity of innovation capacities

We turn now to the term 'innovation capacity'. The capacity of companies in the current context becomes crucial for their performance. It defines a constant need to develop the qualifications of individuals and the organizational or technological skills of companies. The constitution of knowledge includes practical skills through learning by imitation, as well as intellectual capacities acquired in educational and training institutions. It also includes knowledge management through organizational learning, as well as R&D. In other words, innovation capacities include the realization of learning processes through practice (learning by doing), through use (learning by using) or through interacting (learning by interacting), as well as individual learning processes (education and training), controlled directly by individuals. These are inherent prerequisites for innovation processes, even though they do not directly concern them. Direct learning processes are mainly aimed at universities, research centers and R&D laboratories and concern formal organizations, while indirect learning processes are more concerned with internal company learning processes. The similarity between the two processes lies in their social and interactive nature. Finally, learning processes combine four types of knowledge (Lundvall and Johnson 1994): know-what or informational knowledge, know-why or the understanding of social and natural phenomena (scientific knowledge), know-who or the social ability to cooperate and communicate, and finally, know-how or the ability to do something on a practical level (experience). All of these processes, far from being exhaustive, are not only related to the amount of energy spent by actors to solve problems, but also to the expertise that actors have in mastering new knowledge. They consist of efforts to use local knowledge through the capacity to (be able to) internalize foreign knowledge. We speak of domestication of knowledge, rehabilitation and local reappropriation. For this, while knowledge utilization is achieved through capacity building, it also depends on learning opportunities. These capacities, based on constantly evolving demand, develop very rapidly within contexts of learning opportunities: i.e. access to universities, research centers and institutions, and also to national education systems or research projects (Gregersen and Johnson 1997).

The set of capacities shows the great diversity of learning processes that a company can institute, in line with its direct and indirect environment. This diversity is more broadly understood as a "learning culture" (Johnson *et al.* 2003). The latter refers to the daily promotion of learning in all segments of the economy (R&D, production, human resources, institutions, politics): from individual learning to organizational learning, tacit and explicit, formal and informal, in low and medium technology, from the exact sciences to the humanities. It requires the adaptation of knowledge to local conditions and the improvement of these conditions in the economy as a whole. It is through lack of a "learning culture" that innovation capacities are limited and the institutional framework is not well equipped to promote the necessary learning. In other words, valuing learning in all its forms is key to understanding how firms learn.

6.4. Capacities, innovation system and competency building

While innovative capacity has proved the most common expression in the jargon of current authors in the field of innovation economics, the term "skills construction" has appeared in parallel in the economic literature to take advantage of the diversity of forms of learning, and also their uses for productive purposes. Thus the expression "System of Innovation and Competence Construction" (S.I.C.C.) was first presented by the Globelics group in 2002 at an international conference on innovation systems at the University of Aalborg. Lundvall (2013) recently recalled its importance in developing economies by highlighting the importance of formal training, learning by interacting apprenticeships and also of informal activities, influenced by the use of information technologies and communication.

In addition, the geographic setting in which capacity is developed is important. As the concept of the "national innovation system" reminds us, capacities are built and identified at the national level, but are not closed to and from outside. The participation of innovative foreign firms, the links between external innovation networks and the effectiveness of innovation systems in adapting to changes in the global environment are the main measures of the opening up of these national capacities. This openness is also linked to the acquisition of foreign knowledge, to the mobility of human capital or to global value chains (Chaminade *et al.* 2018). As for the presence of foreign innovators, they contribute to reinforcing the heterogeneity of capacities while playing different roles in the host country's innovation. As a result, innovation capacities maintain increasingly complex collaborative links across national boundaries. They are more adaptive and scalable. Like "open" or "globalized" innovation systems (Binz and Truffer 2017), some research points to the role of multinational firms, their activities and their means, which enable SMEs to exchange knowledge and technology through partnerships, and to then absorb and strengthen innovation capacities (Watkins *et al.* 2015). Other studies (Fu *et al.* 2011) characterize the learning processes in which entire local firms and industries connect to global value chains led by multinationals. These local firms can not only learn about globalized market needs, standards or practices, but also about new technological and organizational skills.

Finally, it remains important to position the capacity for innovation in a perspective of economic development, beyond purely quantitative growth objectives or benchmarks related to Science and Technology. Inclusive innovation shows how the development of technologies, coupled with social policies aimed at reducing inequalities, are important levers. Inclusion can be "passive" or "active" depending on the degree to which individuals and communities can play an "active" role in economic development. The capacity for innovation is therefore oriented towards inclusive innovation, to the extent that formal or informal learning processes are allocated qualitative functions around well-being, improving quality of life or reducing poverty. This may be the case when looking at the role of universities in the systemic dynamics of innovation. In some transition and developing countries, the demand for highly qualified personnel is low. This low demand for graduates reflects cultural and social barriers that restrict their hiring. The low demand for knowledge can create stagnation in terms of technical and organizational change. This leads to an unoptimistic logic in which capacities will not have influenced the dynamics of innovation and economic development, which are essential for building an innovation system and making it sustainable in the long term.

6.5. Conclusion

In conclusion, we have understood that capacities are based on learning mechanisms, resulting from the connectivity between those who benefit from new ideas and seek to expand their possible applications, and those who use them and have continually evolving needs. The National Innovation Capacity, through the learning processes it initiates and sustains, plays a major role in the issue of systemic innovation. Not only does its development increase the growth potential of States through the processes of technological absorption and diffusion that it generates, but above all it gives priority to the local knowledge of communities through issues of poverty or inequalities that it can now raise.

6.6. References

Binz, C. and Truffer, B. (2017). Global innovation systems – A conceptual framework for innovation dynamics in transnational contexts. *Research Policy*, 46, 1284–1298.

Casadella, V. and Uzunidis, D. (2018). Les capacités d'innovation comme préalable à la formation d'un système national d'innovation. *Technologie et innovation*, 7(2), 1–15.

Casadella, V., Uzunidis, D., Liu, Z. (2015). *Innovation Capabilities and Economic Development in Open Economies*. ISTE Ltd, London, and John Wiley & Sons, New York.

Chaminade, C., Lundvall, B.A., Haneef, S. (2018). *Advanced Introduction to National Innovation Systems*. Edward Elgar Publishing, Cheltenham.

Fu, X., Pietrobelli, C., Soete, L. (2011). The role of foreign technology and indigenous innovation in the emerging economies: Technological change and catching-up. *World Development*, 39(7), 1204–1212.

Gregersen, B. and Johnson, B. (1997). Learning economies, innovation systems and European integration. *Regional Studies*, 31(5), 479–490.

Johnson, B.H., Lundvall, B-Å., Edquist, C. (2003). Economic development and the national system of innovation approach. *The First International Globelics Conference: Innovation Systems and Development Strategies for the Third Millenium*, Rio de Janeiro, November 2–6.

Lundvall, B.Å. and Borras, S. (1999). *The Globalizing Learning Economy: Implications for Innovation Policy*. European Commission, Brussels.

Lundvall, B.Å. and Johnson, B. (1994). The learning economy. *Journal of Industry Studies*, 1(2), 23–43.

Watkins, A., Papaioannou, T., Mugwawa, J., Kale, D. (2015). National innovation systems and the intermediary role of industry associations in building institutional capacities for innovation in developing countries: A critical review of the literature. *Research Policy*, 1407–1418.

7

Capital – Knowledge Capital and Innovation: Production and Use of Knowledge in Companies

7.1. Introduction

Innovation has become the buzzword of many organizations and economic and social institutions. To be competitive in a changing world, to stimulate growth and to motivate teams, they have to innovate in terms of products, processes, organization, new business methods and so on. The capacity to innovate depends on the constitution and constant strengthening of knowledge capital, defined as "scientific and technical information and knowledge produced, acquired, combined and systematized by one or more companies within a particular productive objective, and more broadly, within a process of value creation" (Laperche 2017). Knowledge capital refers to knowledge accumulated by one or more companies. It is embedded in people (know-how), machines, technologies and routines. It is constantly enriched by information flows. Knowledge capital is more than the sum of its parts: it is a process of cross-fertilization between all these sources of information and knowledge, meaning that the return from the use of this combined set of information and knowledge is higher than the return from the use of each of these individual components taken separately. Knowledge capital is therefore a dynamic concept – a process – that defines knowledge accumulated by one or more companies and is continuously enriched or combined in different ways. This productive objective – value creation – is the main characteristic that transforms knowledge into "capital".

We begin this chapter with a brief definition of knowledge capital. Then, we examine it in relation to other concepts associated with the importance of tangible and intangible resources (knowledge-based capital and intellectual capital) within

---

Chapter written by Blandine LAPERCHE.

companies, with the production and management of knowledge (SECI model, C-K theory, dynamic and absorptive capacities), and with the role of collaboration and openness (open innovation). In each of these cases, we define key concepts and show how knowledge capital differs from them, complements them or is complemented by them. As a result, this chapter allows us to draw the contours of the conceptual landscape associated with the production of knowledge in business economics and management.

7.2. Knowledge capital: toward an understanding of the innovation process

The study of companies' knowledge capital helps to understand how they generate new knowledge and how they transform it into technological, organizational and commercial innovations. Indeed, information is collected on markets through business intelligence strategies, access to patent documents, purchase of technologies and the signing of licenses and other cooperation agreements. It is integrated into the company's knowledge stock through learning processes, the basis for transforming information (as a flow) into knowledge (as a stock) (see Figure 5.1). The use of this stock of knowledge, through transfer to other firms or in the company's production process (e.g. introduction of new products and/or services) depends on market opportunities and the degree of maturity of the technologies developed.

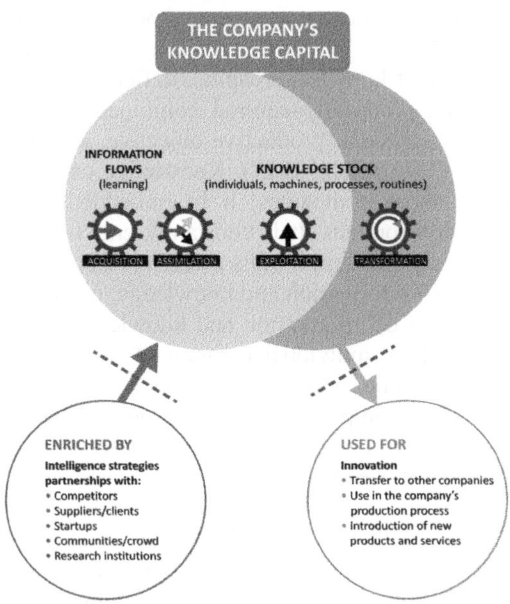

Figure 7.1. *The company's knowledge capital (source: BPI, in Laperche (2017)). For a color version of this figure, see www.iste.co.uk/uzunidis/innovation1.zip*

7.3. Knowledge capital, tangible and intangible assets

The concept of knowledge capital is analytical by nature and aims to deepen the understanding of the content of the "black box" of a company's innovation process. It differs from but complements the concept of "knowledge-based capital" (KBC) proposed by the OECD (2013a). The objective of KBC designers is to list and measure intangible assets in which firms invest, such as data, software, patents, designs, new organizational processes and firm-specific skills. They are divided into three groups: computerized information, innovative property and economic competency (see also Corrado *et al.* 2005). A different classification is also used when studying "intellectual capital", broadly defined as all useful knowledge that can be transformed into value (Edvinsson and Malone 1997). It includes human capital (knowledge, know-how and skills), relational capital (external relations with customers and suppliers) and structural capital (databases, organizational routines and culture).

The objective of "knowledge-based capital" and "intellectual capital" is to demonstrate the economic value of intangible assets, and thus to study their impact on growth and productivity, on the competitiveness of companies and on innovation, in order to promote public policy measures which are more adapted to this broader vision of innovation. However, according to Zambon and Monciardini (2015), most studies on this subject are more focused on the measurement and accounting of intangible assets and neglect the study of their specific role in the value creation process. However, they are useful since they allow for the quantitative evaluation of the contribution of intangible assets. In this sense, they complement our approach to understanding a company's knowledge capital by being more precise about the list of intangible assets that contribute to innovation. However, they need to be linked to other management concepts in order to enact a dynamic vision of the innovation process. Moreover, although intangible assets are central elements to a company's innovation strategy, tangible assets also contain knowledge in the form of "dead labor" embedded in tools, machines and production processes. In our view, these tangible assets are just as essential to the innovation process as intangible assets. From this point of view, our understanding of the use of knowledge capital is broader.

7.4. Knowledge capital and knowledge management within organizations

Many other related concepts can be found in the vast field of knowledge and innovation management. The importance of tacit knowledge and its interactions with explicit knowledge is also at the heart of management studies that focus on the genesis of knowledge within organizations. This is the case, for example, of the work of Nonaka and his co-authors on the genesis and circulation of knowledge within organizations. This is the SECI (socialization, externalization, combination and internalization) model (Nonaka and Takeushi 1995) where innovation in an organization emerges from the interaction between explicit and tacit knowledge, associated with a circulation of knowledge from the individual to the inter-organizational level. We can consider that this process of knowledge creation makes it possible to detail the activities of the central knowledge stock in our understanding of knowledge capital. Similarly, the C-K theory (which stands for concept and knowledge) emphasizes issues of creativity in design and provides further insight into the creation of knowledge within organizations (Hatchuel and Weil 2009; Le Masson and Macmahon 2016).

This work on the production and dissemination of knowledge within organizations is part of resource theory, which has been demonstrated, from its conception, in the work of Edith Penrose (1959). The authors place particular emphasis on the role of competencies (especially key competencies (Prahalad and Hamel 1990)) and capabilities in explaining the competitive advantage of firms. Capabilities which can develop new specific assets gathered in organizational routines are called "dynamic capabilities" by Teece *et al.* (1997). They refer to the "firm's ability to integrate, build and reconfigure internal and external competencies to address rapidly changing environments". The study of how the company's dynamic capabilities are developed is the subject of the cognitive theory of the firm, according to which "knowledge constitutes the most crucial asset and hence, the ability to develop and employ knowledge is the most crucial organizational capability" (Nooteboom 2009, p. 11). Among these dynamic capabilities, absorptive capacity is central to the analysis of the formation of companies' knowledge capital. Absorptive capacity was first defined by Cohen and Levinthal (1990) as a firm's ability to recognize the value of new information, transform it into knowledge, assimilate it and apply it to business purposes. Four dimensions of absorptive capacity are generally identified: acquisition, assimilation, transformation and exploitation (Zahra and George 2002). "Acquisition refers to a firm's capability to identify and acquire externally generated knowledge that is critical to its operations" (Zahra and George 2002, p. 189); "Assimilation refers to the firm's routines and processes that allow it to analyze, process, interpret and understand information obtained from external sources" (Ibid., p. 189); "Transformation denotes a firm's capability to develop and refine the routines that facilitate combining existing knowledge and the newly acquired and assimilated knowledge" (Ibid., p. 190); "Exploitation reflects a firm's ability to harvest and incorporate knowledge into its operations" (Ibid., p. 190).

These four dimensions of absorptive capacity are considered essential to build and maintain a competitive advantage, particularly in the context of open innovation. In our view, absorptive capacity is central to our concept of knowledge capital, as shown in the following figure.

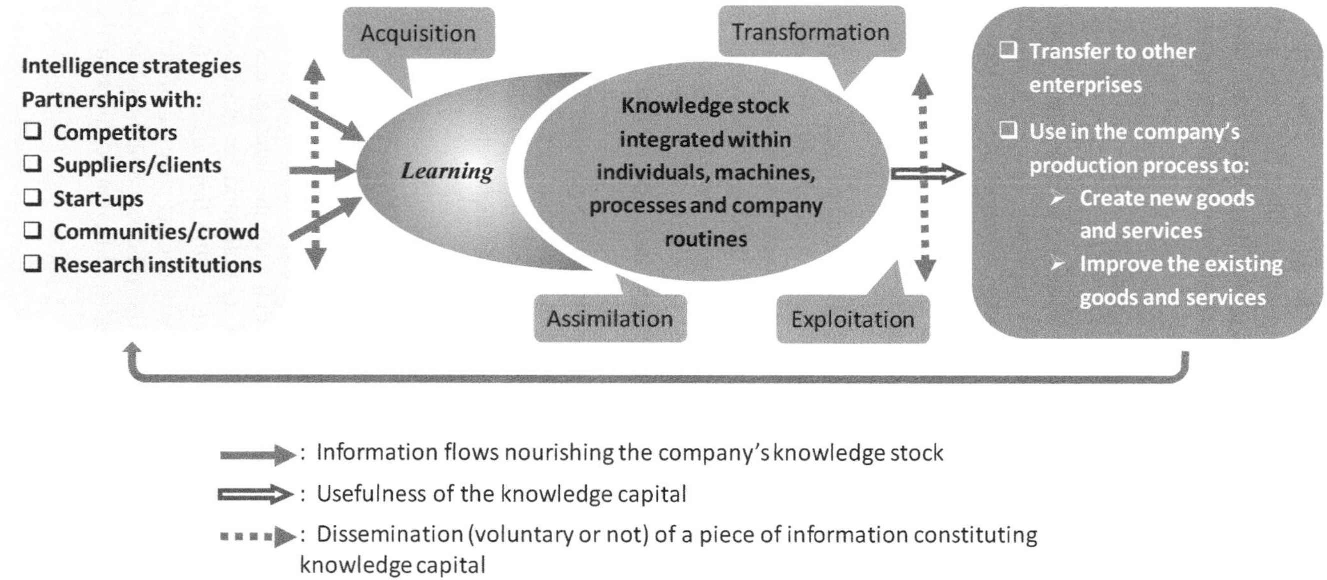

Figure 7.2. *Absorption capacity and knowledge capital. For a color version of this figure, see www.iste.co.uk/uzunidis/innovation1.zip*

The learning process is a way to integrate (Assimilation) information flows that come from outside the company (Acquisition). They are transformed (Transformation) into knowledge and integrated into the company's knowledge stock. This knowledge is then exploited and translated into various forms of innovation or integrated as such into another production process (Exploitation).

7.5. Knowledge capital and open innovation

Multi-partner innovation (or open innovation) is understood here as a generic model integrating all the ways in which a company is open to its environment in order to innovate. It suggests that companies' management of innovation activities has evolved over time from a "closed" process to an "open" process in which "valuable ideas can come from inside or outside the company and can go to the market from inside or outside the company as well" (Chesbrough 2003, p. 47).

According to this author, the open innovation paradigm has begun to replace the old closed innovation paradigm since the end of the 20th century. The logic of the closed innovation paradigm was an internal logic according to which companies financed, generated, developed, built and commercialized their own inventions. Several factors such as the increased mobility of highly skilled workers, the greater availability of private funding for firms, more opportunities to commercialize new ideas, and the more sophisticated skillsets of external suppliers have contributed to the increased questioning of closed innovation. The economic context in which innovation performance and profitability imperatives constrain companies' investment strategies has also led to the rise in collaboration. Open innovation strategies highlight the major role of networks which are considered as generators or stimulators of knowledge. Indeed, companies' knowledge capital is built within these networks.

According to the open innovation model, firms collaborate with multiple partners at all stages of the "interactive" innovation process (design, production and marketing). The analysis of collaborative innovation in an open model integrates two main open innovation processes (Chesbrough 2003; Gassmann and Enkel 2006). The first is known as inbound, or outside-in (OI), which refers to the search for and integration of external resources that feed the internal development of the knowledge stock. The second is known as outbound, or inside-out (IO), which harnesses technological capabilities outside of the firm, using different marketing channels such as licenses, transfer agreements or the creation of new firms. A third process is also mentioned, which is a mixed process combining the Outside-In and Inside-Out processes while bringing together different partners in the same R&D project.

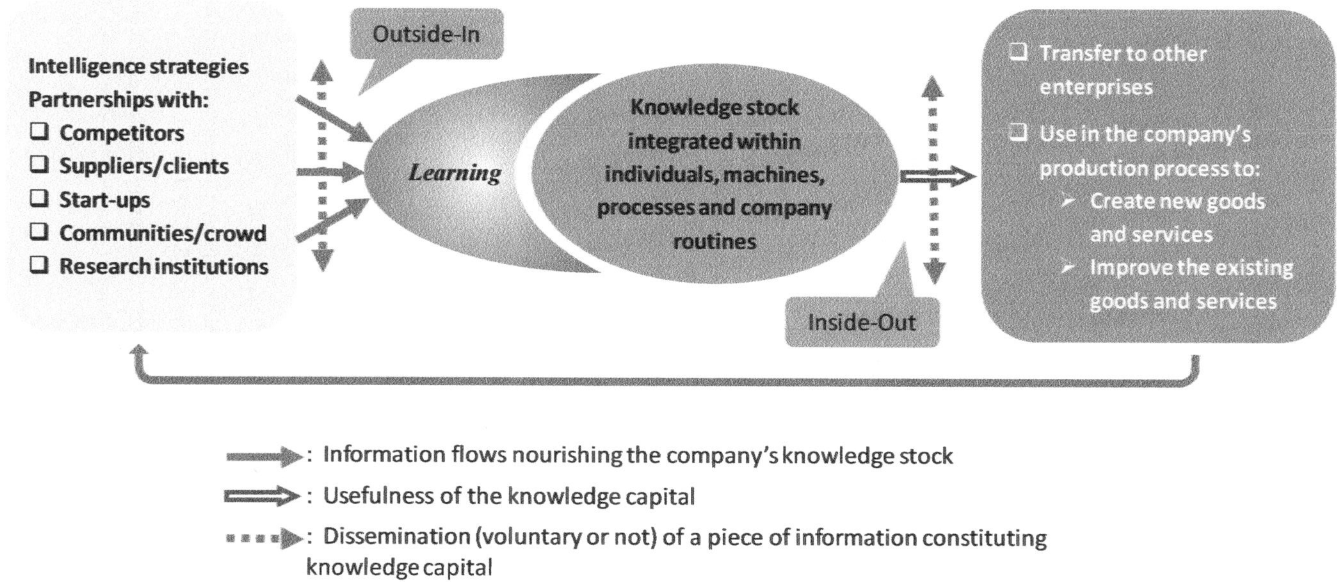

Figure 7.3. *Open innovation and knowledge capital. For a color version of this figure, see www.iste.co.uk/uzunidis/innovation1.zip*

If we return to our knowledge capital framework, we can thus consider that open innovation concerns both of its processes (see Figure 5.3).

Through business intelligence strategies and partnerships with different stakeholders (whether competitors, suppliers, start-ups, customers, research institutions), firms pursue an "Outside-In" strategy, which should help to feed their stock of knowledge. At the opposite end of the spectrum, through transfers to other companies via intellectual property licensing agreements or spin-offs (Inside-Out), firms commercialize and give value to its stock of knowledge.

7.6. Conclusion

In our view, knowledge capital is an effective model for analyzing the innovation strategies of large companies, but also of small- and medium-sized ones. It also makes it possible to understand the role of knowledge and experience in the evolution of their trajectories.

The large number of concepts related to the economy and management of innovation in business shows the importance of training, sharing, combining and using knowledge in the innovation process. This is a response to the long-dominant view of the firm and of production simply as functions articulating undifferentiated stocks of labor and capital, where innovation was not integrated or only accepted as an exogenous element. Researchers' ambitions are to bring about new knowledge or methodologies to improve the understanding of these economic and social phenomena. First, they conduct a specific analysis of the phenomena which they study. It is therefore first and foremost their own understanding of the phenomena which they will approach and present. The purpose of this chapter is to briefly present the contours of an approach to the conceptual landscape of economics and business management, which naturally deserves to be challenged and enriched.

7.7. References

Chesbrough, H. (2003). *Open Innovation: The New Imperative for Creating and Profiting from Technology*. Harvard Business School Press, Boston.

Cohen, W.S. and Levinthal, D.A. (1990). Absorptive capacity: A new perspective on learning and innovation. *Administrative Science Quarterly*, 35, 128–152.

Corrado, C.A., Hulten, C.R., Sichel, D.E. (2005). Measuring capital and technology: An expanded framework in the new economy. *Studies in Income and Wealth*, 65, 11–45.

Edvinsson, L. and Malone, M.S. (1997). *Intellectual Capital. The Proven Way to Establish Your Company's Real Value by Measuring its Hidden Brainpower*. Biddles LTD, King's Lynn.

Gassmann, O. and Enkel, E. (2004). Towards a theory of open innovation: Three core process archetypes. *R&D Management Conference*, Lisbon.

Hatchuel, A. and Weil, B. (2009). C-K design theory: An advanced formulation. *Research in Engineering Design*, 19(4), 181–192.

Laperche, B. (2017). *Enterprise Knowledge Capital*. ISTE Ltd, London and John Wiley & Sons, New York.

Le Masson, P. and McMahon, C. (2016). Armand Hatchuel and Benoit Weil : la théorie C-K, un fondement formel aux théories de l'innovation. In *Les grands auteurs du management de l'innovation et de la créativité*, Burger-Helmchen, T., Hussler, C., Cohendet, P. (eds). EMS Editions Management et Société, Paris.

Nonaka, I. and Takeuchi, H. (1995). *The Knowledge Creating Company*. Oxford University Press, New York.

Nooteboom, B. (2009). *A Cognitive Theory of the Firm. Learning, Governance and Dynamic Capabilities*. Edward Elgar, Cheltenham.

OECD (2013). *Supporting Investment in Knowledge Capital, Growth and Innovation*. OECD Publishing, Paris.

Penrose, E. (1959). *The Theory of the Growth of the Firm*. Oxford University Press, Oxford.

Teece, D.J., Pisano, G., Shuen, A. (1997). Dynamic capabilities and strategic management. *Strategic Management Journal*, 18(7), 509–533.

Zahra, S.A. and George, G. (2002). Absorptive capacity: A review, reconceptualization, and extension. *Academy of Management Review*, 27, 185–203.

Zambon, S. and Monciardini, D. (2015). Intellectual capital and innovation: A guideline for future research. *Journal of Innovation Economics & Management*, 17(2), 13–26.

8

Cluster – Innovative Cluster: Geographical and “Virtual” Proximity in the Digital Era

8.1. Introduction

Geographical and social proximities played a key role in characterizing traditional clusters and industrial districts (Marshall 1920; Boschma 2005). Nonetheless, following the Internet revolution and the diffusion of information and communication technologies, the role of geographical proximity has become questionable (Friedman 2007), laying the foundation for a greater role to be played by other forms of proximity and aggregation (Boschma 2005).

As a result of technological diffusion, we are assisting in the evolution of a clustering phenomenon that implies internal as well as external new dynamics (Fornahl *et al.* 2015). New forms of clusters – beyond the traditional physical location – are arising: these clusters can be defined as “innovative clusters” (Pinch *et al.* 2003; Fornahl *et al.* 2015). These innovative clusters go beyond formalized business links, and interaction and learning processes are not strictly delimited by the physical boundaries of traditional clusters or industrial districts.

Geographical proximity has a limited influence on knowledge flow phenomena: the diffusion of (tacit) knowledge and capabilities is “fluid” and it is not possible to attach constraints or physical boundaries to its circulation (Saxenian 1991). Nowadays, a community sharing norms, values and practices may be geographically dispersed (Pinch *et al.* 2003) and still represent a cluster but in a new form, compared to clusters of the past.

Chapter written by Elisa SALVADOR.

An innovative cluster is thus characterized by weak ties (Granovetter 1973) that enable long-distance travel and go far beyond geographical proximity (Boschma 2005): more actors can be reached and embedded in more effective clustering dynamics. Indeed, very strong ties within a cluster context could negatively impact the performance of the firms in terms of innovation, since the information transmitted within a cluster tends to be redundant, lacking originality, and hence inhibiting creativity. The sense of community (Granovetter 1973; Pinch *et al.* 2003) and membership to an innovative cluster can also be exhibited in the form of a (digital) business ecosystem.

This chapter is structured as follows: a section dedicated to the matter of geographical and "virtual" proximity is followed by a short overview on the influence of the Internet and information and communication technologies on innovative clusters. Finally, some concluding remarks will follow.

8.2. Innovative clusters: the matter of geographical and "virtual" proximity

Clusters' formation has usually been identified in the literature as a key factor in regional development (Porter 1990). The seminal example of Silicon Valley and Route 128 are known worldwide, and so too are the traditional Italian industrial districts (Becattini 1990). Studies appearing at the beginning of the 1900s highlighted that in traditional industrial districts, geographical and social proximities played a key role in network formation, company growth, as well as knowledge diffusion and competitiveness. "Proximity" has always been stressed as a key condition for an area to host a cluster (Salvador *et al.* 2013).

Nonetheless, the Internet and diffusion of information and communication technologies revolutionized this context. New forms of "virtual" agglomerations, like innovative clusters and (digital) business ecosystems, are emerging spontaneously or as a result of forward-looking public policies (Salvador *et al.* 2013). The business ecosystem concept has been developed in the recent literature on complexity and evolutionary economics, and it has been applied specifically within the digital field through drawing an analogy between the biological ecosystem and a population of organizations.

The importance of clusters has again been underlined within the framework of the Lisbon Strategy, launched in 2000. Regional clusters may contribute to the visibility of small firms and help in overcoming the liability of newness. Traditionally, the most successful clusters, like the Italian industrial districts, were a market driven, spontaneous phenomenon; since the end of the 1990s, however, an increasing number of new forms of clusters have been fostered through specific public policies. Business ecosystems, science parks and innovative clusters are among the main representative examples (Salvador *et al.* 2013).

An innovative cluster is based on membership to a dedicated organization with common interest activities, which is identified and managed by a cluster management company. Innovative clusters are dynamic structures, based on sector commonalities/markets and/or the use of similar technologies; they include companies that may also be hosted in a science park (Salvador *et al.* 2013). Nonetheless, the different forms of proximity (Boschma 2005) do not constitute forcedly relevant underlying conditions for innovative clusters. The basis for traditional clusters and industrial districts was predominantly geographical and social proximity – the two necessary (though not sufficient) conditions for their existence – as well as the concentration of active small businesses and a community of people in an identified area with an industrial specialization. Today, however, innovative clusters are no longer the result of the natural integration of communities of people and businesses within the same, delimited geographical and industrially-specialized area. In particular, Marshall (1920) developed three formal reasons for firms' agglomeration in an industrial district and localization within the same area: the presence of specialized local labor; increased provision at local level of non-traded input specific to the industry; and a well-developed flow of information and ideas. While in the past, space played a role in generating location advantages like lower transaction costs and higher productivity, with more efficient use of resources and greater innovative capacity, since the early 1980s technological improvements started to be considered as an element that negatively influenced the importance of geographical distance (Warf 1995).

8.3. Innovative clusters and the Internet and information and communication technologies revolution

Since the 1990s, several authors have discussed the "death of distance" (Cairncross 1997), or "the world is flat" (Friedman 2007). In particular, Cairncross (1997) attempted to underline how the world was changing with the introduction of the Internet and information and communication technologies. The author highlighted the power of these technologies in reducing or eliminating distance as a key factor in business and daily activities. Friedman (2007) argued that the beginning of the 21st century will be remembered for a "flattening" of the world, the death of distance becoming prevalent, making the world small, flat and fast. Globalization and the revolution brought by new digital technologies implies that people, knowledge and resources can be connected instantly at a global level, "flattening" the playing field. Furthermore, following this revolution, knowledge circulation and learning are no longer spatially delimited.

Innovative clusters are designed to stimulate innovative activity by promoting intensive interactions, sharing of facilities and exchange of (tacit and codified) knowledge, as well as expertise. They also contribute effectively to technology transfer and networking activities. Innovative clusters can be managed by a dedicated company that can also be a science park. Innovative clusters can also be based on a membership, they can amass a larger number of organizations (i.e. businesses, universities and research centers) in comparison to science parks. Furthermore, although the innovative cluster members will still require face-to-face contact, this does not require permanent geographical proximity through co-location (Salvador *et al.* 2013). In other words, innovative clusters can be exemplified by digital platforms where members interact through online exchanges, as well as by (digital) business ecosystems.

8.4. Conclusion

The diffusion of information and communication technologies and globalization has reduced the importance placed on geography and revolutionized the organization and structure of the traditional model of various industries. New dynamics and business transformations are thus arising everywhere.

In this context, new forms of aggregation that can be labeled “innovative clusters” are emerging as a complement or a substitute to traditional clusters or industrial districts.

Innovative cluster members share a space that is not forcedly characterized by geographical proximity. It can be said that they share a common context characterized by fluid interactions and rapid exchanges. Face-to-face networks are thus completed or substituted by “e-networks”, as the need for spatial proximity must be made compatible with and completed by the need for connectivity in the Internet and digital technologies age.

In the innovative cluster, the variable “space” is not seen as a boundary but as an advantage, thanks to the Internet and the potential of information and communication technologies.

Proximity has usually been considered to be advantageous for knowledge transmission, as high-tech clusters arose where knowledge was produced. Otherwise, actual and future improvements in the field of information and communication technologies enables us to go beyond geographical proximity for knowledge creation and dissemination, and will also enable further development of this new form of cluster, not limited to specific geographical locations.

8.5. References

Becattini, G. (1990). The Marshallian industrial district as a socio-economic notion. In *Industrial Districts and Inter-Firm Cooperation in Italy*, Pyke, F., Becattini, G., Sengenberger, W. (eds). International Institute for Labour Studies, Geneva.

Boschma, R.A. (2005). Proximity and innovation. A critical assessment. *Regional Studies*, 39(1), 61–74.

Cairncross, F. (1997). *The Death of Distance: How Communications Revolution Will Change Our Lives*. Orion Business Books, London.

Fornahl, D., Hassink, R., Menzel, M.P. (2015). Broadening our knowledge on cluster evolution. *European Planning Studies*, 23(10), 1921–1931.

Friedman, T.L. (2007). *The World Is Flat: A Brief History of the Twenty-first Century*, 3rd edition. Picador, New York.

Granovetter, M.S. (1973). The strength of weak ties. *American Journal of Sociology*, 78(6), 1360–1380.

Marshall, A. (1920). *Principles of Economics*, 8th edition. Macmillan, London.

Pinch, S., Henry, N., Jenkins, M., Tallman, S. (2003). From "industrial districts" to "knowledge clusters": A model of knowledge dissemination and competitive advantage in industrial agglomerations. *Journal of Economic Geography*, 3, 373–388.

Porter, M.Y. (1990). The competitive advantage of nations. *Harvard Business Review*, 68(2), 73–93.

Salvador, E., Mariotti, I., Conicella, F. (2013). Science park or innovation cluster? Similarities and differences in physical and virtual firms' agglomeration phenomena. *International Journal of Entrepreneurial Behaviour & Research*, 19(6), 656–674.

Saxenian, A. (1991). The origins and dynamics of production networks in silicon valley. *Research Policy*, 20(5), 423–437.

Warf, B. (1995). Telecommunications and the clustering geographies of knowledge transmission in the late 20th century. *Urban Studies*, 32(2), 361–378.

9

Collaboration – Collaborative and Open Innovation in Highly Competitive Contexts

9.1. Introduction

Innovation is a key factor in the knowledge economy, increasing the competitiveness of companies through differentiation and the use of specific resources. Since firms can no longer innovate on their own, knowledge that is useful for generating innovations comes from both internal and external sources (Chesbrough 2003).

Collaborative innovation and "open innovation" are concepts that use openness outside the boundaries of the company, involving exchanges with different types of actors. Collaboration and the use of new sources of ideas are at the heart of these concepts. These terms are used interchangeably throughout this chapter.

Open innovation (OI) is defined by Henri Chesbrough as a paradigm set against closed innovation (see Figure 7.1), reflecting a traditional vertical integration model, where Research and Development (R&D) activities are internal to the firm. Vertical integration, as opposed to horizontal integration, is a way of managing the activities that a firm carries out. By integrating the various processes, such as production, processing and product marketing, the firm can view its performance (general or differentiated by activity), as well as its costs for various optimized expense items. Some sectors are more marked by vertical integration than others, such as the agri-food sector on the continent of North America. Fruits and vegetables or dairy industries are traditionally vertically integrated, in contrast to the grain sector.

Chapter written by Camille AOUINAÏT.

The closure of a company's borders to its external environment produces innovative solutions that will be diffused in the traditionally used market (Chesbrough 2012).

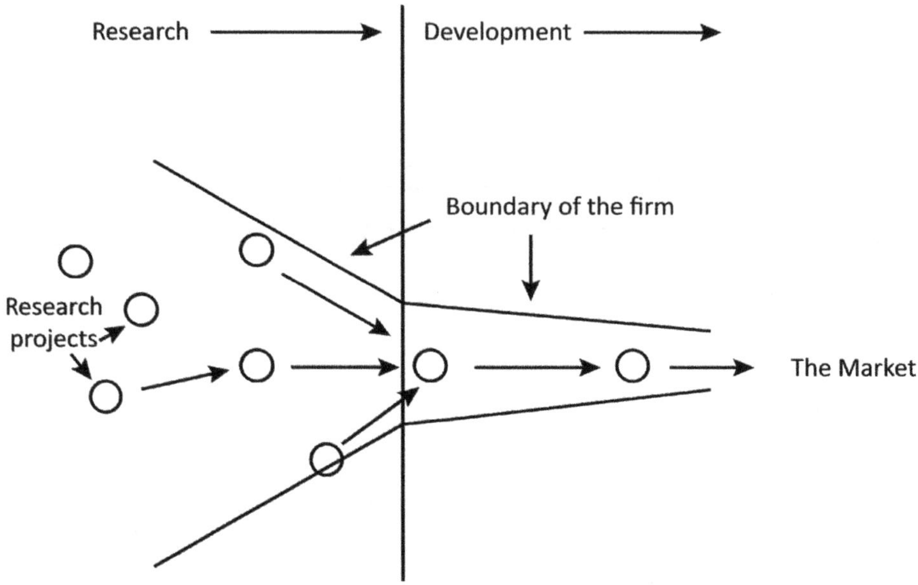

Figure 9.1. *Chesbrough's closed innovation paradigm (Chesbrough 2003)*

Open innovation is a model of collaborative innovation, defined as "the use of purposive inflows and outflows of knowledge to accelerate internal innovation, and expand the markets for external use of innovation, respectively" (Chesbrough 2006). In Figure 7.2, the different exchange flows of information, knowledge and other inputs with the outside world via porous boundaries are highlighted. New sources of technology can be used at any point in the R&D process. Results are distributed through the usual channels, as well as to new markets. This new provision, characterizing open innovation, brings new possibilities of partnerships with actors with various profiles (e.g. firms working on the same market, suppliers or research laboratories).

In this first section of this chapter, the guiding concepts and basic notions associated with open and collaborative innovation are presented. A brief history and the main occurrences in the literature from different fields are then presented. The issues inherent to these concepts are presented in a complementary fashion, before this chapter ends with a final section outlining the conclusions and implications.

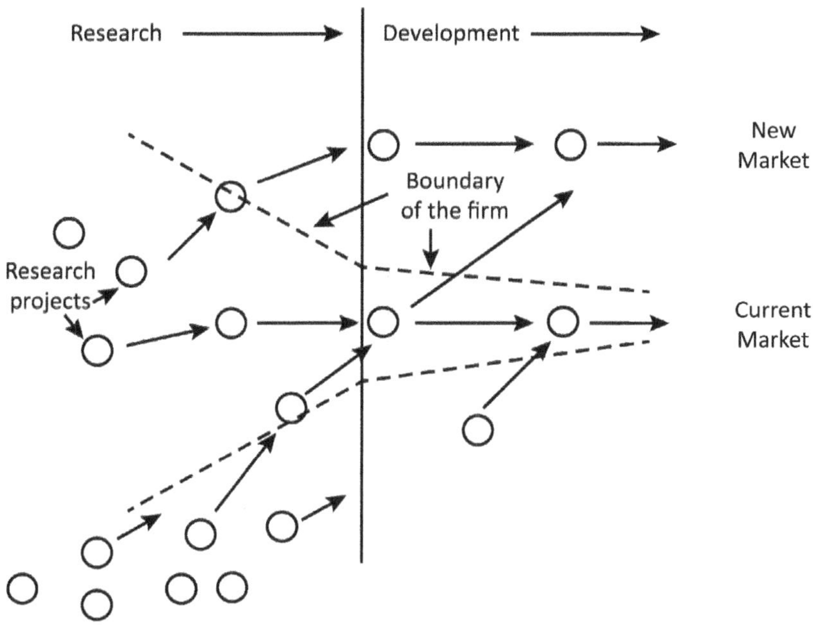

Figure 9.2. *Chesbrough's open innovation paradigm (Chesbrough 2003)*

9.2. Literature review

9.2.1. *History*

Open innovation is a term that appeared in 2003 in Henri Chesbrough's work, notably in the book *Open Innovation: The New Imperative for Creating and Profiting from Technology* (Chesbrough 2003).

The term "open innovation" emerged in parallel with the term "open source"[1], which was applied to software and had known success due to changes in the field. This facilitated the spread of Henri Chesbrough's model, which made significant

1 Open source software is software that is free to use for everyone. This type of software is developed by communities of users for these same users. Since their creation in the 1960s and 1970s, thousands of projects and numerous communities have been developed throughout the world (von Hippel 2001, 2003).

modifications to the Intellectual Property Rights (IPR)[2] used until then (Loilier and Tellier 2011).

According to Chesbrough, several erosion factors have contributed to the decline of the "closed" model. The first concerns the mobility and availability of skilled workers. The second relates to the venture capital market, where specialized companies disseminate innovations through the creation of spin-offs, in particular. Another erosion factor concerns the new capacities of suppliers to carry out R&D activities. Knowledge and other inputs useful for innovation are redistributed differently among different actors (Isckia and Lescop 2011).

Since its inception, the term open innovation has been indisputably used. Chesbrough counted 483 million links when searching for "open innovation" in Google's search engine (Chesbrough 2012). After his first book on *Open Innovation* in 2003, the author turned his attention to *Open Business Models* in 2006 (Chesbrough 2006). According to him, "the business model plays an essential role in the innovation process". The service sector, which is highly remunerative for companies, was then studied from an open innovation perspective. Firms can benefit from positive results by bringing various players together to solve problems and provide solutions, thanks to the diversity of skills and knowledge of each. In the case of the firm Xerox and its Palo Alto Research Center, many projects initiated in the medium and long term failed because the business model at the time was not adapted and the company was unable to obtain the true value of the innovation created.

9.3. Collaborative innovation and innovation ecosystems

Open innovation comes from the field of innovation and technology management and mainly concerns Research and Development. The fields of business strategies and organizational behavior are now engaging with it, highlighting the growing involvement of this theory in the various fields of social sciences, in particular (small and large, high-tech and low-tech firms) (Gassmann *et al.* 2010).

2 The two principal goals of Intellectual Property Rights (IPR) are to protect the innovator from fraudulent use of their innovation and to grant them exclusive temporary rights over the innovation, for example, for 20 years in France and 17 years in the United States. Revenue can be obtained from these IPRs. The control of the diffusion and the commercialization of information relating to the protected product benefit the innovator. The patent is the most studied IPR in existing literature; also common are licenses, author's rights and even brands (Liotard 1999).

According to Isckia and Lescop (2011), the field of business ecosystems is close to that of open innovation. The diffusion of innovation and the central role of companies in a defined ecosystem are spearheads of this field of research, with the essential goal of value creation.

In addition, collaborative innovation enables the creation of innovative projects (Loilier and Tellier 2011). Collaboration enters into co-development logics between various actors with common interests (Isckia and Lescop 2011). R&D is an economic and technological position where the organization of collaborations is strategic. The openness of companies in the innovation process becomes essential.

Moreover, the externalities and impacts of open innovation are distributed within and outside the company's borders. Open innovation can be achieved through two processes: inside-out and outside-in. The first process requires firms to allow unused or little-used ideas to go beyond the firm's boundaries for external use by other actors. The second refers to the opening of firms' innovation processes to various external inputs and contributions (Isckia and Lescop 2011; Chesbrough 2012). As a result, sources for new ideas can be found both inside and outside the firm, for example, by participating in R&D activities or by providing important resources. Collaborative innovation allows for "sourcing", looking for sources of innovation from outside the firm. This underlines the importance of using a variety of information and knowledge search mechanisms to be able to innovate. The use of the network in which companies are integrated is therefore essential to enrich their knowledge base and develop collaborations with various partners (e.g. other companies, universities, research associations).

Moreover, in competitiveness clusters using OI, optimizing innovation capabilities on a collective level is one of the goals (Leroux *et al.* 2014). The time between the creation of an innovation and its introduction to the market can be reduced. This process is therefore beneficial for companies collaborating in these collective actions.

In addition, competitiveness clusters are a grouping on an identified territory of both public and private actors such as small, medium and large companies, training organizations and research centers, working on a common theme, financially supported by public authorities. These clusters aim to promote innovation, develop collaborative projects and foster growth in the territory.

One of the advantages of collaborative innovation lies in the fact that the company opens up to its external environment and becomes more visible to actors who might be interested in collaborating and gaining the specific knowledge and skills required in innovative projects (Loilier and Tellier 2011). However, this model of innovation can play a role in the firm's defined strategies, in terms of the relationships established or to be developed with external partners in order to acquire skills and knowledge and intellectual property modalities (e.g. the degree to which knowledge circulating openly is free to use) (Leroux *et al.* 2014).

Finally, despite the openness of companies to their external environment, they must carry out at least a minimum of R&D internally, in a way that is not defined by studies on the subject, so that they can work on their absorption capacity[3] (Loilier and Tellier 2011; Chesbrough 2012). Indeed, in order to exploit the resources and knowledge collected externally, particularly through established collaborations, firms must be able to reuse them internally (Loilier and Tellier 2011).

9.4. Open innovation versus closed innovation

Open innovation is situated in different problematics today. Indeed, the dichotomy of open innovation versus closed innovation is criticized in many works. It stems, in particular, from the difference in permitted boundaries (whether porous or not) (Dahlander and Gann 2010; Isckia and Lescop 2011; Loilier and Tellier 2011). A model of innovation is neither totally open nor totally closed. Hybrid forms, at the crossroads of the two models of innovation, may exist, as Loiler and Tellier (2011) describe in their paper. This is an intermediate model, combining the public and private aspects used in the open model of open source ("free user participation") and the closed model of traditional firms ("firm ownership of results"), respectively. This model is, however, poorly established because the financial counterpart is at the basis of many business strategies, where the innovator can "capture the income from innovation" according to the model of appropriability chosen.

In addition, OI involves the co-creation of knowledge and innovations as well as knowledge transfer. However, it has been widely studied that knowledge transfer can take several forms, depending on the type of knowledge involved:

3 Cohen and Levinthal defined absorptive capacity as "the ability to recognize the value of new, external knowledge, assimilate it and apply it commercially". This capacity of firms is built over the long term by creating a knowledge base and skills internal to the firm, which are necessary to integrate the new knowledge that is acquired over the course of projects, particularly through Research and Development. This absorption capacity of firms tends to be built on the individual absorption capacity of firm members, to be cumulative and depends on the previous trajectory chosen (e.g. the technological and strategic choices that the firm implements) (Cohen and Levinthal 1990; Lane and Lubatkin 1998).

formalized/codified or tacit/uncodified[4]. Codified knowledge is easily transferable to various contexts because it is not dependent on the agents carrying out this transfer. It is generally recorded or written. Tacit knowledge, on the other hand, is "sticky", dependent on the context in which it was created and/or used and inherent to individuals (von Hippel 1994).

Another criticism concerns the new aspect of the model (Loilier and Tellier 2011). Indeed, it is not particularly innovative to use innovations from outside to benefit companies, as in the case of licensing. Intellectual Property Rights (IPRs) represent "contractual arrangements" that allow firms to benefit from multiple forms of collaboration (Isckia and Lescop 2011). Indeed, IO, because of its structure, involving external actors, allows the redistribution of the costs of the innovation process. On the one hand, R&D costs can be lower. On the other hand, the use of IPR generates revenues.

Nevertheless, it is estimated that only 20% of patents generate 80% of revenues. Not all IPRs are suitable for internal use. Isckia and Lescop (2011) therefore consider that the advantage of open innovation would be to "enhance these 'dormant' patents by offering them to other companies".

Moreover, another limit or frontier of the open innovation model concerns labor mobility, which is an indispensable factor in ensuring the efficiency of project transfers between companies. If staff change firms during a project, they will be able to increase the integration of all the important project data into the new environment (Chesbrough 2012). The erosion factors discussed by Chesbrough can be found here.

Finally, the degree of openness of the model is questioned in the literature. The degree of openness of open innovation remains limited, in the sense that the logic of ownership is still in place. Indeed, in return for financial compensation, a firm can sell its innovations, via licenses, for example (inside-out principle or innovation exit) or acquire them (outside-in principle or innovation entry). This contrasts with the open source model for software, where the publisher of a source code gives up their rights to this code for modification, improvement and joint use by other users. The opening up of this type of model is therefore more widely supported (Loilier and Tellier 2011; Chesbrough 2012).

---

4 Tacit knowledge is said to be non-codified knowledge, acquired through the informal adoption of previously learned behaviours and procedures. This knowledge is usually embedded in individuals and not formally transmitted. Therefore, this type of knowledge is more difficult to transmit than codified knowledge, such as documented and written information (patents, certificates, databases and archives). This explicit knowledge is edited in a formal language and is easily transmissible (Cowan *et al.* 1999; Howells 1996).

Open innovation and collaborative innovation are therefore similar up to a certain level of openness in the model. The collaborations that are possible and necessary to develop and accelerate innovative activities internal to firms may be limited in terms of property rights and conditions predefined by the actors (e.g. type of contractual collaborations, type of partners and partnerships).

9.5. Conclusion

Open innovation, collaborative innovation and other terms used to refer to concepts initially developed by Henri Chesbrough are now widely used in various disciplines, from management to economics and social sciences. Several discussions and criticisms remain open regarding the openness that companies should achieve in innovation processes. Innovation networks can, in this context, be a support for firms and a support to launch innovative initiatives or to put them in contact with key players, in order to promote collaborations that lead to innovation.

Moreover, few studies have focused on the territorial dimension of open innovation (Loilier and Tellier 2011). Networks can be created by integrating local actors that are historically present in the territory and new actors that are identified as useful resources for a project. The use of local facilitators (e.g. local research centers) with the necessary physical proximity is often preferred, as is the case in the industrial district of Emilia Romagna in Italy. In this example, the district makes use of actors at the national and international levels, as well as local research centers. Physical proximity appears to be a necessary and minimum condition for innovation.

Finally, national innovation systems that foster the production of technology, science and knowledge, as well as their diffusion and use, provide a national framework within which firms can innovate, through interactions between the public and private sectors (Casadella and Benlahcen-Tlemcani 2006). Moreover, regional innovation systems also have their part to play in promoting collaborative innovation within more territorialized and scattered frameworks, which are at work in many European territories.

9.6. References

Casadella, V. and Benlahcen-Tlemcani, M. (2006). De l'applicabilité du système national d'innovation dans les pays moins avancés. *Innovations*, 24(2), 59.

Chesbrough, H.W. (2003). *Open Innovation: The New Imperative for Creating and Profiting from Technology*. Harvard Business School Publishing, Boston.

Chesbrough, H.W. (2006). *Open Business Models: How to Thrive in the New Innovation Landscape*. Harvard Business Review Press, Boston.

Chesbrough, H.W. (2012). Open innovation: Where we've been and where we're going. *Research-Technology Management*, 55(4), 20–27.

Cohen, W.M. and Levinthal, D.A. (1990). Absorptive capacity: A new perspective on learning and innovation. *Administrative Science Quarterly*, 35(1), 128–152.

Cowan, R., David, P.A., Foray, D. (1999). The explicit economics of knowledge codification and tacitness. *Industrial and Corporate Change*, 9(2), 211–253.

Dahlander, L. and Gann, D.M. (2010). How open is innovation? *Research Policy*, 39(6), 699–709.

Gassmann, O., Enkel, E., Chesbrough, H.W. (2010). The future of open innovation. *R&D Management*, 40(3), 213–221.

von Hippel, E. (1994). "Sticky Information" and the locus of problem solving: Implications for innovation. *Management Science*, 40(4), 429–439.

von Hippel, E. (2001). Innovation by user communities: Learning from open-source software. *MIT Sloan Management Review*, 82–86.

von Hippel, E. (2003). Open source software and the "Private-Collective" innovation model: Issues for organization science. *Organization Science*, 14(2), 208–223.

Howells, J. (1996). Tacit knowledge. *Technology Analysis & Strategic Management*, 8(2), 91–106.

Isckia, T. and Lescop, D. (2011). Une analyse critique des fondements de l'innovation ouverte. *Revue française de gestion*, 37(210), 87–98.

Lane, P.J. and Lubatkin, M. (1998). Relative absorptive capacity and interorganizational learning. *Strategic Management Journal*, 19(5), 461–477.

Leroux, I., Muller, P., Plottu, B., Widehem, C. (2014). Innovation ouverte et évolution des business models dans les pôles de compétitivité : le rôle des intermédiaires dans la création variétale végétale. *Revue d'économie industrielle*, 146, 115–151.

Liotard, I. (1999). Les droits de propriété intellectuelle, une nouvelle arme stratégique des firmes. *Revue d'économie industrielle*, 89(1), 69–84.

Loilier, T. and Tellier, A. (2011). Que faire du modèle de l'innovation ouverte ? *Revue française de gestion*, 37(210), 69–85.

10

Creativity – Creativity for Innovation: A Mutually Advantageous Relationship

10.1. Introduction

If it seems obvious enough today to associate creativity, this capacity to generate new and original ideas, with innovation, the study of their common history tends to show a rapprochement and a reciprocal influence that strengthens over time. History is marked by the representations that political and economic decision-makers have had of innovation, which, as we shall see, are evolving in the direction of a progressive consideration of the role of the individual. After presenting how the fields of innovation and creativity have gradually come together, and how the former has in a way "instrumentalized" the latter, we will attempt to show how they have reciprocally influenced each other in the way we think about and practice both.

10.2. Increasingly "creative" representations of innovation

Thus, until the end of the 1970s, innovation was thought to only concern advanced sectors (armament, aerospace, nuclear industry, etc.) and large companies. The general issue is the dissemination and application of scientific knowledge to industry at the national territorial level, according to a linear model: fundamental research → applied research → production of innovation. Mainly studied by economists and managers, it is first of all a financial fact, a question of means: public intervention is directive and consists of financially assisting both researchers and industrialists working in areas identified as strategic, and also of facilitating the transfer of knowledge from the academic world to the economic world.

Chapter written by Raphaël BARY.

In a context where innovation is reduced to the development of a new idea that is already present, the question of creativity does not arise, or only to a limited extent – all the more so because, since the work of Guilford (1950), it is a concept that belongs to psychology, which has not yet grasped the object of study that is innovation. Following Schumpeter's thought, which distinguished "invention as the initiator of novelty and innovation as a possible and desirable end of invention" (Carrier and Garand 1996), the emergence of ideas is not part of the innovation process but of invention: they are two distinct and complementary stages. Consequently, the questions of researchers and practitioners in the field focus on aspects related to the identification of inventions and the methods used to select and protect the most interesting ones.

From the early 1980s to the mid-1990s, innovation spread throughout industry and market services. In addition to the financial aspects, there was also a question of both technological (design of new products and processes, technology transfer, etc.) and managerial (participative management, project management, cooperation between firms, etc.) methods. As such, industrial innovation became a research subject for engineering and management – and, through the latter, for the sociology of organizations, the psychosociology of work. In the context of increasing competition, having a new or original idea became a competitive advantage. It was then a question of understanding how ideas "came about" and what facilitated or inhibited this generation from an individual, social and organizational point of view (Amabile 1983).

This was the moment when creativity fully entered into innovation. This was achieved by drawing on theoretical and methodological knowledge that had already been produced, as well as generating new research directions. Thus, if we take the example of creativity techniques, it was in the mid-1980s that brainstorming and synecticism were "rediscovered" (Osborn 1988), at the same time that new methods such as scenarios, crushing and morphological analysis were developed. Group methods were particularly studied and tested in the framework of creativity at work (Vadcard 1996). Their aim was to put individuals in optimal conditions in order to stimulate and promote the expression of their own creativity, but nevertheless, they demonstrated certain limits, especially as they depended on the environment in which they were implemented and, above all, on the creative potential of the participants.

Thus, shortly before the turn of the millennium, the need to take into account the individual dimension of innovation became more strongly felt – all the more so as it became an imperative for all sectors, even public services, which had to adapt to the deregulation of services. Taking this into account raised questions about the skills needed for the act of innovation, including creativity. Thus, new approaches contributing to the knowledge of man were being mobilized, an extension of the cognitive sciences, to better understand the intrapsychic factors and mechanisms of creative production and its expression. Drawing on a whole line of research on the creative process, new studies described the innovator, their ways of thinking, the knowledge feeding the production of ideas and, more broadly, the way in which their interactions with the physical and social environment enabled them to become aware of a problem, to formulate it, explore it and generate a new solution, as well as validate its feasibility and viability (Bary 2002).

10.3. Impacts on creativity of its integration in the field of innovation

Alongside this focus on the innovator and their creativity, innovation research has continued to work on its technological, methodological and organizational dimensions, focusing on making links between these different levels. In this respect, the method of creative problem solving is quite exemplary. This method, born from the work of Alex Osborn (1953) and, later, Sid Parnes (1967), can almost be considered the "mother" of much of today's creative approaches. In fact, based on Osborn's work, which focused on describing the cognitive mechanisms at work in creativity, it proposed a division into phases where divergent and convergent thinking alternate, phases which are more or less found in all creative approaches: identifying the problem, gathering relevant data, generating ideas, evaluating them and preparing to put them into action. The CPS has therefore focused on the mental and intellectual dimension of the generation of new ideas. However, faced with limitations and difficulties in implementing this method, researchers have explored its affective and motivational aspects, thus highlighting their importance in its success (Puccio and Cabra 2009). These are the same factors that depend in part, in creativity at work, on a human context, a system of actors and ways of organizing relationships between people, knowledge and objects. Therefore, just as it is important to have tools that facilitate creative thinking, it is also essential to question the context in which they are used: the relational quality within the team, the representations of creativity within the company, the possibility of exchanging ideas that have not yet been developed, with colleagues, the right to make mistakes, access to new scientific knowledge, etc.

Strictly speaking, the creativity methods themselves were not really impacted by this more complex vision of new idea generation. They always consist of proposing detours to thoughts, in order to avoid going straight to readymade, common, banal ideas; detours by analogies with other fields (Synectic), by the search for solutions opposed to the initial problem (Inversion), by the unconscious (Guided Imagery), by identification with different modes of reasoning (Six Hats Technique), etc. On the other hand, the conditions of their implementation have been profoundly modified in the sense that, nowadays, the use of the creative tool requires a framework that is safe, comfortable and inspiring for the group during the creativity session, as well as before and after, by creating a climate conducive to innovation, a true *management of ideas*.

10.4. The same shared complexity

This historical overview shows how the dominant representation of innovation has played on the role of creativity. Under the effect of a twofold movement, somewhat paradoxically, innovation has become commonplace (by no longer being solely the product of fundamental research and no longer limited to technological breakthroughs) and has become more complex (through a new understanding of its multiple dimensions, their interactions and the emergences produced). In doing so, it has also become more humanized, integrating the creative contribution of the individual more fully. And if, during the "Trente Glorieuses" (the 30 years following the end of World War II in France), engineers and managers invested in the field of innovation drew the knowledge they needed from psychologists, the relationship between innovation and creativity was not only in this direction. The practical and theoretical questions that have emerged with the multiplication of studies on innovation have not failed to challenge the psychology of creativity, thus initiating new avenues of research, particularly in higher education. Thus, understanding how ideas emerge requires questioning different levels. It is already a question of the individual creativity of the teacher who introduces new things into their practice: their motivations to change, the mental processes used to imagine solutions, the particular representations that support the act of innovating, the specific knowledge mobilized, etc. (Cros 2001). It is also about the mechanisms that, within pedagogical teams, facilitate or hinder the expression and concretization of novelty. Thus, the more exchanges there are within a group, the more individual initiatives are known to all and, potentially, recognized. This leads to an exchange of knowledge and practices among colleagues, as it gives innovators the recognition they are waiting for, which supports their motivation to innovate (Bertrand 2014; Viaud 2015). However, organizing meetings and workshops within teams, creating labs or introducing design thinking approaches is not enough to generate sustainable collective creativity. It must also be done within institutions that welcome and promote innovation. This requires the provision of time and material resources (Buabeng-Andoh 2012), which make sense if they are part of an institutional policy that

> leaves the actors free to organize themselves, each at their own level and according to their context; to make them responsible by respecting what is in place; to value initiatives; to provide elements of understanding of these evolutions; to accompany them. (Bertrand 2014, p. 13)

In higher education, as in all sectors, it is less and less imaginable today to understand the mechanisms of creativity without studying the conditions and environments that are favorable to it. Without being at its core, creativity has become one of the dimensions of innovation, and it raises questions for practitioners and researchers at all levels, from the psychology of the individual to the design of public policies.

10.5. References

Amabile, T. (1983). *The Social Psychology of Creativity*. Springer-Verlag, New York.

Bary, R. (2002). Les voix/voies de l'innovation : de la naissance de l'idée innovante à sa matérialisation, une analyse cognitive des pratiques et apprentissages des innovateurs. PhD Thesis, Institut National Polytechnique de Lorraine, Nancy.

Bertrand, C. (2014). Soutenir la transformation pédagogique dans l'enseignement supérieur. Report, Ministère de l'Education Nationale, de la Recherche et de l'Enseignement Supérieur, Paris.

Buabeng-Andoh, C. (2012). Factors influencing teachers' adoption and integration of information and communication technology into teaching: A review of the literature. *International Journal of Education and Development Using Information and Communication Technology*, 8(1), 136–155.

Carrier, C. and Garand, D.J. (1996). Le concept d'innovation : débats et ambiguïtés. *5th International Strategic Management Conference*, Lille, 21.

Cros, F. (2001). *L'innovation scolaire*. INRP, Paris.

Guilford, J. P. (1950). Creativity. *American Psychologist*, 3, 444–454.

Osborn, A.F. (1953). *Applied Imagination: Principles and Procedures of Creative Problem-Solving*. Scribner's Sons, New York.

Osborn, A.F. (1988). *Créativité, l'imagination constructive*. Bordas, Paris.

Parnes, S.J. (1967). *Creative Behavior Workbook*. Scribner's Sons, New York.

Puccio, G.J. and Cabra, J.F. (2009). Creative problem solving: Past, present, and future. In *The Routledge Companion to Creativity*, Rickards, T., Runco, H.A., Moger, S. (eds). Routledge, London.

Vadcard, P. (1996). Aide à la programmation de l'utilisation des outils en conception de produit. PhD Thesis, Ecole Nationale Supérieure des Arts et Métiers, Paris.

Viaud, M.-L. (2015). *Les innovateurs silencieux. Histoire des pratiques d'enseignement à l'université depuis 1950*. Presses Universitaires de Grenoble, Grenoble.

11

Cycles – The Long Cycles of the Economy and the Question of Innovation

11.1. Introduction

Capitalism is a system that cannot support immobility, routine, etc. It cannot be stationary, and can never become so (Schumpeter 1939). Since the 18th century, for many economists innovation has been at the origin of economic growth as well as of its crisis: new technologies, new forms of work organization, new consumer goods, new communication tools and new needs. Periods of decline have followed periods of economic prosperity. A relevant link between innovation and economic growth was highlighted by Schumpeter (1939), who made long cycles a central element of his *Theory of Economic Development* (title of his first book from 1911; Schumpeter 1935). In 1911, in fact, Schumpeter moved from an approach based on static economy to a dynamic one with the concept of evolution. In 1925, Kondratieff published an article on *The Major Economic Cycles,* which set out his theory of long-term movements based on the evolution of wholesale prices since the Industrial Revolution. Nikolaï Dmitrievitch Kondratieff (1892–1938) was a Soviet mathematical economist famous for his theory of economic cycles known as "Kondratieff cycles". He showed that capitalist economies experience long-term cycles (50–60 years) with a period of sustained growth, followed by a period of depression. In 1939 and 1942, Schumpeter merged his own work and that of Kondratieff's into what has been called the "Schumpeterian system".

From the theory of economic cycles, we can retain the fact that innovation can, under certain conditions, be the solution against endemic crises. The logic of the reasoning is as follows: it is necessary to liberate the forces of production, reform the market economy or re-establish its bases of accumulation in order to put the

---

Chapter written by Dimitri UZUNIDIS.

economy back on an upward trajectory. The process of innovation is intrinsic to the functioning of the economic system. According to institutional economists, it involves many stages, connects multiple actors (individuals, businesses and institutions) and combines information and knowledge through learning to give rise, both cumulatively and discontinuously, to new products, processes, services, markets and organizations. The outcome of this process is the entry or retention of the innovator (individual or organization) in the market and the emergence in the economy of new investment and profit opportunities.

In order to understand why technology does not in itself generate continued economic growth, it is necessary to distinguish between technological potential (i.e. everything that technology promises) and the actual use that is made of it. Technological innovation, organization and the models that accompany it are in the realm of what is feasible in a given economic structure; the "scientific and technological potential" of innovation is in the realm of what is conceivable, in the process of restructuring the economy. From this differential are born the long movements of the economy, the conditions of which will be presented in the first part of this chapter, followed by a discussion of the historicity of these "cycles".

11.2. The conditions for cyclical economic development: the key role of innovation

Between 1925 and 1928, Nicolaï Dmitrievitch Kondratieff established the existence of major economic cycles. Each cycle took place in concrete historical conditions. He qualified the major cycles as "ruptures", without completely freeing himself from the concept of equilibrium (Kondratieff 1984). The break with equilibrium was achieved by Joseph Schumpeter, among others.

In the book *Business Cycles* published in 1939, Schumpeter introduced a strong distinction between innovation and invention: it is absolutely irrelevant whether an innovation involves scientific novelty or not. Although most innovations can be attributed to some conquest in the field of theoretical or practical knowledge, there are many that are not. Schumpeter's definition of innovation is very broad. It is a historical and irreversible change in the way things are done. To innovate is to introduce new combinations into the business: manufacturing a new product, introducing a new production method, opening up a new outlet, conquering a new source of raw materials or intermediate products and implementing a new organization (Schumpeter 1987).

The relationship of these forms of change to Kondratieff cycles is that they do not remain isolated events and are not evenly distributed over time. They tend to come in clusters; firstly because some, then most, businesses follow in the wake of successful innovations, and secondly because innovations tend to be concentrated in certain sectors and their vicinity (Schumpeter 1939).

Schumpeter proposed a cycle in four phases: recovery, prosperity, recession and depression. The evolution in general, but more specifically the "boom" or recovery and prosperity of the cycle, is triggered by the appearance of a few pioneering entrepreneurs and then, by osmosis or contamination, by entrepreneurs in "swarms". They make new combinations that spread in clusters (Schumpeter 1987). Swarms and clusters, and the "shock" (Schumpeter 2008) that results from their combined effects, are the main conditions of Kondratieff's ascending phase. Then, the shock gradually decreases in intensity. Growth runs out of steam and the movement reverses, leading to the process of "creative destruction". The crisis appears. Cluster effects have to be on such a scale that the disruptions are consequential, in the sense that they disrupt the existing system, cannot be absorbed smoothly and lead to a specific process of adaptation (Schumpeter 1939). The disturbances to which society is forced to adapt are driven by the entrepreneurs who benefit from them.

In 1942, Schumpeter noted that destruction constantly revolutionizes the economic structure from within by regularly discarding old structures in favor of new ones. It is in this form that it is creative and that it is "the fundamental fact" of capitalism (*ibid.*). It should be noted that Schumpeter's approach is more qualitative than quantitative and more historical than statistical. The Kondratieff cycle is neither repetitive nor deterministic. The intensity of the movement, which is different each time, depends on the spirit of the period, the performance of innovations, the profile of the economic agent and the intensity of the investment multiplier. Through repeated long cycles, the economy evolves, but it is never the same.

Schumpeter emphasized that it is of the utmost importance to have a perfect grasp of the economic history of the time, country or industry before learning from the behavior of time series. General history (social, political and cultural), economic history and especially industrial history are not only indispensable but also, in fact, the most important contributors to the understanding of the problem. All other indicators, materials and methods, statistical and theoretical, depend on history and are useless without it.

On this central point, Schumpeter is in line with Kondratieff's observation. The scheme presented by the latter takes place in the concrete conditions of capitalist society. It begins with the Industrial Revolution and "obeys an internal logic" that consists of replacing and building large infrastructures, whose production requires a long process and exceptional investments. Kondratieff points out that each cycle is not a replica of the previous one: it is characterized by profound changes in the techniques of production and exchange. He notes that during most of the downward phase, inventions appear at a sustained pace, which are exploited industrially at the end of the downward cycle and at the beginning of the upward cycle. He also points out that the upward turnaround corresponds to a broadening of international markets. At the same time, the upward phase of the cycle is richer in social upheavals (wars, political and social struggles) than the downward phase.

11.3. Historical time and periodization of the economy

Following this logic and following Karl Marx, Kondratieff and then Schumpeter introduced historical time in their analyses of the long movements of capitalism; the key word being competition. For Marx, competition requires a continuous expansion of capital and imposes the immanent laws of capitalist production as external coercive laws on each individual capitalist (Marx 1992, Volume I). To avert the danger of its disappearance, the company must innovate and simultaneously grow. Innovation allows the devaluation of capital that is already old and whose profitability is weakening, and creates the conditions for a new wave of investment. The faster the pace of capital renewal accelerates, the higher the marginal cost of capital and the greater the financial needs. The intervention of finance facilitates the merger of capital (centralization) forming global corporations. As a result, the economy tends to develop the productive forces as if they were limited only by the absolute power of society (Marx 1992, Volume II). However, this tendency means that at a certain level of their development, the material productive forces of society contradict the existing production relations (organization of work, trade regulation, competition between businesses, sectoral asymmetries, property relations, etc.). Periodic crises have the effect of putting the scientific and technical potential to sleep or leading to the destruction of part of the existing productive forces. The gap between reality and innovation potential widens. The resumption of growth, after this destruction, will not be possible without profound modification of the bases and norms of social organization (new social organization of work, new rules of competition, new technologies, new institutional forms of administration and regulation of the economy).

The cyclical evolution of the economy proposed by Schumpeter and that of the economists inspired by his work is not mechanical. Not only has regularity never been observed in history, but also the economic causes of the crisis are diluted in extremely contradictory and sometimes violent political relations (Freeman and Perez 1986; Rosenberg 1994; Freeman and Luça 2001). The major transformations of markets are inseparable from profound changes in the social relations of production and ownership. Large-scale technical change is inseparable from the reorganization of society.

The "Industrial Revolution" is linked to the birth of the industrial entrepreneur, defined both as the creator and owner of an industrial company, and as the creator of new combinations of production resources for the introduction onto the market of different types of technological and organizational innovations. Later, according to Friedman (2002), the expansion of the scale of production, markets and companies propelled "large families" with high permanent incomes (wealth, monetary savings, education) to the forefront of the economic scene. The "*bourgeois cycle*" corresponds to the period of the socialization of corporate capital and the rise of "big business", supported by the State and financial institutions (banks, the stock exchange). During the first half of the 20th century, in the United States as well as in Europe, the "*families*" of finance and industry presented themselves as those who triumphed in business. Puritanism and social Darwinism came at the right time to justify the constitution of the elite whose wealth was growing (Boutillier and Uzunidis 2014).

In the 20th century, the "*mercantilist*" and "*interventionist*" cycles corresponded to the opening up of industrial economies to global competition, and to state intervention to defend major industrialists, bankers and national traders (resurgence of protectionism, increase in military spending, new deal, planning and major technological programs, etc.). The result of this increase in the scale of production is the interweaving of the economic and political interests of the state with those of "*big businesses*". Gradually, since the 1930s, the internal markets of the major industrial and international countries have widened, the social division of labor has become more refined, and the social costs borne by businesses and the community, as well as the external savings obtained by companies, have become, along with entrepreneurial opportunities for investment (i.e. for acquiring and combining productive resources), the catalysts or barriers to accumulation; they drive growth and then, by overestimating their potential, become causes of depression. The resulting crisis, materialized by the consequent decrease in the remuneration and opportunities for capital valorization, entails dangers for businesses as well as for the social edifice of capitalism (Schumpeter 2008), while also being a propitious moment for the emergence of new technologies and methods of production, and new social practices. This, of course, presupposes the transformation of the social bases of value creation and accumulation; otherwise, the technological potential previously constituted cannot be fully utilized.

From the middle of the 19th century onwards, economic operations on credit led to a banking system that gradually became independent of industry and commerce. A new market was thus formed, that of surplus financial capital, which gave financial enterprises the possibility of controlling production and trade enterprises. Financial transactions (shares, bonds and other money market securities) expanded. The stock exchanges became centers of decision-making, guiding the strategic and economic policy choices of the states. We propose the term "*managerial*" to qualify the current phase of capitalism, with reference to two phenomena: a) the strengthening of the economic and decision-making power of managers – company directors or state officials – who manage private or public assets and ensure that they are satisfactorily remunerated, from which they benefit as holders of financial capital, in a liberal and globalized context; b) the securitization and marketization of these individual or collective assets, through economic policies of privatization, deregulation and financial innovations that facilitate the growth and centralization of wealth (buyouts, cooperation, coalitions, networks); financial yield now takes precedence over profit (Laperche and Uzunidis 2008).

The transition in time from the primacy of the commercial sphere, then that of industry and finally that of finance over economic activity gives rhythm to economic cycles. This evolution has been supported by social and military conflicts and by voluntary state intervention. Radical technological innovations concentrated in particular sectors and then gradually spread from one sector to another are the result of the general business climate and contribute to its modification. With Schumpeter, the neo-Schumpeterians and Kondratieff, we can identify five major economic cycles since 1780 or, rather, five long movements associated with five waves of radical innovations: textiles, iron and steel; steam at the end of the 18th century; railways in the mid-19th century; electricity, automobiles and chemicals at the beginning of the 20th century; oil, plastics and electric motors in the middle of the 20th century; and microelectronics, biotechnologies and eco-technologies towards the end of the 20th century (see Table 9.1).

	Prosperity	**Recession**	**Depression**	**Recovery**
"*Industrial Revolution*" cycle (textiles, iron, steam)	1787–1800	1801–1813	1814–1827	1828–1842
"*Bourgeois*" cycle (railways)	1845–1857	1858–1869	1870–1885	1886–1897
"*Mercantilist*" cycle (automobiles, electricity, chemicals)	1898–1911	1912–1925	1926–1939	(1940–1950)
"*Interventionist*" cycle (oil, plastics, nuclear)	(1951–1965)	(1966–1975)	(1976–1985)	(1985–1995)
"*Managerial*" cycle (digital technologies, biotechnologies, green technologies)	(1996–2008)	(2008–...)	?	?

Table 11.1. *Economic cycles (source: author, based on Kondratieff, Schumpeter and Neo-Schumpeterians)*

11.4. Conclusion

Technological innovation can play a key role in explaining economic cycles or, better yet, economic movements. For Schumpeter, innovations lead to an increase in the demand for means of production, a decrease in production costs thanks to the introduction of labor-saving machines and, probably, a reduction in the cost of fixed assets through, in particular, the increase and diversification of the quantities of goods produced. The increase in supply capacity leads to an increase in demand due to new consumption needs, favorable expectations of consumers, entrepreneurs and employees, and recourse to credit. The combined increase in investment, distributed income and profits puts the economy on the path of growth. This phase of prosperity, after the initial stimulating effect of radical innovations, will be prolonged by incremental innovations … until the production process is saturated.

However, the term cycle suggests a certain regularity that does not exist in reality. The economy fluctuates permanently. Only an overall vision of society that takes into account the interrelationships between the technical, organizational, social and political spheres allows us to apprehend the real evolution. Hence the importance of the broad definition of innovation and the holistic approach to economics applied by economists of change.

11.5. References

Boutillier, S. and Uzunidis, D. (2014). The theory of the entrepreneur: From heroic to socialised entrepreneurship. *Journal of Innovation Economics & Management*, 14(2), 9–40.

Freeman, C. and Louça, F. (2001). *As Time Goes By. From the Industrial Revolutions to the Information Revolution.* Oxford University Press, Oxford.

Freeman, C. and Perez, C. (1986). *The Diffusion of Technical Innovations and Changes of Techno-Economic Paradigm.* SPRU, Sussex.

Friedman, M. (2002). *Capitalism and Freedom*, 4th edition. University of Chicago Press, Chicago.

Kondratieff, N.D. (1925). Bolschije cycly konjonktury, *Voprossy Konjonktury*, 1, Moscow.

Kondratieff, N.D. (1984). *The Long Wave Cycle*, Dutton. London.

Laperche, B. and Uzunidis, D. (2008). *Powerful Finance and Innovation Trends in a High-Risk Economy.* Palgrave Macmillan, London.

Marx, K. (1992). *Capital.* Vol. I, II, III, Penguin, London.

Rosenberg, N. (1994). *Exploring the Black Box. Technology, Economics, and History*. Cambridge University Press, Cambridge.

Schumpeter, J.A. (1935). *La théorie de l'évolution économique* [*The Theory of Economic Development*, original book published in German in 1911]. Dalloz, Paris

Schumpeter, J.A. (1939). *Business Cycles: A Theoretical, Historical and Statistical Analysis of the Capitalist Process*. McGraw-Hill, New York.

Schumpeter, J.A. (1987). *History of Economic Analysis*. Routledge, London.

Schumpeter, J.A. (2008). *Capitalism, Socialism, and Democracy*, 3rd edition. Harper Perennial Modern Classics, New York.

12

Design – Innovative Design: The Importance of a Methodical Approach

12.1. Introduction

Innovation is a part of our humanity. Since the first tools were carved in prehistoric times, humans have never ceased to innovate in all areas of their existence, thereby contributing to the conception of the world in which they live.

However, in the industrial age, innovation could not remain a random phenomenon. It had to be "domesticated". The emergence of Design Offices at the end of the 19th century was part of a rationalization of the design process, the latter being a multi-step process which, starting from an identified problem, allows the generation of an innovative concept that creates value. More precisely, it contributed to the diffusion of the regulated design model (Hatchuel *et al.* 2006). The latter favors design reasoning based on the application of a system of rules that assures designers that they will be able to design a variety of objects without embarking on costly and uncertain explorations.

While this form of design organization has proven its effectiveness in innovating on parametric performance criteria (faster, cheaper, smaller, etc.), it is not without its critics. First, it locks organizations into finite object models. Closely linked to the above, regulated design leads to the massification of the production of incremental innovations (Forest 2020). However, incremental innovation is no longer a sufficient guarantee to deal with the emergence of disruptive innovation, as shown by the example of Airbnb, which has reinvented all the fundamentals of the hotel industry and challenged established positions. It is precisely this observation that argues for the advent of innovative design, i.e. a design regime that cultivates disruptive

---

Chapter written by Joëlle FOREST.

innovation and opens up the creation of new markets by putting competition out of the game. However, and as we will see in this contribution, engaging in an innovative design approach does not mean "navigating on sight". On the contrary, innovative design implies being methodical in order to arrive at the right port, as we will see from the presentation of the main methods of innovative design that follows.

12.2. What methods should be used to cultivate disruptive innovation in the 21st century?

Claiming that the competition through innovation depends on innovative design should not lead us to think about the latter as a magic solution. Innovative design first requires us to bypass the fixation effect, i.e. to deviate from the models developed by our brain. Indeed, the latter act as restrictive frameworks for innovation because, when designers are faced with a new problem to solve, they tend to reproduce solutions they have previously developed and remain in the dominant design. As James Dyson points out, reproduction is easier than invention. According to him, this is the reason why so many vacuum cleaners still operate from an old dominant design (in this case, the use of a bag that serves to retain dust and dirt, and lets air escape through small holes), which makes them inefficient and disappointing to use. The question then arises of how to emancipate oneself from the fixation effect?

In 1946, using the analysis of 40,000 patents, Genrich Altshuller developed the TRIZ theory (Russian acronym for the Theory of Inventive Problem Solving). The latter is based on two postulates, namely the laws of evolution and contradiction (Choulier and Weite 2011), the second one meaning that a technological disruption results from an uncompromising resolution of a contradiction, being characterized by the fact that the improvement of one parameter implies the degradation of one or more other parameters. However, while contradiction is the starting point for TRIZ, its identification often poses a problem for the designer, who is trapped by the fixation effect, and is unable to think of their problem in a new light. In order to break down psychological stereotypes and support the emergence of contradictions, Genrich Altshuller proposed a number of methods: the miniature men's method and the DTC operators (for Dimension, Time, Cost). Once the technical contradiction has been identified, its resolution is carried out "using a reasoning by analogy facilitated by the use of the TRIZ metabases that are the inventive principles" (Cavallucci 2018). Precisely, it is a question of exploring generic solutions, borrowed from other domains from a matrix (39 × 39), which are listed in rows and columns. The parameters can, by association, characterize contradictions with a number (from 0 to 4) at the intersection, each of them referring to one of the 40 inventive principles identified by Genrich Altshuller, which can act as a catalyst for innovative solutions. One example is Pringle's chips. Procter & Gamble stood out from the competition by preserving the perfect integrity of the chips in their packaging by asking themselves how to combine the need for transport with the, *a priori* irreconcilable, requirement to not touch the chips, taking inspiration from electrostatics. Now, at the end of the chain, the chips are no longer grasped, but are attracted by an electrostatic device, like a sheet of paper sticking to a rubbed ruler.

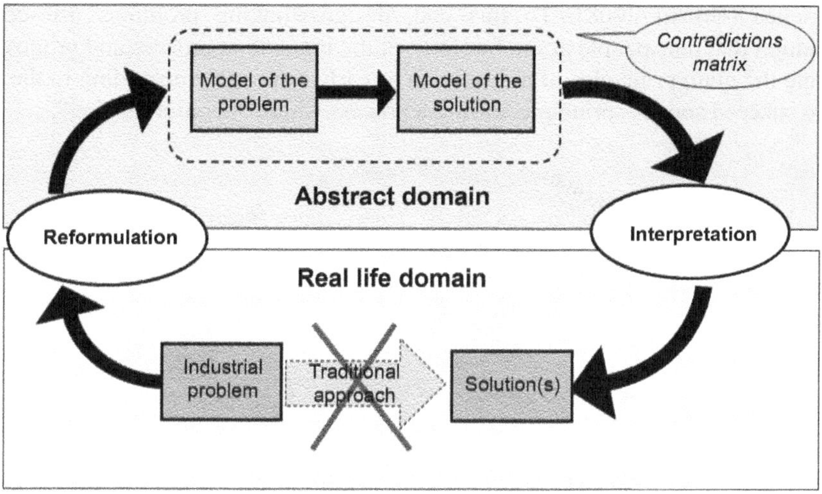

Figure 12.1. *TRIZ approach. For a color version of this figure, see www.iste.co.uk/uzunidis/innovation1.zip*

While TRIZ has its followers (it has been Samsung's main innovation method since 2007 and has allowed it to achieve a strong growth in its turnover), some people deplore the psychological resistance to the basic principles of TRIZ, i.e. the ability of the designer to move away from their industrial problem and develop a model of the abstract problem. Others point out the difficulty of grasping principles that are too far removed from the company's field of expertise. The latest criticisms are related to the fact that TRIZ is not sufficiently market and user-oriented and is solely focused on technical innovation (Yannou *et al.* 2018).

In the early 1990s, the design agency IDEO formalized *design thinking* as a three-step innovation process:

– identifying a problem and understanding its environment;

– finding the concept (the idea that will allow us to answer the problem posed);

– designing the form that will embody this concept.

This was designed to generate innovative concepts that meet the three fundamental criteria of desirability (for the user or the market), technical feasibility and economic viability.

However, as Brown points out, design thinking is not about making an object more attractive at a faster rate than its competitor, but about creating a user experience (Brown 2008). To this end, design thinking promotes user-centric innovation that puts people at the forefront of the innovation process and proposes to validate the main principles of the solution as early as possible according to the "fail fast to succeed sooner" principle, during a process where "iteration is king".

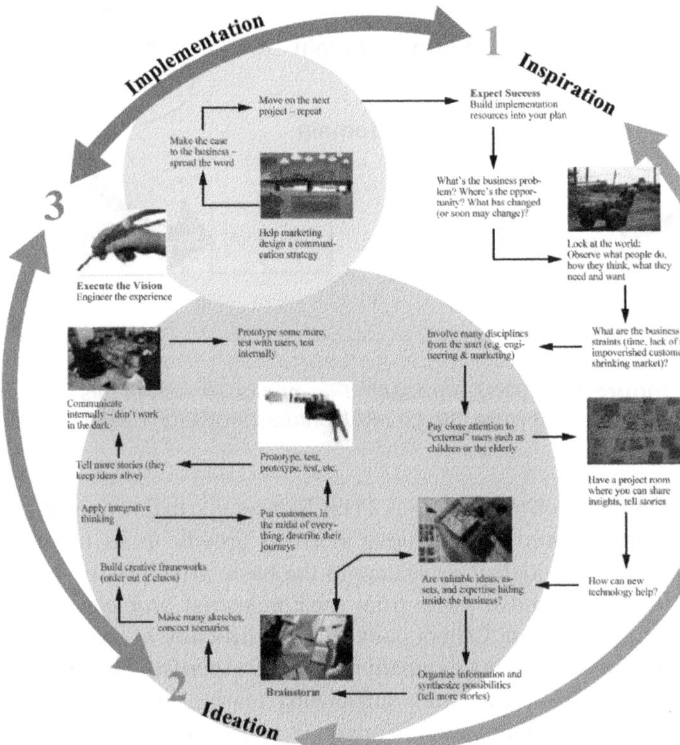

Figure 12.2. *Design thinking (from Brown 2008, pp. 88–89). For a color version of this figure, see www.iste.co.uk/uzunidis/innovation1.zip*

Considered a central pillar of the innovation culture of the world's most innovative companies (Apple, Samsung, General Electric, HP, SAP, etc.), design thinking is not without its critics, however. Bruce Nussbaum, one of the fervent promoters of this approach does not hesitate to speak about "failed experiments".

For their part, Hatchuel, Le Masson and Weil (2006) propose to get rid of the effect of fixation by revisiting the identity of the object. Indeed, the prevalence of incremental innovations is, according to them, linked to the fact that they are part of the register of knowledge exploitation and regulated design, where the identity of the object remains unchanged. However, an innovation such as the Dyson vacuum cleaner or the iPhone involves emancipating oneself from the identity of the object: the bag for the vacuum cleaner, thanks to cyclone technology and the keyboard in the iPhone, thanks to the scrolling function that allows the screen to scroll horizontally and vertically with the touch of a finger. The authors base their subject on the C-K theory.

According to them, it is possible to theorize the emergence of novelty from a theory of reasoning in design, organized around the distinction between two types of space: C space, which represents the space of concepts, and K space, which represents the space of knowledge. Concretely, starting from an identified problem, design reasoning begins with a K–C disjunction that gives rise to a concept and ends with a C-K conjunction, which transforms a concept into knowledge. Redefining the identity of artifacts implies, to put it another way, the generation of expansive partitions, producing a double expansion in concept and knowledge. This double expansion is the necessary condition for the formation of a new object with a broken definition in C because, without a concept, we are condemned to indefinitely explore objects whose definition never changes.

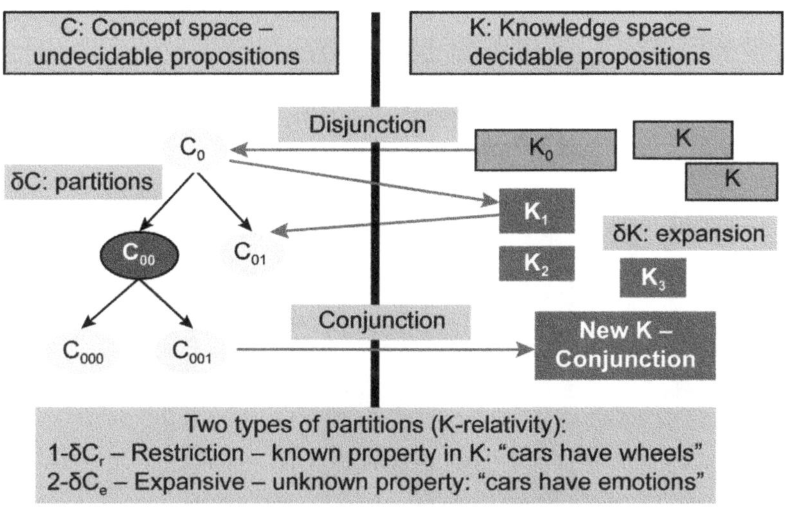

Figure 12.3. *C-K theory (Hatchuel* et al. *2018). For a color version of this figure, see www.iste.co.uk/uzunidis/innovation1.zip*

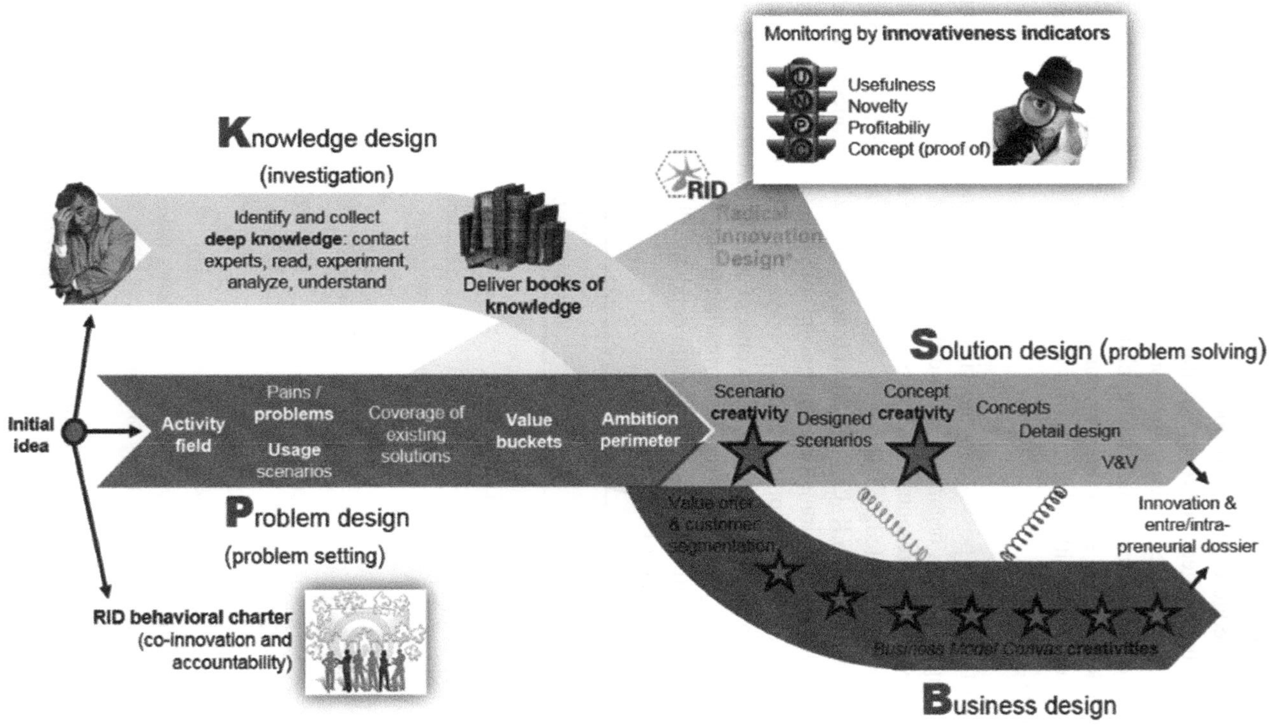

Figure 12.4. *The Radical Innovation Design® method (according to Yannou* et al. *2018). For a color version of this figure, see www.iste.co.uk/uzunidis/innovation1.zip*

However, the C-K theory is not without its critics. Some point out the difficulty of defining the field of innovation, others say that it "says nothing about" how "expansive partitions should be generated from K" (Dubois *et al.* 2019, p. 141), and others finally consider that the concept tree represents more of the history of the genesis of a concept than a concept space and pleads for the social inscription of knowledge production to be taken into account (Coateana *et al.* 2010).

Developed a little over 10 years ago, the Radical Innovation Design® method is a disruptive innovation method driven by uses which, according to Yannou, allows it to significantly differentiate itself from classic methods such as design thinking, CK and TRIZ theories (Yannou 2018).

RID is based on the premise that in order to design innovative artifacts, it is necessary to start from the problems encountered by users, rather than focusing on products and technologies. It is therefore based on the two sub-processes of problem design (exploration of existing problems, uses and solutions) and knowledge (building up skills and knowledge that feeds into problem design) to identify a set of pockets of value (the situation where the gap between the existing and ideal situation is greatest). These allow the definition of the scope of ambition from which the design of the solution and its business model are launched in parallel, as shown in Figure 10.4.

Because it is centered on uses (and is not technocentric), the Radical Innovation Design® method provides the key to innovation. However, because it is anchored in the present, isn't it more favorable in producing incremental rather than disruptive innovations?[1]

12.3. Conclusion

Orchestrating disruptive innovation: this may seem paradoxical as innovation is associated in the collective imaginary with the idea of freedom. However, this is the main lesson of the different innovative design methods mentioned above, to escape random processes such as brainstorming. Indeed, all the methods presented invite us to implement a structured approach, an approach that allows emancipation from the fixation effect, a necessary condition for generating disruptive innovations.

To do this, innovative design involves the art of detouring. First, the art of detouring can be understood as the ability to divert oneself from a clear-cut path

1 We find here one of the criticisms addressed to design thinking of which it shares the user focus.

considered from the dual point of view of systematic design and dominant design. Second, the art of detouring refers to the famous proverb "everything comes to those who wait". Associating our problem with varied knowledge in order to look at it from a new angle, identifying contradictions, cannot be seen as a waste of time, but as a vector to get off the beaten track.

Finally, it should be noted that while innovative design reaffirms the role of knowledge in innovation, it also rehabilitates the role of a form of thought that has long been disqualified by the history that we named creative rationality (Forest 2017).

12.4. References

Brown, T. (2008). Design thinking. *Harvard Business Review*, 84–95.

Cavallucci, D. (2018). La TRIZ, une théorie de l'invention en support des activités de R&D : fondements et méthodes. *Techniques de l'ingénieur*, 6 July.

Choulier, D. and Weite, P.-A. (2011). *Découvrir et appliquer les outils de TRIZ*. UTBM Editions, Belfort.

Coateana, E., Forest, J., Choulier, D. (2010). The engineering design CK theory: Contributions and limits. *22nd International Conference on Design Theory and Methodology*, Montreal, 83–92.

Dubois, S., De Guio, R., Chibane, H. (2019). Differences and complementarities between C-K and TRIZ. In *New Opportunities for Innovation Breakthroughs for Developing Countries and Emerging Economies*, Benmoussa, R., De Guio, R., Dubois, S., Koziołek S. (eds). Proceedings of the 19th International Triz Future Conference, Springer, Cham.

Forest, J. (2017). *Creative Rationality and Innovation*. ISTE Ltd, London and John Wiley & Sons, New York.

Forest, J. (2020). Thinking about the meaning of innovation. In *Innovation for Society: The P.S.I. Approach*, Chouteau, M., Forest, J., Nguyen, C. (eds). ISTE Ltd, London and John Wiley & Sons, New York.

Hatchuel, A., Le Masson, P., Weil, B. (2006). *Les processus d'innovation conception innovante et croissance des entreprises*. Hermes Lavoisier, Paris.

Hatchuel, A., Le Masson, P., Weil, B. (2018). Théorie C-K : fondements et implications d'une théorie de la conception. *Techniques de l'ingénieur*, 10 April.

Yannou, B. (2018). La méthodologie Radical Innovation Design® (en bref, positionnement pour les experts de l'innovation). Research report, Centrale Supélec, Gif-sur-Yvette.

Yannou, B., Lamé, G., Cluzel, F. (2018). Radical innovation design : innover par les usages grâce à l'identification de poches de valeur. In *Valeur(s) et management*, 2nd edition, de Hemmer, O. and Poissonnier, H. (eds). Editions EMS, Paris.

13

Diffusion – Diffusion and Adoption Behavior of Innovations

13.1. Introduction

The analysis of the diffusion of innovations has been popularized in economics since the middle of the 20th century, notably with the work of Griliches (1957). Its starting point is the observation that an innovation is never adopted from the outset by all the economic actors likely to do so in the long run. This is true for companies faced with an innovation process that is aimed at reducing their production costs. It is also true on the part of consumers, when it comes to a product innovation that meets needs that have been poorly or not met until now. The first works were interested in identifying and quantifying the mechanisms that explain this diffusion of adoption over time, which is characteristic of the diffusion phenomenon. A distinction between two types of approaches soon emerged.

On one hand, there is the so-called epidemiological approach, which gives a central role to information, and, on the other, there is the individual choice approach, which emphasizes the heterogeneity of potential adopters. Although this reading was not preponderant at the outset, these two approaches have, as a common denominator, the role of positive externalities between adopters in the phenomenon of diffusion. The recognition of these externalities is essential because it is the basis and the driver of public intervention. Although the analysis initially focused on the diffusion of an innovation taken in isolation, it was later enriched by work on competing innovations. Depending on the approach adopted, this extension has made it possible either to gain a better understanding of the importance of the

---

Chapter written by Marc BAUDRY.

start-up phase of diffusion or to establish a more explicit link with R&D activity and, thus, the genesis of innovations.

The epidemiological approach is presented first, followed by the individual choice approach. The importance of externalities for public policy is then discussed before touching on some extensions.

13.2. The epidemiological approach

The epidemiological approach to explaining the diffusion of innovations is based on the contagion of diseases. It considers an innovation whose adoption would benefit every agent in a given population. However, the adoption of this innovation is not necessarily achieved by all agents because it requires that they be informed beforehand of its existence and its profitability. Information is treated as a public good in the sense that, on the one hand, its use by one agent does not prevent its use by another agent (the non-rivalry property) and, on the other hand, it is not possible to prevent an agent from using this information whenever they have the opportunity to do so. Nevertheless, the information is scarce, because not all agents necessarily have access to it initially. The population of agents is generally assumed to be homogeneous, except that at least one agent initially has information about the existence and profitability of the innovation. Informed agents therefore adopt the innovation, which will reveal its existence and profitability to the other agents with whom they are in contact. This transmission cannot take place within the framework of a market exchange because the value that an agent places on information is only known to them once this information has been revealed to them. There is therefore an informational externality, since each new adopter does not integrate into their economic assessment of adoption the impact that this will have on agents who are not yet informed.

The interest in the epidemiological approach is simply that it has formalized this idea. First, it is assumed that the initial proportion of informed (respectively, uninformed) agents is known, called the prevalence rate (respectively, the non-prevalence rate). If we consider a random encounter of two agents, the probability that this will result in a new adoption corresponds to the joint probability that one of the agents is informed and the other is not. This joint probability is therefore the product of the prevalence rate and the non-prevalence rate. Assuming, for example, that an encounter takes place on every date, this will result in a dynamic of the prevalence rate, which has been shown to correspond to a logistic function of time. The associated trajectory for the prevalence rate typically describes an "S" curve: the early dates are characterized by an increasingly rapid rise in the prevalence rate until the prevalence rate equals the non-prevalence rate, and then the rise continues, but at an increasingly slower rate. This very basic diffusion model has been enriched in different ways.

The first aspect is taking into account the probability that each agent informs themselves and not by meeting another agent. The result is a less symmetrical diffusion trajectory than that of the logistic model. A second aspect is the introduction of a probability that the transmission of information is effective, which was then modeled according to contextual elements, explaining that the diffusion occurs more or less quickly depending on the population under consideration. Chow (1967), for example, considered a price index, corrected for hardware performance, as a contextual element in analyzing the diffusion of computers.

13.3. The discrete choice approach

The discrete choice approach postulates, contrary to the epidemiological approach, that agents are perfectly informed but are heterogeneous as to the profitability of adopting the innovation. The basic model dates back to the analysis of the diffusion of mechanical reapers in North America from the mid-19th century onwards by David (1966) and Davies (1979). The adoption of a mechanical reaper represents a fixed cost that saves on the variable cost of labor; the larger the area harvested, the easier it is to amortize this fixed cost. Assuming, at first glance, that farms differ only in size, only farms above a critical size initially find it profitable to adopt the new equipment. From knowledge of the distribution of farm size, one can therefore deduce the proportion of initial adopters. However, a diffusion mechanism can only be triggered if the first adoptions induce a change for subsequent adopters. This change occurs either through an increase in the gains from the use of the innovation or through a decrease in price. The increase in the gains derived from use is characteristic of club goods, the most telling example of which is the telephone: the higher the number of other users, i.e. people who can be contacted, the greater the satisfaction of a user. This effect is commonly referred to as network externality. The fall in price of a process or product with unchanged characteristics is the result of increasing dynamic returns to scale, often referred to as learning effects: thanks to the experience acquired, the supplier of the innovative product or process sees its marginal production cost fall with the cumulative sum of the units produced previously, which leads it to lower its price. Whether the change occurs via gains in use or via marginal production costs, each new adopter exerts a positive externality for the benefit of agents who have not yet adopted it. In fact, they do not include the positive effect that they will exert in favor of those who have not yet adopted in their adoption decision.

13.4. Public dissemination policies

The epidemiological approach and the discrete choice approach are not incompatible with each other. For example, Jaffe and Stavins (1994) developed a model that takes into account the prevalence of innovative technology in the cost of the technology. In their model, the effect of prevalence is informational; the transmission of information between adopting and non-adopting agents allows the latter to take advantage of the experience of the former to use the new technology more effectively. The article by Jaffe and Stavins (1994) is also of interest in explicitly addressing the influence of public policy. However, these authors are interested in policies to promote eco-efficient technologies that are environmentally justified and independent of the externalities underlying the diffusion. The central role of externalities in the diffusion of innovations calls for specific public policies.

Indeed, as soon as externalities exist, there is a discrepancy between the decisions taken by economic agents and what would be socially optimal. In the epidemiological approach, by neglecting the positive impact in terms of information transmitted to others in their decision to adopt, agents underestimate the collective gains derived from this adoption. If these social gains were integrated into decision-making, the rate of adoption would be higher. In other words, the socially optimal rate of adoption is faster than the rate of adoption in a "laissez-faire" situation. To correct this inefficiency, adopters should be rewarded for internalizing the social effects of their decision. This reward is all the stronger when early adopters are considered, because the cascading informational effect means that the social impact of their decision is greater than for late adopters. The logic is similar for the discrete choice approach, even if the externalities are of a different type. Public subsidy policies for the adoption of innovative products or processes therefore find their theoretical justification here.

A typical example of these policies is the guaranteed purchase price system for electricity produced and put on the grid by wind farms. By guaranteeing a stable price that is higher than the wholesale price, this so-called "Feed-in Tariff" system has increased the profitability of wind farm construction and allowed the large-scale development of this technology. In this particular case, it is learning effects that have contributed to lowering the cost of wind turbines and induced diffusion (Baudry and Bonnet 2019). As the technology has spread, the social gains from new installations have been reduced. This has led states that had instituted the "Feed-in Tariff" system in the early 2000s to reduce or eliminate it. Indeed, in essence, the rationale for adoption support is diminishing as diffusion occurs and the number of agents that can benefit from cascading effects becomes fewer and fewer. Optimal public support is therefore inherently temporary and diminishing.

13.5. Some extensions of the analysis: multiplicity of innovations and institutional framework

The above work has largely focused on a single, well-identified process or product, which facilitates data collection and quantitative analysis. In practice, however, several innovative solutions may be in competition. This raises the question of whether the diffusion of each of them will follow the same trajectory or not. If one of the technologies is also considered to be inherently better, then the question arises as to whether it will prevail over the others. The pioneering work of Arthur *et al.* (1987) is rather pessimistic in this respect. By developing a model built around the concept of Polya's urn, which can be seen as a variant of the epidemiological model with several products or processes, Arthur *et al.* (1987) show that diffusion always converges towards an equilibrium, but that any distribution of the market between these products or processes can be this equilibrium. One response, in terms of public policy, could be to ensure the best possible information on the intrinsic merits of the different solutions, in order to limit the excessively random nature of the choice of early adopters. However, public authorities still need to be intrinsically better informed than other economic agents.

In practice, too, the development and diffusion of a technology is based on a cluster of innovations: starting with a first disruptive innovation, the technology is gradually improved by a succession of incremental innovations. A distinction must therefore be made between the diffusion of a particular innovation and the diffusion of the technology as a whole. Taking up the bases of the approach through individual choices but coupling it with product differentiation, Trajtenberg (1989) proposes a model where the improvement of product characteristics guides adoption choices. The link can then be made between the diffusion of technology and the R&D effort made upstream by innovative firms to improve the product, an effort whose return on investment has been studied by another body of literature dealing with the value of innovations.

Beyond the approaches described above, the literature has focused on the cultural or social institutional factors that can, sometimes, constitute a breeding ground for diffusion and, sometimes, a hindrance. The case of the diffusion of electric vehicles is quite illustrative in this respect. Developed at the end of the 19th century in parallel with vehicles with the internal combustion engine, its diffusion has stumbled and is still stumbling over the question of the concomitant and *ex nihilo* development of a network of recharging stations. In contrast, gasoline was already distributed by drugstores for household use at the end of the 19th century, meaning vehicles with combustion engines could be distributed without strong constraints on fuel supply (Melaina 2007). Another illustrative example is that of the printing industry. It has been established that printing text from movable metal typefaces was developed in the Far East (China, as well as

Korea) independently and prior to Gutenberg's innovations (Hargrave 2013). However, it did not enjoy the same diffusion there because the writing systems of these countries required too many characters to ensure the profitability of the invention. Finally, the issue of diffusion of innovations has generally been seen from the perspective of diffusion between firms. A more limited number of papers also address the equally important issue of diffusion within the same firm.

13.6. Conclusion

The explanations put forward in the economic literature for the adoption of an innovation's diffusion over time, which is characteristic of the diffusion phenomenon, make externalities play a central role. Whether they are informational in nature or result from club or learning effects, they justify supportive public policies specifically oriented towards early adopters. The interweaving of adoption and innovation behaviors in the more general context of an innovation cluster means that these policies are also, partly, innovation policies. However, their effectiveness must be qualified by the institutional environment or the coexistence of competing innovations at the very beginning of the diffusion phase.

13.7. References

Arthur, W.B., Ermoliev, Y.M., Kaniobski, Y.M. (1987). Path-dependent processes and the emergence of macro-structure. *European Journal of Operational Research*, 30, 294–303.

Baudry, M. and Bonnet, B. (2019). Demand-pull instruments and the development of wind power in Europe: A counterfactual analysis. *Environmental and Resource Economics*, 73(2), 385–427.

Chow, G.C. (1967). Technological change and the demand for computers. *American Economic Review*, 57, 1117–1130.

David, P.A. (1966). The mechanization of reaping in the ante-bellum Midwest. In *Industrialization in Two Systems: Essays in Honor of Alexander Gerschenkron*, Rosovsky, H. (ed.). John Wiley and Sons, New York.

Davies, S. (1979). *The Diffusion of Process Innovations*. Cambridge University Press, New York.

Griliches, Z. (1957). Hybrid corn: An exploration in economics of technological change. *Econometrica*, 25, 501–522.

Hargrave, J. (2013). Disruptive technological history: Papermaking to digital printing. *Journal of Scholarly Publishing*, 44(3), 221–236.

Jaffe, A.B. and Stavins, R.N. (1995). The energy paradox and the diffusion of conservation technology. *Resource and Energy Economics*, 16, 91–122.

Melaina, M.W. (2007). Turn of the century refueling: A review of innovations in early gasoline refueling methods and analogies for hydrogen. *Energy Policy*, 35, 4919–4934.

Trajtenberg, M. (1989). The welfare analysis of product innovations with an application to computed tomography scanners. *Journal of Political Economy*, 97(2), 444–479.

14

Disruption – Disruptive Innovation and the Evolution of Competitive Relationships

14.1. Introduction

Over time, many meanings and definitions of innovation have been presented, each one needed to capture a different aspect, a new nuance of innovation, useful for a better understanding of the innovation process for the players involved or the impact on the market. In the first section of this chapter, the key concept definition of disruptive innovation will be presented, and then the impact on the market is shown through relevant examples. In the final section, disruptive innovation is considered in relation to similar and overlapping concepts.

What is a disruptive innovation? First of all, it is not a breakthrough, an important discovery or significant technological development; instead, in this context, disruptive refers to the impact of innovation on the market and on the incumbent competitive advantage. Clayton Christensen, who introduced the framework in a seminal article dated 1995, distinguished between sustaining and disruptive innovation. On one hand, sustaining innovation offers better performance compared with what is already available and targets high-end customers. Innovations can have an incremental nature – small improvements or upgrades made to a company's existing products – or they can be radical, a technological breakthrough enabling a leap forward, thus replacing current products. Disruptive innovations, on the other hand, do not refer to better products offered to established customers; instead, they disrupt and redefine the competition by introducing products that are not as good as the current ones but have some useful features and benefits – typically, they are simpler and cheaper and appeal to new or less demanding customers.

Chapter written by Giovanni ZAZZERINI.

14.2. The disruptive innovation model

A disruptive innovation replaces a product that historically was so expensive and complex that only the high-end market could buy it, with a product that is affordable and accessible to a larger population. Even if the disruptive innovation has a lesser technological performance – at least in the short term – it brings to larger markets, low-end and mass markets, a very different value proposition, changing the competitive scenario of the markets. In fact, disruptive technologies underperform established products from a technological point of view in mainstream markets, but they also have other features that a different market segment value most. In the words of Christensen (1997), "products based on disruptive technologies are typically cheaper, simpler, smaller, and, frequently, more convenient to use". New customers are ready to accept the lower quality for a significantly better price.

For example, in the 1960s Toyota entered the low-end market with the cheap Corona model, disrupting the market for Ford and other American car manufacturers. Then, over the years, the company progressively positioned itself in the high-end market offering high-performing cars. History is now repeating itself; Korean automobile manufacturers such as Hyundai and Kia are stealing market share from Toyota at the low-end of the market.

Figure 12.1 describes the typical disruptive innovation dynamic and its key elements.

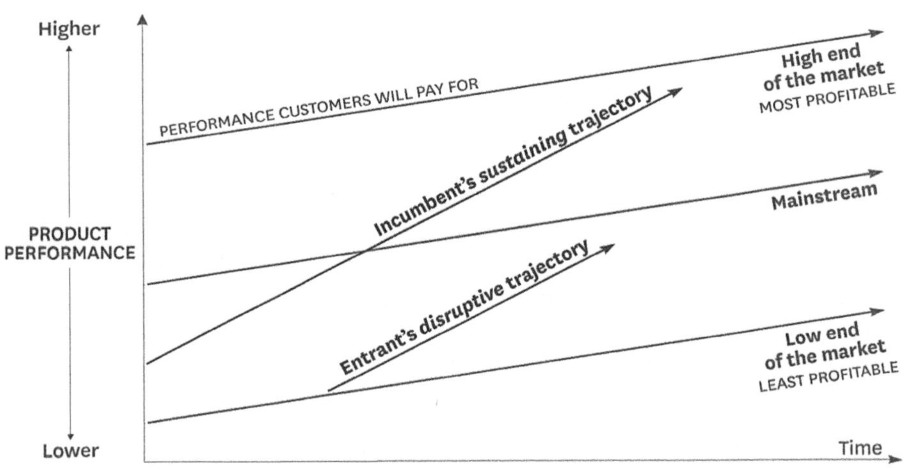

Figure 14.1. *Correlation between product performance level, market profitability and the disruptive innovation dynamic. For a color version of this figure, see www.iste.co.uk/uzunidis/innovation1.zip*

Figure 14.1 shows customer demand trajectories – the blue lines – showing customer willingness to pay for performance; it depicts the level of performance and technological improvements that customers can absorb or that are valuable to them. The red line shows the product performance trajectory, which increases over time.

As shown in the figure, technological progress – the red line – almost always overtakes the line representing the level of performance required by the market, along the different levels. Over time, companies continue trying to make better products that they can sell to their best customers at high-end of the market. Incumbent companies introduce high-quality products targeting the most profitable customers – the high-end market. As illustrated, technologies can progress faster than market demand; this offering "overshoots" the needs of the mass market; it gives customers more than they need or ultimately are willing to pay for, leaving space for newcomers to target less profitable segments neglected by the incumbents. The entrant's disruptive trajectory – the lower red line – better addresses the needs of the low-end market, in terms of good value for money or different features and product characteristics; until the disrupter displaces many of the older companies and becomes the industry's new leader. Then, the new entrant improves the offering and its performance over time, moves up the market and challenges the dominance of the incumbent. This happens because the pace and speed of technological progress surpasses customer demand for better performing technologies. As a result, incumbents produce and offer products that are more advanced than customers want. In this way, there is a gap between the performance demanded by customers and the one provided by businesses, thus leaving space at the low-end of the market where customers are looking at lower performing products, at cheaper prices.

This is exactly what happened when, in 2007, ASUS introduced the first netbook, with a combination of lightweight hardware, Linux-based operating system, solid-state drive (SSD) and relatively low cost, they disrupted the market.

In 2006, the game console market also witnessed a significant disruption. At that time, Sony PlayStation and Microsoft Xbox consoles were controlling market share with an 86.6% total of all units sold. Both of the systems were investing more in performing processors and better graphics for hardcore shooting and sports games, following the technology trajectory represented above. Because of the investments needed in this battle, Nintendo shifted from incremental advancement to a product targeting a different market segment, offering a new experience that shifted demand within the video game industry. The introduction of the Wii console revolutionized the way consumers interact with video games and developed a new paradigm of gaming. This was reflected in a consumer behavior shift; as a result of this change in 2009, Nintendo had reclaimed the top position in the video game industry by capturing 48% of the market share in console sales.

In order to compete with Sony's PlayStation 3 and Microsoft's Xbox 360, Nintendo reinvented video gaming, making it more social, more intuitive and more physically engaging. The feature that sets the Wii apart from both of its competitors is the remote control that connects to the console wirelessly. It is equipped with three-axis acceleration sensors developed by STMicroelectronics, one of the world's leading semiconductor manufacturers, who were able to provide a motion-activated user interface for Nintendo's new home console.

14.3. The innovator's dilemma

Because disruptive products are often commercialized in emerging or insignificant markets, leading companies to follow what their best and most profitable customers want and ask for, they are rarely able to invest in disruptive technologies until it is too late. Existing customers and profits coming from current business hinder investments by established companies in new innovations. However, the market can be attractive to newcomers who have few customers and face fewer competing investment opportunities. As a result, incumbents are typically not motivated to develop their own disruptive innovations that promise lower margins, target smaller markets and introduce inferior products and services that their existing customers cannot use.

This is the dilemma explored by Christensen (1997): "[...] the logical, competent decisions of management that are critical to the success of their companies are also the reasons why they lose their positions of leadership". To avoid this trap, incumbents have to pay attention to disruptive technologies because even if, at the beginning, they enter the market with lower-quality substitutes offered to the least-profitable customers, as the technology improves, they will move up and become competitive with the market leaders. Incumbent companies who see the early signs of disruption have to invest early in the new technology and be prepared to shift when price and performance are acceptable to the mass market. So, ambidextrous organizations have to manage the current business and strengthen relationships with key customers, and, at the same time, they have to create a new division focused on the growth opportunities that arise from the disruption. To manage disruption, companies need to balance the tension between exploiting a core business that generates revenue and exploring new areas where results are uncertain, even if the long-term payoff is attractive.

The example of Netflix helps to explain why incumbents frequently overlook disrupters. When it was launched in 1997, Netflix's initial service was not appealing to most of Blockbuster's customers who rented movies on impulse. Netflix, at that time, had an exclusively online interface and a large inventory of movies, but delivery via U.S. Mail meant that movies took several days to arrive. The service only appealed to small segments: movie lovers, early adopters of DVD players and online shoppers. Then, new technologies allowed Netflix to shift to streaming video content over the Internet, offering a wider selection of on-demand content, coupled with low prices and high-quality; Netflix's offer thus became appealing to Blockbuster customers. It was a classic disruptive path. If Netflix had entered the market targeting the high-end market, Blockbuster's most likely response would have been a vigorous, and probably successful, counterattack. But failing to respond effectively to Netflix's disruptive innovation led to Blockbuster's collapse.

This framework contrasts with the traditional strategy approach where innovators create differentiated goods targeted at customers who can afford to pay more and are willing to do so. Thanks to increased efficiency and economies of scale, these goods can later be offered to mass markets at lower prices. Here, new products are introduced with lesser features than the current offering, but at a significantly better price, attracting customers who will accept lower quality.

The Clayton Christensen model slightly overlaps with the Blue Ocean Strategy by Chan Kim and Renée Mauborgne. In their classic book, *Blue Ocean Strategy*, they suggest that "the best way to beat the competition is to stop trying to beat the competition", meaning that companies should avoid competition in current markets – red oceans – and offer something new – value innovation – to a new market – the blue ocean.

A similar concept is the Big Bang Disruption characterized by the exponential growth and falling costs of new digital technologies, which allows products to be simultaneously better, cheaper and more customized compared to the existing ones. This is demonstrated by the example of Google Maps – both better and cheaper compared to traditional GPS navigation systems – offered by Larry Downes and Paul Nunes in their book, *Big Bang Disruption*.

In conclusion, a disruptive innovation is not a breakthrough or simply a technological advancement, instead it is a bottom-up innovation that delivers a new combination of value, often at a lower price, to a different market segment compared to the one targeted by the incumbent. Eventually, it disrupts the existing market and displaces established companies and products.

14.4. References

Christensen, C. (1997). *The Innovator's Dilemma: When New Technologies Cause Great Firms to Fail*. Harvard Business School Press, Boston.

Downes, L. and Nunes, P. (2014). Big bang disruption. In *Exponential Organization: Why New Organizations Are Ten Times Better, Faster, and Cheaper Than Yours (and What To Do About It)*, Ismail, S. (ed.). Diversion Books, New York.

Kim, W.C. and Mauborgne, R. (2005). *Blue Ocean Strategy: How to Create Uncontested Market Space and Make the Competition Irrelevant*. Harvard Business School Press, Boston.

Porter, M.E. (1985). *The Competitive Advantage: Creating and Sustaining Superior Performance*. Free Press, New York.

15

Ecosystem – Innovation Ecosystem: Generativity, Resilience and Power of Attraction

15.1. Introduction

The concept of the ecosystem is becoming increasingly important in economics and management. Since the pioneering work of Moore (1993), this concept has come a long way. Moore initially referred to a *business ecosystem*:

> A business ecosystem is an economic community supported by a foundation of interacting organizations and individuals – the organisms of the business world. The economic community produces goods and services of value to customers, who are themselves members of the ecosystem. (Moore 1993)

Members of the business ecosystem also include suppliers, major producers, competitors and other stakeholders. These different members (whose capacities and roles evolve over time) tend to align with the directions set by one or more central organizations.

More recent contributions (Adner 2006; Attour and Burger-Helmchen 2014; Autio and Thomas 2014; de Vasconcelos Gomes *et al.* 2018) have suggested going beyond the notion of a business ecosystem, which is considered too focused on the economic interests of a central organization alone, by proposing the notion of an *innovation ecosystem*. An innovation ecosystem perspective is no longer just a question of analyzing how a given organization manages to capture value by

---

Chapter written by Patrick COHENDET.

orchestrating its interactions with various stakeholders, but how a structure of heterogeneous actors (companies, various organizations, informal collectives and individuals) engaged in a process of interactions manages to act on their environment, develop new useful solutions, and collectively co-create value. The notion of an innovation ecosystem differs here from that of an innovation network in that it emphasizes the importance of informal actors (individuals, users, collectives and communities, etc.) in complementarity with formal organizations and institutions (firms, public agencies, centers of research, etc.). The present contribution aims at exploring two main dimensions of innovation ecosystems: the different theoretical approaches of this notion, and the main features of innovation ecosystems (generativity, resilience and the power of attraction).

15.2. Theoretical approaches of an innovation ecosystem

The classical example of an innovation ecosystem is given by Saxenian (1994), when she compares the local dynamics of the evolution of Route 128 and Silicon Valley in the United States in the 1980s. She notes that the largest industrial and research organizations are located around Route 128 in Massachusetts, and that this proximity had everything to do with generating an exemplary innovation dynamic. However, in terms of innovation, growth of high-tech jobs, creation of electronics firms, etc., Silicon Valley clearly dominates Route 128, even though at that time it did not benefit from the presence of many large innovative firms. Saxenian's explanation is that Route 128 corresponds to a system of innovation (presence of formal entities, which maintain contractual relations with each other). This system does indeed produce value creation (through new business opportunities, through the interplay of positive externalities, etc.), but in proportions that are not comparable to the power of the creative dynamics of an innovation ecosystem such as that of Silicon Valley. In this ecosystem, the economic and social dynamic is based on incessant interactions between formal organizations, on the one hand, and informal collectives, on the other hand (such as Steve Jobs and Wozniak in their garage), which are often at the origin of ideas that bring about disruptive innovation. It is from the variety of these permanent interactions that start-ups and new innovation projects emerge with unusual intensity.

Saxenian's contribution illustrates how the work on ecosystems is intended to enrich the notion of the innovation system (Lundvall 1992), which has dominated until now in explaining the diffusion of technologies. The notion of innovation system, particularly in its territorialized versions (national or regional innovation system), is essentially limited to explaining how the nature of interactions between existing institutions conditions innovation trajectories ("how institutions drive action"). This restriction is precisely what justifies the interest today in reasoning in terms of the ecosystem: (a) not only to consider that the dynamics of innovations are based on interactions between existing (formal) institutions, but also to open the analysis to stakeholders of all kinds, including informal groups (user communities, in particular) and individual entrepreneurs who can be the source of disruptive innovations; and (b) not to consider institutions as given *a priori*, but to look at the dynamics of innovation that lead to transforming institutions or to the formation of new institutions, practices and ways of doing things ("how action drives institutions") through dialogue with multiple stakeholders (in the private sector and the public sector): patients, caregivers and families, local entrepreneurs, etc. As underlined by de Vasconcelos Gomes *et al.* (2018, p. 3):

> The concept of innovation ecosystem has increasingly gained ground in the literature on strategy, innovation, and entrepreneurship. Scholars have developed a set of definitions and concepts in a variety of contexts, employing innovation ecosystem with different labels and, in some cases, with different meanings and purposes: digital innovation ecosystem (e.g. Rao and Jimenez 2011), hub ecosystems (e.g. Nambisan and Baron 2013), open innovation ecosystem (e.g. Chesbrough *et al.* 2014), platform-based ecosystem (e.g. Gawer and Cusumano 2014).

Two main approaches to the study of the concept of innovation ecosystem have emerged from this perspective: (1) the first approach investigates virtual ecosystems through the analysis of the role of virtual platforms as a coordination mechanism and supports in an open economy context; and (2) in line with the work of Saxenian (1994) on the dynamics of Silicon Valley, the second approach emphasizes the territorial dimensions underlying the dynamics of innovation within a given ecosystem. This approach has since been enriched by an extended model that emphasizes the role of the social ecology of exchanges that is established at the local level (Carayannis and Campbell 2010).

15.3. Main features of innovation ecosystems

Apart from defining the constitutive components of innovation ecosystems, the literature has also strived to identify the main features that can help academics and practitioners alike to differentiate between ecosystems, while refining their understanding of the main properties that might condition the performance of an ecosystem and influence its internal dynamics. Three major characteristics emerge from the heterogeneous works on the subject: generativity, resilience and the power of attraction (Saxenian 1994).

– *Generativity* can be defined as "the ability of a technology platform or technology ecosystem to create, generate or produce new output, structure, or behavior without input from the originator of the system (and to) produce unprompted change driven by large, varied, and uncoordinated audiences" (Zittrain 2006, p. 1980). Beyond the domain of digitalization explored by Zittrain, this ability seems to express an essential feature of ecosystems of innovation.

– A *resilient* system is the one that can react to adversity (unexpected events, competitive pressure, shifts in dominant technology, crisis, etc.) and evolve in response to the new complex environment. This means that not only can the system manage crises effectively (adaptive capacity), but also, in case of major damage or destruction of some of its (formal) components, these formal entities may also return to an informal state (for instance, communities or informal groups of former employees) before potential transformation into new viable formal entities. In these regards, we also make the hypothesis that the existence of a rich and diversified common pool of knowledge resources, shared between the formal bodies and informal members, plays a major role in the level of an ecosystem's resilience.

– *Power of attraction* stems from the fact that dense interactions between the different heterogeneous stakeholders of an ecosystem might exert a strong power of attraction on external newcomers that contribute to enriching the ecosystem and increasing its innovative potential. Beyond the richness and diversity of its knowledge bases, the power of attraction of an ecosystem can be linked to the effects of "buzz" in a specific industry, "tags" in professional and creative communities, and to the frequency and vibrancy of "events" that renders the density of stimulating knowledge exchange and creation in a specific field and/or territory visible. We could argue that, beyond the interplay of the diversity of actors, contributing to knowledge creation and creativity expected in clusters, the power of attraction helps in maintaining generativity that supports resilience.

In such a perspective, fostering the development of an innovation ecosystem is, in fact, "open innovation" (Chesbrough 2003): the dialogue between stakeholders makes it possible to anticipate developments in the field and to mobilize more intelligence on the understanding of emerging issues. The integration of the various contributions is a source of original solutions, often in a break with traditional approaches. In addition, because these explorations mobilize different types of actors and, in particular, those who use or are affected by the products and services of ecosystem organizations, this model of innovation makes it possible to include the initiatives of entrepreneurs, start-ups and SMEs, and to validate them more quickly and effectively by testing them in context. It also ensures a better shared understanding of the issues at stake for each and a dynamic co-construction of social acceptability.

15.4. Conclusion

For organizations, the growing need to establish and actively participate in innovation ecosystems is explained by the increasing complexity of issues (particularly, in health), the speed of technological change, and the diversity and dispersion of sources of skills and new ideas. In the face of these challenges, an existing institution can no longer focus on itself alone. It must build and maintain an innovative ecosystem for: (1) responding in a relevant and efficient manner to the changing needs of its clients and the increasing complexity of the issues at stake; (2) deepening the question of innovation as a collective and collaborative mechanism for value creation, a vector of efficiency and competitiveness; and (3) capturing the added value generated by ecosystem stakeholders, in particular, by combining knowledge and skills from various sources.

In addition, when an ecosystem actually produces high-impact innovations, it becomes a reference pole and a factor of attraction for the territory, inducing a virtuous dynamic by attracting expertise from elsewhere (as is the case for Silicon Valley in IT, for Seattle or Toulouse in aeronautics, or for Montreal in video games, etc.). Thus, functioning as an innovation ecosystem, by mobilizing distributed knowledge, constantly exploring its innovative recombination, and regularly attracting external expertise to ensure its renewal, becomes a key innovation vector for the resilience and development of the organizations involved, and also of an entire sector and territory.

Such an approach is not without its challenges. The keystone of an innovation ecosystem lies in the expression and recognition by all stakeholders of a common purpose – a shared raison d'être – which justifies a form of solidarity commitment to share knowledge, pool skills, and explore new solutions together to ensure the perpetuation of a common future. This also implies, in order to respond to the ever-increasing complexity of the issues at stake, ensuring the continuous renewal of knowledge bases, stakeholders and practices, in particular, by consciously and voluntarily cultivating openness towards the outside world and towards new actors. Finally, the optimal functioning of the ecosystem will only be possible if each of the stakeholders recognizes the potential value of the contributions of all other stakeholders, "on an equal footing of dignity". The functional principle of required variety – mobilizing more varied knowledge, in dialogue, in order to respond to increasingly complex issues – also presupposes an operational principle of broad mobilization and an ethical principle of respect for the practices, routines, identities and specificities of each of the stakeholders.

15.5. References

Adner, R. (2006). Match your innovation strategy to your innovation ecosystem. *Harvard Business Review*, 84(4), 98.

Attour, A. and Burger-Helmchen, T. (2014). Écosystèmes et modèles d'affaires : introduction. *Revue d'économie industrielle*, 146, 11–25.

Autio, E. and Thomas, L. (2014). Innovation ecosystems: Implications for innovation management? In *The Oxford Handbook of Innovation Management*, Dodgson, M., Gann, D.M., Phillips, N. (eds). Oxford University Press, Oxford.

Carayannis, E.G. and Campbell, D.F. (2010). Triple helix, quadruple helix and quintuple helix and how do knowledge, innovation and the environment relate to each other? A proposed framework for a trans-disciplinary analysis of sustainable development and social ecology. *International Journal of Social Ecology and Sustainable Development*, 1(1), 41–69.

Chesbrough, H.W. (2003). *Open Innovation: The New Imperative for Creating and Profiting from Technology*. Harvard Business School Publishing, Boston, MA.

Chesbrough, H.W., Kim, S., Agogino, A. (2014). Chez Panisse: Building an open innovation ecosystem. *California Management Review*, 56(4), 144–171.

Gawer, A. and Cusumano, M.A. (2014). Industry platforms and ecosystem innovation. *Journal of Product Innovation Management*, 31(3), 417–433.

Lundvall, B.Å. (1992). User-producer relationships, national systems of innovation and internationalisation. In *National Systems of Innovation: Towards a Theory of Innovation and Interactive Learning*, Lundvall, B.Å. (ed.) Pinter Publishers, London.

Moore, J.F. (1993). Predators and prey: A new ecology of competition. *Harvard Business Review*, 71(3), 75–83.

Nambisan, S. and Baron, R. (2013). Entrepreneurship in innovation ecosystems: Entrepreneurs' self-regulatory processes and their implications for new venture success. *Entrepreneurship: Theory and Practice*, 37(5), 1071–1097.

Moore, J.F. (1996). *The Death of Competition: Leadership & Strategy in the Age of Business Ecosystems*. HarperBusiness, New York.

Porter, M.E. (2000). Location, competition, and economic development: Local clusters in a global economy. *Economic Development Quarterly*, 14(1), 15–34.

Rao, B. and Jimenez, B. (2011). A comparative analysis of digital innovation ecosystems. *Proceedings of PICMET'11: Portland International Center for Management of Engineering and Technology – Technology Management in the Energy-smart World*, 31 July–4 August, 1–12.

Saxenian, A. (1994). *Regional Networks: Industrial Adaptation in Silicon Valley and Route 128*. Harvard University Press, Cambridge.

Torre, A. and Zimmermann, J.B. (2015). Des clusters aux écosystèmes industriels locaux. *Revue d'économie industrielle*, 4, 13–38.

de Vasconcelos Gomes, L.A., Figueiredo Facon, A.L., Sergio Salerno, M., Kazuo Ikenami, R. (2018). Unpacking the innovation ecosystem construct: Evolution, gaps and trends. *Technological Forecasting and Social Change*, 136, 30–48.

Zittrain, J.L. (2006). The generative Internet. *Harvard Law Review*, 119(7), 1974–2040.

16

Entrepreneur – The Innovative Entrepreneur as an Actor of Economic Change

16.1. Introduction

Designated as the driving force of economic change and innovation, the entrepreneur has been the focus of economists since the 18th century, when the economy was established as a scientific discipline in its own right in order to ask the fundamental question: How do we create wealth (Boutillier and Uzunidis 2016; Boutillier and Tiran 2016)? The entrepreneur has long been subject to criticism (individualism, personal gain, profit, etc.), however, a kind of empathy is nevertheless evident today, in the era of the entrepreneurial society (Audretsch 2007, 2019). The image of entrepreneurs has not always won the support of economists. Even Smith (1759, 1776) was wary, at least of the entrepreneur whose extravagant behavior could have negative consequences for the economy. Instead, he placed his hopes in the prudent man whose behavior seemed much more reasonable. Subsequently, it was mainly Say (1803) and Schumpeter (1911, 2008) who placed the entrepreneur on a pedestal, but with a very different objective, that of innovating, since according to Schumpeter's famous formula, capitalism is not stationary and can never become so. Almost 100 years separate them. This time lag largely explains the appreciation that both economists may have had for the entrepreneur, since capitalism evolved considerably over this period. The growth in the size of companies has led to a preference for the combination of manager/shareholder to the detriment of a single actor, the entrepreneur. But the fundamental function of the entrepreneur is to create an organization, is it not?

Chapter written by Sophie BOUTILLIER.

More fundamentally, the entrepreneurial economy can be understood as a diptych between the theories that view the entrepreneur as an actor of a desired and controlled change, or as an agent of an economic system, capitalism, which he does not control (or does so with difficulty). Moreover, while the place and role of the entrepreneur have changed considerably in an economy dominated by wage labor, since the 1980s becoming an entrepreneur has become a kind of injunction, backed by appropriate public policies, to guarantee an emerging entrepreneurial society (Audretsch 2007, 2019). It is also in this context that the question of the heterogeneity of entrepreneurship arises with great acuity (Aldrich 2011), because the entrepreneur has a thousand and one faces, and is not necessarily innovative and an actor of change, unless one considers that through their actions they contribute to the creation of new activities and jobs. Managerial capitalism has led to the creation of a class of employees (proletarians and then white-collar workers) whose numbers have increased considerably since the first industrial revolution. For Hayek (1960), this constitutes a danger for the future of capitalism. The economists of the 21st century seem to have learned from Hayek's fears.

16.2. The entrepreneur as an actor of change

The entrepreneur appears, from the outset, as an actor in the change they wanted. Under these conditions, their action is closely linked to the risks they take, unlike other social categories. This is the position that Cantillon (1755) adopts by defining the entrepreneur as the economic actor with "uncertain wages", considering that the other part of society is made up of persons with "certain wages". Smith (1776) subsequently pays little attention to the entrepreneur but expresses his fear, above all else, of the projector who embarks on extravagant projects, such as investing in new technologies. Bentham (1789), on the contrary, glorifies the action of the projector who, through their decisions, contributes to transforming society. In Bentham's portrayal of society, the entrepreneur, like any individual, makes decisions in a way that balances pain and pleasure. The pleasure lies in the expected profit and the opportunity to realize a project. In keeping with this, Say (1803) makes the entrepreneur a producer of utility. They place themselves in an intermediate position between the scientist who produces knowledge and the worker who applies it to industry. The entrepreneur is thus the innovator, the one who transforms a scientific discovery into a consumer good, thus creating markets and jobs.

The development of managerial capitalism at the beginning of the 20th century led economists (Galbraith 1968; Chandler 1977) to abandon the entrepreneur in favor of the manager. As Schumpeter (2008) had already pointed out, modern business needs specialists; the entrepreneur, who concentrates all the roles of shareholder, owner and manager, is no longer relevant. However, Kirzner (1973) has not forgotten the entrepreneur and defends the idea of a company of entrepreneurs, without using this term. No doubt he was influenced by Baumol's (1968) article, according to which the entrepreneur had disappeared from neoclassical economic theory. Indeed, it was an aberration that the innovative entrepreneur was absent from a theory based on individualism and competition. Kirzner returns to Schumpeter's 1911 definition, considering that the entrepreneur does not create profit opportunities but discovers them. Under these conditions, they are in a state of "alertness".

However, the entrepreneur (Baumol 1990) is inserted into an institutional framework that conditions their activity. In an appropriate institutional framework that respects private property, where the State will not attempt to supervise their initiatives, they will be innovative. On the contrary, in the opposite case, they will be unproductive, as their activity will be based on rent-seeking. But whatever the institutional, social, economic and cultural framework, entrepreneurs do not all have the same capacity to identify opportunities (Shane 2003). The discovery of opportunities requires entrepreneurial cognition. The ability to collect, identify and process the right information is essential. The most successful individuals use information corridors and detect information more easily than others because they have prior knowledge that allows them to identify it (the richness and diversity of the social network is crucial). Shane (2003) emphasizes the importance of the cognitive abilities of entrepreneurs to identify opportunities. The individual who becomes an entrepreneur is the one who has been able to take advantage of the socio-economic context in which he is inserted. Thus, Casson (2003) emphasizes that it is the entrepreneur who creates the business. The entrepreneur is the economic actor who makes decisions to combine scarce resources. They intuitively perceive their place in the market, which is different from that of other entrepreneurs. However, accessing information is difficult. The creation of a business appears as a way to get around ignorance by monitoring the exchange. The company is thus a means of collecting information; it is not reduced to a simple unit of production but permitted to search for external sources of information that will feed new ideas and new markets. Furthermore, the company contributes to market transformation, with the entrepreneur participating in the transformation of industries and markets, although not all entrepreneurs have the same resources. The family context, education and career path of individuals have an influence on their ability to carry out their plan. Risk and uncertainty punctuate the entrepreneur's activity. The greater the uncertainty, the more difficult it is to predict the future. Effectuation is an entrepreneur's decision-making process (Sarasvathy 2001). Its rationality is necessarily limited. The entrepreneur does not define a specific goal and then find the resources to reach it or get close to it. They follow the opposite approach: according to the means at their disposal, their experience, their skills, their personality traits and their networks. The entrepreneur develops a project and makes it evolve according to the potential of the moment. The market does not exist; it is staged. The opportunity is not discovered by the entrepreneur; they shape it. The entrepreneur builds their project as they progress in their action and reflection. They are in interaction with their environment, which is thus a socially constructed production. By developing their reflection and their action, the entrepreneur builds their identity and their future, without controlling it, but they adapt by trial and error.

16.3. The evolution of the function of the innovative entrepreneur

In an economy based on individualism and competition, the fittest survive, but even the fittest who, for example, preside over a powerful industrial empire can have their power challenged and questioned by a more enterprising entrepreneur! But the entrepreneur does not act because they are guided by a sense of power, for example, but because the economic system in which they are inserted forces them to do so, a source of negative or positive externalities for society and for themselves. The entrepreneurial profiles distinguished by Smith (1759, 1776), the son of the poor man, the prudent man, the projector, correspond to a typical behavior. These different profiles also reflect different forms of capitalism, where innovation and the risk associated with it are more or less present. The son of the poor man, generally of modest origin, seeks to succeed. The prudent man does not take risks. He does not get into debt to develop his small business. The projector, on the contrary, takes risks, invests in new technologies and gets into debt. He corresponds to the profile of the Schumpeterian entrepreneur … Smith is wary of him. He sees him as a danger to society as a whole. By getting into debt without taking any steps to develop his extravagant ideas, he runs the risk of causing a serious financial crisis that cannot be controlled.

However, the projector’s behavior may not be the result of the entrepreneur’s intrinsic will. He innovates because the economic system in which he is inserted forces him to adopt this behavior. “Accumulate, accumulate, it is Moses and the prophets” (Marx 1867). Capitalism is based on competition. The big eat the small. You have to eat the others (grow) in order not to be eaten. The entrepreneur is a kind of puppet caught up in a logic that they try to master, but which is beyond them. Competition is gradually disappearing in favor of an increasingly concentrated market where the number of entrepreneurs has considerably decreased.

Disappointed by the inability of neoclassical economists to grasp technical change, contrary to the German historical school that he valued, Schumpeter (1911) invented the entrepreneur whose function was to create “new combinations of production factors”, i.e. to innovate. The entrepreneur is the actor of change and innovation. If they do seek to enrich themselves, they also do so by challenge, by play. However, gradually, the function of the entrepreneur is disappearing. They are replaced by a team of specialists in a management company. However, Marshall (1890) envisaged a kind of coexistence between the entrepreneur – innovator, owner and administrator – and the manager, the paid director of the company. He also found that small entrepreneurs could operate in poor neighborhoods to meet the needs of a local clientele. The entrepreneur also has many faces, and may take the appearance of an animal spirit (Keynes 1936). With a herd mentality, they do not evaluate risks and opportunities, but follows the decisions of others. Keynesian entrepreneurs act according to their feelings and emotions, basing decisions on expectations out of their control.

During the post-war growth years, the entrepreneur disappeared from the concerns of economists, with a few rare exceptions (Baumol 1968; Kirzner 1973). McClelland (1961) thus makes the link between a country's entrepreneurial culture and its level of economic development. The need for achievement is the entrepreneur's driving force. However, the economic crisis of the 1970s highlighted the inability of the capitalist economy to create enough jobs, so the solution was in the capacity of the greatest number to create their own jobs. The entrepreneurial society (Audretsch 2007, 2019) gives the entrepreneur back their rightful place. Public policies are emerging to encourage individuals to create their own businesses and jobs. An entrepreneur in rags appears in the economic analysis (which, as Marshall showed, was the reality). Aldrich (2011) also highlights the diversity of entrepreneurs, according to age, gender, career path, family origin and so on. Not all follow the same trajectory. Failures are numerous, while successes are much less so. Aldrich places particular emphasis on entrepreneurs with atypical profiles (women, immigrants in particular), who became entrepreneurs out of necessity, not by choice. He emphasizes the knowledge they have at their disposal, considering it more important than capital. Many entrepreneurs start with very little capital. Moreover, mobilizing the network of social relations provides individuals with low capital endowment with the resources they lack. Aldrich certainly has a more nuanced view of the entrepreneurial society that Audretsch calls for.

The role of the entrepreneur is to permanently ensure the transformation of capitalism. In an economy that relies on growth in order not to disappear, the entrepreneur is the economic actor who fulfils this function. Beyond the Schumpeterian entrepreneur, who is constantly innovating (product, process, technical or organizational innovation), the function of the entrepreneur also fulfils other functions, including that of creating jobs, first and foremost their own, because they are constrained to do so by a logic that they cannot control. The fundamental question that divides the scientific community on this subject is whether the entrepreneur controls this dynamic of change that they have initiated or whether they are the product of an economic and social logic that dictates their behavior and the decisions they take.

16.4. References

Aldrich, H. (2011). *An Evolutionary Approach to Entrepreneurship*. Edward Elgar, Cheltenham.

Audretsch, D. (2007). *The Entrepreneurial Society*. Edward Elgar, Cheltenham.

Audretsch, D. (2019). The foundations of the entrepreneurial society. *Management International*, 23(5), 20–25.

Baumol, W. (1968). Entrepreneurship in economic theory. *American Economic Review*, 58(2), 64–71.

Baumol, W. (1990). Entrepreneurship: Productive, unproductive and destructive. *Journal of Political Economy*, 98(5), 893–921.

Bentham, J. (1780). *An Introduction to the Principles of Morals and Legislation*. T. Payne & Son, London.

Boutillier, S. and Tiran, A. (2016). La théorie de l'entrepreneur, son évolution et sa contextualisation. *Innovations*, 50, 211–234.

Boutillier, S. and Uzunidis, D. (2016). *The Entrepreneur: The Economic Function of Free Enterprise*. ISTE Ltd, London, and Wiley, New York.

Cantillon, R. (1755). *Essai sur la nature du commerce en général*. Institut Coppet, Paris.

Casson, M. (2003). *The Entrepreneur*. Edward Elgar, Cheltenham.

Chandler, A. (1977). *The Visible Hand of Managers*. Harvard University Press, Cambridge.

Galbraith, J.K. (1968). *The New Industrial State*. Princeton University Press, Princeton.

Hayek, F. (1960). *The Constitution of Liberty*. University of Chicago Press, Chicago.

Keynes, J.M. (1936). *The General Theory of Employment, Interest and Money*. Houghton Mifflin Harcourt, Boston.

Kirzner, I. (1973). *Competition and Entrepreneurship*. University of Chicago Press, Chicago.

Marshall, A. (1890). *Principles of Political Economy*. Palgrave Macmillan, London.

Marx, K. (1867). *Capital: A Critique of Political Economy*. Penguin Classics, London.

McClelland, D.C. (1961). *The Achieving Society*. Free Press, New York.

Sarasvathy, S.D. (2001). Causation and effectuation: Toward a theoretical shift from economic, inevitability to entrepreneurial contingency. *Academy of Management Review*, 26(2), 243–263.

Say, J.-B. (1803). *Traité d'économie politique*. Economica, Paris.

Schumpeter, J. (1911). *Theory of Economic Development*. Routledge, London.

Schumpeter, J. (2008). *Capitalism, Socialism and Democracy*. Harper Perennial Modern Classics, New York.

Shane, S. (2003). *A General Theory of Entrepreneurship. The Individual-opportunity Nexus*. Edward Elgar, Cheltenham.

Smith, A. (1759). *The Theory of Moral Sentiments*. A. Millar, London.

Smith, A. (1776). *An Inquiry into the Nature and Causes of the Wealth of Nations*. W. Strahan and T. Cadell, London.

17

Financing – Financing R&D and Innovation

17.1. Introduction

It is a widely held view that a significant number of innovative firms are often denied access to financing (Hall and Lerner 2009, p. 3), even though they could use funds productively if they were available. This so-called "financing gap" is not neutral as it impedes, in return, their creation and growth. Among the reasons explaining the lack of incentives to invest in R&D and innovation, it has long been recognized that such investments are particularly risky and that the cost of R&D is often uncertain. Moreover, the characteristics of innovation are such that innovators face difficulties in appropriating the benefits of their activities. Indeed, the outcome of R&D is random (many projects end in failures) and the returns from innovation are extremely skewed (Scherer and Harhoff 2000). In addition, it is commonly accepted that the social return to R&D is higher than the private level. Faced with these observations, it is necessary to examine what kind of finance is the best to serve the purposes of innovation, and how companies finance their innovation activities. As with other forms of investment, financing for innovation can be provided in a number of ways: through internal resources, which are clearly preferred by companies, through external financing (bank credit, capital venture, etc.), through direct or indirect public support. To answer these issues, this chapter first examines the role of information asymmetries on funding. We then look at the reasons for funding reluctance. Finally, we turn to public intervention to finance innovation.

Chapter written by Béatrice DUMONT.

17.2. Information asymmetries and sources of funding

The issue of the funding structure is meaningless within the framework of orthodox financial theory. Indeed, the Modigliani–Miller theorem (1958) states that, under the assumptions that capital markets are perfect, and in the absence of *taxes*, *bankruptcy* costs, agency costs and *asymmetric information*, any financing structure that combines equity and debt is supposed to be neutral on the value of the company. In other words, in the absence of informational asymmetries in capital markets, internal and external financing are perfectly substitutable, and the type of finance that innovators receive is neutral and cannot affect the rate and direction of innovation.

The removal of these assumptions gives rise to questions about the different forms of finance for innovation. Indeed, the cost of capital may differ by the source of funds and across different types of investments, for instance for taxation reasons. The innovative content of projects to be financed also reinforces the traditional problems of asymmetry of information between an innovative firm and external capital providers, and thus leads to differences between the external and internal cost of capital. Broadly speaking, three categories of information asymmetries can be distinguished:

(i) *Ex-ante* information asymmetries arise because innovators often have better information about their company's prospects, risks and the value of their project, than potential investors. These *ex-ante* information asymmetries are at the origin of an adverse selection phenomenon: due to limited liability in case of failure, increasing the rate of interest deters projects with low risk, whereas projects with similar expected returns, generated with high gains obtained with a low probability of success, still find it profitable to ask for a loan. Aware of this mechanism, lenders may then refuse to finance companies that accept high-cost financing, resulting in credit rationing (Stiglitz and Weiss 1981).

(ii) Asymmetries of information may also arise during the course of the contract. It concerns the management of the project itself. Indeed, many innovation projects fail without any assurance that this is due to the inventor not having done "everything possible", or simply because of "bad luck" (due to unpredictable events). These asymmetries generate principal–agent problems and therefore control costs. As the potential for moral hazard is particularly high for innovative firms, investors require that a manager has as much to lose in the event of failure, so that they can be sure that they will do their utmost despite the impossibility of external control. This means that the existence of information asymmetries between a firm and external capital contributors, in terms of probability of success, anticipated benefits and quality of management involvement, increases the premium for external financing (Leland and Pyle 1977).

(iii) Finally, information asymmetries may appear *ex-post*. Indeed, investors cannot accurately assess the rate of return of a completed project, which may in turn create an incentive for a borrower to adopt opportunistic behaviors, i.e. to put more risky projects in place, or to report less income than actually earned in order to minimize repayments.

In short, information asymmetries between an innovative firm and potential investors materialize in the form of difficulties in accessing external financing in an optimal way, and may have the effect of hampering the innovation effort of enterprises. It is assumed, in economic literature, to be particularly sensitive for young innovative companies that may launch projects that are too risky, or fail to exercise an innovation option. The existence of an anti-selection problem has the consequence of establishing a hierarchy of preferences ("pecking order theory") between different financing methods (Myers and Majluf 1984). More precisely, these authors postulate that companies prioritize their sources of financing, first preferring internal financing, when available (because it is cheaper and by definition, not subject to the problem of anti-selection), and then debt over equity if external funding is required.

17.3. Reasons for funding reluctance

There is solid evidence in empirical literature that debt is a disfavored source of finance for R&D investments. Studies by Hall and Lerner (2009), for instance, show that "firms are either unable or reluctant to use debt finance for R&D investment, which may raise the cost of capital, depending on the precise tax treatment of debt versus equity". Moreover, the lack of collateral further reduces the possibility of debt financing. Indeed, innovation projects encompass a significant proportion of intangible assets, which cannot be used as collaterals. Such assets have high transaction costs and do not allow banks to cover themselves against the risk of failure of a company. As a result, external investors, especially lenders, may be reluctant to finance such projects. Almeida and Campello (2006) show, for instance, that the ability of firms to offer collateral in the form of tangible assets largely determines their access to external financing. The elements mentioned above suggest an important role for retained earnings in the R&D investment decision and that investment in research by firms is positively related to their past cash flow. This means that small firms may be at a disadvantage compared to large firms in innovation, due to their lower internal revenue ("success breeds success"), and they may under-invest in research.

In the presence of market failures, there is potential room for public intervention. More precisely, the State must organize risk-sharing over time and over several projects, in particular by ensuring the smooth functioning of the markets. In practice, direct forms of support such as procurement, subsidies or grants are usually combined with indirect forms of support offered through the tax system.

17.4. Public intervention in finance innovation

Among the various ways in which the public sector can support the financing of innovation, the guarantee of certain financial or bank loans against the risk of business failure is an important one. This modality of intervention makes it possible to separate the function of project selection and that of control, which remains in the private sector, and the risk coverage function that is assumed by a third party guarantee body that is public, but could be a private structure.

Public authorities can also invest in public research systems or place direct orders with industries for national defense purposes, for instance. On average, this last type of financing represents an important part of the public funds allocated to innovation by industrial companies in OECD countries. Public funding is not a substitute for other sources of financing and can be seen as a complement to internal funding. Public funding allows the company to pass the research and development milestone, a period when the probability of failure is highest and profitability is still uncertain. They are less solicited afterwards, as the project progresses, particularly during the industrialization and manufacturing phases.

However, over the last couple of decades, tax incentives, like allowances and credits, as well as other forms of tax treatment of business R&D expenditures, have become a widely used policy instrument by OECD countries, as a key instrument in their policy toolbox for inducing higher levels of business R&D expenditures. As shown by Hall and Lerner (2009), it may be socially beneficial for public authorities to offer tax incentives to companies, especially to small and new firms, in order to reduce the cost of capital they face for R&D investments. One of the most popular mechanisms to do so is the Research & Development (R&D) tax credit. It is by far the first component of public aid for innovation in some OECD countries (Mulkay and Mairesse 2018). Its aim is to reduce the *ex-post* cost of research for firms, and encourage them to carry out more research than they would spontaneously do. Because of the heterogeneity of the structures of R&D tax credits within OECD countries, the magnitude of their economic effects is debated by many economists. The question of the effectiveness of this measure arises first and foremost in terms of its ability to induce more research by firms. A study by the OECD (2018) suggests that tax incentives are associated with additional R&D spending, but involve some degree of crowding out (i.e. firms add proportionally less than the money they receive in compensation to R&D). Firms instead allocate part of the support to other activities. The question whether R&D tax incentives are good value for money often varies on a country-by-country basis. However, it is worth remembering that R&D tax credits had a cushioning effect during the 2008 crisis, by preventing a decline in R&D investment.

17.5. Venture capital

An alternative offered to innovative firms to solve the "financing gap" is financial venture capital (VC). It can be defined as the activity of providing equity capital by specialized investors to privately held, high growth companies. Financial venture capital associates different types of operators (banks, pension funds, large companies or individuals). These investors are bound by multiple clauses, such as a predetermined, finite lifetime of the fund or the impossibility to exit the fund without the consent of all other partners. The purpose of these clauses is to avoid strategic behavior by investors who would have access to better information than other members of the fund and would try to exploit it at the expense of the other members of the fund. Gompers (1995) shows that financial venture capital is targeting a special type of company model, namely early-stage companies developing products with breakthrough/radical innovation where informational asymmetries are significant and monitoring is valuable, enabling them to grow rapidly, leading to significant future profits with a fast growth cycle.

Available industry level data shows that VC investments are mostly concentrated in the ICT sector. However, this type of financing is limited in scope. Indeed, it is accepted that financial venture capitalists will only finance 1% of the projects proposed to them. Moreover, commitment to the venture capital industry is very uneven and the volume of activity is also impacted by tax issues. Indeed, the development of financial venture capital in the United States is often linked to the fact that capital gains taxes are not paid by the limited partnerships. Ultimately, venture capitalists also want to be able to easily exit the firm's capital (through an Initial Public Offering – IPO, a resale to an industrial company or another private equity firm), in order to make their investments profitable by realizing a significant capital gain. Alternatively, an exit may come about via the private equity secondary market. Megginson and Weiss (1991) document that venture capitalists hold significant equity stakes and board positions in the firms they take public, even after the IPO. This pattern reflects the certification they provide to investors that the firms they bring to market are not overvalued.

This financial approach can be supplemented by a possible industrial approach, called a "corporate or industrial venture". It is the intervention of industrial groups in the capital of SMEs with a particular technology that may be of interest to a group in the long term, or in which the group sees an opportunity for further development. These interventions are almost always in the seed capital or creation capital, or even post-creation phases and very little in takeover projects or in companies in strong development. Corporate venture capital often allows companies to prepare for a takeover in three different ways: either directly in the capital of companies via majority shareholdings in a first stage; by investing in dedicated seed capital or venture capital funds; or by encouraging spin-offs.

17.6. Conclusion

Information asymmetries between an innovative firm and potential investors materialize in the form of difficulties in accessing external financing, and may have the effect of hampering the innovation effort of enterprises. Faced with market failures, public authorities have a rather rich toolbox at their disposal to bring the private return on R&D closer to its public return. However, it is usually considered that the public sector must give priority to financing projects that would not have been financed by the private sector (predominance of the subsidiarity aspect), i.e. essentially upstream (research, feasibility, prototypes and start-up), and intervention should be reduced as the project progresses. The private sector should then gradually take over because the closer the project is to the market, the less justification there is for public intervention.

17.7. References

Almeida, H. and Campello, M. (2006). Financial constraints, asset tangibility, and corporate investment. Working Paper No. 12087, NBER.

Gompers, P. (1995). Optimal investment, monitoring, and the staging of venture capital. *Journal of Finance*, 50, 1461–1489.

Hall, B.H. and Lerner, J. (2009). The financing of R&D and innovation. Working Paper No. 15325, NBER [Online]. Available at: https://www.nber.org/system/files/working_papers/w15325/w15325.pdf.

Leland, H.E. and Pyle, D.H. (1977). Informational asymmetries, financial structure, and financial intermediation. *The Journal of Finance*, 32(2), 371–387.

Megginson, W. and Weiss, K. (1991). Venture capital certification in initial public offerings. *Journal of Finance*, 4, 879–893.

Mulkay, B. and Mairesse, J. (2018). Nouveaux résultats sur l'impact du crédit d'impôt recherche. *Study for the MESRI* [Online]. Available at: https://www.strategie.gouv.fr/sites/strategie.gouv.fr/files/atoms/files/rapport_mulkay-mairesse_evaluation_ex-post_du_cir_mesri.pdf.

Myers, S.C. and Majluf, N.S. (1984). Corporate financing and investment decisions when firms have information that investors do not have. *Journal of Financial Economics*, 13(2), 187–221.

OECD (2018). Measuring R&D tax support: Findings from the new OECD tax incentives database. OECD Science, Technology & Industry, Working Paper N°2019-06 [Online]. Available at: https://www.oecd-ilibrary.org/docserver/d16e6072-en.pdf?expires=1579550000&id=id&accname=guest&checksum=58850415BA1E4BBF3D86A3F90A7B5AE4.

Scherer, F.M. and Harhoff, D. (2000). Technology policy for a world of skewed-distributed outcomes. *Research Policy*, 29(4–5), 559–566.

Stiglitz, J.E. and Weiss, A. (1981). Credit rationing in markets with imperfect information. *The American Economic Review*, 71(3), 393–410.

18

Frugality – Frugal Innovation as Inclusive Innovation

18.1. Introduction

Frugal innovation (FI) is a rapidly growing new field of research and is likely to attract more attention in the future. Pisoni *et al.* (2017) noted that there have been 113 articles dealing with FI since 2005; however, there was no research on the matter published before 2004. We observe a significant increase in the number of contributions in 2012, with a peak in 2016. Underdeveloped or emerging economies have the motivation and therefore tend to push individuals and firms to create this type of innovation. The "new fashion" of low-cost solutions has led to firms in the developed world also starting to build up FI-related technological solutions. In this chapter, we use the recent abundant literature mainly inspired by the principles of strategic technology management. Our aim is to briefly review the existing definitions of the phenomenon and, in particular, to shed light on its relationship with environmental issues and sustainability.

18.2. Frugal innovation as a new technological paradigm

The review of existing studies allows us to point out that definitions of FI in relevant literature are converging to the idea that "we do more with less for more people" with FI. Basu *et al.* (2013) state that "frugal innovation is a design innovation process in which the needs of citizens in the developing world are put first to develop appropriate, adaptable, affordable, and accessible products and

---

Chapter written by Christian LE BAS and Sana KHAN.

services for emerging markets". Similarly, Gupta (2011) notes that FI integrates the specific needs of bottom of pyramid (BOP) markets as a starting point and works backward to develop appropriate solutions that may differ significantly from existing solutions designed to address the needs of up-market segments.

It is essential to underline that it is not just a matter of taking advantage of low-cost labor, but also a matter of redesigning products and processes to cut out unnecessary costs (Woolridge 2010). As a result, FI can create new market segments linked to new needs. It sets up an inclusive innovation that is beneficial for resource-constrained economies. On the supply side, the necessary research and development (R&D), contrary to traditional R&D, is minor and requires fewer investments and resources. By contrast, on the demand side, new frugal products match the needs of poorer communities struggling every day with limited income sources. The FI process not only affects the products and services, but also changes the traditional business models in order to work effectively with limited resources which, in turn, offers environmental benefits.

FI, however, is not limited to poorer or emerging countries. Because of the economic crisis in the industrialized world and rising consumption in the developing world, frugality can be turned into an important societal value to increase BOP consumption in both the global North and South (Tiwari *et al.* 2016).

Based on the above discussion, we suggest interpreting FI as a new paradigm in search of less functionality with a certain level of quality matching the needs of poorer (or less rich) people (Le Bas 2020). As a result, we can observe a systematic elimination of "luxury" and unnecessary characteristics of products, i.e. no-frills products. Although engineers and researchers are aiming for a lesser number of functionalities, the core functionalities of the product are always conserved. This means that a frugal product is less sophisticated (Brem and Wolfram 2014) compared to other existing over-engineered solutions available in the market. It must, however, meet the performance level that is needed for it to function and satisfy local conditions. In the next section, we discuss various innovations that meet these requirements.

18.3. Case studies

Health, agriculture, consumer goods and information technology are the main sectors in which FI is particularly relevant. A well-known example is the *ChotuKool* fridge, a small refrigerator, sold by Indian company Godrej. It looks like a computer cooling system rather than a refrigerator. The *GE Lullaby* baby warmer is a low-cost but high-performance baby incubator that regulates the newborn's body temperature and thus reduces infant mortality. It is sold for $3,000 compared to its original high-end version sold for $12,000. It was launched in India in May 2006 and is now sold in 80 countries, including Western European countries. Unnecessary features were removed to reduce prices for the Indian market. Its durability, simplicity and functionality are the key features reflecting its quality. The firm *gThrive* saw the need for and developed an inexpensive, easy-to-use, accurate monitoring solution for farmers. Their solution consists of several portable and wireless *gStakes* that can be installed at different locations within a farm, a *gLink Base Station* for collecting data from *gStakes* and software that stores data on the cloud. *gStakes* measures the level of sunlight, air temperature, soil temperature, soil moisture and electrical conductivity, and transmits it to the *gLink Base Station* via a radio link. Then, *gLink* collects and uploads the data onto the server either by Wi-Fi or by using a cellular phone network. Kokono® is a brand-new product that consists of a rigid shell to protect infants from 0 to 12 months. Thanks to its plastic-based structure, covered with natural fibers, Kokono® isolates the baby from direct contact with the ground, reducing the probability of infections if an infant is spending long periods of time on the floor and thus could be exposed to infectious agents and dangerous animals. It is not only frugal but also sustainable.

Frugal products can include a certain variety. Frugality is often associated with low-end products, but can also be used for the development of high-end products. For instance, let us consider the car industry. In India, the *Tata Nano* car is sold for less than $2,500. It is aimed at low-income consumers wishing to move up from a two-wheeled scooter to a four-wheeled vehicle. Nevertheless, this car would likely not pass the safety tests in Europe and North America. By contrast, KWID, launched by Renault-Nissan in 2015 at the price of € 3,500, can be seen as a frugal high-end product that offers comfort and fulfills different norms. While manufactured in India, it is now sold in Brazil and South Africa.

18.4. Frugal innovation and similar approaches

FI is closely linked with many other concepts that have been subject to investigation recently in the field of innovation. We briefly introduce them here.

– Gandhian innovation: an approach that takes advantage of existing technologies by integrating them into the local context and establishing local expertise through spillovers and collaboration to increase the social wealth of people from the BOP. It was developed for the Indian market and is based on the underlying assumptions of Gandhi, i.e. affordability and sustainable development (Prahalad and Mashelkar 2010).

– Jugaad innovation: according to Radjou *et al.* (2013, p. 45), this type of innovation relies on six principles: "*1.* Find opportunities in an adverse context and transform constraints into opportunities; *2.* Do more with less; *3.* Think and act with agility; *4.* Aim for simplicity; *5.* Involve a marginal population; and *6.* Follow one's own insight and heart". Jugaad innovation is based on ingenious technical developments and improvised solutions that are born out of necessity under the conditions of limited funds and resources. It is considered different from FI, which is more complex.

– Catalytic innovation: an approach that focuses on social change by breaking down existing social and economic structures and creating new market structures, and that helps to develop solutions that are "scalable, sustainable, system-changing" for poorer consumers (Christensen *et al.* 2006).

– Grassroots innovation: a bottom-up development approach that develops ecologically and socially acceptable solutions by connecting people through social or technical networks.

– Reverse innovation: innovation that was first adopted by emerging or poorer countries which then "trickles up" to developed countries when demand is identified in these more affluent markets.

18.5. Frugal innovation as an environmental innovation

The notion of environmental innovation refers to "technologies whose use is less environmentally harmful than relevant alternatives" (Kemp and Foxon 2007). It encourages economic players to take measures to develop new ideas, products and processes that contribute to a reduction of environmental degradation. Recent literature shows that FI clearly has a positive impact on the environment. FI is essentially a special kind of environmental innovation (Le Bas 2020), because it saves material and energy in manufacturing and contributes to the fair management of exhaustible resources. Moreover, due to its relatively lower technological complexity, FI exhibits three important environmental properties: easy repair in case of failure, a possible recovery of end-of-life components and recycling. Figure 17.1 outlines the main mechanisms and the different relationships between FI and its environmental benefits (Le Bas 2010).

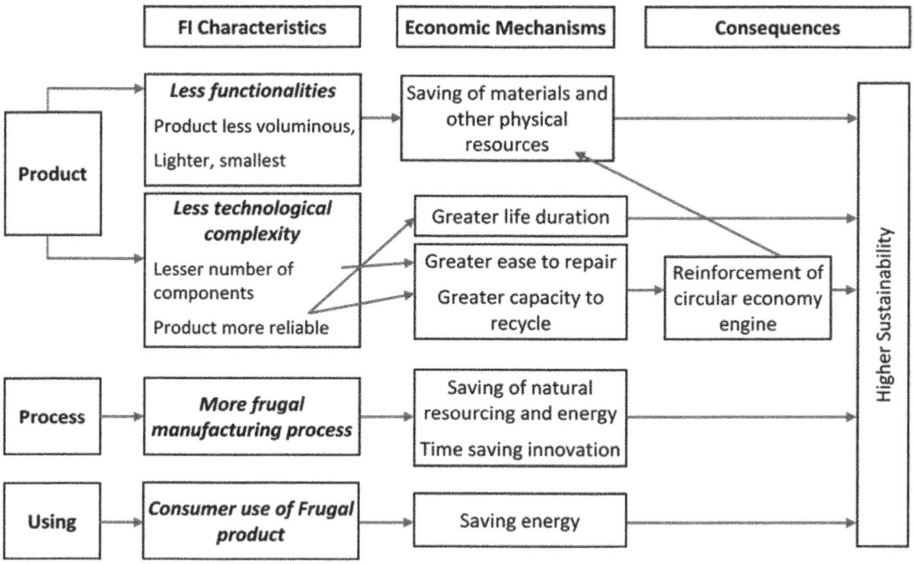

Figure 18.1. *Complex interplay between frugal innovation characteristics: a virtuous circle of positive environmental effects (source: Le Bas 2020)*

18.6. Frugal innovation and sustainability

It is relevant here to include the three key aspects of a firm's sustainability, derived from the triple bottom line approach:

– Economic sustainability refers to various strategies that facilitate resource use efficiently and responsibly, ensuring long-term benefits for all stakeholders.

– Social sustainability refers to practices and goals that enhance social capital and promote societal well-being. Examples are poverty elimination, fair trade practices, human capital development, protecting human rights, etc.

– Environmental sustainability refers to practices and decisions that benefit the natural world or reduce ecological footprint. Various strategies include a reduction in greenhouse gas emissions and pollution, energy conservation, renewable consumption, etc.

Frugal innovation is key to inclusive growth. The frugal innovator acts as a responsible stakeholder. FI drives inclusive growth that builds on cooperation and collaboration among different types of stakeholders and favors sustainable economic development in both developed and developing countries. Moreover, it aims to involve BOP communities in value chains. FI creates locally driven design solutions that can meet local needs such as water, energy and food in a sustainable way. Finally, it can be a source of welfare services to people, including the less affluent, and those primarily from poorer countries. As a result, FI contributes towards social sustainability. We saw in the previous section that FI helps to protect our environment and hence can be considered as an essential element of sustainable development. To sum up, FI is strongly related to the three aspects of sustainability.

18.7. Drivers of frugal innovation: demand-pull and competition effects

FI indicates *a new direction* of technological change and serves the underserved needs of new markets. Firms have more incentives to innovate frugally in a country that has a large population of low-income people. In the tradition begun by Schmookler, a positive variation of demand gives incentives to invest in R&D (inventive activities) and triggers a positive variation of most innovation. In the context of FI, it is innovation that triggers a positive variation of demand in the context of a specific market. In fact, it is the expectations of such a variation in demands that gives incentives to invest in innovation activities. Frugal innovation has the power to trigger a higher volume of consumption, as it provides a change to people's welfare. The idea that variation of demand can be an *economic consequence* of innovation is not new (see the seminal work by Walsh (1984), who indicates that innovations in chemical industries provoke changes in demand levels).

According to microeconomic theory, an economic agent will accept to pay a higher price for a product with incorporated improvements. However, in the case of FI, the opposite is true; thanks to fewer functionalities and lower prices, a consumer will be able to pay for the new product. FI can also be relevant in the context of vertical differentiation in which a firm wants to create products better than their competitors' (Besanko *et al.* 2009). Nevertheless, the aim of FI is not to capture the customers of competitors; it is to create new markets.

18.8. Conclusion

In this chapter, we survey the very recent literature dealing with frugal innovation, which we have shown to be a kind of inclusive technological innovation. We contribute by defining it as a new technological paradigm. We show how it differs from other close types of innovation, and shed light on its relationship with environmental concerns and sustainability issues.

The future of FI could be better understood by splitting it into FI in emerging/developing countries and FI in developed economies (Tiwari and Herstatt 2019). In the former case, FI uses an inclusive approach to serve poorer consumers constrained by resources and low incomes. In the latter case, there is a strong motivation for firms to innovate. People are more aware of environmental issues and hence intend to change their lifestyle in order to encourage sustainable and responsible production and consumption. What Tiwari and Herstatt (2019) call "affordable green excellence" refers to affordability in monetary, infrastructural, environmental and societal terms.

18.9. References

Christensen, C.M., Baumann, H., Ruggles, R., Sadtler, T.M. (2006). Disruptive innovation for social change. *Harvard Business Review*, 84(12), 94.

Haudeville, B. and Le Bas, C. (2016). L'innovation frugale, paradigme technologique naissant ou nouveau modèle d'innovation ? *Innovations*, 3, 9–25.

Haudeville, B. and Le Bas, C. (2018). Développer l'innovation en Afrique et dans les PMA : construire le SNI, encadrer l'innovation frugale, multiplier les systèmes locaux. *Mondes en développement*, (4), 101–118.

Hossain, M. (2018). Frugal innovation: A review and research agenda. *Journal of Cleaner Production*, 182, 926–936.

Khan, S. and Le Bas, C. (2019). Ethics and sustainability in frugal innovation. *Frugal Innovation: A Global Research Companion*, McMurray, A.J., de Waal, G.A. (eds). Routledge, Abingdon.

Le Bas, C. (2016). Frugal innovation, sustainable innovation, reverse innovation: Why do they look alike? Why are they different? *Journal of Innovation Economics Management*, 3, 9–26.

Le Bas, C. (2017). Sustainable innovation and frugal innovation: Exploring the relationships between innovation and sustainability. *Revue d'économie industrielle*, 3, 113–137.

Le Bas, C. (2020). Frugal innovation as environmental innovation. *International Journal of Technology Management*, 83(1,2,3), 78–96.

Pisoni, A., Michelini, L., Martignoni, G. (2018). Frugal approach to innovation: State of the art and future perspectives. *Journal of Cleaner Production*, 171, 107–126.

Prahalad, C.K. and Mashelkar, R.A. (2010). Innovation's holy grail. *Harvard Business Review*, 88(7–8), 132–141.

Tiwari, R. and Kalogerakis, K. (2019). What drives frugal innovation in an economically developed economy? *Frugal Innovation: A Global Research Companion*. McMurray, J.A., de Waal, G.A. (eds). Routledge, Abingdon.

Tiwari, R., Fischer, L., Kalogerakis, K. (2016). Frugal innovation in scholarly and social discourse: An assessment of trends and potential societal implications. Working paper, Center for Frugal Innovation, Hamburg University of Technology, Fraunhofer Center for International Management and Knowledge Economy, Hamburg and Leipzig.

19

Future – The Future of Innovative Technologies: Between Imagination and Technological Ideology

19.1. Introduction

In June 2002, a report sponsored by the National Science Foundation (NSF) and the Department Of Commerce (DOF) entitled "*Converging Technologies for Improving Human Performance: Nanotechnology, Biotechnology, Information Technology and Cognitive Science*" was published and quickly became a great success within the scientific community. It synthesized knowledge in the sectors listed in its title and announced prodigious discoveries in the coming years, particularly in the field of health. Thus, computer science would make it possible to establish increasingly complex and efficient protocols, and the announced advent of biotechnologies and nanotechnologies could significantly increase human life expectancy. The search for what Lucien Sfez called "perfect health" in his book "*La Santé Parfaite*" (Sfez 1995) should constitute a new era for globalized capitalism. Laboratories around the world are competing to develop ever more efficient technologies and treatments, with the aim of increasing human capacity. Large companies, such as Google and the others that make up GAFAM (Google, Apple, Facebook, Amazon, Microsoft), have set themselves the goal of defeating death in the coming decades, through major investments in research and development (R&D). The medicine of the future will be revolutionized by the innovations of these companies, which have flourished in the era of ICT (information and communication technologies). Thanks to nanotechnologies, biotechnologies, information technologies and cognitive sciences, capitalism develops new products and deploys a virtuous system, whose ultimate goal is to push back the frontiers of

Chapter written by Thomas MICHAUD.

death. This document marks a breakthrough for R&D on a global scale, presenting the likely trajectories of major innovations for the coming decades. The increase in life expectancy is announced as inevitable, like man–machine fusion.

This chapter will present the different trajectories envisaged for innovative technologies in the coming decades. Real revolutions are expected in virtual reality, neuro-connection, health and the space industry. Moreover, the imaginary and technological ideologies that accompany these mutations, such as science fiction, cyberculture or transhumanism, will be presented.

19.2. A paradigmatic convergence

The NBIC report proposes to increase the physical and cognitive capacities of the human being through the convergence of nanotechnologies, biotechnologies, computing and cognitive sciences. Medicine should make it possible to extend life expectancy, thanks to genetics and biotechnologies. The myth of immortality is reactivated by this ideology, and allows innovative networked companies to finance research, particularly in the convergence of computer science and medicine. Implants could, in the near future, manage the health of individuals and optimize treatments by quickly alerting doctors at the first signs of physical failure, who would take care of patients before their condition deteriorates. Nanotechnology and genomics also promise considerable progress in the medical sector, as most known diseases can be defeated through these innovations. Jeremy Rifkin, for example, in his book "*The Biotech Century*" (Rifkin 1998), presented the major mutations promised by medical innovations in the coming decades.

As a worthy heir to cybernetics, the Nanotechnologies, Biotechnologies, Information Technologies and Cognitive Sciences paradigm is an intermediate step before humanity's colonization of the solar system. American scientists are a driving force behind the cyborg concept, which has, since the 1950s, been promising the creation of humanoid robots, as well as psychologically and physically augmented humans. The convergence of different disciplines should allow a mutation of humanity towards a transhumanity, or even a posthumanity, designating new species of humans that are capable of living in extraterrestrial environments which are particularly hostile for human bodies used to living on Earth. Transhumans refer to human beings that are augmented thanks to NBIC convergence, without renouncing the characteristics of humans at the beginning of the 21st century.

Virtual reality is also presented as a mutation that could allow humanity to become immortal and evolve in computer simulations. In the future, humans will be neuro-connected to simulations that are so realistic that they will feel as if they are evolving in worlds that allow them to fulfill all their dreams and fantasies. Cognitive immortality would be the consequence of digitizing the mind in these artificial paradises. Under these conditions, the human body is considered to be obsolete.

Cyberculture and science fiction are at the origin of many representations of the future of virtual reality. The invention of the Internet in the 1990s provoked an intellectual ferment in the computer and telecommunications sectors, leading to both intellectual and financial speculation at the end of the last century. Cyberculture brought together scientists, engineers and artists to create prototype technologies with the aim of imagining and inventing futuristic societies, thriving around innovations that would ensure the mutation of the species towards new conditions of existence.

19.3. Technological revolution: the imagined future

The NBIC report was released after the bursting of the speculative bubble on NICTs (new information and communication technologies). Renowned scientists proposed reflections on the future of the many innovations imagined since the end of World War II. This forward-looking plan defined the promising sectors that American and then global R&D had to deal with as a priority. The Human Cognome Project is one of the main aspects of this vision. It is designed to make it possible to study human cognition, with the aim of ensuring the fusion between the human brain and machines. Directing technologies through thought is one of the perspectives of this project, which also envisages deciphering the world of thought, as the Human Genome Project has made it possible to better understand and control DNA. Eventually, human creativity could be optimized, as will intelligence, which will have to be significantly increased to meet the new challenges posed by the exponential growth of artificial cognition.

The replacement of human organs and the monitoring of physiological well-being are at the heart of a program that seeks to establish a utopian society in which perfect health would be ensured by technological innovations. Similarly, the ideal of an optimal communication society must be ensured by innovations that, for example, overcome language and geographical barriers. Telepresence and immersive virtual reality are the subject of major investments in order to avoid physical travel while ensuring optimal communication between individuals. Combined with holography, these communication technologies could be at the heart of a transportation revolution by abolishing distance. The NBIC report announced major innovations and a rationalization of the financial and ecological costs of transportation.

According to the NBIC report, the convergence of the most innovative technologies should lead to a social and individual revolution. Humans are soon to be enhanced, to become more efficient on a physical and psychological level. Societies will also be modified by new technologies. Future inventions will make it possible to solve individual problems, such as diseases, through collective responses. Collective intelligence is bound to be strengthened, to become more creative, thanks to technoscience, before an expansion of humanity in the solar system and in the wider cosmos. However, the NBIC report does not set out a spatial perspective for the species; its projections focus on the expansion of humankind to improve communication and health. This report proposes a long-term program for humanity. Although of American origin, it met with worldwide success, inspiring numerous programs in multiple R&D centers. Although they are competitive, researchers from around the world adhere to common perspectives, to a global research agenda that is proposed and not imposed by the leaders of a technoscience that has been boiling since the end of World War II, and, more recently, since the revolution in personal computing and the Internet.

Companies from Silicon Valley, which appeared at the beginning of the virtual and Internet era, participated in the realization of techno-scientific fantasies, devoting large sums of money to realize visions that were considered pure fiction until the end of the 20th century. The 2002 report constitutes a breakthrough in technological foresight. Indeed, it provides a synthesis of the many imaginings that have accompanied scientific research since the early 1980s. It rationalizes the multiple representations of the future, coming mainly from science fiction, and allows transhumanism to develop, to the point of becoming an important ideology of technological capitalism in the first years of the third millennium. Transhumanism has its origins in "new age" cybernetics, particularly influential in the United States and then in the rest of the world. The NBICs are at the center of American futurology, giving rise to a techno-prophetism serving as a strategic vision for the leaders of the planet.

At the time of writing, this paradigm continues to influence decision-makers, researchers and investors in techno-scientific sectors, promising, for example, to create biocybernetic super-intelligences or immersive virtual worlds, modifying the very nature of humanity. The NBIC report has initially made it possible to rationalize certain fantasies emanating from science fiction, which is often prophetic as well as, sometimes, a little delirious. For example, the theory of singularity, predicting a surpassing of humanity by machines, is the object of collective fears that can lead to collective technophobia. Similarly, the NBIC report demystifies certain technophile fantasies in order to propose a forecast around some major innovations that should fuel the next economic cycles.

NBICs are at the interface between two fictional systems. Transhumanism, justifying major investments in R&D, was an inspiration for the authors of this report. Science fiction is also at the forefront of reflections on the positive or negative consequences of research in computer science, cognitive science, biotechnology and nanotechnology. Fictions prior to the report were restricted, hemmed in by the reality of innovation, and have since entered a new creative, more ideological phase. The NBIC report synthesizes and filters the abundant technical imaginings of the previous decades, in order to pragmatically define the evolutions and the future of science and technological capitalism for the coming decades. This rationalization of the NBIC imaginings also generates a new production of fictions, in the form of a global technological ideology, guiding an R&D that is in a perpetual quest for stimulating objectives and innovations that promise to change the world.

The NBIC report announces an industrial revolution in which the physical and intellectual increase of humanity is a central issue. It sets out the major technoscientific challenges of the next 20 or 30 years. Political decision-makers are strongly encouraged to invest in nanotechnologies, biotechnologies, computing and cognitive sciences, as these sectors are considered to be the most innovative. Since the early 2000s, transhumanism has accompanied the NBIC revolution, which should lead to considerable progress for humanity. Some of the projects resembled science fiction in 2002, with the report being reminiscent of a synthesis of the technical imaginings of the last 20 years. This forward-looking approach to R&D makes it possible to distinguish between unrealistic ideas and pragmatic intuitions in a teeming technical imagination. The NBIC report puts into perspective the most innovative scientific discoveries in order to define the priorities of fundamental and applied research. The Cognome Project, for example, is based on fundamental research into the origin of ideas, with the aim of developing technologies for fusing the human brain with machines, in order to commercialize them. The NBIC paradigm seems to be a synthesis of the most innovative science fiction ideas. However, it goes beyond this fiction to remind us that technoscience is in the midst of change, generating not only popular imaginary representations but also fundamental knowledge, whose practical applications are at the origin of new products that feed markets and stimulate the dynamics of capitalism. Scientific ideologies stem from the techno-scientific paradigm, but also from science fiction, which very often boosts future innovations.

19.4. Conclusion

These prospective trajectories are therefore not merely imaginary, but are aimed at planning ambitious innovation policies at the global level. Americans, leaders in R&D, have presented pragmatic and futuristic discourses through reports as well as through fictions, envisaging the supersession of humanity through research to create superior beings, in a neo-Darwinian perspective. Immersive or medical technologies that are in preparation in laboratories feed numerous fantasies and fears, leading to ethical questions about the future of a humanity confronted with the advent of technosciences and sequences of industrial revolutions. The future that is imagined by researchers and artists is often based on an apology for technology, which is expected to radically change the human being. Living for 300 years, becoming cognitively immortal by downloading our mind into computer simulations or colonizing other planets are projects that should make it possible to fight against death and ensure the survival of humanity in the distant future. It remains to be seen whether science fiction and the blissful faith in technical progress might not generate a Faustian science, motivated more by profit or imperialism than by the well-being of the species.

19.5. References

Banse, G., Grunwald, A., Hronszky, I., Nelson, G. (eds) (2007). *Assessing Societal Implications of Converging Technological Development*. Edition Sigma, Berlin.

Bostrom, N. (2017). *Superintelligence*. Dunod, Paris.

Claverie, B. (2010). *L'homme augmenté : néotechnologies pour un dépassement du corps et de la pensée*. L'Harmattan, Paris.

Kurzweil, R. (2007). *Humanité 2.0 : la bible du changement*. M21 Editions, Paris.

Noyer, J.-M. (2016). *Transformation of Collective Intelligences: Perspective of Transhumanism*. ISTE Ltd, London and John Wiley & Sons, New York.

Rifkin, J. (1998). *The Biotech Century: Harnessing the Gene and Remaking the World*. Jeremy P. Tarcher, Los Angeles.

Roco, M.C., Bainbridge, W.S., Tonn, B., Whitesides, G. (2014). *Convergence of Knowledge, Technology and Society: Beyond Convergence of Nano-Bio-Info-Cognitive Technologies*. Springer Science & Business Media, Berlin.

Sfez, L. (1995). *La santé parfaite, critique d'une nouvelle utopie*. Le Seuil, Paris.

20

Hybridization – Hybridization of Tech-Push and Market-Pull Approaches in Innovation Processes

20.1. Introduction

Innovation practitioners and theorists have ignored the importance of the degree of maturity of demand, of the expression of needs, and have followed the only technology maturity scale, the technology readiness level – TRL (Mankins 1985). Tech-Push approaches are often opposed to Market-Pull approaches. With the DRL (demand readiness level) tool (Paun 2012), the foundations for innovative approaches to hybridization between Tech-Push and Market-Pull are finally laid and available for all collaborative innovation processes. Concrete tools make it possible to accelerate innovation, thanks, in particular to methodologies that support national strategies, as well as companies and innovation networks (Paun 2018): "tools to compensate for asymmetries between players" and "Tech (TRL) and Market Pull (DRL) hybridization".

Choosing to analyze the innovation actors, partners and management tools of different stages in the collaborative innovation process is part of a hybridization methodology that has been well known for a few years ("TRL-DRL"), which also offers solutions to co-qualify together with potential partners and stakeholders, the degree of maturity of both the innovative technologies (TRL) and the demand and needs for innovation (DRL). The discovery of the DRL-TRL tool (Paun 2012), and its first applications in innovation strategies is quite recent thanks to research, innovation and experimentation in the aerospace field. Collaborative innovation has been the subject of numerous scientific works on open innovation (Chesbrough *et al.* 2008) as collaborative processes (Laperche and Uzunidis 2012; Von Tunzelman and Richard 2012), and defined as an organizational process that integrates a variety of

---

Chapter written by Florin PAUN.

public and private actors, sometimes in the form of communities of thought and action that create, share and disseminate different knowledge aimed at creating value through innovation, or incremental disruptions in a diversity of fields.

The theoretical corpus of this article is based on research and experiments originally carried out in France at the *Office Nationale de Recherche et Études Aérospatiales* (Paun 2012), to build a new dynamic of innovation and technology transfer with SMEs, through the integration of "new specific asymmetries of collaborative processes".

An empirical approach allows us to identify not only the conditions of the creation of the demand readiness level and DRL-TRL tool, but also the pioneers of their experimentation and adaptations. Among these major players are Technology Transfer Acceleration Structures, company networks such as Le Mouvement des Entreprises de France, the Pacte Pme (Pacte 2016), as well as visionary schools and leaders (Carole Miranda and Alain Quevreux from the Innovation School of the National Association for Research and Technology, the Toulouse Business School, Paris School of Business), expert training institutions (EUROSAE, DENT Associates, Marcus Evans, Innovation Johnson) and government innovation support structures such as the Parliamentary Conference for Innovation in France and the Business Innovation Center in Indonesia, currently working towards the emergence of a new national strategy for collaborative innovation in Indonesia, democratizing the use of new collaborative tools such as the demand readiness level (BIC and Indonesia 2018).

The methodology and structure is as follows: After recalling how and why this tool was discovered in France, and the way in which economists and practitioners have grasped the question of the importance of hybridization solutions between Tech-Push and Market-Pull approaches, thanks to the creation in France of the "DRL – demand readiness level" concept (Paun 2012), we will then show the analysis and empirical material on the impacts of the DRL-TRL tool on the performance of collaborative innovation strategies, open innovation. In conclusion, we will formulate the potential importance of this tool in the acceleration and agilization mechanisms of all collaborative innovation processes. On the theoretical level, we specify the potential impact of such tools on the evolution and transformation, not only of the management, but also of the evaluation and innovative and sustainable financing of innovation (Letier 2018).

20.2. Definitions of Tech-Push and Market-Pull in the implementation of innovation processes

The understanding of the process of emergence of the demand for technological innovation has long remained an object of secondary study, or the subject of separate analyses, mainly carried out by the humanities and social sciences. Logics of anchoring in the construction of the demand for innovation models and innovation strategies no longer boil down to a linear R&D process.

DRL (demand readiness level) (Paun 2012) is an innovative tool for open-innovation collaborative processes, created in 2009 by Paun as a new scale for expressing the degree of maturity of a demand identified by potential innovation players. This scale, complementing the technology readiness level – TRL (Mankins 1995), shows the stage of conceptualization of a need in a potential market and allows innovation actors to work together to identify an "optimum meeting point" with existing or potential technological (or social and societal) offers. This innovation acceleration tool is designed to measure the degree of maturity of the expression of an identified innovation need in a given market, or in anticipating the creation of a future market. DRL also provides access to an understanding of the behaviors and stages of innovation players in Market-Pull-type approaches. The development of this new scale for maturing innovation demand was conceived in France, when the existing TRL scale (Mankins 1995) proved insufficient for analyzing the licenses signed at the *Office Nationale de Recherche et Études Aérospatiales* (between 2006 and 2014). DRL was used for the first time to determine the degree of maturity of an aerospace technology that can contract its technology transfers most effectively in the various civil sectors of the *Office Nationale de Recherche et Études Aérospatiales'* partner SMEs, thus contributing to increasing the competitiveness of French companies and successfully valorizing research.

20.3. The nine demand readiness level (DRL) stages

(DRL 1) corresponds to the perception of a still undefined lack in the uses of an individual, an SME or other types of economic actors in society. DRL 1 is, by analogy the equivalent of fundamental research, from the first TRL 1 stage on the TRL scale.

(DRL 2) corresponds to the identification of the need for innovation. In market studies, DRL 2 corresponds to studies to identify the expected uses for a new product/service.

(DRL 3) corresponds to the identification of potential functionalities through future products/services. This level is the result of the identification studies of the uses and the construction of the respondents to the needs.

(DRL 4) is the level where the innovation players have already successfully specified and qualified the expected functionalities. We know the level of performance to be achieved on each of the functionalities, as well as integrating the interactions of the respective weights of each of the functionalities in relation to the others.

(DRL 5) is the level at which everything is "at stake" because innovation actors must absolutely identify the "systemic competencies" (Paun *et al.* 2012), in order to successfully translate the expected functionalities for the new product/service into "dynamic functional capabilities" (Paun *et al.* 2012).

The dissociation of "capabilities" into resources, skills and abilities needed to achieve innovations is done at Level Seven (DRL 7).

(DRL 8) identifies the actors belonging to the different types of value-contribution channels that will intervene in the overall innovation process.

(DRL 9) corresponds to the construction of the response in terms of innovation expectations precisely corresponding to the identified need, while contributing to the construction of a technological research project necessary for this co-constructed response, by following the maturity scale of the innovation demand.

20.4. Hybridization and agility of innovation processes

With the DRL scale, which offers an in-depth and dynamic understanding of Market-Pull approaches, and the innovative patented DRL-TRL tool (Paun 2012), we have a new reference system that complements TRL (which is part of Tech-Push) to accelerate and "agilize multi-sector and multi-function innovation processes" in the face of a dynamic of "reducing innovation cycles" (Paun 2018). We can thus better understand and anticipate the actions, stages and specificities of all the players during the different stages of collaborative processes aimed at creating market value and knowledge capital for manufacturers and research laboratories. By articulating the determinants of supply as well as demand (by entrepreneurs and intra-entrepreneurs and their innovation ecosystems), innovation acceleration cycles can be described as "hybrids" (Paun 2018) because of the variation in their magnitude over time, as well as the superposition of classic sectoral innovation trajectories and multifunctional innovation trajectories.

The evolution of humanity is based on disruptive innovation. For example, disruptive innovation in materials has forged the evolution of humankind's eras. We have thus moved, with technological mastery, from the era of stone to that of bronze, iron, steel and probably to that of silicon, graphene and perhaps, the materials of tomorrow (JEDI – Joint European Disruptive Initiative – European MoonShot, December 2018), adaptable and nano-reformable, "living materials".

Demand Readiness Level (DRL)	
Level	**Definition**
1	Sensation or impression of "a lack"
2	Identification of a specific need
3	Identification of expected functionalities of a new product or service
4	Quantification of expected functionalities
5	Identification of systemic skills (including project management)
6	Matching the expected functionalities with the necessary skills to construct the response
7	Definition of skills and necessary resources
8	Identification of experts with the required skills
9	Construction of the response to the need expressed by the market

Source: Florin Poun - Onera

Definition	Level
Systen proven through successful operation tasks	9
Complete system and flight (aeronautics field) qualification using tests and demonstrations	8
Demonstration of a prototype system in an operational environment	7
Demonstration of a system/sub-system model or demonstration of a prototype in a relevant environment	6
Validation of a component and/or a produced artifact in a relevant environment	5
Laboratory validation of a component and/or produced artifact	4
Critical function analyzed and experimented and/or characteristic proof-of-concept	3
Concepts and/or technology applications are formulated	2
Basic principles are observed and reported	1
Technology Readiness Level (TRL)	

Figure 20.1. *"DRL-TRL" tool – the (patented) "agilization" tool for innovation processes through Tech-Push and Market-Pull hybridization (source: Paun 2012). For a color version of this figure, see www.iste.co.uk/uzunidis/innovation1.zip*

If we integrate the system of the two references TRL and DRL, one for the Tech-Push (TRL) approach and the other for the Market-Pull (DRL) approach, we are able to determine the optimum conditions (the sum of the two scales being equal to or greater than 9) and the ideal period for a technology transfer or collaboration agreement (even for disruptive innovation) to be signed in an efficient way for the partners.

It can be stressed that the different levels can only be partially achieved and this is often insufficient to guarantee the success of an innovation project.

20.5. DRL-TRL and its applications to the hybridization dynamics of Tech-Push and Market-Pull approaches

For a product/service to become an innovation, the DRL and TRL levels must be reached imperatively. There are also cases in which valuation agreements for TRL levels lower than 3 have been signed with a new real DRL higher than 5 (i.e. in the presence of a contractor with a high-level project). It can be assumed that in the case of "Market-Pull" projects, the "DRL-TRL" sum limit can probably be less than 9.

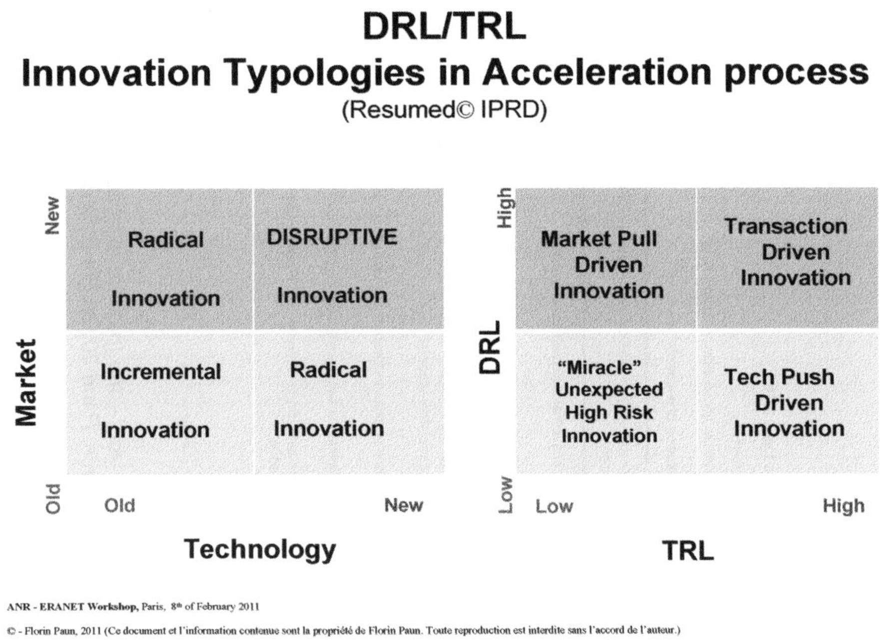

Figure 20.2. *Various uses and adaptations of the DRL-TRL tool for accelerating disruptive innovation in France (source: Paun 2011). For a color version of this figure, see www.iste.co.uk/uzunidis/innovation1.zip*

20.6. Impacts of DRL-TRL

The roles of the different actors in innovation have not been sufficiently analyzed, and the "entrepreneur" alone has taken center stage (Boutiller and Uzunidis 1999). The DRL-TRL tool is consistent with the needs and developments identified by recent research on system innovation theory, which views innovation as a complex system that adapts itself. This approach proposes an understanding of the interactions of innovation systems and, above all, of the actors in their practices that contribute more or less to the performance of global disruptive innovation support systems. Innovation is no longer the exclusive function of the R&D department but the expected behavior and practice shared by all employees and stakeholders (Three Totals Theory, XU 2007).

Innovation strategies are evolving rapidly, and among the pioneers of open (Chesbrough 2008) and collaborative innovation in France are Airbus, Safran, Valeo, Siemens and EDF, as well as the support structures for injecting start-ups into the R&D programs of multinationals and innovative Accelerators (Starburst, the Pegasus Growth Accelerator, the Biz Lab by Airbus and Yann Barbaux' Aerospace Valley, the catalyst for Thomas O'Neal's entrepreneurial initiatives at the University of Central Florida in the United States, the European Space End Project (Co designed by Paun 2019), which have Tanya Suarez' IoT Tribe, the Pole Safe in France, Cluj IT Cluster and the Center for Earth Observation in Bucharest as consortium partners.

The DRL-TRL tools are part of this new dynamic of research as well as the experimentation of new strategies and tools, and are supported by legislative evolution (Loi 2007; Ronan 2010) and institutional innovation (e.g. the strategies of Inter-company Mediation developed by the Mediator Pierre Pelouzet (https://www.economie.gouv.fr/mediateur-des-entreprises/innover-ensemble)).

The DRL-TRL tool enables the agilization of disruptive innovation processes by transforming the simple Distribution Chain of technological value in a single sector into a real "Tree" or "Mangrove Forest" (Paun 2018) with fiscal, organizational and participative management incentives for technological, as well as societal innovation processes in several sectors. Thus, we are moving from Design Thinking to Agile Demo-Tech thinking strategies that promote disruptive innovation. Innovation models are constantly evolving, from C&D ("connect & develop"), "lead user method", "Open Innovation" (Chesbrough 2008) to the Total Innovation Model (Xu 2007), "Hybridization Tech Push and Market Pull – TRL-DRL" (Paun 2012) or "liberated enterprise"-type models, and finally, to Agile Demo Tech Thinking (Paun 2018).

20.7. Conclusion

The challenges of creating the future Europe of disruptive innovation will be the ability to integrate these new tools for accelerating and, above all, agilizing innovation processes at the heart of a new paradigm of collaborative innovation, using budgets and criteria for qualifying and financing disruptive innovation thanks to "Agile Demo-Tech Thinking" (Paun 2018). We integrate the ability to anticipate and change business models, sectors or regions by following "multi-functional innovation trajectories" (not just "one-shot innovations").

The more we integrate (at all stages of the DRL-TRL innovation process) the impacts perceived by one or more stakeholders, the more we increase the capacities and capabilities to "make innovation processes more agile" (Paun 2018). In this way, the resilience of collaborative innovation actors is strengthened.

DRL-TRL can have macroeconomic impacts to transform national innovation strategies. In fact, the more companies and institutions adopt (at the micro level) the tools (DRL-TRL, Impact Readiness Level, Risk and Shared Benefit Contracts, Agile Demo Tech Thinking, etc.) for the agilization and hybridization of Tech-Push and Market-Pull strategies (at the meso-economic level, at the level of regions and sectors, even branches), the more a real "culture of collaborative and agile innovation" emerges from the bottom-up.

The importance of these new collaborative tools and strategies for innovation agilization is that they generate, in a "recursive causality" of new centers of value creation, economic changes at the micro, meso and macro levels, which makes it possible to anticipate the trajectories and cycles of multi-sector and multi-functional innovation. Innovation management is thus based on agile methods of "open and participative qualification" (Paun 2018) that are compatible with economic, social and environmental expectations.

20.8. References

Barbaroux, P. and Liu, Z. (2017). Les dynamiques d'innovation dans les industries aérospatiales et de défense. *Technologie et innovation*. ISTE OpenScience, London.

BIC (Business Innovation Center, Indonesia) (2018). 110 Indonesia's innovations – 2018. Pages on Dr. Paun's thesis on the Hybridization of Tech Push and Market Pull: DRL-TRL, 44-45; "Innovation Strategies: Agile Demo-Tech", Conference, 12 December 2018, Cikarang, Indonesia [Online]. Available at: goo.gl/A562NE.

Boutiller, S. and Uzunidis, D. (1999). La légende de l'entrepreneur. Le capital social, ou comment vient l'esprit d'entreprise. *Éditions La Découverte et Syros*, Paris, 18.

Chesbrough, H., Vanhaverbeke, W., West, J. (2008). *Open Innovation: Researching a New Paradigm*. Oxford University Press, Oxford.

Laperche, B. and Uzunidis, D. (2012). Eco-innovation, knowledge capital and the evolution of the firm. *The IUP Journal of Knowledge Management*, 10(3), 14–34.

Letier, F. (2018). *Comment doubler la taille de votre entreprise*. Edition Eyrolles, Paris.

Mankins, J.C. (1995). Technology readiness levels. White paper. Advanced Concepts Office, Office of Space Access and Technology, NASA, Huntsville, AL.

PACTE PME (2016). Guide de bonnes pratiques en innovation ouverte, 14, 15 [Online]. Available at: https://pactepme.org/media/brochures/guide-innovation-ouverte.pdf.

Paun, F. (2012). The demand readiness level scale as new proposed tool to hybridize market pull with technology push approaches in technology transfer practices, in technology transfer in a global economy. *Springer Series: International Studies in Entrepreneurship*, 28, 397.

Paun, F. (2014). *J'innove, donc je suis ! Visionnaires du XXIe siècle*. Éditions L'Harmattan, 27–92 [Online]. Available at: http://www.ubifrance.fr/0019782343020051+j-innove-donc-je-suis-.html (Launched during the Conférence Parlementaire Innovation, Paris, 2015, Maison de la Chimie).

Paun, F. (2018). Raccourcir les cycles d'innovation. *Technologie et innovation*, ISTE OpenScience, London.

Paun, F., Von Tunzelmann, N., Richard, P. (2012). Asymmetries and dynamic interactive capabilities in technology transfer between ONERA – the French Aerospace LabTM and SMEs. *Journal of Innovation Economics & Management*, 1, 103–137.

Xu, Q. (2007). TIM (Total Innovation Management) – "A paradigm of innovation management in the 21st Century". *Journal of Technology Transfer*, 32(1–2), 9–25.

21

Incentives – Incentives for Innovation: Diversity and Public–Private Combinations

21.1. Introduction

Most sectors of economic activity with high growth potential are subject to competition. At the level of companies as well as at the country level, innovation provides a competitive advantage. The competitiveness of a company results, for example, from good management of the marketing of a finished product, resulting from an efficient and flexible production system at a lower cost. A country's competitiveness depends intrinsically on its stage of development but is correlated with the capacity of potential growth sectors to create export opportunities. These different forms of competitiveness imply returns of significant scale, as well as significant market shares, in relation to competitors. For good planning of research and development (R&D) activities, the forms of incentives put in place play an important role. Taking into account innovation and its purposes, incentives for innovation are defined as all specific measures of policies or strategies that make it possible to obtain a determined behavior from targeted agents, in exchange for one or more advantages that are known in advance. It is therefore a contract between employer and employee to achieve a performance objective resulting from the R&D of an economic activity.

Because of the impossibility of observing and controlling individual or collective research efforts, an incentive mechanism for the production of a new good or process becomes a strategic issue for the success of a project. It is in this respect that the theories relating to innovation incentives attempt to respond to the problem that motivating and rewarding the performance of creativity and research are instruments for obtaining a comparative advantage.

Chapter written by Babacar NDIAYE.

First, we present the theoretical underpinnings that have fostered the development of incentive theory in the form of a typology. Second, we propose an analysis of the different forms of incentives and their applications, according to the characteristics of the firm, the sector of activity and the competition.

21.2. The incentive for innovation and its forms

Originally, agency theory set the framework for the typology of the forms of incentive to be implemented (Jensen and Meckling 1976). The notion of moral hazard due to the asymmetry of information on the agent's real motivations implies setting up incentive mechanisms for innovation. In 1989, Holmström already argued that the agent's utility is an increasing function of his wealth and that he presents an aversion to work and, more particularly, to effort. It is within this framework that the problem of the employee's incentive provided by the employer is of fundamental importance in the theory of innovation.

Throughout the economic literature, three forms of incentives to innovation are highlighted: control and ownership rights (Grossman and Hart 1986; Aghion and Tirole 1994), monetary incentives within the firm (Holmström 1989; Holmström and Milgrom 1991; Manso 2011) and non-monetary incentives (Aghion and Jackson 2016).

The first form of incentive to innovation, also called incentive to production, comes under the theory of contract incompleteness because it is important, when signing an R&D contract, to specify the allocation of control rights and property rights. Thus, the sharing of the fruits of innovation depends on the type of allocation defined *ex ante*, according to the most important motivation so that the agent may adopt the desired maximizing behavior. The producer is thus more motivated to make a major effort to produce knowledge from which they will benefit, through an income, as well as from intellectual property protection guaranteeing them a more or less exclusive ownership right to the product. Consequently, the patent system is an important instrument for encouraging innovation in certain technology-intensive sectors.

However, while the incentive to innovate encourages patenting, it also implies the existence of a temporary monopoly, which limits the use of technology. This temporary monopoly situation results in higher prices than in a competitive situation. The result is a loss of consumer welfare. Thus, when innovation is cumulative, the existence of a patent tends to hinder innovation, because the fundamental invention is protected.

The second form of incentive for innovation depends on performance-related rewards, which encourage the agent to focus on measurable tasks to determine the incentive threshold. Experience with multitasking models allows us to clearly specify priority tasks and classify them. In general, monetary incentives take the form of cash payments linked to a performance-based indicator. This remuneration takes the form of, among other things, the payment of bonuses associated with the achievement of individual absolute performance objectives, bonuses associated with relative performance objectives or monetary compensation based on a team's performance.

However, the different applications related to this model reveal limitations related to the allocation of effort between the agent's routine and research tasks. Thus, monetary incentives are not necessarily more efficient than other forms of incentives for innovation because they lead to a crowding-out effect in favor of other forms of incentives.

The last form of incentive for innovation, the non-monetary incentive, aims to motivate employees without any financial payment. It consists of motivating the agent by introducing mechanisms such as "prizes", "challenges" or "rewards" (Radhakrishnan and Ronen 1999). In this category of incentives, there are tangible non-monetary incentives, that is, rewards in the form of objects or services that the organization grants to an employee when they achieve certain objectives (travel, free meals, access to a company daycare center, etc.), social non-monetary incentives that take into account the value of relationships between employers and employees within the organization and occupation-related non-monetary incentives that motivate employees, to make work more enjoyable. This form of incentive for innovation is increasingly developing in the form of professional recognition, as it represents an essential component of working life. The advantage of this form of incentive is that it has a smaller crowding-out effect on the intrinsic motivation of agents than monetary incentives. In this case, the crowding-out effect is interpreted either as the fact that the increase in monetary incentives is perceived as a sign that the task to be performed will be unpleasant as compared to routine work, or as the fact that the introduction of monetary incentives changes the perception that the employee initially associated with the effort.

21.3. Diversity of applications of incentive forms

In the course of the evolution of the literature, Deci (1975) considers these three forms of incentive to constitute extrinsic motivation. In contrast, intrinsic motivation refers to the agent's desire to feel competent and autonomous (Frey and Osterloh 2002).

Furthermore, economic theory shows that different forms of incentives for innovation have different characteristics, depending on firm size, industry and competitive influence. In particular, the implementation of the theory of incentives to innovation is more present in private firms than in public firms. This finding is linked to the fact that, in a private firm, any action that provides a gain greater than its cost must be carried out at the expense of an unprofitable action: this is the economic logic of the profitability of an investment.

On the other hand, the process of encouraging innovation has some characteristics that are not specific to private investment and that partly justify public intervention. This makes it possible to better manage risks and deal with the irreversibility of investments. In a situation of cumulative innovation, private incentives to innovate are all the more important, as opportunities linked to competitive advantages translate into substantial gains for the leader. This very favorable position in a competitive environment allows the firm to develop outlets and attract the best skills in relation to its core business. As a result, personal recognition linked to effort seems more effective than financial rewards based on the results of an activity: the examples of the Nobel Prize and the Fields Medal are a perfect illustration of this. It is in this context that there are implications related to the theory of incentives.

The first occurrence related to the theory of incentives for innovation is that public intervention in R&D activities has become an important issue, especially for developed countries, in which new technological discoveries are both of national and public security interest. It is with this perspective that the doctrine that tends to support the primacy of incentives for innovation in private organizations tends to dissipate, in favor of incentives for innovation implemented in public institutes, laboratories and research centers.

The second occurrence comes from the process of employers calculating utility optimization. Indeed, the organizations most concerned about the instruments and forms of incentives for innovation generally have the best human skills to promote innovation. This is fundamentally about the motivation and mobility of researchers in their working environment.

21.4. Conclusion

Incentive theory is seen as a set of rules that induce economic agents to exert high levels of effort and eliminate all barriers that promote asymmetric information within an organization. Most studies on the economics of innovation show the importance of taking incentives into account in decision-making. This is how human resource management strategies have emerged in favor of an effective incentive policy. The economic logic of the profitability of an investment explains the fact that incentives for innovation are more present in private companies than in public companies. Beyond the diversity of forms of innovation incentives, the framework of agency theory and its applications has made it possible to highlight the occurrences linked to employer and employee optimization calculations. Consequently, the implementation of an incentive procedure remains an effective way to solve the problem of moral risk. When this incentive is oriented towards innovation, economic agents receive good information on the intrinsic quality of a product or service.

21.5. References

Aghion, P. and Jackson, M.-O. (2016). Inducing leaders to take risky decisions: Dismissal, tenure, and term limits. *American Economic Journal: Microeconomics*, 8(3), 1–38.

Aghion, P. and Tirole, J. (1994). The management of innovation. *The Quarterly Journal of Economics*, 109(4), 1185–1209.

Deci, E.L. (1975). *Intrinsic Motivation*. Plenum Press, New York.

Frey, B.S. (2007). Awards as compensation. *European Management Review*, 4, 6–14.

Frey, B.S. and Osterloh, M. (2002). *Successful Management by Motivation. Balancing Intrinsic and Extrinsic Incentives*. Springer, New York.

Grossman, S.-J. and Hart, O.-D. (1986). The costs and benefits of ownership: A theory of vertical and lateral integration. *Journal of Political Economy*, 94(4), 691–719.

Holmström, B. (1989). Agency costs and innovation. *Journal of Economic Behavior and Organization*, 12, 305–327.

Holmström, B. and Milgrom, P. (1991). Multitask principal-agent analyses: Incentive contracts, asset ownership, and job design. *Journal of Law, Economics, and Organization*, 7, 24–52.

Jensen, M.-C. and Meckling, W.-H. (1979). Theory of the firm: Managerial behavior, agency costs and ownership structure. *Journal of Financial Economics*, 3(4), 305–360.

Manso, G. (2011). Motivating innovation. *Journal of Finance*, 66(5), 1823–1860.

Radhakrishnan, S. and Ronen, J. (1999). Job challenge as a motivator in a principal–agent setting. *European Journal of Operational Research*, 115, 138–157.

22

Indicators – The Complexity of Innovation Indicators

22.1. Introduction

The second half of the 20th century established both the crucial role of innovations in economic dynamics and the role of public policy in encouraging them (Godin 2015). This plebiscite has been reinforced over the last 25 years with the focus of public decision-makers, on the supposed relationship between "competitiveness" and "innovations", following the accelerated dismantling of customs barriers (generalization of free trade agreements) and the rise of so-called emerging countries (with China in the lead). In the reconfiguration of the international division of labor, innovation would make it possible to keep countries with low labor costs at a distance and conquer the market shares in emerging sectors in the face of other advanced economies. The promotion of innovation is also justified by new societal and environmental challenges, such as the fight against climate change and the need for attractiveness at all territorial scales.

The prioritization of innovations on the political agenda has raised the need to measure them, in order to assess the performance of States and compare them with one another. The Organisation for Economic Co-operation and Development (OECD) was a pioneer in this field with the publication of the famous "*Proposed Guidelines for Collecting and Interpreting Technological Innovation Data*" in 1992, which aimed to provide methodological support for the collection and interpretation of data on innovation. Over the course of the various editions (the last and fourth published in October 2019), this guide will gradually be expanded, notably by broadening its scope of analysis beyond technological innovations: the "Oslo Manual" (this is how it is commonly referred to) is now an authoritative reference. Its complementarity with

---

Chapter written by Slim THABET.

another reference system that chronologically precedes it – the "Frascati Manual" (first published in 1963) – makes it possible to cover the innovation process both upstream and downstream. This chapter is structured in two parts: first, we present some of the main indicators of innovation, and then we show its limits through certain biases.

22.2. Presentation of innovation indicators: input and output approach

There are many indicators of innovation, which can be grouped according to different criteria: market pull/technology push (i.e. indicators that focus on innovations related to technological inventions or those in response to unsatisfied market needs), context/outcome/impact (context: environment in which an action(s) takes place; outcome: immediate effect(s) generated by the action(s) on the target(s) and compliance or non-compliance with the expected result(s); impact: longer-term indirect effects), input/output, etc. Each classification has its advantages and disadvantages. In the following discussion, we will rely on the input/output distinction, which is the most widely used.

Innovation flows are part of a systemic process: on a given territory (continent, nation, region, local productive system, metropolis), the production of innovations is not simply the aggregation of independent discoveries. It is the result of a complex, interactive, collective, collaborative and cumulative process that can be accounted for by the "systemic" and "interactionist" approach. The production of innovations is indeed the result of interactions between several actors, and these interactions "make systems". This system is fed by "inputs" (inputs: domestic R&D expenditure, personnel, research effort, i.e. human and financial resources) and generates "outputs" (outputs: innovation rate, patents filed, scientific publications).

Due to the complexity of the issues addressed here, the clarification of the definitions of some commonly used concepts and indicators are required. It is also necessary to draw the reader's attention to certain precautions of use and interpretation (bias).

Research and Development (R&D) is a statistical, economic and accounting category that encompasses the creative work carried out in a systematic way, to increase the sum of human knowledge and develop new applications. It encompasses three activities: basic research, applied research and (experimental) development. Its identification makes it possible to calculate the "domestic expenditure on research and development" (DERD), equivalent to the sum of the financial resources devoted to R&D work carried out on the national territory, regardless of the origin of the funds (domestic or foreign). Part of the DERD is carried out by administrations (DERDA), the other part by companies (DERDC). Any country wishing to be included in international research rankings must calculate this indicator, the methodology of which is set out in the famous Oslo and Frascati Manuals published by the OECD.

Indicators	**Definitions**
Input indicators	
Domestic expenditure on research and development	According to the *Institut national de la statistique et des études économiques* (France), domestic expenditure on research and development (DERD) includes the financial resources (national and foreign: payroll of research and development personnel, operating costs and purchases of equipment needed for R&D) mobilized for the performance of research and development work on the national territory by administrations (DERDA) and the company sector (DERDC).
Research staff	This is the total workforce of public administrations and companies (teacher–researchers, researchers, engineers, technical or administrative support staff, etc.) that carry out research and development work.
Research effort	This is the ratio of DERD to Gross Domestic Product (GDP).
Output indicators	
Innovation rate	The innovation rate is obtained from the biannual European Community Innovation Survey (CIS). It corresponds to the ratio of the number of companies (with at least 10 employees in technological services, industry, transport-warehousing and wholesale trade) that have introduced an innovation (whether a product, process, organizational or marketing) to the total number of companies in the field concerned.
Patent	According to INSEE, a patent is a tool that protects a technical innovation, i.e. a product or process that provides a solution to a given technical problem.
Scientific publications	Scientific publications refer to the different types of communications that researchers make about their work to their peers and to an expert audience. These papers are recorded in databases and are validated by the scientific community through an independent peer-review process.

Table 22.1. *Innovation indicators: presentation and comments*

22.3. Main limitations of innovation indicators

By relating DERD to GDP, we obtain the "research effort" (or "technology intensity", or even "R&D intensity") of a given entity (nation, region, etc.). This is the key indicator, the most widely disseminated; the one that serves as a standard. However, it must be examined carefully because it has some important limitations.

First, we examine its level. The United Kingdom and the Netherlands have a research effort of around 2%, far behind the high-performance South Korea and its 4%, even though these countries are known for their active (applied) research. Territorial comparisons are always difficult. They mask biases due to "structure effects". A territory may show a lower research effort due to a stronger economic specialization in sectors with an intrinsically lower technological intensity. For example, in 2009, the difference between Germany and France in terms of research effort was mainly explained by the different sectoral compositions between the two countries (Le Ru 2012).

If, as discussed above, the relative level of technological intensity matters (taking structural effects into account), its evolution and impact must also be carefully examined. Research effort is primarily an indicator of investment, not performance. It does not account for the effectiveness of the results obtained, nor does it tell us anything about important qualitative dimensions, such as tacit knowledge exchange between actors, the density of interpersonal relations and trust within networks. As researcher Mazzucato (2013) has shown, in the 1970s, Japan had a much lower technological intensity (2.5% of its GDP) than the USSR (4%, mainly in the armaments and aerospace sector). Nevertheless, spending by the State and companies was much more efficient and spread throughout the entire economic fabric. The strategic role of the public authorities and "public–private" interactions proved to be decisive.

Another example is Nokia, an information and communication technology multinational that is now in tatters. The group accounted for 40% of Finland's DERD in 2011, one of the world's most R&D intensive countries (3.6% technological intensity in 2012). The country's poor record (three consecutive years of recession between 2011 and 2014, and a steady decline in technological intensity since 2009, while it has been rising across the OECD as a whole) is not unrelated to the considerable weight that the former telecoms giant had occupied in its economy and R&D (concentration effect bias).

Research and development activities are aimed at implementing innovations in several forms. Economists distinguish between two main types: technological and non-technological. "Technological" innovations correspond to product (or service) and process innovations. Organizational and marketing innovations are "non-technological".

It is certainly preferable to have high R&D budgets to foster innovation, but the link is not necessarily mechanical and strictly proportional. Rightly considered highly innovative, Denmark is a country that, until the mid-2000s, had a modest R&D ratio (close to 2% of GDP). Yet, its innovations are driven by activities that are not necessarily high-tech and did not necessarily require heavy R&D budgets. Moreover, while the relationship between R&D and innovation is strong, the influence also works the other way around: the will to innovate also drives R&D. The research effort is therefore partly endogenous: this is the case in many sectors (such as the automobile industry).

The number of patents filed is also another criterion for assessing the effectiveness of R&D, at both the micro and macro levels. We must be careful not to mechanically believe that the higher the number of patents filed by an institution or nation, the more innovative it is (Kabla 1994; Le Bas and Pénin 2015). A firm, for example, may very well innovate without patenting and, conversely, it may patent abundantly (as part of a market strategy) without innovating as much as a result. Moreover, patenting practices differ widely across countries or territories. When Japan grants 400,000 patents per year, France only registers 12,000. Even when compared to the number of inhabitants (or employees) or the number of companies, the gap is very high. It is largely explained by the fact that the Land of the Rising Sun grants much narrower patents, often for each component of a new product, whereas in France, there is a tendency to only patent the new goods or service as a whole. For international comparisons, it would therefore be better to limit oneself to certain types of patents – even if, again the indicator is imperfect – such as the so-called "triadic" (OECD) patents, i.e. those filed at the same time by the European, American and Japanese patent offices, which are considered to be of better quality. Finally, the number of patents is also influenced by cultural factors or industrial structures: some countries patent more than others, such as Switzerland; some sectors also patent much more than others, such as the pharmaceutical industry or the electronics industry (measurement bias).

22.4. Conclusion

The decisive role conferred on innovations for growth, competitiveness and social and environmental issues means that indicators are needed to measure their effects. There are many such indicators, the most widely used being those relating to the inputs and outputs of innovation systems, whether local, regional or national. Far from being "black boxes", these systems are in fact fed by "inputs" (human and financial resources) and generate "outputs" (innovation rate, patents filed and scientific publications). However, although indispensable, these indicators must be handled with care, as they have limits that must be kept in mind so as not to misinterpret them. These limits are due to various biases related to structural effects, concentration effects and measurement.

22.5. References

Godin, B. (2015). *Innovation Contested: The Idea of Innovation Over the Centuries*. Routledge, London and New York.

Kabla, I. (1994). Un indicateur de l'innovation : le brevet. *Economie et statistique*, 275–276, 95–109.

Le Bas, C. and Pénin, J. (2015). Brevet et innovation : comment restaurer l'efficience dynamique des brevets ? *Revue d'économie industrielle*, 151(3), 127–160.

Le Ru, N. (2012). Un déficit d'effort de recherche des entreprises françaises ? Comparaison France–Allemagne. *Information note "Enseignement supérieur & recherche"*, 12, 09.

Mazzucato, M. (2013). *The Entrepreneurial State. Debunking Public vs Private Sector Myths*. Anthem Press, London and New York.

OECD (2015). *Frascati Manual 2015: Guidelines for Collecting and Reporting Data on Research and Experimental Development*, 9th edition. OECD, Paris.

OECD and Eurostat (2019). *Oslo Manual 2018: Guidelines for Collecting, Reporting and Using Data on Innovation*, 4th edition. OECD/Eurostat, Paris and Luxembourg.

23

Information – Information for Innovation: Strategic, Competitive and Technological Intelligence

23.1. Introduction

Any innovation process cannot take place without an informational input and this can take many different forms (panoramic patent report, trend analysis, market positioning, product image, etc.). In the limited, but already important framework of a product innovation, the provision of a useful informational supply in a timely manner is already a complex problem to solve. However, even in this more limited framework, informational supplies are varied. They can be classified into three categories: "traditional monitoring" carried out in support of innovation processes, "creative monitoring" linked to the use of a creative process, and the more general or more specific "strategic innovation monitoring". In order to understand these different variants, we will first discuss the concept of monitoring. Then, some possible links between traditional monitoring (such as strategic, competitive and technological monitoring) and an innovation process will be considered. Finally, we will discuss the specificities of information retrieval in an innovation framework and the particular cases of creative and strategic innovation monitoring.

23.2. The monitoring concept

Generally speaking, monitoring is an informational research and surveillance activity in accordance with the legislation in force, which shares many common

---

Chapter written by Stéphane GORIA.

features with journalistic investigation (interrogation of sources, verification of sources and data, cross-checking of information analysis, synthesis, etc.). It is not espionage since it excludes any illegal action. Unlike journalistic investigation, its raison d'être is to provide an answer to the information needs of a company, institution or association.

Monitoring is first about methods and then about resources. Although platforms, software and other dedicated digital tools can be of great help, it is the monitoring and its purpose that must determine the tools used. In terms of the universe of information resources to be explored, the Web and all the technologies related to the Internet are unavoidable but not necessarily sufficient. Thus, any person in charge of monitoring must ask themselves about the knowledge and information already present in their organization, the human resources they can call upon (experts, users and non-users) and the interesting physical sites to visit.

These aspects are taken into account by all members of the company who must be aware of them in order to pass on new and useful information to some of their employees or managers. It is therefore important that a monitoring strategy be implemented at all levels of the company.

23.3. "Traditional" monitoring and innovation

There are many types of monitoring that can be described as "traditional" (strategic, technological, market, product, regulatory, legislative, etc.), as they are not specifically designed for innovation but they can contribute to it. These monitoring activities participate in the innovation process in a diffuse way, as an informational support for related activities. In the same vein, other monitoring systems can contribute to the innovation process, in particular by reporting the appearance of new elements or the disappearance of others (monitoring of suppliers, customers, subcontractors, distributors, partners, competitors, investors, etc.). Similarly, some forms of monitoring observe players, products and trends taking place in the company's environment (monitoring of opinion leaders, economics, raw materials, patents, reputation, etc.). Their objective is not to innovate, but the changes they report can be interpreted as having a strong impact on the innovation process (Blanco and Le Loarne 2009).

To summarize all of these cases, useful information related to innovation can take the form of:

– an opportunity alert (appearance of a new need, a potential supplier, a payment, etc.);

– a threat report (development of a potential breakthrough innovation, difficulties with a supplier, change in alliance configuration, etc.);

– additional information to inform a decision (following the identification of a weak signal, a discussion, an intuition, etc.);

– an observation carried out systematically, when the opportunity arises or following a request, concerning practice benchmarks or a discovery report.

All of this information plays an important role in the innovation process, even if it is not usually focused on contributing to it. When this is the case, the treatment to be given to it is more specific.

23.4. The search for information and innovation

Carrying out a monitoring activity or searching for information related to an innovation amounts to solving a particular problem. In order to provide a relevant answer, it must first be well understood. Its formulation must be questioned, reformulated and, if possible, tested (response prototyping). To make it easier to process, it can be reformulated to consist of three parts: (1) the subject of the research/monitoring; (2) the type of information provision(s) requested and the recipients associated with it; and (3) the constraints, preferences and priorities to be respected (including deadlines or frequency, format, fields to be explored or avoided, criteria and alert thresholds). Once the responses have been obtained, they will feed into a monitoring plan that will categorize them and link them to sources to be interviewed or monitored, resources to be exploited and other complementary information.

If the understanding of the subject requires significant reflection, it is preferably performed on site and in direct contact with the people in charge of innovation. The most practical way to do this is to first consider the supply to be produced. This must be thought out according to the stage(s) of the innovation process to which it is to contribute. This helps to identify recipients and information needs that may be overlooked.

Once this is done, the most delicate point to deal with is the subject of monitoring. This amounts to analyzing it from several different angles, involving a series of questions for each case. In a schematic way, the subject can be assimilated to a system composed of at least one element: a thing (material or immaterial), a concept (something abstract or that does not exist), a technology, a group of individuals, etc. The subject can also be assimilated to a system composed of at least one element. This system is then subject to 5W-2H type questioning (Who? When? Where? What? Why? How? How much?). Then, the system is approached and questioned from another angle, such as its interest or usefulness. To do this, it is sufficient, for example, to add "for" in front of each of the interrogative pronouns of the previous questioning (e.g. For whom? For when? For where?) or to deepen its chain of causality both upstream and downstream of the system. In these cases, it is a matter of understanding the system's raison d'être, the needs it must meet and its weaknesses (anything that could cancel out its reason for being) (Goria 2017).

If the questions are not directly associated with a stage of innovation, it is because the subject is implicitly linked to the ideas of novelty or alternative choices. In this case, the information seeker must try to think like the entrepreneur, the designer, the inventor or the artist. This is why they must use forms of analysis found in creativity or design techniques, such as analyses: functional, morphological, compositional, super-systems and sub-systems, past and future, user/customer experience, etc. Similarly, when exploring new markets, they must approach their identification and segmentation differently (Millier 2015). In order to do this kind of work as effectively as possible, it is best for qualified people to work with them on one or other aspect of the problem to be addressed.

23.5. Creative monitoring

Beyond the exploration of a subject related to a stage of innovation, certain forms of monitoring (or strategic intelligence, competitive intelligence, etc.) can be designed to inspire or be carried out by the creatives themselves. Trend monitoring is one of the strong points of this approach and gives rise to various productions: trend analyses ("simple" or joint), semantic mapping, trend or mood boards, etc.

From another point of view, it can be a question of identifying those who create, carry, make or are at the origin of new trends. All new creators, inventors, artists can be monitored according to profiles and criteria to be defined. They will most often be spotted through their productions or their network(s), directly or with the help of comments that others will make about them or their production.

Some creative forms of monitoring concern mapping and the search for new, forgotten or non-existent solutions. According to the C-K theory (Agogué *et al.* 2013), the role of information such as this is to identify knowledge (what exists) and explore concepts (what does not exist). Concepts are associated with a particular informational provision, justifying their status by showing that apparently nothing about them exists. In addition, inspiring information that can be associated with concepts can be searched for among visions of the future proposed by science fiction or solutions provided by nature (biomimicry).

In addition to the monitoring of weak signals, certain signals can be picked up directly from indicators of the development of certain new products, such as risks of technological, sectoral or societal disruptions. In the same way, in addition to these signals, analysis of routine signals can highlight stagnation of practices, design, technologies, etc. (Goria 2017). These signals are linked to a date that indicates the appearance of an element that has become unavoidable. They alert to creative opportunities and risks of rupture, even if they do not indicate the form they will take. They can also relate to internal company processes and the evolution of practices, their routinization and adequacy, over time, as well as those employed externally.

23.6. Strategic innovation monitoring

In addition to the creative forms of monitoring, there are other forms specifically oriented to contribute to strategic innovation. They target the strategic innovation orientations of competitors, or directly nurture strategic thinking aimed at innovation.

They can aim to position the company's innovation strategies in relation to its environment. This can be done through creation and adaptation of a reading grid used to estimate different forms of innovation implemented according to several criteria, such as contributions, disadvantages and risks of employment and non-employment, associated successes, companies employing them or the products/services that result from them. It can give rise to a mapping of practices and innovation around a category of products, processes, practices or companies, to which it is preferable to add a temporal dimension in order to reveal certain variations.

In support of this monitoring, certain accompanying tools can be put in place, including visual information management. Digital or physical tables, as well as entire rooms can be dedicated to it. These rooms can take the form of "war rooms" or spaces for creativity and information acquisition. In these cases, the walls can be used for Kanban-type teamwork organization charts, mind maps, user experience maps (UX maps), trend maps, idea displays, strategic frameworks, etc. Tables and other spaces are used to accommodate computer workstations and brainstorming workshops in the form of activities, some inspired by games (Lego serious play, Playmobil Pro, etc.), others not (Business origami, Hivemind or Hivemind SOLO, 3D immersion, etc.) to approach problems from a different perspective (Williams 2015).

More rarely, this type of room is a place for strategic reflection based on the analogy of battle or war. Reflections and mapping are carried out there in the spirit of combat marketing where the positions of products or companies are associated with those of armies and the field with mental representations of customers. In a similar vein, simulation exercises in the form of business war games can be carried out. They put at least two teams in opposition to one other to envisage different ways of approaching a problem by including certain chains of causality. The debriefing that follows should encourage participants to propose answers to questions such as: What if? These answers and the recommendations that complement them constitute a body of information that can then be used (Oriesek and Schwarz 2016).

23.7. Conclusion

There is a wealth of information that is useful for the innovation process. It can take the form of a specific contribution or a more general one that influences the entire innovation system. Some of this information comes from the search for information, others aspects from internal or external environmental monitoring, or even from reflections resulting from prospective studies. Beyond these practices, monitoring can contribute to a strategy of influence. It will contribute to this by mapping actors or monitoring the progress of operations of the company, its partners and competitors. In the same way, monitoring can be responsible for strengthening the company's information security capacity. In connection with innovation, it can, for example, keep abreast of new vulnerabilities in systems, techniques or strategies, but above all anticipate new forms of attack, risk and vulnerabilities. Finally, at the level of general management of available Big Data, original cross-referencing of data will enhance its content and reveal new avenues for innovation (Monino and Sedkaoui 2016).

23.8. References

Agogué, M., Arnoux, F., Brown, I., Hooge, S. (2013). *Introduction à la conception innovante : éléments théoriques et pratiques de la théorie C-K*. Presses des MINES, Paris.

Blanco, S. and Le Loarne, S. (2009). *Management de l'innovation*. Pearson Education France, Paris.

Goria, S. (2017). *Methods and Tools for Creative Competitive Intelligence*. ISTE Ltd, London, and John Wiley & Sons, New York.

Millier, P. (2015). *Segmenter les marchés du futur : la méthode de segmentuition*. Pearson Education France, Paris.

Monino, J.L. and Sedkaoui, S. (2016). *Big Data, Open Data and Data Development*. ISTE Ltd, London, and John Wiley & Sons, New York.

Oriesek D.F. and Schwarz, J.O. (2016). *Business Wargaming: Securing Corporate Value*. Routledge, Padstow.

Williams, P. (2015). *Visual Project Management*. Lulu Press, Morrisville.

24

Invention – Shared Inventions and Competitive Innovations

24.1. Introduction

Since the last quarter of the 20th century, new types of inventions have emerged significantly. They were increasingly based on "knowledge sharing", "cooperation between different actors", "reuse of forgotten inventions" and support from socio-political powers via societal dynamics. These new categories of inventions were the result of new invention processes. These new processes were based on "sharing trajectories" or (more recently) on "sharing networks" such as the S.C.O.T. Program (von Hippel 1986) or, finally, on "technological trajectories" defined as modes of action and the linking of all inventors.

The nature of innovations has also undergone significant change that will lead to new categories such as strategic innovations, disruptive innovations, disruptive strategies and strategic revolutions (Roy 2005). Introducing new links between shared inventions and competitive innovations, these new concepts and their reciprocal links will thus be defined:

– Definition 1: "A shared invention is produced by actors of different origins, actors with different knowledge gathered in shared intelligences. This production is helped by social dynamics developing the cohesion of these inventions and the reinvention of old or abandoned techniques" (Vigezzi 2019a).

– Definition 2: "A competitive innovation is produced by actors belonging to rational social groups, groups allowing the combination of their past experiences, their insertions and their professional contacts, a combination motivated by social

Chapter written by Michel VIGEZZI.

dynamics promoting competition and seeking to complement existing inventions by building their legal protections" (Vigezzi 2019b).

– Definition 3: These societal dynamics are defined as "changing relationships of forces, relationships of forces that can be analyzed by understanding the historical dynamics that determine their social, economic and cultural formations..." (Balandier 2004, p. 12).

24.2. From invention sharing to shared invention

The notion of sharing inventions was introduced more than four centuries ago by Giorgio Vasari, a well-known painter who analyzed the shared elements in the apprenticeships of painters, sculptors and architects, based on the sharing of styles and techniques of painters, sculptors and architects during those apprenticeships. This dimension of sharing was developed at the end of the 20th century by M. Hérold (1999), an art historian seeking to define the plural responsibilities of the aspect and realization of works of art. The notion of shared invention was then used in other fields such as economics, management, sociology and history, and was further refined with the work of D. Edgerton, C. McLeod and J. E. Bessen. We thus moved from training based on copies of "works of art" to new co-productions. Sharing became one of the foundations of inventions, now a central element in a phase to be followed by that of competitive innovations.

The concept of "shared invention" was thus born from a particular scientific sector, "history of art", a sector evolving with the development and multiplication of scientific programs in the field of "Humanities, Arts and Social Sciences" (HASS). It also developed in other scientific fields, with tools for analysis and action allowing for new definitions of the concept of "shared invention". Recent works such as those of Andrew Feenberg, David Edgerton and Christine McLeod (Edgerton 1999; McLeod 1999; Feenberg 2014) were applied by J. E. Bessen and Alessandro Nuvolari to business strategy, standards, interoperability and the reciprocal sharing of inventions between inventors (Bessen and Nuvolari 2013, p. 2).

The concept of shared inventions was then enriched by the notion of "Creative class groups", groups that create links between inventions considered as collective intelligences (Florida 2014) allowing the production of shared inventions and the creation of "industrial atmospheres" (a notion conceived by Alfred Marshall in 1919 in *Industry and Trade*). More recently, "Communities of thinkers" (Mokyr 2016), "reinventions" (Feenberg 2017) and analyses of the relations with other components of inventions, such as "New economic history" (a discipline born in 1977 favoring the application of cliometrics and econometrics to history), definitively confirmed the role and interest of these collective intelligences.

Other works on the "global insertion of agents" (Anido Freire 2018, p. 311) focused on new concepts such as "the transformations in innovation systems induced by globalization", "new macroeconomic solidarities", "creative globalization", "partnership between organizations within the framework of this globalization", getting closer to Stéphane Callens' "organization born global" (Callens 2018, p. 19), concepts born of the "collaborative economy", "groupings of forms of collaboration" that can be close to "positive civic dynamics" (Callens 2018, p. 106 and 112) and compatible with the notion of shared invention.

Theodore Koury and Erin G. Pleggenkuhle-Miles, demonstrating the existence of positive links between patent results through a study of 11593 patents produced by 256 companies in the biotechnology industry between 1985 and 2006, reinforced the concept of shared invention by associating it with the notion of *common inventions* (inventions similar to shared inventions) (Khoury and Pleggenkuhle-Miles 2011). More recently, Theodore Koury, Erin G. Pleggenkuhle-Miles and Jorge Walter showed that, in the biosciences, cost–benefit ratios were better for firms that used shared inventions (Khoury *et al.* 2017). Some shared inventions are thus called "shared" because these shares are mainly at the level of the production of the inventions and not at the level of their usage. They are thus based on the interventions of different actors seeking inventions meeting identical objectives and on the reuse of forgotten inventions.

From these evolutions, we can take away the list of the most important principles at the heart of shared inventions:

– the existence and effectiveness of societal dynamics corresponding to the production of shared inventions or to the incentive to seek these types of inventions;

– the provision of cumulative and coherent contributions from these different actors;

– the sharing of knowledge exchanges from different sectors and fields necessary for the invention sought;

– the creations and adoptions of other shared inventions or their components;

– the recourse to old and abandoned inventions that can be reinvented.

This sharing will therefore be based on knowledge, funding, the experience of gatherings of potential inventors and the ownership or memory of forgotten inventions, in a logic of production of inventions (Le Fevre 1987, pp. 33 and 68). Going beyond the "original combination of imitations" (Tarde 1890, p. 565), the shared invention will become an object that can be shared and used for different purposes. It will thus be an object characterized by one or several "sharing trajectories" and will be inserted into groups or networks of cooperation and sharing. All in all, these different attitudes, this knowledge sharing, cooperation between different actors and support from political powers via societal dynamics, would lead to a particular sharing, a sharing of the creation of inventions that will take the form of "sharing trajectories" or (a later notion) "sharing networks" such as the S.C.O.T. Program (von Hippel 1986) or "technological trajectories" defined as modes of action and the linking of actors (Amendola and Gaffard 1988).

24.3. From innovation to competitive innovation

Originating in the closing years of the 20th century (Hamel and Prahalad 1994), the concept of competitive innovation was developed within the management sciences and William Baumol considers it a systematic and indispensable activity (Baumol 2002). This "new game for firms" (Roy 2005, p. 99) was quickly integrated into a whole that remained close to the "new sectoral orthodoxy" that has sometimes been described as "strategic deconstruction", a notion that has been applied in the case of Logan and Burgundy wines (Hamel and Prahalad 1994).

This notion of competitive innovation is mainly used to identify growth opportunities and analyze changes in the balance of power within a sector… (Christensen and Bower 1995) and (Christensen 1997). According to Christian Marmuse, these competitive innovations are the result of "a reflection based not on the study of the greatest number, but on the identification of the specific characteristics of each organization" (Marmuse 2011, p. 14).

Based on these analyses, Dahan classifies competitive innovations into three levels according to their degree of radicality and the difficulties they encounter, distinguishing three types of strategy:

– incremental competitive innovation (knocking out competitors at their own game);

– radical competitive innovation (challenging the rules of the competitive game);

– strategic revolution (avoiding all forms of competition by creating one's own sector of activity) (Dahan 2005, p. 6).

Following a different logic, Jacques-Henri Coste differentiates competitive innovation from disruptive technical innovations and those born of individual initiative (Coste 2006, p. 122) because they are highly responsive to the constraints of an environment structured by a competitive logic. Following the same logic, Lee Fleming *et al.* show that these innovations depend on creativity, defined as a set of past experiences, professional integration and professional contacts of the actors concerned (Fleming *et al.* 2007).

Some authors insist on the fact that this creativity relies on the existence and cohesion of networks linking the actors concerned and on the consideration of the diffusion of competitive innovations, diffusion based on horizontal sharing (Sosa 2011).

They also show that strong and diversified links between operators working in close collaboration facilitate the creation of certain innovations that can be broken down into four criteria: incremental, radical, architectural (Le Loarne and Blanco 2011, p. 26) and strategic, referring to the search for "*core competencies*" that make it possible to forget or rebuild a difficult past (Hamel and Prahalad 1990, p. 84).

24.4. From societal dynamics to the links between shared inventions and competitive innovations

Few analyses have addressed the links between shared inventions and competitive innovations. Nevertheless, the article by Cohen S. K. and T. Caner shows that knowledge sharing has positive effects on "disruptive innovations" and reinforces the positive effects of a firm's production (Cohen and Caner 2016, p. 29), as the existence of networks and the participation of operators working closely together also enhances creativity.

The strength of the links between shared inventions and competitive innovations depends on a third set of factors that has undergone major change since the 1970s: societal dynamics. Precisely defined by G. Balandier, they are both "dynamics inherent to the social system" and/or "structures" (see above). This allows "societal dynamics" to be a major factor in the development of inventions and innovations and, above all, in their cohesiveness. These societal dynamics thus allow the development of efficient relations between techniques, societal relations and forms of work, which are necessary cohesions for technical changes and new forms of production and work (Vigezzi 2019a, 2019b).

These cohesiveness factors can be classified into different sets, which can be summarized in Table 23.1.

The cohesion of these shared inventions and competitive innovations is therefore based on the sharing of knowledge, the management of intra- and intersectoral competition, the management of competition and the management of technological change, all within the framework of the companies concerned.

Societal dynamics	Shared inventions	Competitive innovations	Cohesion factors
Societal dynamics encouraging shared creation	Creation of new technologies through the sharing of knowledge and know-how		Creation of knowledge-sharing groups and reinvention of certain forgotten techniques
Assistance in the transformation of the invention into an innovation and its transfer to different markets	Innovations created according to growth opportunities and changes in the balance of power within a sector… in order to successfully transform shared inventions into competitive innovations and to protect these innovations		Effective management of competition within and between sectors
Economic and social policies regarding cohesiveness and the management of technological change	Modes of management of technological change: allowing for the effective, balanced and equitable sharing of products and the results of these technological changes both at the level of invention and innovation …while defining the ways in which the social, economic and cultural dimensions of the societies concerned operate		

Table 24.1. *Cohesion factors necessary for the creation of shared inventions and their transformation into competitive innovations*

24.5. References

Amendola, M. and Gaffad, J.L. (1988). *La dynamique économique de l'innovation.* Economica, Paris.

Balandier, G. (1974). *Anthropologiques.* Presses universitaires de France. Coll, Sociologie d'Aujourd'hui, Paris.

Callens, S. (2018). *Creative Globalization.* ISTE Ltd, London and John Wiley & Sons, New York.

Dahan, N. (2005). *XIVème conférence internationale de management stratégique.* Pays de la Loire, Angers.

Edgerton, D. (1998). De l'innovation aux usages. Dix thèses éclectiques sur l'histoire des techniques. *Annales. Histoire, sciences sociales*, 4–5, 815–837 (translated into English in 1999 in *History and Technology*, 16, 1–26).

Feenberg, A. (2014). *Pour une théorie critique de la technique.* Eds. Lux/Humanités, Montreal.

Hamel, G. and Prahalad, C.K. (1994). *Competing for the Future.* Harvard Business School Press, Boston, MA.

von Hippel, E. (1986). Lead Users: A Source of Novel Product Concepts. *Management Science*, 32, 791–805.

Khoury, T.A. and Pleggenkuhle-Miles, E.G. (2011). Shared inventions and the evolution of capabilities: Examining the biotechnology industry. *Research Policy*, 40(7), 943–956.

McLeod, C. (1999). Negotiating the rewards of invention: The shop-floor inventor in Victorian Britain. *Business History*, 41(2), 17–36.

Uzinidis, D. and Vigezzi, M. (2020). Des inventions partagées aux innovations concurrentielles : réseaux et stratégies d'automatisation des entreprises. *Revue marchés et organisations*, 3(39), 111–139.

Vigezzi, M. (2019a). Inventions partagées et innovations concurrentielles. *Innovations : revue d'économie et de management de l'innovation*, 2(59), 243–260.

Vigezzi, M. (2019b). *World Industrialization: Shared Inventions, Competitive Innovations and Social Dynamics.* ISTE Ltd, London and John Wiley & Sons, New York.

25

Knowledge – Knowledge Management in Learning Innovative Organizations

25.1. Introduction

Knowledge management (KM) is the process of coordinating talent, systems and organizational structures in order to innovate and create value according to a strategic vision. Through KM processes, the capabilities of knowledge workers can be developed through better organizational systems and structures that enable learning, sharing, communication and innovation. KM leads to more agile, adaptive organizations that create value for customers and shareholders by identifying market opportunities and by developing innovative products, services, processes and business models. This requires attracting, developing and retaining talented knowledge workers whose values and beliefs converge with the organization's strategy and culture, and who are capable of translating the organization's strategic vision into innovation. It also requires the ability to learn with the surrounding ecosystem. As such, KM is an interdisciplinary field at the crossroads between anthropology, sociology, information technology, philosophy, economics, human resources management and psychology. This interdisciplinarity is both its greatest strength, as it allows a multi-perspective approach to the problem of organizational learning and innovation, as well as its greatest weakness, as it creates a heterogeneous field of research and managerial practices.

KM is as ancient as humanity. The act of identifying strategic knowledge and preserving it evolved with the history of information storage methods: initially by oral tradition, then in writing and then in print. The advent of modern computing systems, however, exponentially increased the volume, the speed and the complexity of the information we can now collect and store in modern organizations. The

---

Chapter written by Marcos LIMA.

diffusion of local area networks and the Internet in the 1990s made sharing this information and learning at a distance as inexpensive and easy as talking to a neighbor. Nonetheless, the human ability to transform this massive amount of data and information into actionable knowledge remains constrained by the limits of individual brains and the barriers of space and time to human socialization. This chapter discusses the role of humans, technology and organizations in the process of capturing value from KM.

This chapter is divided into four sections. We begin in section 25.2 by defining KM and knowledge from an organizational perspective. We then discuss a few historical KM frameworks. In section 25.4, we present three important KM concepts: learning organizations, KM strategies and KM tools. In the conclusion, we look at future perspectives for KM research.

25.2. Knowledge and management

In an organizational context, knowledge can be defined as the mental evaluation that leads to informed actions with the purpose of creating value. Value can be created by better understanding customer needs and expectations and managing organizational resources in order to deliver products and services to fulfill those needs. As knowledge is one of the most valuable, rare and difficult to imitate resources an organization can manage, KM is strongly anchored in the tradition of the resource-based view (RBV) of the firm. Underlying this view is the notion that knowledge can be managed like any other resource, such as people, money or materials.

This claim could lead to several controversies depending on one's definition of knowledge. If the definition given above is accepted (i.e. knowledge as a mental evaluation process), then KM is ultimately about the management of people capable of mental evaluations. In this perspective, KM would best be designated as a field of human resource management, organizational psychology and sociology. However, many streams of KM practitioners prefer to treat knowledge rather as data or information, which can be more easily managed using data processing and information technology systems. Data can be defined as objective facts about events. Information is a compilation of data, yielding messages with purpose and meaning. Data and information can indeed be planned, allocated and controlled like any other resource. Mental evaluations, however, take place in the minds of the knowers, and therefore cannot be dissociated from them. Furthermore, knowledge is indissociable from human organizations, with their interdependent structures of learning and knowledge reproduction.

This ambiguity has led to three schools of thinking about KM: a) the techno-centric approach, which assumes that tacit knowledge can be codified and made accessible to decision-makers; in this approach, KM is about optimizing information systems to support decision-making; b) the personalization (or organizational approach), which assumes that tacit knowledge cannot be completely codified; in this approach, KM is about attracting, developing and retaining talented knowledge workers who will use organizational systems to learn and create value; and c) the ecosystems (or inter-organizational) approach, which assumes that the codified knowledge within an organization is only a fraction of the overall knowledge base necessary to successfully achieve an organization's objective; in this approach, KM is not only about sharing knowledge internally, but also constantly seeking learning opportunities beyond organizational borders. These cumulatively more complex approaches to KM follow roughly the evolution of KM as a discipline, from its inception in the 1990s to the current state of the art.

25.3. History of KM frameworks

One of the earliest attempts to systematize the process of KM is Nelson and Winter's (1982) comparison of intra-organizational learning routines to the gene code in the cells of a living organism. In their evolutionary perspective, a good fit between an organization's decision-making routines and the environment could lead to a higher rate of survival (successful adaptation of certain types of organization). Thus, adapted routines lead to successful decisions, resulting in an organization's ability to grow (i.e. reproduce its genetic code). Conversely, poorly adapted organizations (i.e. whose learning routines and decisions are poorly adapted to environmental change) are condemned to disappear.

Cohen and Levinthal (1990) developed this notion further with their concept of "Absorptive Capacity" (AC). The authors define AC as an organization's ability to assimilate and apply new knowledge to gain competitive advantage. AC can thus be considered as the skillset required to use tacit and explicit knowledge to learn about the strategic environment and solve critical problems leading to better organizational performance. This framework uses a systems perspective, describing absorptive capacity in terms of input (the ability to acquire knowledge from multiple sources), process (an organization's overall ability to learn) and output (its ability to use knowledge to create value). The absorptive capacity framework is widely used in innovation research to discuss competitive advantage.

Nonaka and Takeuchi (1995) created one of the most widely used frameworks in the early days of KM to explain how these learning routines take place inside organizations. Known as the SECI model (an acronym using the initial letters of each stage of the framework), it portrays knowledge transfers from tacit to tacit (socialization), from tacit to explicit (externalization), from explicit to explicit (combination) and from explicit to tacit (internalization). The authors describe a knowledge spiral of sharing through organizational dialogue, collective reflection, networking and experimentation. The notion of "dynamic capabilities" (Teece *et al.* 1997) contributed to later stages of KM research by emphasizing an organization's ability to combine internal and external competences in order to exploit collaborative arrangements. Recent authors (see the summary by Dalkir 2013 or Massingham 2020) point out that these learning processes do not happen in the void, however. They must be framed in a context of flexible organizational structure designs, agile information technology systems and a culture of learning and trust. They also highlight the importance of learning with external sources such as partners, suppliers, customers, research centers and competitors. Combining internal and external learning environments facilitates knowledge transfers which form the innovation capabilities of an organization.

The succession of these frameworks illustrates how KM evolved from a linear, techno-centric approach to a more organizational approach in which several variables (human resource policies, structural design, culture, performance metrics) play an increasingly more important role. It culminates with an ecosystem-centric approach that emphasizes inter-organizational learning and capability development.

25.4. Key KM concepts

A number of key concepts are subjacent to these overall KM frameworks. This section gives a brief overview of some of the most important ones.

25.4.1. *Learning organizations*

Emerging in the 1980s and popularized by Peter Senge (1990), the concept of a learning organization emphasizes a firm's ability to learn from experience, adapt to change and grow its innovation capabilities. It is important not to confound organizational learning (the process of creating and transferring knowledge) with the learning organization itself, which enables this process through adapted strategies, flexible structures, a culture of sharing, information systems that facilitate collaboration and learning and key metrics for learning and performance. There can be organizational learning in contexts that would not qualify as a learning organization.

Learning organizations constantly update their problem-solving skills through experiential learning and knowledge sharing. They develop different learning styles (Kolb 1984) based on concrete experience and abstract conceptualization. Teams in learning organizations are very diverse, often making use of four complementary learning styles: a) diverging learners are creative individuals, capable of empathizing with customer needs; b) assimilating learners are logical, they can organize data and create rational models for framing innovation problems and opportunities; c) converging learners are pragmatic, they can lead to solutions and roadmaps; and d) accommodating learners favor trial-and-error approaches to problem solving and testing ideas in the real world. Innovation teams in learning organizations combine these styles in order to better identify unmet needs of their customers/stakeholders, developing competitive solutions accordingly.

25.4.2. *Knowledge management strategies*

Two major knowledge strategies are emphasized in the KM literature: learning by exploring (pursuing new knowledge to develop new forms of value creation) and learning by exploiting (refining existing knowledge to expand or enrich the current form of value creation). Ambidextrous organizations are capable of exploiting current business models, on the one hand, while exploring new ones, on the other hand. In competitive environments with low pressure to innovate, organizations may be able to survive merely by exploiting existing knowledge. This demands less sophisticated KM approaches than aggressive environments, in which exploring new avenues of growth is as important as competing in the existing ones.

In the techno-centered perspective which was prevalent in the early years of KM research, knowledge strategies focus on developing information technology tools that facilitate the codification and communication of data, information and knowledge. A more personalized vision of this process is embodied by the constructivist perspective, which requires people to actively interact with each other to construct intersubjective meaning. In this perspective, knowledge cannot be dissociated from the knowers and their actions: in the process of doing resides the greatest opportunities for learning.

In Nonaka and Takeushi's model (1995), the processes of socialization, externalization and combination are key to foster knowledge internalization by individuals, who then will re-share this knowledge by amplifying the spiral from the individual to the group, from the organizational to the inter-organizational learning space. This could lead to the creation of Communities of Practice (CoP), a group of people who share a deep interest or passion concerning certain topics and share their learning experience by applying the four types of knowledge diffusion in the SECI model.

CoPs typically have the following common characteristics: they share a common goal (to improve the performance of the group by applying best practices), they require a high degree of commitment (trust, interest, credibility, ethical behavior) and they usually take place in a real or virtual sharing space (face-to-face study groups, online storage resources, blogs, wikis, forums). In order to create these sharing communities, it is necessary to develop both human capital (people with the right knowledge, skills and competences) and social capital (networks of trust, as well as the quantity and quality of the relationships therein).

25.4.3. *Knowledge management tools*

The field of KM has accumulated a number of tools that have evolved along with the sophistication of information technology systems over the last quarter of a century. In the 1990s, these tools tended to revolve around local area network solutions such as corporate portals (intranets), data warehouses and knowledge repositories. In the 2000s, Internet-based solutions like voice-over-IP, chats, groupware, blogs and wikis became increasingly popular to facilitate sharing among communities of practice. In the last decade, artificial intelligence and big data have emerged as major trends, swinging the pendulum from the more people-focused perspective back to the more techno-centric approach to KM.

One of the greatest challenges of KM is to measure the value created by KM activities. It is quite easy to acknowledge that the hundreds of billions of dollars of valuation of companies like Microsoft or Google are largely attributed to their intangible assets (know-how, brand, technology) rather than the sum of their tangible ones (inventory of goods, material resources and other assets that appear in balance sheets). It is much more difficult, however, to break down those intangible assets and quantify their contribution to value creation. The Balanced Scorecard (BSC) by Norton and Kaplan (1996) is one of the most widespread tools in the domain of knowledge measurement. It takes into account not only the financial results, but also three other key dimensions of value creation: a) customers and customer perceptions; b) processes and the effective use of technology to lower costs and increase productivity; and c) learning and renewal, including the innovation capabilities. The BSC places the vision and strategy at the center of the evaluation process and focuses on the evolution of human and social capitals as predicting factors for innovation and success.

25.5. Conclusion: perspectives for KM

The field of KM has evolved constantly over the last few decades from a narrow focus on information technology solutions, to a more human-centered approach to knowledge sharing and ultimately an innovation ecosystem perspective. In spite of these advances, empirical evidence of the impact of KM remains inconclusive. The interdisciplinary nature of the field, its very high ambitions and the intangible nature of its object all converge to make KM a controversial and underdeveloped field. According to certain estimates (Massingham 2020), the word "knowledge" associated with "management" appears in fewer than 2.3% of the articles published in the top 20 management journals in the last 20 years.

Questions about how knowledge assets create value remain unanswered. Yet the need to account for the role of intangible assets in the value creation process has become greater as we transition from an industrial era into a knowledge economy in which information-based business models predominate. The techno-centric approach alone will certainly not provide clear answers to this question. The human-centered approach may help gain insights from sociology, cognitive psychology and organizational behavior, but it will certainly not produce a how-to guide to implementing KM processes. A hybrid approach, coupling both technology and people in a wider context of innovation ecosystems, is required to move this field forward.

25.6. References

Cohen, W.M. and Levinthal, D.A. (1990). Absorptive capacity: A new perspective on learning and innovation. *Administrative Science Quarterly*, 35(1), 128–152.

Dalkir, K. (2013). *Knowledge Management in Theory and Practice*. Routledge, London and New York.

Kaplan, R.S. and Norton, D.P. (1996). Linking the balanced scorecard to strategy. *California Management Review*, 39(1), 53–79.

Kolb, D.A. (1984). *Experiential Learning: Experience as the Source of Learning and Development*. Prentice Hall, Upper Saddle River.

Massingham, P. (2020). *Knowledge Management: Theory in Practice*. Sage, London.

Nelson, R.R. and Winter, S.G. (1982). *An Evolutionary Theory of Economic Change*. The Belknap Press of Harvard University, Cambridge, MA.

Nonaka, I. and Takeushi, H. (1995). *The Knowledge-Creating Company: How Japanese Companies Create the Dynamics of Innovation*. Oxford University Press, Oxford.

Senge, P.M. (1990). *The Fifth Discipline: The Art and Practice of the Learning Organization*. Doubleday, London.

Teece, D.J., Pisano, G., and Shuen, A. (1997). Dynamic capabilities and strategic management. *Strategic Management Journal*, 18(7), 509–533.

26

Location – Local Innovation Issues and Priorities for Public Intervention

26.1. Introduction

Since the 1980s, development policies have been strongly oriented towards the organization of territorial socio-economic dynamics based on the promotion of innovations. They are then manifested as a delegation of fields of competences from the central services to the regional and sub-regional services in employment, industrial development, education or research. The objective is to adapt to the new requirements of the modern economy by mobilizing local communities to implement a form of governance that aims first and foremost to make the most of local resources and know-how.

From the point of view of the literature, these movements (decentralization, regionalization) are industrialization policies based on the promotion of innovation: national innovation systems (Casadella and Uzunidis 2018), territorial innovation policies, territorial governance of innovation, regional innovation systems, etc.

However, in spite of the polysemy of the names, these different concepts refer to a singular phenomenon and present common characteristics. In the face of increasingly fierce global competition, they reflect the pressing need felt by States, encouraging them to focus on boosting innovation by linking territorial resources to create an environment conducive to the emergence of R&D projects that promote economic growth and job creation. Territoriality refers to the provisions that implement a spatial delimitation of territories and a redefinition of the modes of intervention granted to the organizations in charge of promoting innovation.

Chapter written by Cheikh Abdou Lahad THIAW.

Thus, localized innovation is similar to a concept that makes it possible to mobilize a territory's resources in order to encourage cross-transfer between the worlds of scientific research and industry. It is operationalized in various formats: clusters, competitiveness clusters, technopoles, technology parks, etc.

The purpose of this chapter is to examine the public actions undertaken to address innovation issues at a localized (sub-national) level. It proposes an analysis of innovation policies considered as a mobilization of resources and skills to drive territorialized economic development.

26.2. Innovation policies adapted to territories

The issue of territorial governance of innovation has been the subject of different conceptual approaches in the social science literature. Reflecting a desire to foster sustainable economic development based on the promotion of innovation, it is the subject of different theoretical and operational variants. Nevertheless, the *ultimate* objective remains more or less the same, namely to provide territories with a high and constant level of economic development through the promotion of innovation.

Indeed, the conceptual paradigms and theoretical models referring to territorial innovation development policies are disparate and temporal. Today, the objective shared by the modernized versions of these public policies is "to increase economic competitiveness by embedding on a specified territorial basis three resource actors of innovation: companies, public and private research centers, and education organizations" (Thiaw 2018).

From a conceptual point of view, the terms policy, territory and innovation can refer to various meanings and definitions. Thus, in addition to the work of semantic clarification necessary to grasp these notions, we are also working to mobilize the main theoretical corpuses in order to proceed, from the point of view of the literature, to a discernment of the evolution and operationalization on the economic sphere of territorial innovation policies (TIP). This analytical structuring allows us then to project ourselves into a prospective discussion process that examines the topicality of these policy models and the impact of economic and technological developments.

By policies, we understand public initiatives taken by public authorities to drive economic development. In territorial forms promoting innovation, they are similar to structuring the actors of a territory around innovation ecosystems. Known as Territorial Innovation Networks (TINs), these policy application ecosystems benefit from efforts by public authorities to promote innovation and a localized development dynamic over portions of local, regional and national territories.

This way of localizing economic activities has existed for more than a century with industrial districts (Marshall 1890; Becattini 1979), clusters (Porter 1998), innovative environments, local production systems and other more recent examples such as competitiveness clusters.

From our review of the literature emerge several classifications taking into account disparate conceptual logics. Two of them are of particular interest: the first considers a historical evolution based on the progress of economies and the transmutation of development priorities according to the eras; the second is based on principles of characterization based on strategic inclinations around innovation.

According to the first classification, the territorialized networks developed by development policies of a given period depend on the development factors in force and the ongoing economic progress. Thus, when the density of the production industry conditioned the competitiveness of nations and their economic development, the networks were "production" oriented. Territorial Production Systems are defined as the organization of a set of productive units (firms, research and training centers, interface organizations, professional organizations, etc.) deciding to join together to generate an overall productive dynamic through the exploitation of their geographical proximity and the creation of market and non-market relations of varying intensity. These network models differ from the others because they derive from the local development theory. In this category, we distinguish industrial districts (Torre and Tanguy 2014), the concept of flexible specialization, new industrial spaces and local productive systems.

Subsequently, the strengthening of innovation as a central driver of the economic growth of nations and the competitiveness of companies gave way to networks more marked by the preponderance of its driving factors. With the acceleration of the process of globalization of economies and the metamorphosis of the factors of firm competitiveness in the early 1990s (innovation, ICT and the knowledge economy), territorial innovation systems emerged as the main means of stimulating the economic growth of nations and mobilizing the variables essential for the competitiveness of modern firms. Indeed, the changing contours of the contemporary economy impact on the ways in which it generates factors of growth and competitiveness (Thiaw 2018). Having become the central theme of new forms of *territorial networks,* innovation constitutes a focal point dealing with the prospects for territorial development. Today, the configuration of territorialized networks is presented as the organization of a set of actors and entities (companies, public and private organizations, institutions) interacting to generate together new economically useful knowledge, which they use and disseminate as part of their production processes.

The second classification is the work of Moulaert and Sekia (2003) who distinguish three families of models of territorialization of innovation. The first includes *innovative environments*, *industrial districts* and *local production systems*. These are distinguished by their great capacity to generate dynamic innovative firms and by the primordial role played by institutions in the research processes as well as the partnerships required in the innovation processes. The second brings together forms of territorial networks close to the concepts of "Broader Systems of Innovation" (Edquist 1997) and "Regional Learning Economy" (Cook and Morgan 1998). Its operating mechanisms are akin to a transfer of the principles of institutional coordination of sectoral and national innovation systems to a regionalized level of development. The third specifies the "*new industrial spaces*" (Saxenian 1994) which are closer to Porter's cluster model (1998). The cluster concept evokes a spatial grouping within an agglomeration (cluster) of firms located in the same industry or value chain.

Thus, innovation coupled with the notion of territory broadens the initial concept of territorial systems of production to the benefit of territorial systems of innovation. The latter now represent a construct used as a generic name evoking the different regional models of innovation in which local institutional dynamics play a significant role (Moulaert and Sekia 2003, p. 291).

Concerning the notion of territory, this covers various contours referring to geographical, economic, sociological and political dimensions. It can be defined as a geographical space with natural, cultural and economic particularities monopolized by groups of individuals who take possession of its resources and develop material means and symbolic expressions (Thiaw 2018). As a result of the action of appropriation that characterizes it, the territory recovers a historical perspective that evokes the "experience", "practices" and "meanings" that are granted to it.

In the context of localizing innovation, the local or regional territory is favored as the geographic space targeted by policies to promote innovation. Thus, it is the object of massive support to boost competitiveness by irrigating the national economy with targeted benefits in order to generate innovation and jobs.

By territorial innovation policies, we mean the efforts of public authorities to identify, at the local level, key resources and skills as well as the associated levers of action, and then to structure local actors in order to implement a localized innovation system to stimulate territorialized economic development.

26.3. The territorialized priority of innovation

Today, "local development depends on innovation in territories" (Godet *et al.* 2018). The strengthening of the hazards of globalization and the opening up of markets, coupled with the "globalization" of production factors, are causing a strong metamorphosis in the framing angle of territorialization models, which leads public authorities to question the predominance of models of territorialized innovation networks that are more or less nomadic (Thiaw 2018). Similarly, with the removal of borders brought about by the digital industry, the various technological advances and the possibilities offered in terms of teleworking lead to the consideration of other forms of networking of organizations without a common spatial base. In other words, it seems legitimate today to question the relevance of issuing territorial innovation policies that allow the networking of actors located in distant geographical areas. That is, localized innovation for territorial economic development could be driven by partners located on distant geographical bases, but who decide to work together in order to pool their skills and meet common innovation challenges.

Indeed, what is sought in the spatial localization of innovation is more the generation of externalities between partners who are physically close, and the ease of pooling authorized by the geographical proximity of their resources and skills. In other words, the ultimate objective remains the search for complementarity around the spatio-temporal interactions of actors located in the same industrial, scientific, institutional, political and social context. However, their non-physical grouping and the non-geographical circumscription of their interactions may not have a negative impact on their modalities of intervention in innovation processes. Indeed, territorial innovation policies aim to bring partners together according to their perimeters of involvement in the key stages of the innovation process, and their effects "rely on the skills (scientific, technological, organizational, etc.) and resources (financial and/or cognitive) contained in each of the elements of the system, and on the nature and intensity of the interactions developed between them" (Depret *et al.* 2010).

26.4. Conclusion

Today, innovations appear to be more optimized when they are deployed in territorialized networks. If disparate theories have been conceptualized and operationalized on territorial innovation policies, they are mainly oriented towards a spatial conception: industrial districts (Marshall 1890; Becattini 1979), clusters (Porter 1998), innovative environments, local productive systems and competitiveness clusters, etc.

Nowadays, with the opening up of markets and the globalization of production factors, the angle from which models for the territorialization of innovation are framed has been seriously disrupted, leading public authorities to question the possibility of implementing concepts that are more or less nomadic. Indeed, it is now possible to envisage models that go beyond physical boundaries to focus solely on variables related to the skills and resources of actors, in order to foresee a networking of actors without a common spatial basis. Open Innovation, a concept in which innovation projects can be launched using internal technologies, or external ones with partners that may be located in geographically distant countries, is a relevant example.

This evolution of models opens up new analysis grids and new perspectives for the development of innovations, even if it can make innovation processes more complex. It can also be a positive response to the economic constraints that force firms to go beyond their borders to acquire valuable knowledge to complement their innovative capabilities. Subsequently, it offers interesting pragmatic possibilities for developing countries faced with the challenges of revitalizing their scientific heritage and industrial parks.

26.5. References

Becattini, G. (1979). Dal settore industriale al distretto industriale : alla ricerca dell'unità d'indagine della economia industriale. *Rivista di Economia e Politica Industriale*, 1.

Casadella, V. and Uzunidis, D. (2018). Les capacités d'innovation comme préalable à la formation d'un système national d'innovation. *Technologie et innovation*, 3, 1–15.

Cooke, P. and Morgan, K. (1998). *The Associational Economy: Firms, Regions and Innovation*. Oxford University Press, Oxford.

Depret, M.-H., Hamdouch, A., Monino, J-L., Poncet, C. (2010). Politiques d'innovation, espace régional et dynamique des territoires : un essai de caractérisation dans le contexte français. *Innovations*, 33(3), 85–104.

Desmarteau, R. and Saives, A.-L. (2008). Opérationnaliser une définition systémique et dynamique du concept de modèle d'affaires : cas des entreprises de biotechnologie au Québec. *Actes de la XVIIe conférence internationale de l'AIMS*, 28–31 May, Nice.

Edquist, C. (1997). *Systems of Innovation: Technologies, Institutions and Organizations*. Pinter Publishers, London.

Godet, M., Jarry, B., Chabaud, D. (2018). Innovation et territoires : les limites de la "métropolarisation" en France. *Population & avenir*, 738(3), 4–7.

Marshall, A. (1890). *Principles of Economics*. Macmillan and Co., London and New York.

Moulaert, F. and Sekia, F. (2003). Territorial innovation models: A critical survey. *Regional Studies*, 37(3), 289–302.

Porter, M. E. (1998). *Competitive Advantage: Creating and Sustaining Superior Performance*. Free Press, New York.

Saxenian, A. (1994). *Regional Advantage: Culture and Competition in Silicon Valley and Route 128*. Harvard University Press, Cambridge.

Thiaw, C.A.L. (2018). *L'innovation localisée pour le développement économique du Sénégal*. Éditions Harmattan, Paris.

Torre, A. and Tanguy, C. (2014). Les systèmes territoriaux d'innovation : fondements et prolongements actuels. In *Principes d'économie de l'innovation*, Boutillier, S., Forest, J., Gallaud, D., Laperche, B., Réseau de Recherche sur l'innovation, Tanguy, C., Temri, L. (eds). Peter Lang, Brussels.

27

Market – Market Innovation: Opening and Controlling New Markets

27.1. Introduction

Subscriptions for home delivery discovery boxes, products developed using consumer communities, customization of products and services, self-scanning in supermarkets, bulk distribution, producer stores, ephemeral stores, collaborative platforms promoting consumer-to-consumer (CtoC) transactions, nudges, etc. are all current examples of commercial innovations. Far from being exhaustive, this list highlights the dynamic evolution of commerce and the multifaceted nature of commercial innovations. This observation is in line with Gallouj's (2004) conclusions, which underline the richness and diversity of innovative devices in commercial organizations.

The shortcut to not commit would be to reduce business innovation in the introduction of a new product or technology in a given sector. Although these forms of innovation have been the subject of much research, the contours of business innovation are much broader. Thus, Choukroun (2012) considers that commercial innovation brings progress to mankind in its way of living, trading and being.

In the first approach, the term "innovation" implies a novelty, a relatively strong break from what was previously proposed. As for the adjective commercial, it specifies the field of application of this novelty, commerce. Commercial innovation answers the question "how to do things differently", both with the object of the exchange and in the very construction of this commercial exchange.

Chapter written by Béatrice SIADOU-MARTIN.

It can concern technical and technological aspects, as well as social, organizational and informational aspects.

A historical perspective on the forms of exchange of goods and services highlights "trade revolutions", defined as events in which commercialization in a given sector evolves to meet consumer needs differently (Moati 2011).

Department stores, symbols of modernity and progress, constituted a "commercial revolution" during the 19th century. They became key players in the retail trade. Their emergence can be explained by sociological, technical, technological, informational and organizational changes such as urbanization, the development of means of transport, especially railways, and mass production. We will first consider the factors that explain and enable the emergence of commercial innovation.

Nowadays, many connected objects have not progressed beyond the idea or prototype stage, due to the lack of a significant potential market or an efficient business model. Regardless of how new or ingenious an idea may be in terms of commercialization, it is still a risky action in this phase of adjustment between supply and demand. It is essential to question the characteristics of commercial innovation and the conditions for its success. This is the subject of the second part of this contribution.

27.2. Factors that foster business innovation

Many factors explain this imperative for business innovation on the part of companies. First, one of the explanatory factors for innovation concerns the current and future, or prospective understanding of markets. Dupuis (2002) emphasizes this point by indicating that innovation implies this "visualization of the market" dimension as well as the methods for gathering these insights or weak signals. As such, innovation is a strategic nature because the firm must not simply defend its market share and its current position even though it is currently in a favorable position.

This is in line with the Schumpeterian approach, which considers innovation as a process of "creative destruction". Thus, by appearing, an innovation leads to the disappearance of a product or an activity, but in parallel, allows the emergence of another product or activity. This vision is found in the classic product approach in marketing literature, based on the product lifecycle marked by four successive stages: launch, growth, maturity and decline.

Innovation means analyzing weak signals and consumer insights, in order to find new growth opportunities and, without doubt, bring new markets to the fore. Without this proactive attitude, the company could risk being in trouble because of a new entrant and a business proposition that would better satisfy the needs of consumers. In the end, it is the market, or more precisely, it is the consumer who judges the relevance of innovations by buying and, above all, re-purchasing the products and services offered, or by visiting distribution points. This behavioral loyalty should also be accompanied by attitudinal loyalty, which makes it possible to build a true relationship with the brand.

In addition, market conditions, characterized by turbulence and competition, drive the need to renew the terms of trade and seek commercial innovation. This innovation then allows an escape from intra-typical competition on existing markets, a redesign of the role of the players, and the creation of new sources of differentiation. Thus, the boundaries between, on one hand, the companies in charge of designing, manufacturing and distributing products and, on the other, the individuals, who take on the role of receiver as buyer and/or consumer, are gradually blurring. Consumption is a structuring element for individuals, and they wish to "give meaning to their consumption" by taking on new roles.

In addition, the spatiotemporal framework of the exchange must be questioned because it sheds interesting light on commercial innovations. Thus, Gallouj (2007) analyzes the commercial innovations implemented by mass retailing by considering "household time use". He shows that the innovations respond to three trajectories: the liberation and enrichment of time (e.g. drives, self-scanning), outsourcing (e.g. ready-made products, fruit and vegetable cutting departments), and finally a combinatorial trajectory.

This example perfectly illustrates the change from the dichotomous paradigm that is built on the opposition of the "shopping experience" and "e-shopping experience" to the ubiquitous paradigm. The ubiquitous paradigm can be broadly summarized by the acronym ATAWAD, which means "anytime, anywhere, any device", in other words, consuming anywhere, anytime and through any physical or electronic interface. Badot and Lemoine (2013) describe the "meta-shopping experience" that "forces retailers to understand what consumers expect from each channel and to integrate it into an overall offer. The lived experience is then no longer strictly linear because the consumer will then pilot an 'omni-channel experience' that makes sense and corresponds to the expectations they have of each mobilized channel" (p. 4).

Under the combined effect of these different influences, the commercial relationship is undergoing strong changes.

27.3. The multifaceted nature of business innovation

In 2005, the Oslo Manual emphasizes this multifaceted nature by proposing to define an innovation as “the implementation of a new or significantly improved product (good or service), or (production) process, a new marketing method, or a new organizational method in business, workplace organization or external relations”. Thus, four categories of innovations are identified: product or service, process, organization and marketing. More specifically, the latter category corresponds to the implementation of a new marketing method involving significant changes in the design or packaging, placement, promotion or pricing of a product.

Thus, the marketing literature proposes several typologies of commercial innovations, which are summarized in Table 27.1.

More recently, researchers have focused on sources of business innovation. In his typology proposed in 2007, Gallouj (2007) adopts a broad vision and declines commercial innovation according to seven dimensions, which are the new sales method, the new sales format, the new product, the new service, the new internal process, the new external process and the application of new technologies. In the same way, Choukroun (2012) identifies seven sources of commercial innovation in distribution, which are the product, the concept, the animation, the online customer link, the organization model, the partnerships and the productivity wheel.

There is also the question of the diffusion of commercial innovation. Rogers’ (1983) work identifying five consumer profiles (innovators, early adopters, early majority, late majority and late adopters) highlighted the role of peers in this diffusion. Indeed, commercial innovation leads to pedagogical support from the creator and cognitive, social and behavioral learning from the user-consumer. Although the technology has been perfected for many years, retail chains are using human resources to support self-service checkouts.

Defined in these terms, business innovation is a key element in the life of companies: an interesting catalyst for internal entrepreneurial dynamics and a lever for consumer loyalty. Indeed, Diallo *et al.* (2015) show that business innovations have an impact on relational variables such as brand and place attachment.

Authors	Typology of innovation	Illustration
Badot and Cova (1992)	– Incremental innovation that introduces a small difference from previous proposals – Radical innovation based on a technological disruption – Social innovation that challenges buying habits – Technical innovation that changes the relationships between the actors in the supply chain	While the tablet can be described as an incremental innovation, the introduction of the smartphone into the cell phone market is an example of disruptive innovation The "Ruche qui dit oui" wants to "re-create a link between consumers and producers" and relies on digital tools for order management
Dupuis (2002)	– Innovative concepts that allow us to rethink the "seller–consumer" interface, a new sales format – Innovation of flows that offer to rethink vertical relationships – Organizational innovation – Relational innovation relating to the modification and improvement of the links between actors in the sector – Architectural innovation, a combination of the different forms already identified	Many commercial innovations can be considered as architectural innovations. Thus, the concept entitled "Le Comptoir", developed by Boulanger, led this distributor to rethink its range, the "vendor–consumer" interface as well as the technological equipment of these points of sale, including interactive terminals for ordering products or picking them up
Moati (2011)	– New store formats – Re-founding of the modes of organization of the commercial enterprise – New business models	The development of the Internet has allowed the emergence of the freemium marketing strategy. For example, some mobile applications are completely free for the user, but derive their profitability from data exploitation or advertising revenues
Gallouj (2004)	– Extensive logic: adding services to the basic service – Limiting or purifying logic: reducing the level of service and withdrawing benefits that are deemed secondary – Logic of intensive innovation: adding new technologies, or better exploiting existing technologies – Logic of combinatorial innovation: combinations of the previous forms	If the luxury hotel industry renews itself by adding new services, the low-cost model corresponds to this limiting logic

Table 27.1. *Typologies of market innovation*

27.4. Conclusion

This presentation highlights the multifaceted nature of business innovation and underlines its relevance to corporate strategy. By mobilizing different resources (human, financial or informational), commercial innovation challenges the internal entrepreneurial dimension.

Nevertheless, the academic literature needed an in-depth review. Thus, the CREDOC study invited us to perceive commercial innovation "as a field of study to be favored in order to observe the changes at work within the commerce and distribution sector" (2015, p. 38).

In fact, many avenues of research can be identified. First, Diallo *et al.* (2015) show that although forms of business innovation appear to be the same in different cultural systems, the perceived sources of innovation appear to be different. This cross-cultural issue deserves further investigation. Second, the issue of the diffusion of this commercial innovation is an interesting avenue of research: is this development based on sectoral mimicry? Is it identical according to the nature of the business innovation? Third, commercial innovation can appear as a complex innovation that combines several dimensions, which has been highlighted under the term combinatorial model or architectural innovation. Is it possible to establish typologies of these forms? Are they more efficient?

27.5. References

Badot, O. and Cova, B. (1992). *Le néo-marketing*. ESF éditions, Montrouge.

Badot, O. and Lemoine, J.F. (2013). Du paradigme dichotomique de l'expérience d'achat au paradigme ubiquitaire. *Recherche et applications en marketing*, 28(3), 3–13.

Choukroun, M. (2012). *Les dynamiques de succès de la distribution : l'efficacité par le pragmatisme et l'innovation*. Dunod, Paris.

Dembo, A., Hebel, P., Vittori, A., Capon, G., Duchen, P., Lehuede, F. (2015). L'innovation commerciale face aux attentes des consommateurs : quelles évolutions depuis 2011 ? *Cahiers de recherche du CREDOC*, 50.

Diallo, M.F., Seck, A.M., Sall, F.D. (2015). L'innovation perçue et ses conséquences dans les centres commerciaux modernes d'Afrique : l'exemple du Sénégal. *Management avenir*, 7, 57–79.

Dupuis, M. (2002). Innovation dans la distribution : les paradoxes de la prospective. *Revue française de marketing*, 188(3), 61–68.

Eurostat, O. (2005). *Manuel d'Oslo : principes directeurs pour le recueil et l'interprétation des données sur l'innovation*. OECD Publishing, Paris.

Gallouj, C. (2004). Innovations et trajectoires d'innovation dans le grand commerce : une approche lancastérienne. *Innovations*, 19(2), 9–25.

Gallouj, C. (2007). Innovation commerciale et usage du temps des ménages : un cadre conceptuel. *Innovations*, 1, 179–204.

Moati, P. (2011). *La nouvelle révolution commerciale*. Odile Jacob, Paris.

Rogers, E.M. (1983). *Diffusion of Innovations*, 3rd edition. Free Press, New York.

28

Model – Business Models for Innovation Strategies

28.1. Introduction

A "business model" can be simply defined as the activities that determine how an organization functions. More specifically, it describes the logic or rationale embedded in the way an organization creates value and how it obtains revenues from the value created. Value is created when an organization fulfills customer needs and/or meets other stakeholder expectations. These value-creating activities include the establishment of partnership networks, the combination of valuable resources and the continuous pursuit of process improvements in order to create a competitive value proposition. The value proposition and how it is delivered must be constantly adapted to market expectations in order to generate competitive advantage and sustainable growth. In the end, every business model must address Peter Drucker's fundamental questions: who (is the customer), what (do they value) and how (we can make money out of this value equation at the lowest cost with appropriate quality).

The process of recombining these activities in new ways that deliver superior value is called business model innovation. There is a consensus among innovation experts that innovative technologies and ideas *per se* have little economic value without a competitive business model to bring them to market (targeting the right people through the right channels, with adequate pricing and revenue models, with efficient resources and activities and with a competitive partnership and cost structure).

Chapter written by Marcos LIMA.

It is important to distinguish between "business model innovation" (BMI) and "innovative business models" (IBM). While BMI is the everyday pursuit of constantly improving the value creation rationale of an organization, often by imitating and adapting existing competitor strategies, innovative business models (IBM) bring a new-to-the-world way to create value. For instance, when Disney decided to launch their streaming service in 2019, thus changing the rationale for the delivery of content from DVDs to cloud-based streaming, they were doing business model innovation by replicating Netflix's success formula. From Disney's perspective, this can be considered a business model innovation in the sense that it completely changed the way it delivers content. This innovation was not, however, an innovative business model. Netflix had pioneered the streaming business model several years ago.

This chapter is divided into six parts. We begin by briefly discussing the history of business models as a construct and how it has evolved over recent decades. We then present a typology of business models' elements and how they are interrelated. In section 28.4, we emphasize the distinction between new business model design, typical of entrepreneurial firms in their early development stages, versus business model reconfiguration, which more mature companies are bound to do in order to remain relevant over time. In the final two sections, we warn against the danger of "business model inertia" and the importance of constantly updating our business model as a source of competitive advantage.

28.2. A brief history of the evolution of business models

Teece (2010) argues that business models have existed since pre-classical eras. Until the advent of the Internet, most business models consisted of manufacturing goods or providing services through traditional retail channels and with rather linear supply chains. The process of creating value often consisted simply of buying and selling goods or labor. Most industrial-age business models relied on this one source of revenue.

In the late 19th century, newspapers introduced the advertising revenue model that would later be imitated by radio and TV. Known as a double-sided business model, this strategy allowed the possibility of offering content at a lower cost (or even for free) to a large base of content consumers and selling their attention time to advertisers. An interdependence is established between the two sides of this type of model: the bigger and more loyal the audience, the more the advertising revenue.

In the 1950s, Diners Club created an innovative double-sided business model that generated revenues from both merchant fees and customer membership. Later, credit cards like Visa and Mastercard specialized in gathering and selling data about their users, thus creating a triple source of revenues. In the 1960s, Xerox experienced vertiginous growth by leasing expensive copying machines and charging on a pay-per-copy basis to millions of businesses across the globe, an example of product-service-system (PSS) business model innovation. In this type of value creation process, the user has no upfront costs of buying a product, but rather subscribes to an all-inclusive service that includes the product, its maintenance and upgrade. Rolls Royce adopts a similar business model for its turbines, selling "hours of flight" with highly specialized maintenance included for the duration of the lifetime of its products.

The 20th century was filled with such examples of innovative business models. However, starting in the early 2000s, the fast adoption of Internet technologies (and the disintermediation opportunities they created) opened the gates to an unprecedented flood of business model innovation opportunities. The connected-localizable-computer-in-your-pocket era of smartphones pushed this trend further: suddenly it was possible to have a plethora of free (or freemium) online services based on advertising, low-cost airlines that circumvented proprietary global distribution systems, free next-day delivery of millions of products from e-commerce platforms, car sharing services that are more effective and convenient than traditional taxis and person-to-person real estate marketplaces that would compete with traditional hotel chains. These post-industrial organizations became profitable not only by creatively leveraging their own resources but also (and above all) by weaving complex supplier and partnership networks using the informational cloud as a platform for value creation.

Open innovation business models (Chesbrough 2010) are an incarnation of the possibilities created by post-industrial trends of the new millennium. Once very protective of all their intellectual property, companies like IBM, Tesla and Procter and Gamble have realized that establishing licensing agreements to key technologies (and sometimes even giving them away or open sourcing them) created value by establishing common standards, increasing market potential and facilitating shared gain opportunities for multiple actors in an ecosystem. Linux is an example of an open-source software system that allows multiple stakeholders (developers, distributors, business consulting services) to co-create value around a free, commoditized product.

Hardly ever used before the 1990s, the phrase "business model" thus became commonplace in business schools and innovative companies at the dawn of the 21st century, as cloud computing, connected devices, Big Data and artificial intelligence all converged to create a post-industrial economy in which complex combinations of information, technology and marketing expertise gave rise to new corporate empires, as well as several start-up ecosystems competing to incubate the next generation of Internet giants.

28.3. Types of business model innovation

According to the Boston Consulting Group (2009), there are six essential components to any business model, divided into two categories: a) value proposition components (target segments, product or service offering, revenue model) and b) operating model components (value chain, cost model, organization). Each one of these six components offers different innovation possibilities. The three types of value proposition innovations are:

– targeting innovation (also called position innovation). Addressing the "who we serve" question, this strategy consists of adapting an existing value creation process to an underserved customer segment. Examples could include an "AirBnB for pets" or a "Netflix for children";

– product or service innovation: addressing the "what we do" question, this strategy consists of improving product attributes to adapt it to changing customer expectations or gain competitive advantage. Heinz's upside-down ketchup bottle is a trivial example of how incremental product innovation can create value by slightly changing the packaging;

– revenue model innovation: addressing the "how we can make money" question, this often consists of shifting the burden of funding an organizational activity from one customer to another. Thus, advertisers pay for the costs of Google's infrastructure in exchange for the privilege of inserting contextualized messages in ubiquitous free online services such as YouTube, Google Search and Adsense-enabled third-party websites.

On the operating model side, the three business model innovation types are:

– value chain innovation ("how we co-create value with our partners"). This approach could involve, for instance, using integrated information systems to increase the speed, reduce the cost and improve the variety of products available. Zara's fast fashion model allows them to have an unprecedented flexibility in offering trendy clothes by combining economies of scope and scale with its supply chain;

– cost model innovation ("how we can become more efficient"). Low-cost airlines are an example of how, using the same technology, human resources and materials, EasyJet gained competitiveness by improving the distribution, logistics and pricing mechanisms of typical air travel incumbents;

– organizational innovation ("how we can recombine our resources, systems and structures to become more efficient"). Holacracy organizations are an extreme example of this kind of business model innovation. By eliminating most hierarchical barriers and trusting a bottom-up approach to problem solving, Zappos created a flexible, agile and innovative organizational model that combined competitiveness with employee satisfaction and motivation.

These sources of value creation are by no means self-excluding: they can and should be combined in the process of designing innovative business models or developing business model innovation.

28.4. Business model design versus business model reconfiguration

Massa and Tucci (2013) make an important distinction between two types of business model innovation: business model design (BMD, defined as the creation of a business model for a newly formed organization) and business model reconfiguration (BMR, defined as recombining the elements of existing business models in more mature organizations). Not all BMD or BMR result in a business model innovation, however: to be considered as such, the output of the business model design or reconfiguration should address *unmet* needs of customers or stakeholders, thus providing superior value. Increased competitiveness is the ultimate measure of successful BMD or BMR.

BMD is typical of entrepreneurial start-ups. It involves agile experimentation with product and process innovation, measuring feedback from prototypes and quickly adjusting the business model accordingly. Business model designers ask several "what if" questions and try real-world experiments to test solutions to unmet needs. A small percentage of new BM designs will be so successful in addressing those unmet needs that they will eventually disrupt incumbents in the industry, becoming the new incumbents.

BMD typically uses one or several of the following frameworks/developing tools:

– business model canvas – created by Alexander Osterwalder and his PhD supervisor Yves Pigneur (2010), this framework quickly became the standard tool to design new business models among entrepreneurs, in great part thanks to its intuitive, visual nature (Lima and Baudier 2017);

– design thinking – based on the principles of empathizing with customer needs before brainstorming solutions and creating/testing prototypes, design thinking has strongly influenced both start-up BMD and advanced product development processes in mature organizations (Brown 2009);

– lean start-up – initially adopted by software developers, this approach is focused on a cycle of building minimum viable products, measuring the fit between customer expectations and perceptions and then improving on the original ideas based on customer feedback (Ries 2011).

All three frameworks share the principles of "testing before you build it" that permeate most business model design processes among innovative start-ups of the 21st century. They tend to follow a pattern that Sarasvathy (2001) calls "effectuation": a process in which actors favor small-scale action over long periods of reflection and analysis when creating innovative business models. According to this perspective, data for business model design must come from real-world, first-hand experiments rather than secondary databases or armchair insights.

According to Amit and Zott (2012), business model reconfiguration can happen in three (non-excluding) ways: a) adding new activities; b) combining existing activities in new ways or c) changing the parties involved in value creation (suppliers/partnership network). Other BMR examples can be found in the BCG types described above. Larger organizations are increasingly adopting business model design tools to reconfigure their existing value creating strategies. However, more mature businesses often lack the agility and the cultural "blank slate" of start-ups that could allow them to design innovative business models from scratch. They must therefore reconfigure their existing activities while taking into account the inertia of their existing business models. So-called "ambidextrous" companies manage to exploit their existing business model while exploring new ones.

28.5. Business model inertia

When a company fails to change its business model in the face of a changing environment (market, economy, competitors, socio-cultural trends, technology), they often fall prey to what may be called the "sleeping frog syndrome" (an allusion to the age-old tale of a frog that slowly adapts to the changing water temperature in a cooking pot, falls asleep and dies before it realizes the water is boiling).

As Clayton Christensen explained in his classic "innovator's dilemma" (1997), successful companies tend to become enthralled by the "dominant logic" of their current business models, preventing managers from identifying new opportunities and threats that could eventually disrupt them. The initial margins of new business models are often unattractive for prosperous incumbents. They prefer rather to overserve premium customers in the high end of the market, leaving less profitable customers to new entrants with different business models. As these competing business models mature, however, they become more profitable thanks to lower operating costs and better value propositions, eventually forcing incumbents off their captive markets.

An antidote against business model inertia is the ambidextrous experimentation (exploration) of new business models in parallel to the exploitation of existing value creation processes (Chesbrough 2010). The three frameworks of business model design exposed above could be used in these cases to experiment with different business model innovation scenarios. However, it is important to keep these experiments "safe" from the intervention of stakeholders invested in the historical business model, lest they try to use their power and influence to abort any threat from the emerging new business. Thus, business model innovation in mature organizations often requires creating competitive spin-off structures and protecting their different resource allocation strategies and organizational culture. Knowing how to manage this transition from a dying business to a new business model is a delicate balancing act that requires commitment, vision and persistence on the part of incumbents.

28.6. BMI and competitive advantage

According to Amit and Zott (2012), business model innovation is an under-utilized source of future value creation. Considering its strategic importance, it should be treated as an important source of sustainable competitive advantage. Indeed, competitors often find it more difficult to imitate a whole value creation process than simply copying a new product or service. Furthermore, the practice of constantly experimenting with new business model scenarios can attune managers to the threats of competitors developing their own innovative ways of addressing unmet customer needs, thus facilitating the implementation of preventive measures.

Developing business model innovation is not the same thing as pursuing a competitive strategy. The former focuses on the reconfiguration of internal resources and activities, whereas the latter focuses on adequately positioning a company's value creation process relative to external opportunities and threats. According to Teece (2010), coupling a company's competitive strategy with its business model analysis is key to protecting competitive advantage in a fast-paced, technologically volatile environment. It is important therefore not only to experiment with new business model scenarios but also to understand how a rival's business models are designed, in order to explore and exploit opportunities that would be hard to replicate by competitors (or else unpalatable to them because of their current positioning in terms of customer expectations, supplier agreements and partnerships).

28.7. Conclusion: perspectives in BMI research

Still in its infancy, the concept of business model innovation lacks theoretical foundations in business studies (Teece 2010). This is an interdisciplinary topic that has enjoyed growing attention from researchers in marketing, strategy, human resources, economics and finance. In spite of the academic prominence of business model innovation in the last decade, executives still tend to focus on product, service or process innovation. With this limited perspective, they neglect to evaluate their organization activities as an integrated, interdependent value creation process. The success of Internet-era companies has shown how superior results can be obtained by using new technologies to redesign or recombine resources, activities and partnership networks, on the one hand, with novel customer segments, value propositions and revenue models, on the other.

However, history has also shown how innovative ideas and technologies decoupled from a viable business model are unlikely to succeed. Mature businesses must learn from the experimentation processes of start-ups. They must constantly question their current flow of value creation, finding opportunities to deliver superior value at lower costs internally, while scanning the strategic environment for competitive threats and unmet customer needs. Ambidextrous companies must learn how to exploit existing business models while developing innovative approaches to value creation. Leaders of these organizations must create a safe haven for experimentation in spin-off business units, giving them the freedom to develop their own organizational culture and structure in order to yield alternative (sometimes cannibalizing) strategies of value creation.

28.8. References

Amit, R., Zott, C., Pearson, A. (2012). Creating value through business model innovation. *MIT Sloan Management Review*, 33(3), 40–50.

Brown, T. (2009). *Change by Design: How Design Thinking Transforms Organizations and Inspires Innovation.* Harper Collins, New York.

Chesbrough, H. (2010). Business model innovation: Opportunities and barriers. *Long Range Planning*, 43(2–3), 354–363.

Christensen, C. (1997). *The Innovator's Dilemma: When New Technologies Cause Great Firms to Fail.* Harvard Business Review Press, Boston, MA.

Lima, M. and Baudier, P. (2017). Business model canvas acceptance among French entrepreneurship students: Principles for enhancing innovation artefacts in business education. *Journal of Innovation Economics Management*, 2(23), 159–183.

Massa, L. and Tucci, C. (2013). Business model innovation. *The Oxford Handbook of Innovation Management*, 20(18), 420–441.

Osterwalder, A. and Pigneur, Y. (2010). *Business Model Generation*. Wiley, New York.

Ries, E. (2011). *The Lean Startup: How Today's Entrepreneurs Use Continuous Innovation to Create Radically Successful Businesses*. Crown Business, New York.

Sarasvathy, S.D. (2001). Causation and effectuation: Toward a theoretical shift from economic inevitability to entrepreneurial contingency. *Academy of Management Review*, 26(2), 243–263.

Teece, D.J. (2010). Business models, business strategy and innovation. *Long Range Planning*, 43(2–3), 172–194.

29

Network – Networks and Development of Innovation Processes

29.1. Introduction

The work of Project SAPPHO (Rothwell 1972) was the first to identify the importance of access to external sources of information when a company wishes to innovate. The distinction between information and knowledge, and then the gradual recognition of the importance of knowledge as a central resource in innovation processes, led to recognition that companies do not possess all the knowledge necessary for their innovation processes internally. Firms are thus led to cooperate within the framework of networks in order to innovate as soon as they lack certain knowledge.

In this chapter, we will essentially deal with the role of innovation networks, which will be defined as formal cooperations between innovative firms and other organizations, either firms – other businesses in the group, customers, suppliers, consulting firms – or public research organizations. The fact that the cooperation is formal does not necessarily imply a contract (still a minority case in many industrial sectors), but that there is a cooperation project involving jointly defined objectives and the pooling of means or resources, as well as a long-term relationship between organizations, as opposed to informal interactions that are ad hoc in nature.

In the first part, we will see how evolutionary approaches have produced fine analyses of the innovation process within companies. However, they have taken little account of the environment as a contributor or creator of innovation resources. In the second part, we will show that, conversely, regional sciences have reiterated the importance of space and territories in innovation processes.

Chapter written by Delphine GALLAUD.

29.2. Knowledge, learning and innovation network

Richardson (1972) was the first author to identify the need for comapanies to cooperate in innovating when they seek to develop complementary activities that are not similar to those they already carry out. Teece (1992) picks up this argument that the cause of cooperation is the need to develop complementary activities, as well as the need to access knowledge and skills held by potential cooperation partners, since knowledge is supposed to foster innovation by enabling firms to modify their product, process or organization. Initially, the work was oriented towards identifying the useful actors to be mobilized in the innovation processes, putting forward customers, suppliers, competitors, consulting firms or research organizations. Jensen *et al.* (2007) then introduced the distinction between two major types of innovation processes: science-based ("science-technology-innovation (STI)" mode) and practice-based ("doing-using-interacting (DUI)" mode). In both modes, companies rely both on their internal knowledge and on cooperation with external sources. In the first mode, the internal learning process takes place mainly in the firm's R&D department and mainly involves engineers and qualified personnel. It is based on the mobilization of factual scientific knowledge, and formalized knowledge. In terms of cooperation, it mobilizes public research organizations. Internally, the second mode is based on a knowledge production process linked to learning-by-doing, and trial and error; it mobilizes all the firm's personnel since it is a learning process carried out in the course of the routine production process. In terms of cooperation, it mobilizes information from client–supplier interactions (identified in the work of Lundvall (1985)). These two modes are mobilized in a different way according to the sectors or the size of the firms, as well as according to the type of innovation that a firm seeks to introduce during its development process. The interaction mode is globally dominant because innovations are most often incremental. Sectors based on economies of scale (scale-intensive) and those dominated by suppliers will make greater use of this mode (Pavitt 1984). Science-based sectors, on the other hand, (which are globally less numerous in the economy) make greater use of the STI mode. Jensen *et al.* (2007) also identified a significant number of firms that are able to mobilize both learning-by-doing and STI-type learning and are the most successful in introducing innovations.

In the early 2000s, the open and collaborative innovation model (Chesbrough 2003) reinforced this argument about the importance of external sources of innovation. But it went beyond this by proposing, above all, an integrative model of the innovation process that encouraged companies to optimize the production of innovations by using several processes simultaneously. First of all, it suggested they should seek to multiply informal interactions, so as to increase opportunities for detecting innovations but, at the same time, use "free revealing" of innovations to competitors, so as to encourage them to provide information on their own innovations. Second, they should seek to mobilize cooperation to develop innovation projects. Finally, they must use technology markets, either to acquire opportunities to develop an innovation on the basis of knowledge produced by other firms, or to protect their innovations.

But the open and collaborative model of innovation, while it presents itself as an integrative model of the variety of innovation processes by encouraging firms to mobilize both external sources, i.e. informal interactions, and formalized cooperation, actually places more emphasis on external sources. Indeed, they are considered to be a way of developing innovation that would be more novel than formalized cooperations. Access to external sources, which often seems easier for organizations than cooperation because it is less formalized, can also present difficulties. This access can be achieved through social network monitoring; however, this takes time, as only large companies have the opportunity to set up this type of monitoring. In the same way, free revealing makes it impossible to make the most of lead times over competitors.

Some firms that develop their innovations more slowly do not have the opportunity to participate in informal exchanges of this type. Furthermore, the incentive to multiply external sources of information does not necessarily take into account the time needed to maintain contacts and obtain information (which can be lengthy), nor does it take into account the differentiated quality of the contacts. Multiple sources can result in "noise", inefficient information and, after a period of time, also lead to redundant information. Finally, informal interactions in fact frequently take place through the interpersonal networks of individuals, which are generally quite homogeneous and provide little variety in information sources.

Thus, this model seems to be becoming a managerial standard for organizational innovation. It therefore seems important to abandon the idea of a single innovation model so that the variety of innovation processes between large firms and SMEs can be taken into account, depending on the sector as well as on the spatial location of the firms.

Numerous studies have therefore emphasized the positive role of networks in fostering the development of innovation through the production of new knowledge. However, knowledge has been recognized as having the role of a strategic resource for companies, giving them a competitive advantage as a result of its tacit nature, which is not easily transferable from one firm to another. From this point of view, cooperation, which is supposed to require knowledge sharing, or even joint production of knowledge by companies, also presents risks for them, the main one being the expropriation of their know-how, including through the use of patents by one of the cooperation partners. A relatively high number of cooperations therefore experience significant delays in finalizing the cooperation project, or even the total cessation of the cooperation during the project.

Evolutionary approaches have produced advances in the analysis of innovation processes; however, they have not integrated the question of the role of space in the formation and sustainability of networks.

29.3. Local innovation networks

In the 1980s, the success of Italian districts, based on the geographical concentration of SMEs inserted in a process of division of labor and cooperating to innovate, showed the importance of space in innovation processes. Following the same model, Silicon Valley has become emblematic of this type of operation. This paved the way for the recognition of space and geographical proximity, giving rise to the development of approaches to innovative milieus (Aydalot 1986) and later to clusters. In all of this work, in order to innovate, companies mobilize local networks involving client/supplier firms and also other industries and services (consulting, in particular) as well as local research. But this research also quickly highlighted the fact that for the learning process and the production of knowledge to be sustainable over time in the local productive system, it was imperative that it also be open to the outside world and that cooperation networks also exist with actors located outside the cluster; thus maintaining the variety of knowledge which is one of the most important sources of innovation.

These approaches have the advantage of highlighting the importance of space and territory in the production of innovations and of no longer considering space as a simple reservoir of resources, but as the place of the production and possible disappearance of productive and innovation resources.

More recently, the importance of local innovation networks has been emphasized, but within the framework of a finer geographical mesh: urban space. Indeed, according to some authors, such as Florida *et al.* (2016), cities, especially the largest among them, i.e. metropolises, have become the only place where innovation can be developed. Peripheral territories, especially rural areas, would no longer have sufficient resources to innovate. The population density and the variety of industries favoring Jacobs' externalities in a limited geographical space within urban areas would favor informal interactions and allow the development of local innovation networks based on dense interactions between members. In addition, cities concentrate skilled workers, especially those from the creative class, who would be the most innovative according to these authors. By contrast, peripheral areas would be under-resourced in relation to all of these advantages.

However, work comparing the introduction of innovation in urban and rural spaces shows that innovation is developed in all types of spaces. Shearmur (2015) proposes a model of innovation based on the value of the information obtained.

Innovators in cities would use market sources but provide a form of information that is quickly outdated: they would be rapid innovators, developing incremental innovations. By contrast, innovators located in peripheral areas would rely primarily on internal sources to develop their innovations, and therefore contribute less frequently to the cooperation network. When they mobilize it, they use the same actors as in urban spaces, including knowledge-intensive services (Shearmur and Doloreux 2015). However, they form cooperations with firms located at a distance, generally in large urban centers. Differentiation of innovation processes lies mainly in the fact that in urban areas, innovators form networks with market sources, whereas in peripheral areas innovators mobilize more institutional and scientific sources. In fact, Florida *et al.* (2016) essentially put forward an innovation process based on external sources, therefore based on informal interactions that would be easier to mobilize in urban space, whereas Shearmur describes an innovation process based more on formalized cooperations that is mobilized by companies in peripheral spaces.

The network in peripheral spaces does not operate by primarily mobilizing geographical proximity – since the organizations with which the innovative company can cooperate are not necessarily present in these spaces – but by resorting to other forms of proximity: organized, social or institutional proximity (Boschma 2005). This has become possible due to the development of technology that allows the multiplication of remote interactions (e-mails, videoconferencing, etc.) and due to the mobility capacity of the actors to interact when necessary during the cooperation. Thus, the need for geographical proximity in innovation networks has often been overestimated, especially since this proximity is generally associated with the co-location of actors, i.e. what the school of proximity (Gilly and Torre 2000) qualifies as permanent proximity. However, geographical proximity can also be temporary (Gallaud and Torre 2005).

Finally, the positive effects of geographical proximity are often overestimated and, conversely, its negative effects are often underestimated. An excess of proximity can lead to involuntary spillovers or even industrial espionage, and in the long-term, lock-in effects frequently appear (Boschma 2005), "trapping" firms that use knowledge provided by the neighborhood into trajectories that are no longer innovative. Geographical proximity is only a potential and a facilitator of coordination if it does not rely on other forms of proximity: organizational, social and institutional.

29.4. Conclusion

Access to external sources of knowledge has become essential to foster innovation processes. But it can take several forms, the two main ones being the use of informal interactions and formalized cooperation. However, the most recent models, in particular that of Chesbrough (2003), even if they propose that firms use all knowledge acquisition processes, in fact place more emphasis on informal interaction processes than on cooperation. Yet this model tends to become the standard for understanding innovation processes both in research and in firms. The role of informal interactions becomes overestimated and, above all, the innovation process tends to be thought of as a single process, whereas there are a variety of innovation processes corresponding to different strategies for companies.

In addition, the numerous works that have developed on cooperation networks have also tended to partially obscure the importance of internal innovation processes. The network cannot be a total substitute for the lack of absorptive capacity. There is still little work that explains how companies should articulate internal and external knowledge. The description of learning processes often targets only one of these two aspects. Finally, some of the negative effects of cooperation often seem to be lessened, particularly for SMEs, which have fewer means of protecting their innovations, both legal and informal, which, contrary to what is often asserted, can prove costly.

Second, most of the work on networks concerns the innovation process aimed at introducing technological innovations. However, innovation is more varied than this and also integrates organizational, marketing and institutional forms. Very few studies analyze the specificities of the production of this type of innovation and, even fewer, the type of cooperation used by firms. Finally, most of the work targets the manufacturing industry, whereas services constitute the dominant economic activity in developed countries, and they are still largely under-studied, particularly public service activities. However, the specificities of the innovation process can be quite numerous, to the extent that the innovation process is described by some authors as a “do-it-yourself activity”.

While regional science approaches have had the merit of reintroducing the role of space and territories and geographical proximity as places for producing innovation resources, these variables have often been equated with the co-location of actors. However, actors are increasingly mobile in geographical space and they have increasingly more access to technologies that allow them to relax the constraint of localization, which has benefited the development of cooperation between distant organizations.

The current societal context, in connection with the objectives of ecological transition, will probably lead public policies to increase incentives to reterritorialize productive activities, which should increase the formation of local innovation cooperation networks, but formed on the basis of the articulation of geographical proximity with other forms of proximity: organized and institutional, in particular.

29.5. References

Aydalot, P. (1986). *Milieux innovateurs en Europe*. GREMI, Paris.

Boschma R. (2005). Proximity and innovation: A critical assessment. *Regional Studies*, 39(1), 61–74.

Chesbrough, W. (2003). *Open Innovation: The New Imperative for Creating and Profiting from Technology* [Online]. Available at: https://s3.amazonaws.com/academia.edu.documents/30503779/open_innovation.

Gallaud, D. and Torre, A. (2005). Geographical proximity and circulation of knowledge through interfirm relationships. *Scienze Regionali*, 4(2), 5–25.

Gilly, J.P. and Torre, A. (2000). *Dynamiques de proximité*. Editions L'Harmattan, Paris.

Jensen, B., Johnson, B., Lorenz, E., Lundvall, B.A. (2007). Forms of knowledge and modes of innovation. In *The Learning Economy and the Economics of Hope*, Lundvall, B.A. (ed.). Anthem Press, London.

Lundvall, B.A. (ed.) (1985). *The Learning Economy and the Economics of Hope*. Anthem Press, London.

Pavitt, K. (1984). Sectoral patterns of technical change: Towards a taxonomy and a theory. *Research Policy*, 13(6), 343–373.

Richardson, G. (1972). The organization of industry. *The Economic Journal*, 82(327), 883–896.

Rothwell, R. (1972). Factors for success in industrial innovations from project SAPPHO – A comparative study of success and failure in industrial innovation. *Journal of General Management*, 2(2), 57–65.

Shearmur, R. (2015). Slow innovators and information value. *Growth and Change*, 46(3), 424–442.

Shearmur, R. and Doloreux, D. (2015). Central places or networks? Paradigms, metaphors, and spatial configurations of innovation-related service use. *Environment and Planning A: Economy and Space*, 47(7), 1521–1539.

Teece, D. (1992). Competition, cooperation, and innovation: Organizational arrangements for regimes of rapid technological progress. *Journal of Economic Behavior & Organization*, 18(1), 1–25.

30

Organization – Modern Innovative Organizational Structures

30.1. Introduction

Today, technology innovation is the result of a complex system of organizational structures, the first formed around 1870 with the creation in Germany of R&D laboratories for the development of new dyes. In this case, a certain number of researchers were looking for possible and continuous technological innovations and not simply the realization of a single inventive idea. In the same period, another industrial R&D laboratory was created in Germany by Carl Zeiss in 1876 for optical applications. At the same time, in 1876, Thomas Edison created the famous research laboratory at Menlo Park (New Jersey). Many other R&D laboratories appeared, especially in the USA, where within the first 20 years of the 20th century there was the creation of 526 facilities for R&D (Basalla 1988). In the same period in the USA we saw the birth of a new activity consisting of supplying R&D services to industry with the creation of contract research laboratories, the first being Arthur D. Little founded in 1909, followed by the Mellon Institute in 1913, and in 1929, the Battelle Memorial Institute created at Columbus (Ohio), a contract research laboratory that would see a great expansion after World War II (Bohem and Groner 1972).

In the first half of the 20th century, R&D activity was characterized mainly by industrial laboratories, supported by some collaboration with universities, and by contracted research activities in the USA. During World War II, in the USA there was also the creation of three major national laboratories at Los Alamos, Oak Ridge and Hanford for the Manhattan Project, probably the greatest R&D project ever made, for the creation of the atomic bomb. These laboratories were also involved

---

Chapter written by Angelo BONOMI.

after the war in R&D for civil applications. Important changes occurred in the second half of the 20th century with the entry of numerous actors other than industry into the development of new technologies such as public and private research laboratories, universities and contract research organizations.

The generation of technology innovations was no longer only from industrial R&D laboratories in conditions of secrecy and competition, but also from co-developments among companies, contract research with universities and laboratories, trade in patents and licenses, corporate venturing funding in what it has been called a distributed innovation system (Haour 2004) accompanied by business model innovation in an open innovation system (Chesbrough 2003). In this situation, there was the birth of a new organizational structure for innovation, the *start-up–venture capital* system with new strategies in financing innovations, and later, at the beginning of the 21st century, the formation of the industrial platform system introducing a new type of relationships, characterized by a continuity of offer and demand of new technologies between the platform and the firms accompanied by an exchange of knowledge. In this chapter, we present a brief description of the three cited organizational structures including their models.

30.2. Organizational structures for innovation

It is possible to present models of these three main organizational structures for technological innovation, the first concerning the R&D projects system, the second the start-up–venture capital system, and the third the nascent structure called the industrial platform system. Such structures shall not be considered alternative for technological innovation but evolutive. In fact, the start-up–venture capital system includes R&D activities, especially when it has technological objectives, and industrial platforms also include R&D activities and possibly start-ups. These three organizational structures are described in the following sections.

30.2.1. *Industrially financed R&D project system*

The R&D activity may be considered at present the most important innovating system organizing flows of knowledge and capital to produce new technologies. A model of the R&D process is presented in Figure 30.1 and consists of an input of financed projects, some abandoned and others successful in producing new technologies. Knowledge generated by both successful and abandoned projects, combined with technical, scientific or other knowledge, generate innovative ideas that may be transformed into R&D project proposals submitted and then selected for financing. New technologies are used with the availability of industrial capital producing returns on investments. Industrial capital combined possibly with public funds make available investments for financing selected R&D project proposals, closing the knowledge and capital cycles (Bonomi 2017). This R&D model is project-based, R&D investments may be seen as the sum of project costs registered in a territory in a certain period of time, and the cost of development of a new technology as the sum of costs of the sequence of projects generating the technology. The knowledge generated by the R&D activity is for the model the driving force for the generation of innovative ideas for R&D projects and assumes various forms (Bonomi 2017). A mathematical simulation of the R&D model shows that it is necessary that a critical minimum number of R&D projects obtain statistically at least one new used technology and even more for a successful technology (Bonomi 2017a). Following the model, the economic growth of a territory does not actually depend simply on R&D investments, which should be considered rather a means, but on the intensity of generation of innovative ideas, which depends on the efficiency of exploitation of knowledge by the territory, and of course by adopted strategies, availability of capital and a suitable industrial organization.

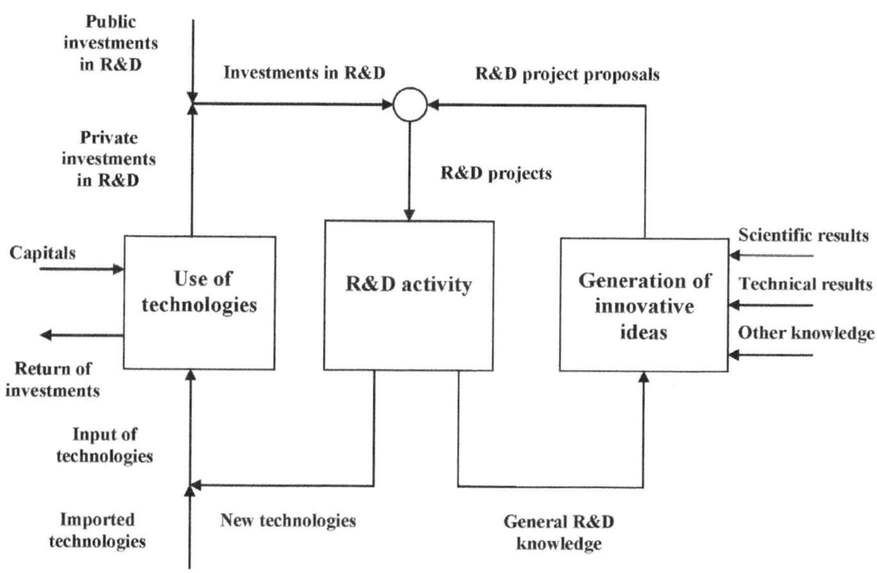

Figure 30.1. *Model of the R&D activity*

30.2.2. *Start-up-venture capital system*

This start-up–venture capital system is composed of start-ups financed by venture capital, and it represents another way to make technological innovations that may be considered an evolution of the industrial R&D projects system. Start-ups are companies but with an activity similar to a project being a single non-repetitive enterprise undertaken to reach an objective, called an exit, within a limited time and capital availability. Start-ups with technological objectives differ from R&D projects because they do not only perform R&D but also business model developments suitable for the developed technology. Start-ups have as an objective the reaching of an exit consisting of selling the technology with its business or of collecting capital to become an industrial company. Venture capital has strategies completely different from those of industrial capital financing innovation through R&D projects as it develops technologies in order to sell them and not for their exploitation. From this point of view, venture capital with its strategies represents the most radical aspect of the start-up–venture capital system with respect to the R&D projects system (Bonomi 2019). The start-up–venture capital system may be characterized by a financing cycle starting with start-up project proposals to venture capital, selection of financed start-ups that in part reach an exit and in part are abandoned. The return of investment to venture capital obtained by selling start-ups may be used to refinance new start-ups. If the return of investment is high enough to cover investments made in successful and abandoned start-ups with good margins, there is an autocatalytic development of financing capabilities and then of new technologies boosting economic growth. Besides this capital cycle, there is for the start-up–venture capital system also a knowledge cycle, similar to that of R&D, consisting of knowledge formed in either successful or abandoned start-ups useful for the creation of new start-up projects but consisting not only of technical but also of business model knowledge. Venture capital is characterized by two important types of strategies: the first, typically American, that selects start-ups on the basis of their potential return of investment and validity of the start-up team; the second, typically European, selects start-ups on the basis of the probability of success although at present in Europe the American-type strategy is increasingly widespread. The American-type strategy is characterized by a rate of failure of about 90% of financed start-ups, while for the European-type strategy, the rate is about 70%. In spite of this difference, the American-type strategy is more efficient because of the much higher return of investment attained from successful start-ups. That may be attributed to a know-how that American venture capital has accumulated during the long time of operation in the start-up–venture capital system with great experience in selection and monitoring the financed start-ups.

30.2.3. *Industrial platform system*

The industrial platform system is based on a new form of technology development based on continuous relationships between offer and demand of new technologies, and it may include R&D projects and start-ups activities. In fact, industrial platforms derive from a general platform system (Cicero 2017), largely applied in social and economic activities as well in informatics and communication technologies, and its industrial version is spreading in the implementation of enabling technologies for Industry 4.0. The platform structure is composed of the owners of the platforms and its partners that have a continuous relationship with the owners supplying services, in particular technologies in the case of industrial platforms. Peer producers are the other actors supplying technologies as partners but not with a continuous relationship with the owners. Furthermore, in the platform structure, there are the peer consumers that represent the firms needing new technologies. Peer consumers are linked by a continuous relationship with the platform supplying new technologies, as well as exchanging with the platform information and experience useful to solve customers' problems and to develop further new technologies. Externally, there are the stakeholders of the platform, entities interested in platforms and promoting or regulating their activities.

30.2.4. *Comparison of the various organizational structures*

It should be noted that the various formed organizational structures are not alternative but rather evolutive, and their formation is a response to the evolution of various types of technology innovations, linked to their degree of radicality and exigences to improve efficiency in the offer of new technologies. While the industrially financed R&D projects system and the start-up–venture capital system present radical differences in the way of financing technology innovation, the industrial platform system does not introduce new forms of financing but new forms of relationships based on a continuity of offer and demand of new technologies. With regards to the start-up–venture capital system, it has the advantage of developing business models suitable for the developed technology, and it is not limited in the innovations by existing strategies of firms financing R&D projects. On the other hand, the start-up–venture capital system is economically sustainable only with new technologies with a relatively high ROI that is possible with a relatively high degree of radicality of innovation. The R&D projects system is, on the contrary, well suited to technology innovations with a limited degree of radicality and lower need for investments. This is confirmed by the fact that the big companies tend to limit their R&D to their core business looking for possibly more radical innovations in the start-ups market (Branscombe *et al.* 2000). Industrial platforms are only at the beginning of their diffusion, but it seems that their potential success depends on the availability of infrastructures such as the Internet, big data and cloud computing offering possibly a continuous link based on IT contributions. Their diffusion might change the innovation environment by important shifts: from science to business toward business to business in technology transfer, from research to firms toward research to platforms, and from technological competition among firms toward competition among platforms. In Figure 30.2, we have resumed the different fields of suitability of the R&D and start-up–venture capital systems with respect to the radical degree and the potential return on investment of the developed technology, while for the industrial platform system, being a system of relations, its suitability is independent of the radical degree or potential return of investment of the technology.

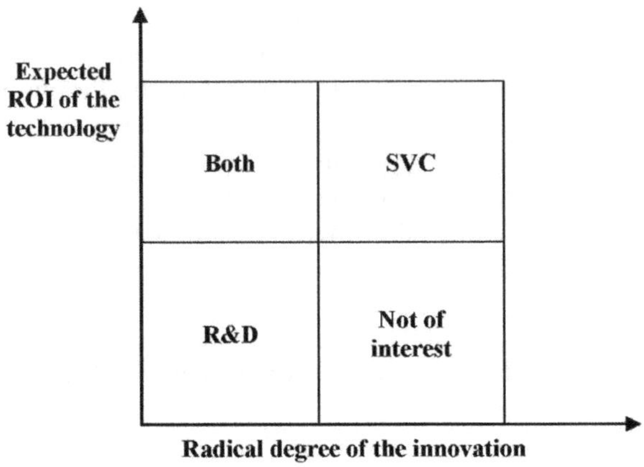

Figure 30.2. *Field of suitability of R&D and SVC organizational structures*

30.3. Perspectives

Summarizing the perspectives of the three structures discussed above, it is possible that in an open innovation economy, the start-up–venture capital system will gain importance with respect to the R&D system because of the contemporary development not only of a technology but also of a business model suitable to the technology. However, a possible large diffusion of industrial platforms might disrupt the actual R&D and start-up–venture capital innovation systems because firms might satisfy their needs of innovations by links with many different platforms, active in different types of technologies needed by the firms, while peer producers might offer innovations to many platforms. In this case, platforms become concentrators and diffusors of an enormous amount of knowledge boosting the generation and improvement of new technologies.

30.4. References

Basalla, G. (1988). *The Evolution of Technology*. Cambridge University Press, Cambridge.

Boehm, G. and Groner, A. (1972). *Science in the Service of Mankind, The Battelle Story*. Lexington Books, Lanham, MA.

Bonomi, A. (2017a). A mathematical toy model of the R&D process: How this model may be useful in studying territorial development. IRCrES Working Paper, 6.

Bonomi, A. (2017b). A technological model of R&D process, and its implications with scientific research and socio-economic activities. IRCrES Working Paper, 2.

Bonomi, A. (2019). The start-up venture capital innovation system: Comparison with industrially financed R&D projects system. IRCrES Working Paper, 2.

Branscombe, L., Morse, K., Roberts, M., Boville, D. (2000). Managing technical risk: Understanding private sector decision making on early stage technology-based projects. NIST GCR 00-787, US Department of Commerce.

Chesbrough, H.W. (2003). *Open Innovation: The New Imperative for Creating and Profiting from Technology*. Harvard Business School Press, Boston, MA.

Cicero, S. (2017). From business modeling to platform design [Online]. Available at: https://platformdesigntoolkit.com/platform-design-whitepaper.

Haour, G. (2004). *Resolving the Innovation Paradox: Enhancing Growth in Technology Company*. Palgrave Macmillan, London.

31

Paradigm – The Techno-scientific Paradigm: The Ethical Control of the Technological Progress

31.1. Introduction

The concept of technoscience was developed by the Belgian philosopher Hottois (2013), following the work of Lambright in *Governing Science and Technology* (1976). The history of this term is the subject of the introduction to the book *Généalogies philosophique, politique et imaginaire de la technoscience* (Vrin 2013). The concept is connoted by a prospective and futuristic dimension. The technoscientific era designates a particular mode of knowledge production, oriented by the instrumentalization of discoveries and scientific research for practical and technological purposes. While some actors denounce the effacement of pure science in the face of more practical research, others believe that this system facilitates the emergence of new concepts, in a productive system increasingly oriented by Research and Development (R&D), in companies or institutions motivated by the search for profitability and profit. A true culture of innovation allows permanent technical progress, thanks in particular to the stimulation of a collective imaginary named "technoscience-fiction" by Hottois. The technoscientific era succeeded an innovation system based on cybernetics since the end of World War II. It prolongs research in the space, computer science and telecommunications sectors, for example. NASA is the archetype of the technoscientific research center, a producer of important innovations in the space sector. Thus, in the 1980s, the term "Big Science" became synonymous with the term "technoscience". Hottois regrets that his concept subsequently spread by modifying its initial meaning. At the end of the 20th century, it was used to denounce the excesses of neo-liberalism and

---

Chapter written by Thomas MICHAUD.

technological capitalism, and to caricature the American system of scientific knowledge production.

The techno-scientific paradigm will be the subject of a historical review since its appearance in the 1970s. It has allowed major innovations, such as the Internet, to flourish for more than 20 years, also raising managerial and political questions about the ethical control of technical progress. Notably, the concept was reappropriated by critics of the neoliberal order, who used it, for example, to contest possible technocratic abuses emanating from the dominant players in the economy.

31.2. The controversial techno-scientific gigantism

The concept of technoscience has been necessary in deciphering the innovation process since the 1970s. The grouping of R&D activities in large networked centers around the world makes it possible to speed up discoveries, and to carry out pharaonic projects, such as the Human Genome Project, or to envisage the establishment of human colonies on other planets. Some research activities require heavy investments that only the State can make. However, the latter's difficulties may generate a transfer of R&D to private actors. A colbertist approach justifies the intervention of the State to carry out policies envisaging a radical change in the territory over several decades, or even several centuries. Technoscience enables the merging of skills on a large scale and the optimization of productivity.

The concept does not, however, systematically designate a fertile system for innovation. The term has been recuperated and influenced by actors ideologically opposed to economic liberalism. The technosciences are accused of resting on a system that alienates workers and on a travesty of the meaning of the history of technology. Science no longer serves to produce knowledge without seeking economic interests through the development of marketable technical innovations. Ecological criticism of the productive system thus takes a dim view of the setting up of a megamachine, in Mumford's sense, which could lead to natural disasters, as well as to the collapse of human civilization (because of the complexity of a system that could not withstand epidemics, or phenomena that could wipe out the millions of people specialized in managing the technical system). Collapsology is a discipline that emerged at the end of 2010 to criticize the omnipotence of technosciences. It provides a summary of the criticisms of the productive system since the 1970s. Authors such as Jacques Ellul, Alain Gras and Lewis Mumford are concerned about the future of a humanity increasingly dependent on technology.

Technoscience is the subject of divergent opinions, revealing its influence in developed societies. Followers of the ideology of progress believe that the fusion of science and technology, in what Alain Gras calls technical macro-systems, can be virtuous and improve the living conditions of its supporters. However, a blissful faith in technoscience can generate major difficulties and a reversal of technology against humanity. It is not uncommon to find imaginary representations of a science without conscience. "Technoscience-fiction" warns members of developed societies, faced with a loss of control over machines, that these could become enemies of humanity and lead it to destruction. Technosciences have been developing since the end of World War II and the demonstration of American power as the mistress of nuclear fire. Following the destruction of Hiroshima and Nagasaki, many scientists have questioned the meaning of their research activities. Engineers and decision-makers realized the need to set up ethics committees in order to limit the risks of developing Faustian science.

The warning signs of a drift of the technical system towards a form of soft totalitarianism can be found in the movement of technocrats in the 1930s in the United States. In several of his books, the American futurist Jeremy Rifkin warns about the risk of turning innovations against their creators. For example, in *The End of Work*, he shows that the technical system will eventually replace humans in repetitive tasks, especially in industry. This mechanization makes it possible to reduce production costs and disseminate as many innovations as possible to improve living conditions. On the other hand, it leads to the replacement of a large number of jobs and a form of impoverishment of the workforce that is no longer necessary. Technosciences have radically changed the planet, but have also generated perverse effects, such as social criticism, the destruction of ecosystems and global warming. The control of the technoscientific system raises the question of the advent of a potentially liberticidal technocracy.

31.3. Technocracy and technicism

Technocracy is a form of social organization advocated by engineers, who see it as a way to control the population with a view to accelerating R&D. Their approach is justified by the acceleration of discoveries, of the innovation process, and thus of social progress, if all living forces are oriented towards technocratic policies. This approach is in line with an ideology designated as neoliberal by neo-Marxist critics. The latter, associated with ecologists, believe that the seizure of power by scientists and engineers can lead to condemnable abuses. The technocracy envisaged in the interwar period was not extended at the end of the conflict. However, the advent of technosciences became inevitable. It was accelerated by the Cold War and the space race. A period of research euphoria led to major innovations, including considerable progress in the computer and telecommunications sector, with the creation of the Internet.

The technoscientific era developed from the late 1970s to the late 1990s, before being replaced by the NBIC paradigm (nanotechnology, biotechnology, information technology and cognitive science). Such concepts are generated by a community of researchers building technopolitical thinking. Scientists have acquired influence and have developed a philosophy that ensures the synthesis between their innovative ambitions and their contribution to the organization and life of the city. Technopolitics and technoscience go hand in hand to reflect on the modalities of social control in a world where a few technology companies (including GAFAM, Google, Apple, Facebook, Amazon, Microsoft) govern the existence of a large part of the population. The most revolutionary innovations also have their dark side, if they are instrumentalized by unethical actors. Thus, some decision-makers regularly call for the dismantling of companies like Google, insofar as their innovations could harm individual freedoms. The virtual technostructure is very promising for some, but danger for others, who consider that it could lead to a totalitarian society, if private information were in the possession of a dictatorship or a liberticidal regime.

31.4. Technosciences and innovation in debate

Technosciences are at the center of a technopolitical debate that is increasingly present in developed societies. Technological ideologies accompany innovations, with a view to instrumentalizing technical imaginations that trivialize innovation and make it easier to obtain funding. The territories controlling the most advanced technologies also have more political power. Space policies are an example of techno-scientific practice in full evolution, which could in the coming decades, extend capitalism to other heavenly bodies such as the Moon or Mars. However, R&D must obtain the agreement of the population to commit large sums of money to develop innovations that will allow humanity to expand into the cosmos. Hottois felt that Latour's work (1989) helped spread the concept of technoscience in America and around the world. Bachelard did not use this term, but developed theories designating this form of organization. In *Le nouvel esprit scientifique* (1934), he placed the new scientific spirit under the influence of mathematics and technology. He used the term *technical science* to designate contemporary science.

The question of how technosciences work is at the center of ethical, political and managerial reflections. While they are at the center of innovation processes in developed societies, they also contribute to the stability and renewal of global capitalism. This characteristic, which is the subject of much ideological criticism, also raises questions of the philosophy of science and epistemology: is there such a thing as pure, archetypal science, devoid of any connection with financial and economic interests? Is all science necessarily linked to its material and commercial extension, i.e. technology? Moreover, the imaginary that accompanies the progress of science and technology is also guided by the practices of the productive system. The term "technoscience-fiction", used by Hottois to define the fictions at the center of the functioning of this form of capitalism, is appropriate insofar as the intrigues that develop there revolve around utopian technologies, or purely scientific theories. Between science fiction, technoscience fiction and technofiction, the technical imaginary is revealing of the orientations of a productive system based on more or less technicist or scientific R&D.

The instrumentalization of science by technophile policies is ensured by the spread of ideologies such as transhumanism, inspired by multiple imaginaries, most of them coming from science fiction. Politics and management are intimately linked in the development of major industrial projects in which technoscience contributes to meeting complex challenges. It is advisable to consult the article on innovative technologies and on the imaginary and innovation, among others, to understand the interrelationships between technoscientific public policies, the development of innovative technologies by companies and a global imaginary that feeds the discourse on technical progress. If the technosciences era gave way to the NBIC paradigm in the early 2000s, it also generated an abundant imagination, preparing humanity and the scientific community for the challenges of the next economic cycles. The Fourth Industrial Revolution is heralded as the phase following the NBIC period, starting in 2020. Cycles lasting about 20 years are based on ideologies and imaginaries that economists and politicians must anticipate and interpret in order to ensure gentle systemic mutations, without violent crises that often occur in economic history. Any review of the age of technosciences is unquestionably marked by the deployment of information technology and the Internet. It was also characterized by a slowdown in the race for space. The Cold War faded and the world did not experience any major conflicts, leaving a peaceful world, conducive to continuous technological innovation and faithful to the visions of brilliant entrepreneurs, who made Silicon Valley the territory for the development and deployment of technical systems that brought about revolutionary changes in the organization and prosperity of human societies.

31.5. Conclusion

Technoscientific innovations have brought about major social and economic changes. They remain at the center of new developments, particularly in the medical sector, and nourish a rich and influential imagination to ensure the integration of these technologies into society. However, the notion of technoscience remains negatively connoted insofar as it is based on the instrumentalization of science by economic interests, and on the fact that it is tied to technology. A return to fundamental research, to pure science, is indeed an imperative to conceive new theories and new concepts allowing for a radical renewal of world visions, and thus, in the longer term, to imagine new and innovative sociotechnical systems. Nevertheless, the age of technosciences has left a major imprint in the history of contemporary societies, allowing the emergence of many technologies. Space research, biotechnologies, nanotechnologies, cognitive sciences and computer science drew the foundations for their development in the 1980–1990s, and are destined to continue to develop in the future to enable humanity to continue to mutate towards new conditions of existence, for example, towards a virtual and multiplanetary civilization.

31.6. References

Bensaude, V.B. (2009). *Les vertiges de la technoscience*. La Découverte, Paris.

Ferenczi, H. (2001). *Les défis de la technoscience*. Complexe, Brussels.

Goffi, J.-Y. (2007). *Regards sur les technosciences*. Vrin, Paris.

Hottois, G. (2013). *Généalogies philosophique, politique et imaginaire de la technoscience*. Vrin, Paris.

Lafontaine, C. (2008). *La société post-mortelle : la mort, l'individu et le lien social à l'ère des technosciences*. Le Seuil, Paris.

Lambright, W.H. (1976). *Governing Science and Technology*. Oxford University Press, Oxford.

Latour, B. (1989). *La science en action*. La Découverte, Paris.

Mumford, L. (1974). *Le mythe de la machine*, 2 volumes. Fayard, Paris.

32

Pattern – Linear, Interactive and Hybrid Patterns of Innovation

32.1. Introduction

The identification of activities related to innovation, the analysis of their organization, interactions and their representation in the form of "models" emerged when innovation became a subject of economic study in its own right. For a long time, technical progress was perceived as belonging to the world of engineers, who are compared to "Prometheus" giving fire to humans. Only its effects on growth and employment were studied by economists. But the recognition of its role led to the opening of a "black box" (Rosenberg 1982) in order to better understand the mechanisms by which innovation emerges and spreads throughout the economy and the factors that stimulate or hinder it. All of this in order to define not only policies but also managerial strategies capable of promoting innovation and, consequently, the competitiveness of firms and economic growth.

The purpose of this chapter is to present the main "models of innovation". It begins with the linear model of innovation, which uses a succession of basic and applied research and activities of technological development to explain the genesis of innovation. We then explore interactive models of innovation, which emphasize the links between different phases of the innovation process and the wider considerations of the market. Finally, we discuss the hybridization of these models, depending on the context or the fields concerned.

Chapter written by Blandine LAPERCHE.

32.2. The linear model of innovation

The organization of the multiple activities that form part of the innovation process (research done by scientists or researchers, the applications of engineers, the launch activities carried out by companies' marketing departments) was initially conceived in the form of a linear model where each phase of research and development followed one another (see Figure 32.1).

In this figure, each phase pursues a goal and is carried out in a different place (universities or public research laboratories for basic research, industrial laboratories for applied research and technological development). The three phases mark the progression of scientific and technical discoveries, from the birth of the idea of a product or service to its design and, eventually, its distribution. These phases represent the passage from a stock of knowledge produced by fundamental research to invention resulting from applied research, and then to innovation. For Kline and Rosenberg (1986), these events can be visualized as flowing smoothly in one direction, as if they were the "precepts" of Christianity.

The origin of this linear model is often attributed to the report of the Director of the U.S. Office of Scientific Research and Development V. Bush "*Science: The Endless Frontier*" (1945). However, as detailed by Godin (2006), Bush focused on the relationship between science and socio-economic progress, a detailed description of which does not appear in this report. In his article, Godin traces the history of this model and outlines its three essential stages. The first began at the start of the 20th century and lasted until 1945, marked by the ideal of "basic research" and the links between pure and applied research. A second stage began in the 1930s and continued until the early 1960s, when a third term – development – appeared, giving rise to this three-stage model of innovation: basic research – applied research – development. The third stage from the 1950s onwards extended the model to include production and diffusion activities. Ultimately, according to Godin, the model owes less to Bush's report than to the work of industrialists, consultants, business schools and, eventually, economists, who took up the issue later. Similarly, the author emphasizes the role played by the production of statistical tools in the stabilization, diffusion and longevity of this model, first by the National Science Foundation (NSF) in the United States and then by the OECD (first publication of the Frascati Manual in 1963): "Statistics solidified a model in progress into one taken for granted – a social fact" (Godin 2006). Other contributions to the linear model should also be mentioned, namely those of Furras (1948) and Maclaurin (1953), recalled by Balconi *et al.* (2010).

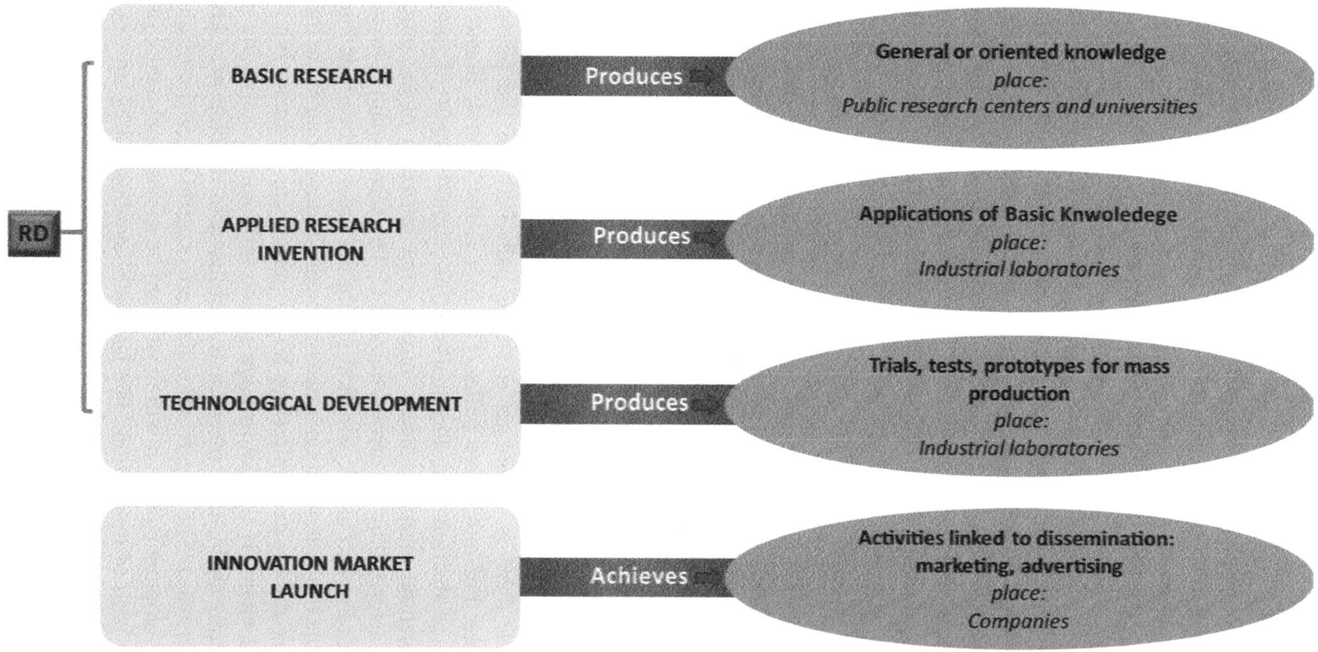

Figure 32.1. *The linear model of innovation (source: author). For a color version of this figure, see www.iste.co.uk/uzunidis/innovation1.zip*

32.3. Towards interactive models

The linear model has been strongly criticized because it did not allow for feedback between each phase and because the role of demand was neglected, only being considered at the end of the process. It seemed to correspond to the neoclassical theoretical representation of growth, in which technical progress is considered to be outside the sphere of economics. From the 1980s onwards, technical progress and innovation began to be understood as more endogenous phenomena. Interactions (contractual, as well as through the increased mobility of scientific and technical work) between public and private institutions devoted to scientific and technical activity became more involved in the analysis of the process of innovation. These are designed according to interactive and systemic models that emphasize the interactions between the R&D phases and wider considerations of the market (consumer tastes, quality requirements) throughout the process leading to innovation (Kline and Rosenberg 1986; Rothwell 1994; the latter highlights five models of innovation since the 1950s).

In these models, technology evolves as it is disseminated. Bringing an invention to market generally leads to multiple improvements that are essential to its success. Similarly, while scientific developments are often decisive in generating innovation, it can also take place without an established scientific theory preceding it. Kline and Rosenberg (1986) cite the example of the bicycle, which was a key innovation despite the absence of a theory explaining the stability of a rider in relation to their bicycle. These authors provide the best-known representation of the interactive model of innovation (see Figure 32.2).

In this model, there is no longer a single path between the phases of the innovation process, but rather five paths. The first is the central, linear path that links design to production and the market (the central chain of innovation). However, the potential market is taken into account upstream of the process; this main path is characterized by the arrows marked C. The second path is juxtaposed to the first by the feedbacks f and F, which highlight the links and various interactions between each stage of the innovation process. Scientific developments in the form of knowledge that is already available (link K) do not appear upstream but "irrigate" the entire central chain. If this knowledge is not sufficient to solve the problems posed in the central chain, then research is mobilized to develop new knowledge (K-R links) (third way). The fact remains that science can be at the origin of new technological developments, which will most often be of a radical nature (arrow D); this is the fourth path of innovation. The last path, symbolized by arrows I and S, highlights the fields that technological innovations can open up for research.

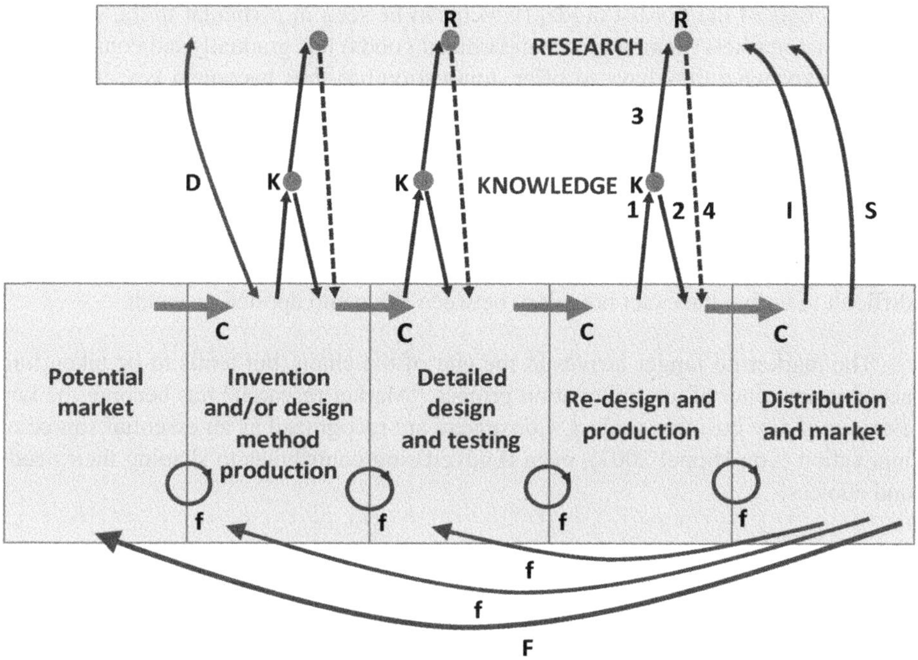

Figure 32.2. *The interactive model of innovation (source: Kline and Rosenberg 1986). For a color version of this figure, see www.iste.co.uk/uzunidis/innovation1.zip*

The different phases of research are so intertwined that the terms basic research, applied research and development have disappeared in favor of "research" or "R&D". This can be explained by the growing rapprochement between the academic world and the business world. On one hand, universities and public research centers have a new mission of the commercialization of research, which should strengthen their contribution to economic growth and allow them (if this was not already the case) to build up their budgets autonomously. This encourages them to carry out not only basic research but also applied research that is more likely to be of interest to companies. On the other hand, the pivotal period of the 1970s was marked by the exhaustion of the Fordist mode of production based in particular on the mass production of standardized goods. This model, dominant in the post-war growth years, justified price competition. It was well suited to a linear model of innovation in which major basic and applied research programs, mainly associated with the military field, provided techniques that could be enhanced on a large scale in the form of new products and processes.

The crisis of the Fordist model (which can be seen in particular in the saturation of national markets' demand for standardized goods) has gradually led companies to seek to vary what they have to offer. Innovation has thus become a key element of their strategy. The opening and liberalization of markets (goods and services, financial, labor) in the 1980s made innovation the driving force behind competition between firms on the global market. Hence, the willingness of firms to cooperate more closely with public research, on one hand, by increasing their internal research staff, and, on the other, by financing public research so as to have exclusive access to its results as soon as possible. In practice, then, it is becoming increasingly difficult to define the exact boundary between basic and applied research.

The market no longer arrives at the end of the chain, but tends to be taken into account upstream of any innovation project. "Market research" has become the key element of any business project. Consumers are recognized as an essential source of innovation (von Hippel 2001), even if advertising contributes to shaping their needs and choices.

The nature of technological change is another factor that explains the blurring of the boundary between R&D phases and justifies the existence of an interactive model of innovation. In biotechnology or genomics, for example, the boundary between R&D phases is becoming increasingly blurred. Research conducted in universities and public research centers therefore naturally combines theoretical and practical aspects and makes the results more attractive, leading to the emergence of numerous university spin-offs. These fields of research, which combine theory and practice, are becoming increasingly numerous today (biotechnology, innovation technology, artificial intelligence, etc.). The awareness of researchers of the possibility of linking the two activities, as well as the financial resources generated by the commercialization of their research results (which will enable them to fund their future research work), has thus accelerated the closer association between basic and applied research.

32.4. Hybridization of linear and interactive models of innovation

However, a complete reconsideration of the linear model is the result of superficial analysis of the writings of the authors behind it, and an overly restrictive interpretation of the notion of linearity, according to Baconi *et al.* (2010). Linearity does not imply that the market intervenes only at the end of the process. Similarly, interactivity does not mean that all activities take place at the same time. Finally, the issue is not that of questioning the role of science in the creation of new products or services. However, depending on context or the concerned fields, different activities may play a more or less important role, and on a different time frame. Technological advances can also influence scientific work (e.g. the development of vaccines often precedes their scientific understanding) or scientific discoveries can be translated into new technologies long after they have been disseminated. The genesis of innovation does not follow a strict and unwavering rule.

On the other hand, according to Godin, alternative models to the linear model, such as the interactive model, are more like “modern art” than true analytical frameworks (Godin 2006). Innovation indicators still measure the different activities integrated into the linear model and those that seek to measure knowledge flows, and interactions between actors in the innovation process are still in their infancy. The longevity of the linear model can also be explained by the primacy of R&D in public innovation policies (Joly 2017). The example of the objective set in Europe by the Lisbon Strategy to reach 3% of GDP leads, according to him, to the implicit or explicit assertion that “science is the solution, society is the problem”. It is then society that must become more entrepreneurial and more enthusiastic about new technologies (Joly 2017). Moreover, according to him, it is in the interest of the drivers of innovation to remain attached to this linear model. This is true for researchers, since the linear model values fundamental research. It is also true for firms, which are the main beneficiaries of public innovation policies, by being awarded a high share of support intended to transform research into goods and services and, beyond that, into competitiveness and growth.

One of the reasons for the longevity of the linear model also lies in its simplicity, as pointed out by the two authors we have cited. To continue this line of thought, we can refer to the fact that to manage their innovation projects, companies (especially the largest ones) very often use a scale developed by NASA in the 1970s (and further developed since) (Mankins 2009). This technological readiness level (TRL) scale was originally intended to be a tool for evaluating technological programs, showing their different stages and has been adopted by many organizations, both public institutions and companies. It comprises nine steps, from the most basic research (TRL1) to the application of technology in real conditions (TRL9), and is similar to a linear model. However, this linear representation of activities does not prevent interaction between the different phases.

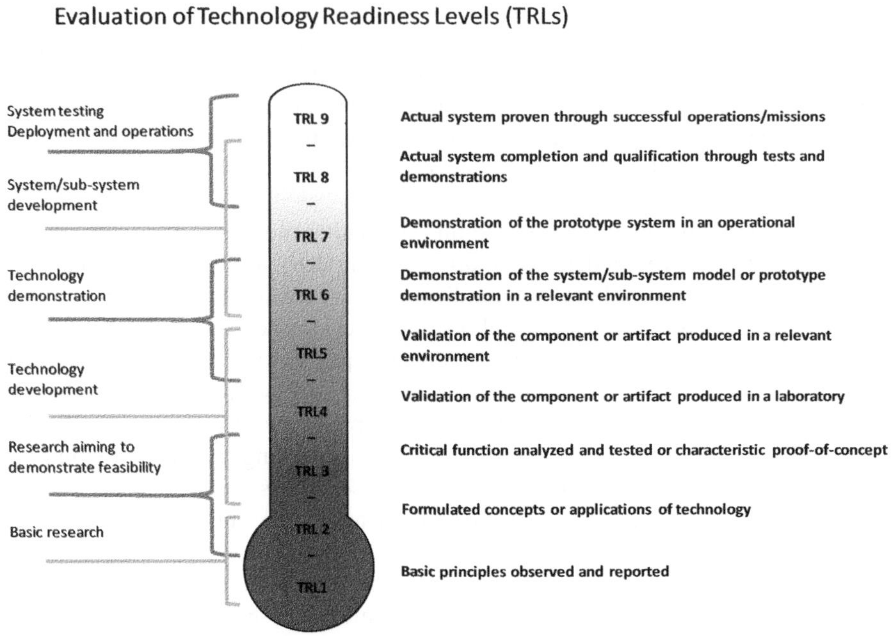

Figure 32.3. *The technology readiness levels (TRLs) scale (source: Mankins 2009). For a color version of this figure, see www.iste.co.uk/uzunidis/innovation1.zip*

32.5. Conclusion

The value of comparing different innovation models is manifold. They have made it possible to overcome the opposition between the "technology push", which emphasizes the role of science and technology in the development of innovations, and the "Demand pull", which gives a key role to changes in markets and consumer needs. Innovation is thus seen as a systemic phenomenon in which different stakeholders interact in time frames that can vary from one field or context to another. This leads Carac *et al.* (2009) to propose a "multi-channel interactive model", which also emphasizes the various forms of learning and the role of interface structures inside and outside a firm. The latter aim to facilitate the collective process of innovation emergence. While the practical application of the interactive model of innovation is therefore not widely observable, it has become important in both analytical and conceptual terms and has paved the way for the analysis of the interacting networks inherent to the process of innovation.

Secondly, analysis of these models shows that they are largely focused on technological innovation, and integrate other forms of innovation to a lesser extent. These appear at best as ancillary, even though they represent the most common forms of innovation. Criticism of the linear model could thus reflect the growing interest of firms in non-technological forms of innovation, as well as in minor forms of technological innovation.

Finally, we must note that criticism of the linear model does not, lead to a questioning of the role of science in the process of technological innovation and the great majority of authors stress that, on the contrary, it is crucial to it. However, it "irrigates" the process, rather than always being at the origin of it. This is no doubt also due to changes in the functioning of the institutions that produce scientific advancement, but it is science itself that is called upon to deal with economic, political or health crises. Major scientific and technological programs often resurface to cure the ills of capitalism.

32.6. References

Balconi, M., Brusoni, S., Orsenigo, L. (2010). In defence of the linear model: An essay. *Research Policy*, 39, 1–13.

Bush, V. (1945). Science: The endless frontier. Office of Scientific Research and Development [Online]. Available at: https://www.nsf.gov/od/lpa/nsf50/vbush1945.htm.

Caraça, J., Lundvall, B.A., Mendonça, S. (2009). The changing role of science in the innovation process: From Queen to Cinderella? *Technological Forecasting & Social Change*, 76, 861–867.

Furnas, C.C. (1948). Research in industry. In *Its Organization and Management*, Van, D. (ed.). Nostrand Company Inc, New York.

Godin, B. (2006). The linear model of innovation: The historical construction of an analytical framework. *Science, Technology & Human Values*, 31, 639–667.

von Hippel, E. (2001). Perspective: User Toolkits for Innovation. *Journal of Product Innovation Management*, 18(4), 247–257.

Joly, P.B. (2017). Beyond the competitiveness framework: Models of innovation revisited. *Journal of Innovation Economics and Management*, 22, 79–96.

Kline, S. and Rosenberg, N. (1986). An overview of innovation. In *The Positive Sum Strategy: Harnessing Technology for Economic Growth*, Landau, R. and Rosenberg, N. (eds). National Academy Press, Washington, DC.

Maclaurin, W.R. (1953). The sequence from invention to innovation and its relation to economic growth. *Quarterly Journal of Economics*, 67, 97–111.

Mankins, J.C. (2009). Technology readiness assessments: A retrospective. *Acta Astronautica*, 65, 1216–1223.

Rosenberg, N. (1982). Inside the black box: Technology and economics. Cambridge University Press, Cambridge.

Rothwell, R. (1994). Towards the fifth-generation innovation process. *International Marketing Review*, 11(1), 7–31.

33

Persistence – The Economic Analysis of Persistent Innovation

33.1. Introduction

Technological innovation is a fundamental source of growth at the firm, sector and nation levels. Analysis of the drivers and underlying mechanisms of innovation persistence, the fact that firms innovate continuously, can relevantly improve our understanding of both long-run industry dynamics and the expected effects of policies for R&D. The issue of innovation persistence has in recent years attracted growing interest from scholars. Several factors have been associated with the presence of persistence in innovative activities: firm size, profitability and the intensity of R&D activities, confirming the hypothesis that the accumulation of knowledge over time tends to induce persistent innovative behavior and that the availability of internal funds enhances the ability to continuously engage in innovation. The increasing availability of firm-level data on innovation activity, through the series of European Community Innovation Surveys, has improved our capability to investigate the sources, forms and consequences of innovation persistence.

The topics we deal with are: the definition of innovation persistence, why this notion is debatable, the issues linked to the measurement of the phenomenon and its explanative frameworks. Finally, we address the relation between innovation persistence and the *path* and *past* dependence.

33.2. Persistent innovation: definition

The meaning of innovation persistence can be easily illustrated by Figure 33.1.

Chapter written by Christian LE BAS.

	T		*t+1*
(1)	Innovation	→	Innovation
(2)	Innovation	→	No innovation
(3)	No innovation	→	Innovation
(4)	No innovation	→	No innovation

Figure 33.1. ***Innovation persistence***

We assume two time periods, *t* and *t+1*, and two options for the firm under observation, innovate or do not innovate, four cases are possible. In case 1, the firm innovates persistently. In cases 2 and 3, the firm is a sporadic innovator. Case 4 outlines the fact that the firm never innovates. In the latter case, the firm is not viable. In the sporadic process of innovation, process (3) is less relevant than process (2). A firm that does not innovate in time t is unlikely to survive to *t+1* or, if it survives, it will not have the resources to invest in technological activities. The probability of such a firm innovating in *t+1* is very weak. In process (2), the firm has innovated but has not transformed the innovation into enough economic success (profits) to reinvest in technological activities. The firm may have modified its strategy inefficiently.

The standard framework for assessing innovation duration is based on patent race. In this literature, we find that technological dynamics is explained by two effects with opposite consequences. The first is the "replacement effect". In general, firms are reluctant to innovate in period *t+1* because they are afraid of cannibalizing rents arising from innovations created in *t*. The second is the "pre-emption effect"; firms receive incentives to innovate in *t+1* (after innovating in *t*) in order to exploit innovations carried out in *t* more effectively. In contrast, the evolutionary framework for assessing innovation duration focuses on learning capabilities and on the interactions between behaviors and economic selection mechanisms. Two types of innovation regime are distinguished: entrepreneurial and oligopolistic. Innovation largely occurs within small entrepreneurial firms, but the firm mortality is high. In the oligopolistic regime, innovation occurs in the R&D department of large oligopolistic firms, which have longer economic lives than small entrepreneurial firms. It is argued that a small firm will innovate over a shorter period of time than a large firm. The fact that some firms innovate over a short period of time and others over a long period of time is normal in an industrial environment characterized by diversity and variety.

33.3. Why is the notion of innovation persistence debatable?

From an empirical point of view, the duration of the period of time in which a firm is observed is crucial for characterization if it is persistent. The longer the time period, the weaker the probability that a firm stays on an innovative path. In the context of innovation persistence, the definition of innovation is problematic. What type of innovation is concerned? Only technological? Should we include improvements that affect firm organization in the definition? Marketing innovation? New types of innovation which recent European surveys throw light on? Where a firm is concerned, the longer the time period under observation, the larger the changes in the firm structure. For instance, over a long time period, a firm modifies its borders. As a result, it is relevant to study persistence in the context of firm growth and structural change (merger and acquisition, vertical concentration, de-verticalization, product differentiation).

33.4. Measurement of the phenomenon

This point is controversial. Academics support the idea that innovation persistence is weak. By contrast, some others think that it is strong. The reason for these opposed views might be the underlying question of method, which we have outlined in the previous section. Moreover, the empirical studies use various quantitative indicators as patents, R&D expenditure, innovation counts and total factor productivity. Using different methods with different data gives unlike trends. Nevertheless, we provide some empirical data on the scale of innovation persistence.

Latham and Le Bas (2006) provided an empirical patent analysis that allows us to explore why some industrial firms innovate over a short period (two or three years) and others innovate over a long period (more than 10 years). They outline information concerning the panel of 3,347 industrial firms (or their laboratories) observed over the period 1969–1985, which have been granted patents by the United States Patents and Trademarks Office at some time during this period. A firm can patent over one or several periods. The time distribution of patenting periods reveals an important feature: 3,902 periods, or 73%, are very short one-year periods (matching sporadic innovator behavior). When the length increases from 2 to 15 years, the number of periods decreases steadily. There is a small spike for the longest period (16 years). This means that a lot of firms innovate over a short time period. Only a few are persistent.

Le Bas and Poussing (2014) built an empirical analysis providing two important qualitative results:

1) A complex innovator is more persistent as an innovator than a single innovator. Complex innovators develop their advances around the product and

process technologies that they master. By contrast, a single innovator improves either their products or processes.

2) There is a process of persistence with respect to environmental technological innovators. They are more persistent than standard technological innovators. This provides grounds for thinking that there are two important factors behind the process of persistence: stricter regulation, and a firm's consideration in favor of sustainable development (linked to Corporate Social Responsibility). That finding underlines the importance of regulation, which remains necessary, even for triggering and maintaining the process of persistence.

33.5. Explanatory frameworks

The literature envisages three main frameworks. The first that has been put forward is the hypothesis of "knowledge accumulation": past experience in innovation is a positive factor implementing currently successful innovations (a type of dynamic which increases returns). By innovating, firms explore a process of learning and discover new ideas by recombining old ones. Past innovation becomes the source of further innovations. The firms lead to the creation of dynamic capabilities (according to Teece: the firm's ability to integrate, build, and reconfigure competences to address changes in the competitive environment) which favor innovation persistence. For instance, a major innovation will feed the creation of minor technological improvements in the future. Another approach is the "success breeds success" hypothesis which asserts that innovation feeds profitability, which later funds innovation activities. The commercial successes of innovation have a long-lasting effect on firm profitability. This is a positive for financing innovation in the following years. It has been observed that systematic innovators earn profits above the average and have a strong incentive to keep innovating and earning profits above the average. Recently, Antonelli and his colleagues built an additional explanatory framework relating to the concept of sunk costs in R&D activities (Antonelli *et al.* 2012). At each time period, a firm faces the choice between investing or not investing in R&D activities. A firm deciding to engage in R&D/innovation activities has to incur start-up costs that are usually not recoverable. They provide essential motives for entering and staying in a specific regime of persistent R&D activity.

Of course, these frameworks about the source of innovation persistence provide a complementary and self-reinforcing explanation. As a result, "knowledge accumulation" and the "success breeds success" hypothesis interplay give rise to a virtuous circle.

33.6. Innovation persistence and the significance of economic evolution: path and past dependence

The nature of the innovation process is both past-dependent and path-dependent in essence. Past dependence means that the characteristics of the processes that are analyzed and their results are fully determined by their initial conditions. The Mansfield epidemiological model of innovation diffusion provides a good example of this. Once the number of firms in the industry under observation are given, the speed of diffusion is provided by deterministic parameters, and this stays the same over the process of epidemic diffusion. By contrast, with path dependence, economic dynamics remain marked by a series of unpredictable "accidents". As a consequence, the past narrows the scope of possible outcomes, shaping the path where evolution can take place. In such dynamics, the agent reaction to a small accident is recognized to be of crucial importance. Of course, pure past dependence and pure path dependence are exceptional; path and past dependence are in fact interrelated.

Innovation persistence would tend to be past-dependent, in the sense that the future innovative dynamic is not fully determined by the nature and characteristics of the first innovation that starts the sequence. Many contingent factors such as evolving market conditions, institutional change and managerial styles affect the evolution.

33.7. Conclusion

In this text, we note the diverse definitions related to innovation persistence. We show the importance of the issues linked to the measurement of the phenomenon and provide a clear overview of the main explanative frameworks. Finally, we address the relation between innovation persistence, designed as an important evolutionary trend related to the firm and the *path* and *past* dependence dynamics.

Firm innovation persistence is crucially related to firm dynamic capabilities, according to the frame put forward by Teece and Pisano. These capabilities draw on organizational routines that are path-dependent and under the effect of self-reinforcing mechanisms. But as Teece and others tell us, managers can act creatively and strategically to shape the firm's path. Only firms with dynamic capabilities can innovate persistently over a long time period. But having innovated and modified their industrial context, the firms create more difficult environments in terms of the cost of innovation. The making of dynamic capabilities is a means to overcome these costs. The authors put forward the idea that individuals are critical for the formation of dynamic capabilities. As a result, it may be that they are equally critical of firm innovation persistence (Antonelli *et al.* 2012).

33.8. References

Antonelli, C., Crespi, F., Scellato, G. (2012). Inside innovation persistence: New evidence from Italian micro-data. *Structural Change and Economic Dynamics*, 23(4), 341–353.

Antonelli, C., Crespi, F., Scellato, G. (2013). Internal and external factors in innovation persistence. *Economics of Innovation and New Technology*, 22(3), 256–280.

Latham, W. and Le Bas, C. (2006). *The Economics of Persistent Innovation: An Evolutionary View*. Springer, Berlin.

Le Bas, C. and Poussing, N. (2014). Is complex innovation more persistent than single? An empirical analysis of innovation persistence drivers. *International Journal of Innovation Management*, 18(1), 1–22.

Le Bas, C. and Scellatto, G. (2014). Firm innovation persistence: A fresh look on the frameworks of analysis. EINT Introductory paper. *The Economics of Innovation and New Technology*, 23(5–6), Special Issue on innovation persistence, new research perspectives.

Le Bas, C., Mothe, C., Nguyen-Thi, T.U. (2015). The differentiated impacts of organizational innovation practices on technological innovation persistence. *European Journal of Innovation Management*, 18(1), 110–127.

Lhuillery, S. (2014). Marketing and persistent innovation success. *Economics of Innovation and New Technology*, 23(5–6), 517–543.

34

Policy – Reinventing Innovation: From Criticisms of the Traditional Paradigm to Policy Transformation

34.1. Introduction

Over the past 15 years or so, the field of innovation has experienced an exceptionally intense semantic proliferation. Whereas innovation was traditionally technological, nowadays it is distributed, bottom-up, social, responsible, frugal, inverse, by withdrawal, etc.

In this chapter, it is proposed that such an abundance demonstrates a fundamental shift linked to two changes. On the one hand, the central paradigm of innovation is the subject of a series criticisms, first brought about by peripheral players but which are now the subject of lively debate at the heart of innovation studies. To put it simply, the dogma that innovation is always good is giving way. While Joseph Schumpeter saw innovation as a process of creative destruction (the creative effects of novelty surpass the destruction of resources – jobs, machines, skills, etc. – that it provokes), some specialists suggest that the destructive part (the social and environmental damage of "progress") can systematically supplant the creative part (Soete 2013). Consequently, it is not enough to maximize the pace of innovation. It is necessary to ensure that it brings the expected social and environmental benefits. The second change is therefore the renewal of innovation policies, marked in particular by what should be called the turning point of "directionality", i.e. the need to promote innovation processes that respond to major societal challenges.

Chapter written by Pierre-Benoit JOLY.

After establishing these two points, this chapter concludes by identifying the factors that boost the transformation of innovation policies.

34.2. Criticisms of the central innovation paradigm

Innovation – literally the introduction of novelty – is generally defined as an invention that has found its users. In common usage, innovation is associated with economic competitiveness, with markets, with patents. The central paradigm of innovation is based on the notion of creative destruction. This paradigm corresponds to the dominant way of designing the process, of teaching it and of constructing, implementing and evaluating policies. In this context, even if it has negative effects, innovation is always good. While many studies have widely questioned this, innovation is still generally considered a linear process in public policy, from research to market. This is particularly apparent in the way innovation statistics are constructed (see the famous OECD Oslo Manual) or, even more so, in the widespread use of management instruments which – like the well known technology readiness levels (TRL) invented by NASA – reinforce the perception of innovation as a linear process.

The critical analyses that are being developed within the field of innovation studies now make it possible to better grasp the narrowness of these conceptions and to think about innovation differently. In this sense, we have shown elsewhere that the central paradigm of innovation rests on several deeply rooted beliefs (or myths) that determine the way innovation policies are designed and implemented (Joly 2019).

The first myth is that technological innovation, because it is the source of economic competitiveness, is the best answer to major societal problems. This belief is an extension of the trickle-down theory. Like this theory – which tells us that when the rich get richer, society as a whole benefits – the idea here is that innovation as the source of economic competitiveness will, through the trickle-down effect, provide the solution to major societal problems. This belief is also strongly associated with technological solutionism, i.e. the idea that technology is the source of solutions to problems generated by technology. In this sense, innovation is a promise. The second myth is that innovation is a linear process, largely determined by the increase in the stock of knowledge, notably linked to emerging technologies (yesterday computer science and biotechnology, today Big Data, artificial intelligence and synthetic biology). The third myth is that innovation is always good: the inevitable amount of destruction is always compensated by what innovation allows us to create.

These founding myths are common to both the Schumpeterian model of the heroic entrepreneur and the more contemporary model of innovation systems. In all cases, the only thing that counts is the pace of innovation, which must be maximized and measured by a series of indicators (patents, creation of companies by researchers, the share of innovative SMEs, R&D spending, etc.). These indicators play a crucial role because, by providing a measure of the effectiveness of the policies implemented, they have a normative value. However, authoritative indicators, such as the ranking of innovative countries by the European Commission (Innovation Union Scoreboard), have been clearly established (Edquist and Zabala 2015). The direction – or orientation – of innovation does not matter since what matters first and foremost is to increase the wealth and competitiveness of companies on the markets, the rest will follow! However, environmental degradation (manifested in particular by climate change and the collapse of biodiversity) and increased inequality show this is not the case. The ecological and inclusive transition that we are promised will not come naturally from an increase in the pace of innovation. This requires, on the one hand, a revision of the central paradigm in order to think about a broad-based innovation, both in its processes (distributed, bottom-up, interactive innovation, etc.) and in its objectives (social, sustainable, responsible, frugal innovation, etc.). On the other hand, it requires transforming research and innovation policies so that they do not stick to the short-lived promise of solutionism but rather build public policy instruments dedicated to orienting innovation towards the major challenges facing society.

34.3. Transformations of innovation policies: directionality and social innovation

Criticisms of the central innovation paradigm are fueling a renewal of innovation policies. We have discussed elsewhere two sources of transformation: the democratization of innovation linked to the active role of creative communities and the responsibility for research and innovation, particularly promoted by the European Commission since the beginning of the 2010s (Joly 2017, 2019). Here, we focus on two complementary sources of transformation: the return of directionality in innovation policies and social innovation. Traditionally, innovation policies aim to create a framework that is conducive to the concretization of new ideas with a view to bringing them to market. This means addressing so-called market failures by funding basic research from public funds, protecting intellectual property through patents, fostering partnerships between public research and industry, and supporting innovation. In France, the research tax credit is the preferred instrument of innovation policies, with public investment of €6 billion per year, with no conditionality on the direction of innovation.

Over the past 10–15 years, Europe, the United States and most OECD countries have affirmed the need to direct research and innovation towards addressing "big challenges". Take the example of the European Commission. The need for European research to address major societal challenges is mentioned in the Green Paper on the European Research Area adopted by the Commission in April 2007. The Lund Declaration of 2009 called for European research to focus on "big challenges" (in areas such as global warming, scarcity of energy, water and food supplies, an aging society, public health, pandemics and security) instead of the traditional thematic approach that prevailed before. The European Research Framework Program H2020 (2011–2017) has been built on this basis, with 45% of the budget devoted to "major challenges". During preparation of the next Horizon Europe Framework Program, it was decided to go further in this direction with the design of "missions". The Lamy report proposed a mission- and impact-oriented approach to address global challenges (Lamy 2017). While societal challenges can be seen as the broader goal or benefit sought (e.g. combating climate change), missions represent a more narrowly defined set of activities that are intended to produce a verifiable outcome on a planned time scale that can be used to measure progress in addressing the societal challenge. The Expert Group on the Economic and Societal Impact of Research and Innovation (ESIR), established in 2017 to advise the Commissioner for Research and Innovation, has played a key role in the development of mission-oriented research and innovation policy (Mazzucato 2018).

This shift towards directionality is based on theoretical contributions that allow us to appreciate the importance of the necessary changes:

– *Innovation does not necessarily mean the introduction of something new, but may involve the implementation of alternatives that have been excluded by lock-in phenomena linked to the technique and to dominant players*. In this case, innovation policy is an unlocking policy. Here we can cite the work of Andrew Stirling (2008), who draws on STS and the history of technology and reminds us that we must take into account the multiple possible directions of innovation, identify the lock-in effects that prevent the exploration of alternative trajectories and find ways to open up the innovation process. This consideration of directionality later inspired the STEPS Centre's "Sussex Manifesto" (2010).

– *Directionality requires going beyond traditional silo approaches and coordinating different areas: research policy, innovation policy and sectoral policy*. In this sense, Weber and Rohracher (2012) have proposed the term "transformational system failure" to underline the need to consider the justification for public intervention not only from the perspective of the traditional approach to market failures, but also the need to orient innovation to solve major societal problems or challenges. This leads the authors to identify several components of failures, namely: directionality failure, demand articulation failure, policy coordination failure, and reflexivity failure.

– *The response to major challenges cannot be achieved by adapting existing systems but requires profound systemic changes.* In a programmatic article, Schot and Steinmueller (2018) (at the crossroads of transition studies and innovation studies) suggest that a new generation of so-called transformative innovation policies is needed. Transformative innovations cannot be decreed: they require that a wide range of options (well beyond the narrow limits set by dominant actors) be explored through a set of social experiments. Policies which support transformative innovations require adaptability, reversibility, learning and anticipation.

It is easy to understand the distance between an innovation policy that takes directionality seriously and current policies oriented towards major challenges. It is essential to reduce this distance; otherwise, there is a risk that such policies will be nothing more than empty promises.

The link with the enlargement that social innovation can bring can be made if we stick to a definition that associates it with three major changes[1]:

– open and inclusive innovation processes in which users and, more broadly, citizens or groups of citizens play an active and deliberate role;

– an innovation in which social transformations play a central role, with technology only supporting them;

– an innovation whose objectives are not reduced to private values but take into account collective issues, including major societal challenges.

Social innovation thus constitutes both an end in itself, for the values of openness and inclusiveness, and a means to implement the set of social experiments essential to explore and promote alternatives to the dominant socio-technical systems.

34.4. Conclusion

Innovating differently is not only a possibility, it is also an imperative. In this sense, this chapter has shown that innovation critics are now at the heart of innovation studies and that this change is accompanied by major transformations in innovation policies. However, this should not be misunderstood. Innovation systems and the policies linked to them do not change easily because they are subject to powerful interlocks that are as much due to socio-cognitive factors (cultural elements, knowledge, routines, etc.) as to the interests of the dominant players.

1 See the European SI-DRIVE project – http://www.si-drive.eu/

The intensification of this fundamental movement will be mainly due to three elements. Research on innovation will make an essential contribution by showing the limits of current policies and the importance of alternatives, including social innovations. To do so, it will be essential to develop metrics and indicators adapted to both a broader conception of innovation and directionality. Second, it is essential to develop a set of policy experiments, at different scales, in order to accelerate learning processes and gain experience of these policies. Finally, there are likely to be policy opportunities, particularly in times of crisis that destabilize dominant systems. From this point of view, the crisis linked to the COVID-19 pandemic should be seized as an opportunity.

34.5. References

Edquist, C. and Zabala-Iturriagagoitia, D. (2015). The Innovation Union Scoreboard is flawed: The case of Sweden – Not the innovation leader of the EU. CIRCLE Papers, Lund University, Sweden.

Joly, P.B. (2017). Beyond the competitiveness framework? Models of innovation revisited. *Journal of Innovation Economics Management*, 1, 79–96.

Joly, P.-B. (2019). Reimagining innovation. In *Innovation Beyond Technology*, Lechevallier, S. (ed). Springer, Singapore.

Lamy, P. (2017). LAB – FAB – APP – Investing in the European future we want. Report, European Commission, Brussels.

Mazzucato, M. (2018). Mission-oriented research & innovation in the European Union: A problem-solving approach to fuel innovation-led growth. Report, European Commission, Brussels.

Schot, J. and Steinmueller, W.E. (2018). Three frames for innovation policy: R&D, systems of innovation and transformative change. *Research Policy*, 47(9), 1554–1567.

Soete, L. (2013). Is innovation always good? In *Innovation Studies – Evolution and Future Challenges*, Fagerberg, J., Martin, B.R., Andersen, E.S. (eds). Oxford University Press, Oxford.

STEPS Centre (2010). Innovation, sustainability, development: A new manifesto. Manifesto, STEPS Centre, Brighton.

Stirling, A. (2008). "Opening up" and "closing down". Power, participation, and pluralism in the social appraisal of technology, *Science Technology and Human Values*, 33(2), 262–294.

Weber, K.M. and Rohracher, H. (2012). Legitimizing research, technology and innovation policies for transformative change: Combining insights from innovation systems and multi-level perspective in a comprehensive "failures" framework. *Research Policy*, 41(6), 1037–1047.

35

Property – Intellectual Property and Innovation

35.1. Introduction

Intellectual property rights (IPRs) are a set of legal norms that an inventor or creator can use to protect, compensate and preserve the rights attached to the creations of the mind. IPRs are divided into three categories. First, copyrights and related rights, which cover literary and artistic works. Second, industrial property that covers utilitarian creations, such as patents and plant breeders' certificates. Third, distinctive signs such as trademarks, industrial designs, domain names or appellations of origins. These three categories have been supplemented over time by a *sui generis* system of protection, i.e. a special form of protection regime outside the known framework, to remedy the inadequacy of protection for certain needs, like, for instance, semiconductors and databases, as well as indigenous and traditional knowledge. The importance of IP was first recognized in the Paris Convention for the Protection of Industrial Property (1883) and the Berne Convention for the Protection of Literary and Artistic Works (1886). The promotion and protection of intellectual property is indeed supposed to spur creation and innovation and be a driver of economic gross and job creation.

The implementation and the respect of IPRs have, however, attracted increasing attention both in academic circles, as well as in public policy debates over the past decades. On one hand, piracy and counterfeiting, and also IP litigation are on the increase and are likely to reduce the incentives to create and invent. On the other hand, the fast growth of sectors in which innovation and appropriability play a key role, and also reforms in the national and international legal frameworks, have resulted in an expansion of the field of patentability and in a strengthening of IPRs.

Chapter written by Béatrice DUMONT.

This has resulted in a risk of over-protection (Beckerman-Rodau 2011) and may lead to limiting the dissemination of works and the use of innovations. Criticisms mainly concentrate on the patent system and the force behind proposals to abolish it, on the basis that no argument proves that the patent system is significantly profitable for innovation (Boldrin and Levine 2008) and that it could even be a "tax" on innovation (Jaffe and Lerner 2004). In order to examine these issues, this chapter first looks at the mechanism of IP. We then analyze the multidimensional impact of protection on innovation. Finally, we turn to the new roles of IPRs.

35.2. IPRs: some imperfect but unmatched mechanisms

The question of why inventions and artistic works need protection, and whether IPRs are prompting or restricting creation and innovation is a difficult one. Initially, the economic literature (Arrow 1962; Nordhaus 1969) has concentrated on patents and their effects on R&D investment decisions, and more precisely on technical progress. As highlighted in the seminal paper by Arrow (1962), the main problem when it comes to innovation is that of appropriability and relates to the public characteristics of good knowledge. Indeed, innovation is generally considered to be the result of a "flash of genius", which, from an economic point of view, is regarded as the production of information. Information has two characteristics: it is non-excludable and its consumption is non-rival. These features imply that social returns from R&D are higher than private returns, especially because, without protection, rivals would presumably be able to imitate the invention at a much lower cost than the initial R&D cost. This means that from a welfare point of view, the community loses out because goods that could have found an outlet will not be produced and thus, there is useless rationing.

By striking a balance between the interests of innovators and creators and the wider public interest, the IP system aims to foster an environment in which creativity and innovation can flourish. In practice, by offering an exclusive right for a limited period of time, IP laws resolve these two problems sequentially. In a first stage, the legal mechanism of IP makes the invention excludable. It means that users need to get a license and to pay royalties to use the protected goods. In a second stage, the IP right falls into the public domain, everyone can access it free of charge. As a result, there is a compromise between, on one hand, the incentives to create and innovate (dynamic efficiency) and the dissemination of the results obtained (static efficiency). However, this sequential processing is necessarily imperfect. In order to limit the problem posed by non-excludability, the duration of legal protection must be infinite, while it must be zero to eliminate the problem posed by non-rivalry.

As the granting of an exclusive right of limited duration is an imperfect mechanism, why use it? Wouldn't there be better instruments? In the presence of both non-excludable and non-rival goods, economic theory prescribes to use subsidies or sponsorships. The problem here is that the removal of the deadweight loss is achieved at the cost of taxation on other goods, which has the effect of introducing distortions in other compartments of the economy. Moreover, the amount of subsidy offered is not perfectly adjusted to the social value of the innovation. Intellectual property is a second best, but there is no better alternative to date.

35.3. The multidimensional impact of protection on innovation

In the specific case of patents, three elements can be highlighted with regard to the impact of IP protection on innovation. The first element is the duration of protection. Patent duration is a means of controlling the extent of the rights granted to innovators. The TRIPS Agreement sets this period at 20 years. Prolonging this period would provide additional profits to innovators and thus, theoretically increase their incentives to innovate. The conclusion that follows is: why do patents not last indefinitely? Among the reasons often underlined, the deadweight loss resulting from monopoly pricing is key (Nordhaus 1969).

Another important element is the breadth of protection. This concept allows the definition of where the "boundary" lies, between what is protected by the patent and what is not. It presupposes the existence of elements describing the patented invention, made known to all by the publication of the patent document. This is a key patent parameter as it measures nothing less than the direct economic impact of the patent on competition, i.e. the use that the innovator can make of it. Intuitively, a broad patent is a way to strengthen incentives for innovation, but is there an optimal breadth? The question at stake here is whether to guarantee a given level of incentive, it is better to have short and broad patents or long and narrow patents? There is a indetermination in the economic literature *vis-à-vis* this issue. Indeed, some studies show that a narrow patent of infinite duration is preferable to a short and broad patent, to ensure a given level of incentive (Gilbert and Shapiro 1990).

Conversely, other studies (notably, Gallini 1992) show that a broad patent for a short period of time is better because it provides better protection against counterfeiting. It is indeed costly for imitators to enter a market if the patent is broad because it increases the cost of imitation. Broadly speaking, what studies show, however, is that by limiting the breadth of a patent, patent offices allow the development of a competitive fringe, bypassing it without infringing it. The interest is to encourage marginal extensions that have not been considered by the patent applicant, that meet a need, but are not necessarily innovative enough to justify a new patent.

The third element of IP protection is patent height. This concept is closely linked to both the definition of what is patentable (i.e. the level of innovation required for a patent to be granted) and the notion of incremental innovation. It relates partly to the tradeoff between the protection of first generation versus second generation inventions. If the criteria of novelty and inventiveness are strictly applied, only significant advances will be patented. Conversely, if the interpretation is too lax, there is a risk that small patents will multiply and hinder future progress.

Besides these elements, it is worth stressing that IP laws create exclusive and transferable rights. Indeed, IPRs not only have an incentive function, but they also facilitate the trade of technologies and thus, their diffusion. From an economic point of view, transferability is as important as exclusivity because it allows the asset to be used by those who value it best (including competitors via licensing) and favors a division of labor. The negotiation of IP transfers and its effects on efficiency is the subject of the Coase's theorem, which states that negotiation leads to an efficient allocation of resources when property rights are clearly defined and there are no transaction costs, regardless of the initial distribution of rights. The problem is that IPRs are not always well defined. Indeed, inventions or creations have a less precise scope than, for example, plots of land. Public authorities have two complementary means of action to promote efficiency when transaction costs are positive. They may attribute the right of ownership from the outset to those who are best placed to benefit from it, or they may seek to facilitate the exchange by reducing transaction costs. This explains why non-technical ideas and theories are kept in the public domain. This avoids the need to negotiate with an IP owner every time a sentence is spoken or reasoning is developed. Similarly, for joint innovations, patent pools are a way to issue a single license to users, while saving costs.

35.4. The new roles of IPRs

The question of whether the traditional incentive role of patents is confirmed in practice has been the subject of many empirical works. Surveys of U.S. innovative firms by Levin *et al.* (1987) and Cohen *et al.* (2000) notably show that patents are not deemed to be the most effective protection mechanism in many industries, although they rank high in the pharmaceutical and chemical sectors. These authors show that firms value secrecy, lead times or complementary sales, more than patents in most sectors. In the same vein, Arundel (2001) shows similar results in the EU. First-mover advantages are deemed as the most effective mechanism to protect innovation, and participation in cooperative R&D arrangements reduces the probability that a firm would prefer secrecy to patents. Among the reasons for not trusting patents, the costs of applying and defending patents prove to be important reasons for not patenting, especially among SMEs.

Although patents are not the most effective method for protecting innovations, many firms employ them anyway. These findings have led economists to analyze the so-called "patent paradox" stemming from the gap between the relative ineffectiveness of patents as an appropriability mechanism and the sharp rise in patents applications in the last three decades. Hall and Ziedonis (2001) show that the increase in patent propensity in the semiconductor industry is not only due to a willingness to protect and appropriate the results of inventions, but can also be explained by a "strategic" use of patents. This translates into patent portfolio races in order to reduce concerns about "patent hold up", use of patents as "bargaining chips" in order to negotiate access to external technologies on more favorable terms with third parties, strategies of patent blocking to increase rivals' costs into a particular technological trajectory, to enhance reputation as a technological leader or for small firms to attract venture capital. To put these studies in perspective, it is worth stressing that, in practice, firms tend to use more than one appropriability method. Different instruments not only coexist, but are also compatible with one another (Cohen *et al.* 2000).

The question of the relationship between productivity gains, R&D and patenting has led to contradictory findings. In this regard, the fragmentation of ownership of highly complementary rights can lead to an under-exploitation of patented inventions. This result is known as the tragedy of the anti-commons (Heller & Eisenberg 1998), to underline that there is both opposition ("too much property" vs. "no property") and similarity (social inefficiency with under-exploitation vs. over-exploitation) with the tragedy of the commons. These findings also led some authors like Boldrin *et al.* (2011) to conclude that the patent system is inefficient for promoting innovation.

35.5. Conclusion

Only looking at innovation through the lens of patents introduces a bias, since not all innovations are necessarily patented. However, today, in the eyes of some economists, the idea that IP has flaws that are getting worse prevails. Statistics about patents have created the idea of an exponential demography of patents which seems out of control. Until recently, economists were skeptical about the positive effect of patents on innovation. Some economists now fear that stronger IPRs could lead to a slowdown in innovation. From being an incentive tool, IP has indeed become a disruptive factor, at least in some sectors, as illustrated by the rise of IP litigation. This ambivalence of intellectual property rights has long been recognized. However, the inability to develop an alternative sustainable mechanism may be seen as "default" proof that IPRs are the best system.

35.6. References

Arrow, K. (1962). Economic welfare and the allocation of resources for invention. In *The Rate and Direction of Inventive Activity: Economic and Social Factors*, Universities-National Bureau Committee for Economic Research, Committee on Economic Growth of the Social Science Research Council (ed.). Princeton University Press, Princeton, NJ.

Arundel, A. (2001). The relative effectiveness of patents and secrecy for appropriation. *Research Policy*, 30(4), 611–624.

Beckerman-Rodau, A. (2011). The problem with intellectual property rights: Subject matter expansion. *Yale Journal of Law and Technology*, 13(1), 1–89.

Boldrin, M. and Levine, D.K. (2008). *Against Intellectual Monopoly*. Cambridge University Press, Cambridge.

Cohen, W.M., Nelson, R.R., Walsh, J.P. (2000). Protecting their intellectual assets: Appropriability conditions and why U.S. manufacturing firms patent (or not). NBER Working Paper, 7552.

Hall, B.H. and Ziedonis, R.H. (2001). The patent paradox revisited: An empirical study of patenting in the U.S. semiconductor industry, 1979–1995. *The RAND Journal of Economics*, 32(1), 101–128.

Heller, M. and Eisenberg, R. (1998). Can patents deter innovation? The anticommons in biomedial research. *Science*, 280, 698–701.

Jaffe, A.B. and Lerner, J. (2004). *Innovation and Its Discontents: How Our Broken Patent System Is Endangering Innovation and Progress, and What to Do About It*. Princeton University Press, Princeton, NJ.

Levin, R.C., Klevorick, A.K., Nelson, R.R., Winter, S. (1987). Appropriating the returns from industrial R&D. *Brookings Papers on Economic Activity*, 18(3), 783–832.

Nordhaus, K.J. (1969). An economic theory of technological change. *American Economic Review*, 59(2), 18–28.

36

Proximity – Impacts of Geographic, Organizational and Cognitive Proximities on Innovation

36.1. Introduction

The *Ecole de la Proximité* (School of Proximity) was founded in France in the mid-1990s with the primary objective of integrating the role of space in economic analysis. It is no longer a question of assimilating space as a simple cost linked to distance or land, and therefore as an obstacle that must be overcome, but of perceiving it, first and foremost, as a system of economic relations. The analysis shifts, no longer focusing on what separates but first on what associates. In addition to the space that generates costs which limit coordination, there is also the idea of a space that offers resources to which proximity gives access. For this dynamic and for others (like the work on innovative environments developed in this volume), the behavior of actors must be analyzed in terms of their place in the space, and therefore their situation in relation to various other actors, groups or organizations (Torre and Talbot 2018). It supposes that location in a given space is likely to reinforce and/or destroy interactions between actors.

The *Ecole de la Proximité* has endeavored to analyze the successes and failures of clusters in a context where permanent innovation appears to be the solution for rich countries to cope with increased competition. The creation of specific local resources, which by their nature cannot be redeployed, is a way of anchoring companies in a territory. Specific knowledge of a very tacit nature is a paradigmatic

---

Chapter written by Damien TALBOT.

example of such local resources, as geographical proximity gives access to them. Therefore, this School poses the following question: Is it necessary to be close to innovate?

To answer this question, we present the positive and negative effects of geographical proximity on innovation, then non-geographical proximities, before concluding.

36.2. A geographical proximity that plays favorably on innovation, without being indispensable

We distinguish several categories of proximities. Thus, geographical proximity refers to the distance in kilometers that separates two or more actors. It is measured by including two categories of elements in the analysis: on the one hand, objective elements such as the temporal, communication and monetary cost of crossing the distance, and on the other hand, a subjective element, since it is ultimately based on a judgment made by individuals on the nature of the distance separating them (Torre and Rallet 2005; Talbot *et al.* 2020).

This geographical proximity between actors co-located in metropolitan areas with varied sectoral structures would make local knowledge from private and public research accessible. This proximity facilitates face-to-face relations, which are known to make tacit exchanges more fluid, reduce the risk of opportunism by accentuating the possibilities of control, and promote the progressive construction of trust over the course of successful coordination and thus the dissemination of knowledge (Breschi and Lissoni 2009). These same actors also benefit from public and private service infrastructures and human capital that is always spatially concentrated and not very mobile. As a whole the firms' capacity to innovate is therefore increased.

Geographical proximity thus has a potentially positive effect on innovation, but it is not indispensable. As proof, the most innovative actors often maintain strong collaborations with partners located at a distance, freeing themselves from the constraint of geographical proximity, in some cases even deliberately to escape the local confinement by diversifying their links (Bathelt *et al.* 2004). Geographical proximity can even hinder innovation if, for example, a region is locked into a rigid trajectory, as is the case for highly specialized regions: concentration on one sector of activity, one technology, can prevent the emergence of a new development path (Boschma 2005). In order to innovate, they call upon non-geographic proximities.

36.3. Other proximities have both positive and negative effects on innovation

The actor is present both "here and elsewhere", since one can be "close" to someone while being geographically distant. Proximity therefore has a non-geographic dimension. The number and nature of non-geographic dimensions vary according to the authors. For example, Boschma (2005) distinguishes four types of non-geographical proximity: (1) he defines cognitive proximity as having a similar and/or complementary knowledge base; (2) actors belonging to the same organization or organizational form share organizational proximity; (3) institutional proximity refers to conforming, in one's actions, to the same institutions, formal or informal, such as laws, rules, customs and values; and (4) social proximity measures individual membership in the same social network. Table 36.1 summarizes the different forms of proximity.

Dimensions	Definition
Geographical proximity	Belonging to the same geographical area
Cognitive proximity	Sharing similar and/or complementary knowledge
Organizational proximity	Belonging to the same governance structure
Institutional proximity	Sharing formal and informal institutions
Social proximity	Belonging to the same social network

Table 36.1. *Dimensions of proximity according to Boschma (2005) (source: author)*

In order to innovate collectively, the actors mobilize all or part of these interlinked proximities between them (Boschma and Frenken 2010). Cognitive proximity can, for example, compensate for a spatial dispersion of actors collaborating on an innovation project. This identity of knowledge bases drives collaborative innovation because it allows actors to absorb new knowledge: their cognitive bases must be close enough to the knowledge to be acquired in order to understand it, verify its usefulness with respect to that already possessed internally and, ultimately, learn it. There is therefore a positive relationship between cognitive proximity, absorption capacity and knowledge transfer.

However, if too much cognitive distance prevents collaborative innovation, too much cognitive proximity is detrimental to such interactions. Direct similarity between knowledge bases reduces the value of the exchanges for the actors involved. Moreover, the creation of new knowledge requires dissimilar and complementary bodies of knowledge to limit redundancies and to generate new ideas (Boschma and Frenken 2010). The aim is to avoid cognitive short-sightedness, preventing companies from seizing new opportunities offered by emerging technologies (Nooteboom 2004). Thus, cognitive proximity has a positive effect on innovation up to a certain point, and beyond this point it becomes a hindrance (Cassi and Plunket 2014).

In the case where cognitive proximity plays a positive role in innovation, governance problems may arise. In order to exploit the complementarity of knowledge, collaborative innovation generally brings together various agents with divergent interests (large groups, SMEs, public laboratories, universities, etc.). In concrete terms, any innovation relationship involves three risks (Nooteboom 2004): (1) actors lose the investments made specifically for this innovation if the collaboration ends; (2) an opportunistic partner may use the results of the collaboration for their own benefit; and (3) knowledge may be unintentionally diffused (knowledge spillover). Organizational proximity, which is the source of common governance, is therefore essential to contain these risks (Beaugency and Talbot 2018).

> [It] brings together the agents participating in a given activity within the framework of a particular structure. […] is deployed within organizations – firms, institutions, etc. – and, where appropriate, between organizations linked by a relationship of economic or financial dependence or interdependence – between companies that are members of an industrial or financial group, within a network, etc. (Kirat and Lung 1995, p. 213).

This governance structure has the effect of controlling stakeholders by limiting the risks of opportunism and the legal and economic autonomy of its members, thus making a secure innovation relationship possible. For example, by organizing the circulation of information and creating technological monitoring systems, the absorption capacity of the actors improves. And, by stabilizing the relationship, it also nurtures the trust that is built step by step.

However, as with geographical and cognitive proximity, strong organizational proximity can limit interactions to overly specific domains, while asymmetry resulting from the size of the actors potentially leads to difficulties in retaining information (Nooteboom 2004). A highly hierarchical network of organizations can become a closed system that reduces access to new knowledge, limits learning or does not offer sufficient organizational flexibility to implement innovations. It is therefore necessary to arbitrate between control and the autonomy of the actors.

Two other forms of proximity can play a role in innovation. Institutional proximity is associated with the political and institutional framework that governs interactions. It includes both "rules of the game" (legal framework and rules) and the idea of a common culture (language, ways of seeing the world, common representations, belief systems, mental maps, categorizations and classifications) at the level of a country, cluster or industry. Speaking the same language, having a legal framework protecting intellectual property rights and a national policy providing tax incentives helps innovation by securing relationships. Sharing the same institutional environment leads to the development of similar behaviors. This similarity, as well as a conservative culture, can hinder adaptation to changes in the environment. Thus, institutional inertia can lead to a lock in that prevents change (Boschma 2005). Institutional proximity then plays a negative role by preventing the appearance of new behaviors.

Economic relations in general, and innovation relations in particular, are always "embedded" in a social network. Social proximity measures this embeddedness. Family ties, friendship, belonging to a network of former students, etc. perpetuate the relationships of innovation that are nourished by the commitment of each individual. They are a source of trust and therefore of knowledge exchange. Social proximity limits the risk of opportunistic behavior because the social cost of such behavior is high, as sanctions can be severe and can go as far as exclusion from the group. Conversely, excessive devotion can lock an actor into pre-established behaviors, to the detriment of their own capacity for innovation, or lead them to underestimate the risk of opportunistic behavior, making them more vulnerable to it (Boschma 2005).

36.4. Conclusion

To conclude, it should be noted that the different proximities are dependent on each other (Torre and Rallet 2005; Boschma and Frenken 2010). In the case of innovative clusters (see Chapters 8 and 41 in Volume 1, and Chapter 33 in Volume 2), geographical proximity between two individuals can reinforce their social proximity, since friendship is nourished by frequent encounters, and thus deepen their mutual trust. The other proximities are also mobilized by the stakeholders of the clusters – since the actors rely on common knowledge bases (cognitive proximity) – around a project (organizational proximity) that can support a regional innovation system (again, see Chapter 33 in Volume 2 for more on this subject) or an intense local culture (institutional proximity). In this case, proximities strengthen each other. They can also compensate for one another: for example, strong organizational proximity thanks to information technology (think of Electronic Data Interchange, EDI) compensates for the spatial dispersion of organizations engaged in a collective innovation process, allowing knowledge to be exchanged over long distances. A common culture (belonging to the same industry, for example) also compensates for significant geographical distance. They can finally destroy each other. Geographical proximity can generate conflicts within neighborhoods or regarding use of space, putting an end to an innovative collaborative network that constitutes organizational proximity.

36.5. References

Bathelt, H., Malmberg, A., Maskell, P. (2004). Clusters and knowledge: Local buzz, global pipelines and the process of knowledge creation. *Progress in Human Geography*, 28(1), 31–56.

Beaugency, A. and Talbot, D. (2018). Proximité cognitive et knowledge spillover dans l'avionique. Une analyse à partir des brevets et des publications scientifiques. *Innovations*, 55(1), 223–246.

Boschma, R. (2005). Proximity and innovation. A critical assessment. *Regional Studies*, 39(1), 61–74.

Boschma, R. and Frenken, K. (2010). The spatial evolution of innovation networks: A proximity perspective. In *The Handbook of Evolutionary Economic Geography*, Boschma, R. and Martin, R. (eds). Edward Elgar, Cheltenham.

Breschi, S. and Lissoni, F. (2009). Mobility of skilled workers and co-invention networks: An anatomy of localized knowledge flows. *Journal of Economic Geography*, 9(4), 439–468.

Cassi, L. and Plunket, A. (2014). Proximity, network formation and inventive performance: In search of the proximity paradox. *The Annals of Regional Science*, 53(2), 395–422.

Kirat, T. and Lung, Y. (1995). Innovations et proximités : le territoire, lieu de déploiement des processus d'apprentissage. In *Coordination économique et apprentissage des firmes*, Lazaric, N. and Monnier, J.-M. (eds). Economica, Paris.

Nooteboom, B. (2004). *Inter-firm Collaboration, Learning and Networks. An Integrated Approach*. Routledge, New York.

Talbot, D., Charreire-Petit, S., Pokrovsky, A. (2020). La proximité comme perception de la distance. Le cas de la télémédecine. *Revue française de gestion*, 46(289), 51–74.

Torre, A. and Rallet, A. (2005). Proximity and localization. *Regional Studies*, 39(1), 47–60.

Torre, A. and Talbot, D. (2018). Proximités : retour sur 25 années d'analyse. *Revue d'économie régionale et urbaine*, 5/6, 917–936.

37

Responsibility – Responsible Innovation in Corporate Strategy and Public Policy

37.1. Introduction

Innovation and responsibility: how to reconcile these two increasingly juxtaposed terms, both in public innovation policy and in private companies? This association is relatively recent, even though each of the two terms, taken separately, has been in use for a long time. It has been introduced with the expression "RRI" (responsible research and innovation) in research and innovation policy, particularly in Europe. The concept has undergone considerable development since the early 2000s, in various forms. It refers to the responsibility of researchers and innovators, and also interacts with the concept of companies' corporate social responsibility. Here, we present the genesis of the concept in research and innovation policy and then in companies.

37.2. Responsible research and innovation policy

The link between science, technology and society has long been taken into account by philosophers. Some of them, such as Francis Bacon, have attributed a positive effect on society to technology (Stilgoe *et al.* 2013), while others, such as Habermas or J. Ellul, have denounced the power of technology over society. Most sociologists and technology philosophers today agree that science, technology and society cannot be considered as independent spheres. The advent of new controversial technologies such as biotechnology, nanotechnology, and even information and communication technology has renewed debates. This change has been accompanied by an increased awareness of environmental issues and a new

---

Chapter written by Leïla TEMRI.

questioning of the responsibility which researchers and innovators have in this regard. These changes have been reflected in research and innovation policy, particularly, but not exclusively, in Europe. Thus, the OECD recently published a recommendation on responsible innovation in the field of neurotechnology, "the first international standard in this field"[1]. This development is based on two major trends considered to be the foundations of the notion of responsible research and innovation.

37.2.1. *The responsibility of researchers and innovators in science and technology*

The question of the responsibility of scientists was raised at the end of World War II after the first use of the atomic bomb (Durbin 1992). It led to the creation in 1976 of the Committee on Scientific Freedom and Responsibility by the American Association for the Advancement of Science (AAAS), whose members published numerous articles in the association's journal, "Science". The responsibility of engineers was starting to be considered, raising many questions about the ethics of the research carried out by scientists and engineers. The philosopher Hans Jonas highlighted the need to question the future consequences of the implementation of techniques and not only their immediate effects, extending the temporal horizon of responsibility (Jonas 1990). He also recommended taking the current and future interests of other actors, who are now called stakeholders into account.

37.2.2. *Technological assessment: from autonomous technology to the social construction of techniques*

The second foundation of responsible research and innovation is the evaluation of technologies or "Technological Assessment" (TA). This trend emerged in the United States in the 1970s. It aimed to identify the potential risks of new technologies in order to prepare or compensate for them, not to avoid them, since technology was then considered to have its own dynamics, independent of society (Grundwald 2011). According to this author, however, in responsible innovation, this approach is complemented by considering the ethics of responsibility, and by the Science, Technology and Society (STS) movement, which requires inter- and transdisciplinary approaches. By the 1980s, the idea of the existence of a social construction of science and technology was accepted. Habermas's (1973) work, followed by the German sociologist Ulrich Beck's book on risk society *Risk Society: Towards a New Modernity* (Beck 1992), denouncing the increase in

1 https://www.oecd.org/fr/sti/tech-emergentes/recommandation-innovation-responsable-dans-le-domaine-des-neurotechnologies.htm [accessed 25/03/2020].

technological risks to the wider society, reinforced the need to involve society more in evaluations of technology and in the definition of its goals, so that these changes would be in line with its values (Pellé and Reber 2013). This implies questioning the prerogatives of experts and public institutions in technological decisions, and introducing more reflexivity.

37.2.3. *Responsible research and innovation in policy*

Since the early 2000s, there has been an increase in citizen participation in the governance of research and policy innovation, in order to ensure the legitimacy of public decisions in scientific matters. In the United States, it has developed around nanotechnology research programs, leading to the establishment of the concept of responsible research and innovation, supported by the *National Science Foundation*. Other countries such as the United Kingdom, the Netherlands and Japan have followed suit. European research programs, in particular the H2020 program that began in 2014, have made significant contributions to its development. von Schomberg, often considered as the promoter of the concept in European policies, provided its first definition (Von Schomberg 2011). Currently, the European Commission proposes:

> Responsible research and innovation is an approach that anticipates and assesses potential implications and societal expectations with regard to research and innovation, with the aim to foster the design of inclusive and sustainable research and innovation.[2]

It places particular emphasis on six key dimensions of RRI:

– public commitment to collaboration between research, industry, policy and civil society;

– gender equality, particularly in research;

– scientific education from the earliest age;

– open access/science to make results more available to everyone;

– ethics, in order to ensure a high societal value of research and innovation;

– research and innovation governance that ensures respect for the other five dimensions.

2 https://ec.europa.eu/programmes/horizon2020/en/h2020-section/responsible-research-innovation [accessed on 05/04/2020].

In addition, the innovation process must meet the following four criteria:

– the diversity and inclusion of different categories of actors early in the process;

– anticipation and reflexivity, in order to consider the future impacts of research and innovation as early as possible and to act better accordingly;

– openness and transparency, on methods, results, implications of research and innovation;

– responsiveness and adaptation in order to change ways of thinking and behaving, in line with changing conditions, to better align action with the needs expressed by stakeholders and audiences.

The concept is still being developed in other countries, such as Australia, where it has been adopted by the CSIRO (Commonwealth Scientific and Industrial Research Organisation), Canada, Germany and Brazil.

37.3. Responsible innovation in companies

In companies, the origins of responsible innovation can be found, as in the case of RRI, in the work of philosopher Hans Jonas (1979), but also in the concept of corporate social responsibility or CSR (Pavia 2012). Initially, CSR focused primarily on the link between business and society. The term "Corporate Social Responsibility" first appeared in the 19th century with the advent of large industrial companies with varied shareholders (Aggeri *et al.* 2005). From the 1920s onwards, questions were raised about the responsibility of companies and their managers, particularly with regard to their employees, often by industry leaders such as Ford, Edison, Sloan and Chester Barnard. They generated philanthropic action, often of inspired by Protestant belief. The first academic works in this field were written by Howard Bowen, an American economist, who laid the first foundations in his book *Social Responsibilities of the Businessman* published in 1953. The book is today considered as the starting point of the Business and Society movement in the United States. Bowen asks businesspeople to consider the impact of their decisions on the well-being of society (in the broadest sense), of which they are a part, and of what will later be called the "stakeholders" of their activities. He defines social responsibility as "the obligations of businesspeople to conduct policies, make decisions, or take actions that are desirable in terms of the goals and values of our society" (Bowen 1953).

The development of this concept, during the 1960s and 1970s, occurred in a context where the legitimacy of the large firm as a form of organization of economic activities was being strongly questioned in the United States (Aggeri *et al.* 2005). The concept of "stakeholder", developed by Edward Freeman in 1984 in the book

Strategic Management: A Stakeholder Approach, constitutes another major advance in the theoretical conception of CSR.

At the same time, starting in the 1970s, the Meadows report "The Limits to Growth"[3] laid the foundations for what would later become sustainable development by explicitly introducing the question of the limits of natural resources and thus raising the question of the environment. The report of the United Nations Commission on Environment and Development "Our common future" (or the Bruntland Report) then popularized this notion throughout the world, in both economic and political fields. The question of the future consequences of current actions was explicitly raised. Sustainable development is based on the three now well-known pillars: society, environment and economy. It was a British consultant, John Elkington, who made the connection between sustainable development and CSR, transposing the three pillars into the context of a company, under the name of the "Triple Bottom Line": Profit, Planet, People (economic prosperity, environmental quality and social justice). The company must perform well in these three pillars, which are still today the foundation of CSR, although other dimensions, such as governance, are also taken into account. The European Commission considers that corporate social responsibility is "a contribution by business to sustainable development" (Commission des Communautés européennes 2002).

Work on responsible innovation in companies is more recent than work devoted to RRI in European R&D programs. Ingham (2011), one of the pioneers of this issue, places responsible innovation within a sustainable development and CSR framework, and defines it as "the voluntary and proactive integration of social and environmental considerations into strategies, behaviors and processes that produce new and better performing solutions through the productive development and use of resources, that result in the creation of 'societal' (economic, social, and/or environmental) value". RRI places particular emphasis on two types of innovation: that which is environmentally relevant, also called eco-innovation or green innovation, and social innovation. According to him, responsible innovation can be classified as: technological, non-technological, mixed and systemic (i.e. combining different types of innovation).

Lubbernick *et al.* (2017) point out, however, that in the context of business, it is necessary to distinguish between responsible innovation and social or sustainable innovation, or, in this case, environmental innovation. These three types of innovation are similar in terms of their aims, which are to respond to current major challenges. The major difference between responsible innovation and the other two types of innovation lies in the predetermined nature of norms and values considered

3 Also known as "LTG".

desirable to guide innovation in the second case, whereas in the first, it is a deliberative process carried out along with all relevant stakeholders. We do not define democratic governance of innovation as a criterion for responsible innovation within a company. While it is desirable, its concrete implementation seems difficult to achieve in the current political and socio-economic system. These difficulties are related, on one hand, to transparency, as the competitive advantage of the firm may be called into question by disseminating fundamental information, and on the other, to the inclusion of all relevant stakeholders, for practical reasons, and because the weight of shareholders is generally preponderant in the decision making process of a company. Moreover, in responsible innovation, stakeholders must be able to contribute to influencing the trajectory of innovation at any time, which is not necessarily the case in environmental or sustainable innovation. Anticipation must also be part of responsible innovation in a business context. It requires that stakeholders be involved in defining what is considered desirable in society and what the role of the company and its innovations may be in the future. However, responsible innovation does not exclude the possibility that the innovation may have unexpected negative implications, which are particularly difficult to avoid.

37.4. Conclusion

The link between the concepts of RRI, in research policy and responsible innovation in companies, is now well established. For research and innovation policy, the origin of this link lies in reflections on the responsibility of scientists, engineers and innovators, on one hand, and in the assessment of technology on the other. It has generated a lot of research, particularly in Europe, and development of innovation policy. In business, responsible innovation is based on sustainable development and CSR, but the concept has not yet stabilized, neither in theory nor in practice. In any case, according to promoters, it truly represents a paradigm shift.

37.5. References

Aggeri, F., Pezet, E., Abrassart, C., Acquier, A. (2005). *Organiser le développement durable*. Vuibert, Paris.

Beck, U. (1992). *Risk Society: Towards a New Modernity*, translated by Ritter, M. Sage Publications, London.

Bowen, H.R. (1953). *Social Responsibilities of the Businessman*. Harper & Brothers, New York.

Commission des Communautés européennes (2002). *Communication de la commission concernant la responsabilité sociale des entreprises : une contribution des entreprises au développement durable*, COM(2002), 347–2002/2261(INI).

Durbin, P.T. (1992). *Social Responsibility in Science, Technology, and Medicine*. Lehigh University Press, Bethlehem, PA.

Grunwald, A. (2011). Responsible innovation: Bringing together technology assessment. *Applied Ethics, and STS Research, Enterprise and Work Innovation Studies*, 7, IET, 9–31.

Habermas, J. and Ladmiral, J.R. (1973). *La technique et la science comme "idéologie"*. Gallimard, Paris.

Ingham, M. (2011). *Vers l'innovation responsable : pour une vraie responsabilité sociétale*. De Boeck, Brussels.

Jonas, H. (1990). *Le principe responsabilité : une éthique pour la civilisation technologique*, translated by Jean Greisch, Cerf, Paris.

Lubberink, R., Blok, V., van Ophem, J., Omta, O. (2017). A framework for responsible innovation in the business context: Lessons from responsible, social and sustainable innovation. *Responsible Innovation*, 3, 181–207.

Pavie, X. (2012). *Innovation-responsable : stratégie et levier de croissance des organisations*. Editions Eyrolles, Paris.

Pellé, S. and Reber, B. (2013). Great (Governance of responsible innovation) 321480 – Theoretical Review – Deliverable D2-2 [Online]. Available at: https://ec.europa.eu/research/science-society/document_library/deliverable_2.2.pdf.

von Schomberg, R. (2011). Prospects for technology assessment in a framework of responsible research and innovation. In *Technikfolgenabschätzen lehren: Bildungspotenziale transdisziplinärer Methoden*, Dusseldorp, M. and Beecroft, R. (eds). Wiesbaden, Vs Verlag, Berlin.

Stilgoe, J., Owen, R., Macnaghten, P. (2013). Developing a framework for responsible innovation. *Research Policy*, 42(9), 1568–1580.

38

Revolution – Innovations and Industrial Revolution

38.1. Introduction

The term "industrial revolution" refers to the profound transformation of the economies of Europe, North America and then Japan that began in the 19th century. This revolution was characterized by the strong growth of both industrial production and of the share of industry in the GDP and the active population. The production of cotton yarn, for example, tripled (in value) in France between 1830 and 1870, quadrupled in Great Britain and quintupled in the United States. This industrial age is associated with the spread of machinery, technical progress and innovation. But what was the role of this technical revolution in the industrial revolution? We will first question the notions of technical revolution and industrial revolution: what are we talking about? Where does the idea that the industrial revolution was the fruit of a technical revolution come from? Second, since innovations rarely arise in technical deserts, they must also be compared with the techniques already in use in order to grasp the roughness of their diffusion. Finally, industrial revolution and innovations can only be understood through a multifactorial analysis that takes into account context effects.

38.2. From the technical revolution to the industrial revolution: what is the history?

For some economic historians, the case is watertight: it was the technical revolution that made the industrial revolution possible and was its primary cause. The succession of inventions and innovations is said to have been the driving force

Chapter written by Cédric PERRIN.

behind this industrial revolution and behind economic growth since the 19th century (Landes 1969). This blueprint leads to the identification of several industrial revolutions to which clusters of innovations are associated: the first industrial revolution at the turning point of the 18th and 19th centuries around the steam engine and coal, the flying shuttle, the locomotive and so on, then the second industrial revolution at the end of the 19th century with the invention of the automobile, aviation, telephone, cinema, electricity and oil, even a third and, for some authors, a Fourth Industrial Revolution in the second half of the 20th century around the atom and computing and then the Internet network.

This Promethean interpretation of industrial history was established as of the 19th century. Marked by the penetration of machines into industry and by numerous technical innovations, economists, journalists and writers saw in this liberation of technical progress the origin of the transformations they witnessed and which they began to describe as an industrial revolution. 19th-century England, which owed much of its power and economic domination to its industries, then built a veritable mythology of the industrial revolution and the heroic inventor (MacLeod 2007). Rival economies, and France in particular, responded by putting forward their national inventors; Denis Papin thus became the inventor of the steam engine, rather than the Englishman James Watt.

These technical pantheons have durably popularized the idea that technical progress was the source of the industrial revolution. In the 1960s, as new technical developments accompanied the strong economic growth of the *Trente Glorieuses* (30-year period in France following in the end of World War II) and the dissemination in homes of new objects that profoundly transformed lifestyles, historians devoted their research to shedding light on the role of technical innovations in these industrial revolutions that had been taking place for more than a century and a half. Books on the history of technology are still available today, organized on the chronological succession of inventions. This narrative retains its supporters because it is in harmony with today's culture of innovation and the public authorities' special attention to new technologies. The idea that we are experiencing a digital revolution is in line with the industrial revolutions that preceded it and reactivates those discursive, even ideological mechanisms.

Nevertheless, the idea that technical innovations could be the driving force behind industrial revolutions, or even history, since the 19th century has been strongly discussed and revised by historians. It evokes the question of the origins of this technical revolution itself, which takes the form of a spontaneous generation, and more generally of the causes of innovation. But why did men and women start inventing the new technical devices and new artifacts of the so-called industrial revolution? To the Promethean account of the industrial revolution, historians can raise three main sets of objections: to the notion of the industrial revolution itself, to the rate of diffusion of innovations, and to other factors of economic and social transformation.

The concept of the industrial revolution has gradually imposed itself in the vocabulary and is still used for its heuristic value, but can we really talk about industrial revolution? Industrial, yes. Revolution, that is less certain. Except in England, but here again with nuances, nowhere has the progress of industry had the speed, nor the radicalism, implied by the idea of revolution, i.e. a complete reversal. Mutations have been much more progressive, even slow, and are more a result of evolution than of revolution. In France, for example, the most industrialized country in Europe after the United Kingdom, which was the first to embark on this process at the end of the 18th century, the overwhelming majority of the population (74%) was still rural, and industry employed just over 20% of the working population around 1850.

While industry was growing, the European population remained predominantly rural and agricultural until late in the 19th century, and well beyond in many countries. It is therefore appropriate to speak of industrialization rather than industrial revolution. Moreover, this industrialization did not follow a single, linear model. The countries did not repeat the English model in turn, at a date that could conveniently be identified in the manner of Rostow's take-off. Industrialization has followed different paths and modalities in different regions.

38.3. The discontinuous diffusion of innovations in the face of the techniques in use

Second, technical innovations have not progressed at a rapid and uniform pace. The pace of their diffusion does not coincide with the growth in industrial production. The chronology disproves the pattern of a technical revolution at the origin of the industrial revolution. In Normandy, for example, one of the main areas of the textile industry in the 19th century, mechanical looms only gradually supplanted manual looms. The diffusion of innovations rather follows industrialization. It responded to the needs of industrial development, more than causing it. The growth of industrial production stimulated innovation and technical progress.

In the textile industry, the creation of bottlenecks along the production chain fueled the technical progress that made it possible to overcome them. The growth in demand for textile products led to the improvement of weaving by mechanizing it to produce more and faster, but from then on yarn production became insufficient and had to be perfected to keep up with this demand. This pressure was then passed downstream to the printing of fabrics. Similarly, the growth of the industry created new energy needs that the old resources, those of rivers and forests, were no longer enough to meet in late 18th-century England, and which made coal mining significant.

Conversely, the old techniques have long remained in use (Edgerton 2013). The industrial revolution was partly made with old techniques. In Catalonia, which was poor in coal, textile factories – whose prosperity made this region the main industrial center of the Iberian Peninsula – were established near rivers and hydraulic power operated their machines. On a global scale, coal consumption continued to grow in the 20th century, long after the emergence of the new energies of oil and electricity. In many cases, economic growth was achieved by mobilizing, at least initially, old techniques and perfecting them. Industrialization was therefore not achieved exclusively by deploying radical technical innovations, but by hybridizing available techniques. Technical innovations and old techniques coexisted during the "industrial revolution". Industrialists first drew on the repertoire of techniques they had mastered to increase their production and only abandoned them in favor of new processes when these brought a decisive advantage.

In the French alpine regions, metallurgy developed, reached its peak and continued until late in the 19th century by producing natural steel, i.e. with charcoal, whereas the industrial revolution and English coke-ironing seemed to condemn it because of its supposed archaism (Judet 2019). Attempts by engineers to introduce coke cast iron, which was poorly mastered, poorly adapted to alpine ores and poorly accepted by the workers, were failures, and it was thus by mobilizing the resources of their territory and the possibilities of the technical system in place that the region's forge masters responded to the growing demand for metallurgical products. It thus appears that the industrialization of Europe was carried out using various techniques and operating knowledge according to places, periods and contexts, and not only thanks to the introduction of new techniques.

However, from the end of the 19th century, the relationship between science and technology and the progress of industry was transformed with the appearance of the industrial research laboratory. While the first industrialization had been carried, for the most part, by small and medium enterprises, the end of the 19th century saw the emergence of large companies with greater financial resources who created their own laboratories. These new firms employed engineers on fundamental research programs and their industrial applications. They were then able to develop new products, or even entire industrial sectors such as electricity applications or image and sound reproduction processes. RCA, Telefunken and Marconi, for example, competed to market the first television sets in the 1930s.

38.4. When the context stimulates innovation

The work of economic historians invites us to go beyond a too narrow technical explanation of industrialization by taking into consideration other factors, such as population growth, transformations in agriculture, the expansion of consumption and markets, the role of capital, colonial trade and the development of international commerce, particularly during the first globalization (Verley 1997). The demographic transition, due to progress in food, medicine and individual and collective hygiene, led to strong population growth in Europe and the United States, reinforced here by the contribution of immigration, and at the same time to a widening of markets.

Progress in agriculture improved the incomes and purchasing power of a population that was still predominantly rural. More numerous, better fed and better cared for, and with slightly higher purchasing power, Europeans and Americans began to consume more. Demand for industrial products thus increased. It first turned towards the satisfaction of basic needs such as clothing, thus stimulating the production of textile industries and then those of everyday consumer goods (shoes, household items, food, etc.). In addition, in order to improve their yields, farmers became consumers of industrial products by buying fertilizers, ploughs, seeders and other agricultural machinery, also stimulating production and innovations in the chemical industries, on the one hand, and mechanical and metallurgical industries, on the other hand.

In addition, the profits from the colonial trade, including the slave trade, made capital available to create industries that enabled the re-export to the rest of the world of processed products of higher value than the raw materials of colonial origin: printed sheets and fabrics rather than raw cotton, for example. Historians now place greater emphasis on the role of markets in explaining the industrialization of Europe.

38.5. Conclusion

Technical innovations are a major characteristic of the industrial revolution or more precisely of the progressive industrialization of the economy and societies throughout the long 19th century. However, they should not be locked up in a technical determinism that would make them the trigger of an industrial revolution. Historians have shown the importance in the emergence of industry of other factors such as the rise of consumption and markets. Technical progress therefore appears rather as a response to the progress of industry. In order to increase their production, entrepreneurs had to improve their techniques and innovate. Above all, industrialization can only be understood through a sum of complex factors that intertwine their effects, not in the search for a single and determining cause such as technical innovations. Finally, in the light of history, it is probably necessary to reconsider the promises that accompany the deployment of the digital revolution, so as not to turn it into a technical mythology for the present day.

38.6. References

Edgerton, D. (2006). *The Shock of the Old. Technology and Global History Since 1900.* Profile Books, Oxford.

Judet, P. (2019). *La nébuleuse métallurgique alpine (Savoie-Dauphiné, fin XVIIIe-fin XIXe siècle). Apogée, déclin et éclatement d'un territoire industriel.* Presses universitaires de Grenoble, Grenoble.

Landes, D.S. (1969). *The Unbound Prometheus: Technological Change and Industrial Development in Western Europe from 1750 to the Present.* Cambridge University Press, Cambridge.

Macleod, C. (2007). *Heroes of Invention. Technology, Liberalism and British Identity, 1750–1914.* Cambridge University Press, Cambridge.

Verley, P. (1997). *La révolution industrielle.* Gallimard, Paris.

39

Services – Defining Service Innovation

39.1. Introduction

Today, service innovation is seen as a catalyst for growth in activities in the tertiary sector, as well as in the primary and secondary sectors.

Service innovation has become popular with the service transition strategy, described as "servicization", "servitization", "servicizing" or the "new service economy", and which, for a manufacturing company, no longer only offers the sale of goods, but the sale of an integrated offer of products and services in order to increase their use value. Service innovation also enables service companies to revitalize their competitive positions.

Many social science authors refer to service innovation, but few venture to define it because it does not conform to the categories usually used to identify innovations (radical vs. incremental innovation; process vs. product innovation). Moreover, service innovation can cover a wide variety of forms: social innovation, organizational innovation, methodological innovation, marketing innovation, innovation in external relations, intangible process innovation, intangible product innovation. Finally, other terms are sometimes used to refer to service innovation, such as non-technological innovation or invisible innovation.

Several categorizations of service innovation have been proposed. While the first categorizations were not adapted to service innovation, much progress has been made since then to isolate the characteristics of service innovation and to take the biases related to the intangible aspects of service innovations into account (Gallouj and Savona 2008).

Chapter written by Céline MERLIN-BROGNIART.

The first section reports on the specificities of services, and their consequences on innovation and innovation processes, before presenting the main definitions of service innovation. The second section presents the typologies of service innovation and the different types of work devoted to service innovation.

39.2. From the specificities of services to the definitions of service innovation

The specificities of services make it difficult to apply traditional concepts of innovation. The immateriality of the service reflects the fact that the service is a process or an "organization". The service is a social construction that produces different effects over time (immediate effects and long-term effects) and in varying degrees of materiality. It is therefore difficult to distinguish between product and process innovation, or organizational innovation. It is also difficult to assess the degree of novelty of the innovation and to evaluate its economic effects. Service innovation is easy to imitate and is therefore more difficult to protect (Gallouj 1994). Interactivity reflects the fact that the client participates in the production of the service to varying degrees. As a result, the client can contribute to innovation, especially when the innovation is simultaneous with the service delivery process (ad hoc innovation). The co-production of innovation raises problems of organization of innovation and appropriation of innovation.

The literature on service innovation emphasizes the interactivity of innovation processes and the fact that the service delivery process and the innovation process are sometimes confused. In this case, innovation is only recognized *a posteriori*. The organization of the service innovation process can therefore take different forms: planned, intentional innovations, by means of R&D services, or the creation of multi-actor project groups, which can integrate the customer, or by means of open innovation; emerging service innovations, such as "bricolage" models, practice-based innovation and ad hoc innovation, in which innovation is not planned. Service innovation can also be developed in innovation networks, especially non-technological networks, in which a multitude of public and private actors are partners.

The definitions of service innovation are based on an analytical breakdown or on the purposes of service innovation. In order to gain a better understanding of services and to avoid the product–process distinction, Gallouj and Weinstein (1997) proposed applying a Lancasterian-inspired representation of the product, based on characteristics and competences to service innovation. These authors represent the product (good or service) as the linking of vectors of technical characteristics [X] (composed of the organization's tangible and intangible systems), and mobilize the firm's competences [C] (some of which concern the ability to combine different technologies, and others being used directly). This combination allows the consumer to obtain the final (or service) characteristics [Y]. The service relationship is an important element of the service. In some cases, a vector of the customer's competences [C'], articulated with that of the provider, accounts for this relationship. This model makes it possible to analyze both pure services, based solely on the provision of competences and knowledge in co-production with the recipient of the service, without mobilizing technical characteristics, and product–service delivery systems. This definition has the advantage of showing that service innovation can involve a multitude of changes in an existing service. Innovation can be achieved when one or more elements of these vectors can be improved, added, removed, combined or dissociated, or when the service is formalized (Gallouj 2002; Gallouj and Savona 2008). Other authors have focused on service innovation as process and outcome. Drawing on Schumpeter's work, in particular the three fundamental conditions characterizing an innovation, Toivonen and Tuominen (2009, p. 893) define service innovation as:

> a new service, or a renewal of an existing service, which is put into practice and provides benefit to the organisation that has developed it; the benefit usually derives from the added value that the renewal provides the customers.

39.3. Typologies and theoretical variations of service innovation

Snyder *et al.* (2016) studied 43 categorizations of service innovation and concluded that these typologies addressed four themes: degree of change, type of change, novelty and means of service delivery. The degree of change (radical vs. incremental) is present in most typologies. According to the authors, it can be related to changes in supply, range extension, or new markets, differences in technology or the achievement of consumer needs. Some authors attach novelty to consumer involvement or associate radical innovation with a totally new offer. In these typologies, the type of change essentially corresponds to the distinction between innovation in product–service, process, organization and market, in accordance with the Oslo Manual. Other authors add the categories of distribution, strategy and management. Still, other authors distinguish interactive innovations (external, related to the service concept) from supporting innovations (internal, related to service production). The third theme, the novelty of the service innovation for the market or the firm, is more ambiguous and relative to the firm under consideration. The last theme, the means of service delivery, focuses on the organization, indicating the role played by the Internet or by people in the delivery of the service, or the stage in which the innovation takes place (the production process, the development process or the current organization of the firm). The authors find that little research focuses on the value provided by service innovations to consumers, not on the financial performances generated by these innovations.

Historically, a synthesis of research on innovation in services can be represented by the pendulum of assimilation, demarcation and integration (Gallouj 1994). The immaterial nature of service innovation has long contributed to its exclusion from the innovation literature, which was then focused on technological innovation (assimilationist perspective). The use of analytical tools dedicated to manufacturing innovation for services has thus led to an underestimation of the impacts of service innovation, in services and by services (because services make few technological innovations, few patents and little R&D). A second wave of work (a perspective of differentiation or demarcation) has instead sought to isolate the intrinsic characteristics of services in order to deduce the specific forms of innovation in services, such as *ad hoc* innovation, innovation in new fields of expertise or innovation in formalization (Gadrey and Gallouj 1998) by focusing on the purest services, such as knowledge-intensive services. These works have the identification of non-technological forms of innovation in common, which escape the traditional tools. Other works, which are rather empirical and specific to a given sector, are classified in this perspective of differentiation insofar as they develop "local theories" based on the specificity of services. These works concern complex services, combining a large number of elementary services, such as tourism or mass distribution. The last wave of work (integrative perspective) seeks to develop an analytical framework that is useful for analyzing innovation concerning both goods and services. This work identifies the informational or service value of goods, or considers the functions rendered by hybrid solutions or packages in which goods and services are sold and consumed together. The functional approach to service activity, for example, is particularly well suited to describing the innovation trajectories of service activities involving packages of goods and services (Gallouj 1999).

Another aspect of service innovation is linked to new economic models and is mainly related to the issue of "sustainable" service innovation. Service innovation is perceived as a new development logic to respond to social and environmental issues (Calabrese *et al.* 2018). This emerging field of research would rather fall into the integrative category, in the sense that there is a great deal of work being done on product–service systems. This research suggests that innovation generally involves system change, in the sense that partnerships or networks are sought to create value through the development of new sustainable service solutions. Thus, models such as functional sales, product–service systems and eco-efficient services are based on a strategy of value migration towards the production of new functionalities associated with products. The other categories selected by Calabrese *et al.* underline the importance of design in innovation or the role of technology in developing environmentally oriented service innovation. In French, the denomination "*innovation servicielle*" is sometimes used as a synonym for "service innovation", but in the context of sustainable services, the term "service innovation" tends to be used in another sense. French research on the economics of functionality and cooperation defines service innovation ("*innovation servicielle*") as the construction, generally by a group of actors, of a response to a territorial expectation or challenge (health, mobility, etc.), in relation to the beneficiary or beneficiaries of the service. This local character makes service innovation difficult to imitate, and it is intended to be "inspiring".

39.4. Conclusion

The synthesis of the literature on service innovation reflects the complexity of services. This complexity extends to service innovation, which makes it difficult to propose a comprehensive definition of service innovation. Different typologies of service innovation are therefore proposed, with particular attention paid to the forms and degree of change (or even rupture) associated with service innovation.

Research on service innovation is still young and raises new questions. The specific characteristics of services, combined with the often multidimensional nature of the performance sought by stakeholders, raise the question of evaluation. The dimensions constituting service innovation are often heterogeneous, made up of elements that are at once tangible, intangible and sometimes singular. Value creation is also the basis for thinking about new business models. The question of the recipient of value creation needs to be explored in greater depth: value can be created for different stakeholders, such as customers, employees, shareholders, partners and communities. Recently, Galloujand Djellal (2018) identified 15 potential research issues on service innovation, grouped into three sub-groups: *societal issues* include social innovation, environment, population aging, development of emerging countries, religious trajectory, gender issues and ethics; other issues are *structural and organizational*, service innovation can be cross-cut with entrepreneurship, employment, intelligent service systems and innovation networks; finally, service innovation involves a number of *methodological and didactic issues* such as service activities that are still little analyzed by research, multidisciplinarity, new evaluations and training in service innovation.

39.5. References

Calabrese, A., Castaldi, C., Forte, G., Levialdi, N.G. (2018). Sustainability-oriented service innovation: An emerging research field. *Journal of Cleaner Production*, 193, 533–548.

Gadrey, J. and Gallouj, F. (1998). The provider–customer interface in business and professional services, *The Services Industries Journal*, 18(4), 1–15.

Gallouj, F. (1994). *Economie de l'innovation dans les services*. Editions L'Harmattan, Logiques économiques, Paris.

Gallouj, F. (1999). Les trajectoires de l'innovation dans les services : vers un enrichissement des trajectoires évolutionnistes. *Economies et sociétés*, 5(1), 143–169.

Gallouj, F. (2002). *Innovation in the Service Economy: The New Wealth of Nations*. Edward Elgar Publishing, Cheltenham.

Gallouj, F. and Djellal, F. (2018). Fifteen challenges for service innovation studies. In *A Research Agenda for Service Innovation*, Faridah, D. and Faïz, G. (eds). Edward Elgar Publishing, Cheltenham.

Gallouj, F. and Savona, M. (2008). Innovation in services: A review of the debate and perspectives for a research agenda. *Journal of Evolutionary Economics*, 19(2), 149–172.

Gallouj, F. and Weinstein, O. (1997). Innovation in services. *Research Policy*, 26(4–5), 537–556.

Snyder, H., Witell, L., Gustafsson, A., Fombelle, P., Kristensson, P. (2016). Identifying categories of service innovation: A review and synthesis of the literature. *Journal of Business Research*, 69, 2401–2408.

Toivonen, M. and Tuominen, T. (2009). Emergence of innovations in services. *The Service Industries Journal*, 29(7), 887–902.

40

Social – Social Economy and Social Innovation

40.1. Introduction

The literature on the economics and management of innovation has essentially dealt with innovations with an economic scope (technological, service, organizational, on business models) allowing either an improvement in the competitiveness of firms and/or territories or the creation of new market opportunities. Two types of limitations can be associated with this. First, it restricts the analysis to innovations that have an impact on systems governed by a market order or by public action. As a result, innovations that essentially produce their effects via other economic mechanisms such as reciprocity are ignored. Second, the processes of creative destruction associated with the dynamics of innovation have essentially been highlighted in their economic dimension while minimizing their social dimension (calling into question modes of social organization, the social status of individuals, etc.). The notion of social innovation aims to take these analytical limitations into account, as well as to compensate for the possible deleterious consequences of innovations with economic implications. This chapter aims to define the contours of these innovations and to present the processes and actors involved in their production.

After a reminder on the state of research on social innovation in economics and management, we will propose, in the second part of the chapter, a definition summarizing the main research in the field. In the third part, we will discuss their production, insisting on the different logics of governance of the associated creative processes. In the fourth part, we will develop the roles played by social economy organizations in the latter. In conclusion, we will highlight two major issues: the governance and the measurement of social innovations.

Chapter written by Paul MULLER.

40.2. Research on social innovation in economics and management

Although it first appeared at the end of the 19th century (Godin 2012), it is only since the beginning of the 21st century that the notion of social innovation has raised real interest in the academic community. Since then, research in economics and management has been divided into three main areas of analysis (van der Have and Rubalcaba 2016):

– *The role of social innovations in solving contemporary social and technological challenges, above all from a sustainable development perspective.* This area is concerned with the roles social innovations play, and their possible interactions with other forms of innovation, in favor of environmental preservation and social development through the reduction of inequalities in all their forms.

– *The links between social innovation and territorial development.* This area discusses the role governance processes and institutions play in social innovation or the role of social innovation in social cohesion and local democracy. One line of thought focuses more particularly on the shortcomings of development policies based solely on innovations of economic scope. In doing so, the analysis also focuses on the definition of policies incorporating social innovation as a development axis.

– *Research on creativity.* This area is particularly interested in the creative processes associated with the production of social innovations, from their genesis to their implementation.

All in all, social innovation covers a heterogeneous body of research for which it is impossible to make a summary assessment within the framework of this contribution. This is why, in the remainder of this chapter, we will focus on research on the production of social innovations related to creativity. As we will see in the following section, the production of social innovations is fundamentally a process involving various stakeholders: the initiators of the innovation, the beneficiaries, as well as public and private actors or collective entities, whether formal or informal. This raises questions about the underlying collective processes and, more particularly, about their governance.

40.3. Defining social innovation

Despite the multiple definitions of the concept, we adopt Moulaert's (2009) definition: "the development of new responses to needs expressed by particular social groups, and which cannot be satisfied or even recognized by the market and by public institutions." Its interest lies in the fact that it summarizes three of the main characteristics of social innovations, distinguishing them from innovations of economic scope (Hillier *et al.* 2004; Bouchard 2006; Harrisson and Vézina 2006; Pol and Ville 2009). First, social innovation is primarily aimed at improving the living conditions of the social groups concerned by providing solutions adapted to their needs and problems. This implies in particular that it cannot be based solely on an isolated product or service, but on a global solution, which may involve a set of adapted products and/or services.

Second, since its main purpose is not economic, traditional economic actors (firms, the State and local authorities) are not in a position to respond directly to the need expressed, either because there is no prospect of sufficient profits to be made or because the nature of the need is such that a public actor is not able to propose an appropriate response. However, this does not mean a total absence of traditional economic coordination mechanisms, which can intervene, for example, through support for the initiators of social innovation projects.

Third, by its very nature, social innovation results from collective processes requiring collaboration with the public concerned. It is, therefore, embedded in a given social context that is often local. Moreover, it often leads us to put into question the socio-economic rules, or even the collective thought models in force in the environments concerned. This is particularly the case with local currencies, which contribute to a broader questioning of the status of money and labor prevailing in Western capitalist societies.

Finally, a distinctive feature of social innovation from forms of innovation with economic scope is that it is not necessarily associated with a criterion of absolute novelty. It can consist of mobilizing and adapting old practices to the social context. Nevertheless, it can build on these other forms of innovation, particularly technological and service innovation. In particular, mention can be made of frugal innovations, which are often technological or service innovations based on the expression of a social need.

40.4. The production of social innovations: "top-down" and "bottom-up" logics

Like most innovations of economic scope, creative activities are consubstantial with the production of social innovations and are part of collective dynamics within ecosystems involving multiple actors. We can therefore identify two different creative logics, top-down and bottom-up.

A top-down logic is based either on social entrepreneurship or patronage of large private structures (business or family foundations) or on public authorities, for which they play a steering role. They thus emanate from structures embedded in multiple and complex economic relationships with various types of public or private structures. This type of social innovation, therefore, starts from an "*upperground*" in the sense of Cohendet *et al.* (2009), corresponding to an economic "level" in direct contact with the for-profit and public sectors. As a result, social innovations associated with such a logic can be expected to be of limited social scope. Indeed, by being initiated by existing socio-economic structures, they do not fundamentally challenge the rules prevailing within existing socio-economic systems, which may hinder the real contribution of the innovation for the targeted public (Richez-Battesti and Vallade 2012).

Faced with the shortcomings expressed by the top-down logic, social innovations can develop according to a bottom-up logic, also known as *grass-roots*. Close to the target population, this logic favors co-construction with the latter. The advantage of this approach is that, by taking the target population as a starting point, it is supposed to be the one most able to meet its needs. From this point of view, this type of social innovation emanates from an "*underground*" made up of individuals carrying out activities outside of any formal structure with an economic aim (Cohendet *et al.* 2010): collectives of individuals, neighborhood associations, etc. (Cohendet *et al.* 2010).

However, the limitation of this production logic is that, starting from a very small scale (individual or small collective), social innovation can have difficulty diffusing and being appropriated at higher collective levels. This is notably because social innovations coming from the *underground* must first be translated in the sense of being understood at the *upperground* level. Indeed, to be able to extend and produce their effects, they need active support from the *upperground*, made possible, for example, through the provision of financial, material or relational resources (Grandadam *et al.* 2013). Given their respective weaknesses, top-down and bottom-up logics are often mobilized simultaneously and in a complementary manner in the production of social innovations. This is particularly observed in the context of mobility in France, with, on the one hand, the development of state plans and platforms aimed at encouraging public and private initiatives and, on the other hand, the development of local mobility solutions by the public concerned. However, whether these processes follow top-down or bottom-up logics of social economy, organizations are central actors.

40.5. The roles of social economy in the production of social innovations

Social economy organizations, which are made up of associations, cooperatives, foundations and mutual companies, play a central role in the production of social innovations. This role is not only at their instigation but also through intermediation activity. Their capacity to produce social innovations is above all linked to their legal statutes, which are based on free membership, democratic management, limited lucrative activity and solidarity. This implies that they are places for social experimentation for which the processes of producing innovations are not primarily aimed at finding an economic advantage: competitive advantage or the creation of new markets. On the contrary, their innovation activity may be underpinned by an objective of providing services to their members, which is frequently the case in cooperatives. They, therefore, contribute to the common interest of their members. In other cases, they may respond to needs expressed within populations in a precarious situation, following the example of social entrepreneurs. Their function thus contributes to the search for general interest.

In addition, social economy organizations assume an intermediation role in facilitating the diffusion of social innovations coming from the *underground*, either towards other potentially interested populations or towards the *upperground*. To this end, their contribution takes various complementary forms (Muller and Tanguy 2019). First, they contribute to filling the "structural holes" of a social network by bringing together actors who would otherwise not have had the opportunity to meet. Second, they establish or reinforce trust between actors by helping to reduce the risks associated with the development of new relationships (risks of moral hazard and of adverse selection). Third, they facilitate the dissemination of social innovations by acting as brokers. They facilitate the circulation of various resources, whether ideas and knowledge or financial and physical resources. Moreover, they "translate", adapt and organize social innovations so that they can be appropriated by the structures of the *upperground*. This makes it possible not only to facilitate their financing but also their dissemination on a larger scale.

40.6. Conclusion and issues

Although it brings together processes similar to innovations of economic scope, social innovation, and its production differs from the latter in that, by definition, its main objective does not lie in the search for competitive advantage or the creation of new markets. On the contrary, it lies in the satisfaction of social needs not covered by traditional economic mechanisms. Moreover, it gives rise to collective processes involving different types of actors (concerned social groups, actors at their own instigation, organizations supporting and diffusing innovations) characterized by different rationalities and logics of action. As a result, the production of social innovations raises several issues, among which are those of their governance and evaluation.

A first issue deals with the problem of the governance of production processes. Beyond the classic problems of governance of collective innovation processes, there is a specific challenge for social innovation, relating to its evolution within ecosystems. Indeed, as we have seen in the previous sections, the production of social innovations involves actors, each occupying different positions within ecosystems and prioritizing top-down or bottom-up logics. Beyond their adaptation, the processes of vertical diffusion of social innovations can give rise to a questioning of their very purpose. This can be a source of conflict between actors at different levels. Indeed, as soon as the actors of the *upperground* have to take into account the economic viability of the social innovation to appropriate it, actors of the *underground* can consider these actions as weakening the innovation or limiting its impact.

A second issue is the problem of the evaluation and the measurement of its results. This issue is essential because the use of indicators makes it possible, in particular, to justify the mobilization of resources to produce social innovations by evaluating their socio-economic impact. However, by solely concentrating on economic dimensions, "traditional" indicators of innovation, such as those taken from the Oslo and Frascati manuals, do not make it possible to account for their social dimension. The effectiveness of social innovations is evaluated according to existing economic criteria and indicators, which are not necessarily relevant. In particular, there is a great risk of under-evaluating the social impact. Hence, an important issue among professionals in the social economy sector is to define sets of indicators to better assess the social impact of innovations.

40.7. References

Bouchard, M.J. (2006). L'innovation sociale en économie sociale, R-2006-01. Collection Recherche, Chaire de recherche du Canada en économie sociale, Université de Montréal, Montreal.

Godin, B. (2012). Social innovation: Utopias of innovation from c.1830 to the present. Working Paper 11, Project on the Intellectual History of Innovation, Montreal.

Harrisson, D. and Vézina, M. (2006). L'innovation sociale : une introduction. *Annals of Public and Cooperative Economics*, 77(2), 129–138.

van der Have, R.P. and Rubalcaba, L. (2016). Social innovation research: An emerging area of innovation studies? *Research Policy*, 45(9), 1923–1935.

Hillier, J., Moulaert, F., Nussbaumer, J. (2004). Trois essais sur le rôle de l'innovation sociale dans le développement territorial, Abstract. *Géographie, économie, société*, 6(2), 129–52.

Moulaert, F. (2009). Social innovation: Institutionally embedded, territorialy (re)produced. In *Social Innovation and Territorial Development*, Diana, M., Frank, M., Jean, H., Serena, V.C. (eds). Ashgate, Farnham, England, Burlington, VT.

Pol, E. and Ville, S. (2009). Social innovation: Buzz word or enduring term? *The Journal of Socio-Economics*, 38(6), 878–885.

Richez-Battesti, N. and Vallade, D. (2012). Éditorial. Innovation sociale, normalisation et régulation. *Innovations*, 38, 5–13.

41

Space – Innovation in Urban or Rural Spaces

41.1. Introduction

The geography of innovation shows a massive trend: the spatial concentration of innovative organizations as innovations. Since the 1980s, certain regions have been identified as highly innovative. Silicon Valley and Route 128 are emblematic examples of these regions, or, in Europe, Cambridge, Île-de-France and Baden-Württemberg.

But if we refine the geographical mesh, innovations are in fact concentrated at the level of cities, especially the largest ones, namely metropolises and large urban areas (Balland and Rigby 2017). This demonstrates the existence of an urban hierarchy between innovative cities (few in number) and non-innovative cities. According to Florida *et al.* (2016), most of the innovations in the US and since 1975 have been produced in the urban areas of the San Francisco Bay Area and, second, in New York City. Firms have also relocated from peri-urban areas such as Silicon Valley to dense urban spaces, in response to the demand for proximity between leisure activities, work and the need for quality schools for the creative class, which is over-represented among workers of innovative firms (Florida *et al.* 2016). Innovative firms would even relocate exclusively to a few select neighborhoods in urban centers, which are the most well resourced in terms of these different amenities. Companies that have benefited from venture capital follow the same relocation pattern.

Chapter written by Delphine GALLAUD.

Thus, the resulting increase in rents has a distancing effect and pushes smaller businesses toward lower-rent spaces, i.e. especially towards peri-urban or rural areas. This trend toward overconcentration in a few metropolises is, however, less clear in Balland and Rigby's 2017 study, which shows a concentration of innovation in a small number of urban areas, but not as marked as those in the San Francisco Bay area.

There could thus exist a very strong urban hierarchy in which a few metropolises occupy the top of the pyramid in terms of innovation production. Conversely, firms located in remote or peripheral areas could face constraints in accessing innovation resources, due to the low population density in these areas and lower variety of available resources.

However, research based on the introduction of innovations by firms shows, on the contrary, that it appears in all types of urban, peri-urban and peripheral or isolated rural spaces (Shearmur 2015). Moreover, analysis of rural entrepreneurship shows a dynamism in the creation of businesses in peripheral areas. What is the real situation regarding the innovation capacity of companies located in different types of areas?

41.2. A concentration of innovation in urban spaces?

Beyond the agglomeration aspect, the urban space is also a creator of innovation resources. Florida *et al.* (2016), in particular, take up elements related to Jacobs' (1969) analyses of externalities. The urban environment provides access to inter-industrial spillovers, an argument also taken up in the work on related variety (Frenken *et al.* 2007, cited by Eder 2019). However, the innovation process is facilitated by access to external sources for innovation, i.e. information from customers, suppliers and consulting firms (knowledge-intensive business services or KIBS) (Shearmur and Doloreux 2014). In addition, a dense and culturally diverse urban environment would promote informal interactions between residents and would be a source of new ideas for innovation and knowledge opportunities. These interactions would be fostered by new spaces for encounters between actors such as co-working spaces. Florida *et al.* (2016) thus insist on the role of geographical proximity between potentially innovative urban residents and between residents and innovation resources.

The development of the open and collaborative innovation model (Chesbrough 2003) has also resulted in a renewed emphasis on the need for geographic proximity. In this model, firms are encouraged not to rely solely on their internal resources to develop innovations but to seek to mobilize all possible sources of innovation. This is achieved through formal cooperation and, above all, through the use of informal exchanges of knowledge, based on the model of the free software sector, i.e. what Chesbrough (2003) describes as "free revealing" as opposed to innovation procedures based on secrecy that allow companies to stay one step ahead of competitors. These informal interactions would allow firms to "optimize" opportunities to detect innovations and thus promote the regular introduction of innovations into the market.

However, the model of innovation associated with urban space seems to go beyond an open model of innovation, toward a production of innovation that would be associated less with a particular firm than with individuals. The organization becomes very porous in some works, or even disappears completely, to be replaced by innovative entrepreneurial individuals detecting innovation opportunities in third places such as co-working spaces.

Finally, if the urban environment is a creator of knowledge and potential resources for innovation, it must, in order to foster the dynamics of regular introduction of innovations, rely both on internal resources and on connections to global networks, i.e. articulating what Bathelt *et al.* (2004) call local "buzz" and global pipelines. This has reopened the debate on the possibility of using substitution between the two types of channels; can an environment without local "buzz", such as peripheral spaces, then rely on a strong connection to global networks?

In summary, the model of innovation in urban spaces that emerges from current texts presents technological innovation (of products or processes), often radical, protected by patents. Innovative firms located in the city are industrial firms engaged in high-tech activities or, more rarely, service firms. They employ a high proportion of skilled workers. The innovation process mobilized by these firms is open and collaborative; it relies on the mobilization of external resources, in particular knowledge-intensive service activities, as well as on informal interactions related to new working environments such as co-working spaces. This process would require significant geographical proximity between actors, which echoes the arguments used to justify the importance of clusters, but shifting the geographical scale from a region to an urban area.

41.3. An underestimation of the innovation of firms located in peripheral areas?

Thus, according to the authors mentioned previously, in particular Florida *et al.* (2016), innovation would develop only in the most important urban spaces and would be almost impossible to develop in other types of spaces. However, works that use a comparative perspective on the introduction of innovation between rural and urban spaces challenge this postulate. Companies located in peripheral rural spaces, i.e. those furthest from large urban centers, are as innovative as firms located in cities (Shaermur 2015; Tanguy *et al.* 2015). This is linked to the fact that innovation does not depend solely on external resources, but that in order to benefit from these resources, firms must have an internal absorption capacity (Cohen and Levinthal 1990). However, absorption capacity does not depend on location in a given space, but on a firm's strategy.

Innovation in peripheral areas is thus largely underestimated. Firstly, because there is no consensus on the definition of peripheral spaces, beyond a definition based on low population and resource density, as opposed to that of urban spaces, which is fairly coherent despite statistical variations in measurement (Eder 2019). This leads to a real difficulty in establishing stylized facts about the introduction of innovations according to the type of space. Secondly, the difference in the rate of innovation introduction according to the type of space is also due to the indicators for measuring innovation. The most commonly used is patenting. However, this is only a partial measure of innovation, since the patent is granted for the invention, the upstream stage of the innovation. It does not automatically reflect the fact that a novelty will be introduced to the market. Furthermore, it is recognized that a patent can be used strategically: in this case, the aim is not to protect an innovation but to block competition by preventing it from developing its innovation. Finally, it is possible to patent products or processes, which correspond solely to forms of technological innovation. However, there are also non-technological forms of innovation, in particular organizational or marketing innovation (Oslo Manual, 2005) and even, in the case of services, "do-it-yourself" innovations. This type of innovation is generally more common in SMEs and in companies in low-tech sectors, which are more often located in rural rather than urban areas. By contrast, companies that patent are often large, in high-tech industrial sectors and are more frequently located in cities.

When using the rate of innovation introduction as an indicator, a different representation is obtained from that given by the geography of innovation. Firms located in all types of spaces innovate, but often according to differentiated processes. Shearmur (2015) proposes a model of innovation based on the value of the information obtained. Innovators in cities would use market sources but they would provide a form of information that would quickly become outdated, they would be rapid innovators, developing incremental innovations. On the contrary, innovators located in peripheral areas would rely primarily on internal sources to develop their innovations and, when in need of additional knowledge, they would make greater use of cooperation, particularly with scientific or institutional sources, and by selecting partners. Their model is adapted to the use of knowledge that expires less quickly than commercial sources of innovation. Their innovation process seems slower but more stable; it provides them as many innovation opportunities as firms located in cities. However, if the company seeks to grow by increasing the size of its market for innovation, there is a likelihood that all or part of the innovative firm will relocate to the urban area where the catchment area is located, which in this case gives an advantage to urban spaces. But the company can also remain located in a peripheral area and seek cooperation with companies located in the city, particularly the distributors of the product.

Thus, it is the geographical proximity between potentially innovative actors and innovation resources that would be the fundamental advantage of urban areas. The argument is the same as the one that justified the importance of clusters but on a different geographical scale. However, this argument equates geographical proximity to the co-location of actors, i.e. to what the school of proximity (Gilly and Torre 2000) qualifies as permanent proximity. However, geographical proximity can be temporary (Gallaud and Torre 2005). The development of ICTs and, above all, the mobility of actors puts the need for co-location into perspective, as actors move around to access the resources they need to innovate. Shearmur and Doloreux (2014) thus show that two-thirds of the innovators surveyed provide knowledge-intensive services outside their city and therefore travel to access them, or interact heavily, via ICT, with these service providers. Finally, the positive effects of geographical proximity are overestimated in the argument for the role of cities and the negative effects are often underestimated, when excessive proximity can lead to unintended spillovers or even industrial espionage. As a result, in the long term, lock-in effects frequently appear (Boschma 2005), "trapping" firms that use knowledge provided by the neighborhood in trajectories that are no longer innovative because the sources of knowledge are no longer sufficiently varied. Geographical proximity is only a potential and a facilitator of coordination if it does not rely on other forms of proximity: organizational, social and institutional, which questions the argument relating to informal interactions that would be more frequent in cities. These interactions only exist if forms of organized and social proximity have been created by the innovative actors.

41.4. Conclusion

If firms in peripheral spaces seem less innovative than those in urban spaces, it is often because of the indicators used to measure innovation, as well as too-frequent reference to the fact that the innovation process is unique. Some researchers tend to set the open and collaborative model as the norm for firms, whereas in reality, innovation processes are differentiated, particularly according to the location of companies in a given type of space.

Furthermore, many studies still underestimate the possibility of using the mobility of actors, and information and communication technologies, to overcome possible constraints of localization, as they remain too focused on the location of organizations instead of analyzing their innovation processes. Finally, it seems there is an urgent need to construct a shared definition of what a peripheral or remote space is, so as to stabilize stylized facts about the introduction of innovations in different types of space.

These two elements would make it possible to develop a more relevant diagnosis for public policies. In particular, while innovation can be fostered by the use of ICTs, a policy guaranteeing infrastructure development and territorial coverage can promote innovation just as much as a policy for financing innovation. Similarly, taking into account the variety of innovation processes would make it possible to adapt policies more precisely to the different spaces and promote territorial development, particularly in peripheral areas.

41.5. References

Balland, P.A. and Rigby, D. (2017). The geography of complex knowledge. *Economic Geography*, 93(1), 1–23.

Bathelt, H., Malmberg, A., Maskell, P. (2004). Clusters and knowledge: Local buzz, global pipelines and the process of knowledge creation. *Progress in Human Geography*, 28(1), 31–56.

Boschma, R. (2005). Proximity and innovation: A critical assessment. *Regional Studies*, 39(1), 61–74.

Chesbrough, W. (2003). *Open Innovation: The New Imperative for Creating and Profiting from Technology*. Harvard Business School Press, Boston, MA.

Cohen, W.M. and Levinthal, D.A. (1990). Absorptive capacity: A new perspective on learning and innovation. *Administrative Science Quarterly*, 35(1), 128–152.

Eder, J. (2019). Innovation in the periphery: A critical survey and research agenda. *International Regional Science Review*, 42(2), 119–146.

Florida, R., Adler, P., Mellander, C. (2017). The city as innovation machine. *Regional Studies*, 51(1), 86–96.

Gallaud, D. and Torre, A. (2005). Geographical proximity and circulation of knowledge through interfirm relationships. *Scienze Regionali*, 4(2), 5–25.

Gilly, J.P. and Torre, A. (2000). *Dynamiques de proximité*. Editions L'Harmattan, Paris.

Shearmur, R. (2015). Slow innovators and information value. *Growth and Change*, 46, 424–442.

Shearmur, R. and Doloreux, D. (2015). Central places or networks? Paradigms, metaphors, and spatial configurations of innovation-related service use. *Environment and Planning A: Economy and Space*, 47(7), 1521–1539.

Tanguy, C., Gallaud, D., Martin, M., Reboud, S. (2015). Quelle est la propension des entreprises à coopérer pour innover et à quelles échelles spatiales ? Une analyse des entreprises agroalimentaires françaises sur la période 2006–2008. *Revue d'économie régionale et urbaine*, 3, 453–479.

42

Standardization – Standardization and Innovation Management

42.1. Introduction

While innovation is nowadays commonly defined as the action of inventing or creating something new, we can wonder whether or not there is a model that facilitates the emergence and development of innovation, that can be the subject of some form of systematization or standardization, independently of the type of organization. But what are we talking about when we talk about standardization? It is a voluntary process for developing specifications based on a consensus between all interested parties (industries, including SMEs, consumers, trade unions, public authorities, etc.). It is carried out by independent standards bodies, acting at national (ANSI, BSI, AFNOR, DIN, AENOR, etc.), European (CEN) and international (ISO) levels. Standards for management systems provide recommendations or requirements to which organizations can refer in order to improve their processes. These standards can be applied to any organization, large or small, regardless of its products or services as well as its sector of activity. Reflection on the standardization of innovation is carried out within the framework of international working groups, which ultimately results in a family of standards on the issue of innovation management (ISO 56000 Series). ISO is an independent non-governmental organization with members from the national standards bodies of 164 countries (ISO 56002). It is the reflections and discussions resulting from these working groups as well as their working methods that we propose to develop in this chapter in order to explain the main principles to be followed when we want to improve our innovation processes.

Chapter written by Laure MOREL.

First, we will present the context that prevailed during the development of the draft standard for innovation management at the global level, as well as the prerequisites for the implementation of a dynamic of innovation in an organization. Second, we will show how the choices made by the experts involved in the drafting process led to a recommendation standard that respects the organizational agility required for the implementation of any innovation management system.

42.2. Prerequisite for standards applied to innovation

It's time for innovation! This sentence sums up the situation facing organizations that want to remain competitive, develop or simply not disappear in the relatively long term. While the 1960s saw the development of work around project management and the 1980s around quality, the 2000s were the years of innovation management. This craze was reflected in several forms and in particular by the establishment of standardization committees at several levels: national, European and international. The latter gave rise to the publication of standards, such as the European standard CEN/TS 16 555-1 "Innovation Management System", initiated in 2008 by AENOR (Spanish standardization agency), drafted by the European Technical Committee CEN/TC 389 and published in July 2013.

The objective of a standard is above all to list in a single document the good practices that will enable an organization to better understand an object and to unify its definitions and representations. As emphasized in the introduction, it is a voluntary and consensual process of developing specifications within commissions proposed by the national bodies of standardization, which are made up of experts from all backgrounds and professions.

More specifically, we will present the results of the reflections, since 2013, on innovation, its definition, management and evaluation at the international level (ISO – International Organization for Standardization).

The international committee for standardization of the innovation process is French in origin. Faced with a growing need to better control innovation and its supporting processes, AFNOR (French Association for Standardization) decided to pilot a draft standard in innovation management at the ISO level. Indeed, AFNOR is the association that represents France at the ISO and the European Committee for Standardization (CEN). The ISO/TC 279 Technical Committee was created in December 2013, with the mission of developing a series of standards (ISO 56000 SERIES Innovation Management) to cover all fields related to innovation management, and thus try to answer fundamental questions that organizations may ask themselves.

42.2.1. *What exactly is innovation?*

According to the ISO 56000 document entitled "Terms and references", innovation is a new or modified entity that creates or redistributes value. By entity, we mean a product, service, process, organization, business model, etc. Value can take several forms: financial, non-financial, image, strategic advantage, knowledge acquisition, intellectual property, etc.

42.2.2. *Why do you want to manage the innovation process?*

According to a study by McKinsey *(Harvard Business Review*, September 2016), 84% of the world's executives say innovation is important. However, 94% admit that they are dissatisfied with their company's innovation performance and do not have the tools and methods that would enable them to remedy this situation and to face the new challenges arising from globalization in particular.

Indeed, the latter has exacerbated aspects facing companies such as:

– global competition and consumer demand are forcing companies to innovate on a regular basis;

– the multiplicity of information requires companies to make choices in order to set up effective monitoring activities;

– the pace of technological change and the emergence of new entrants in all sectors constantly challenge the existing players.

Innovation no longer only concerns products or processes resulting from R&D, it is becoming multiple and multifaceted and affects all sectors of the company.

Innovating no longer requires only technical mastery, but also marketing, sales and legal know-how, etc.

It is therefore a question of moving from a "traditional" innovation management process to a stabilized and reproducible process allowing the implementation of methods and tools to create the most favorable conditions for the development of concrete innovations.

In a nutshell, managing innovation means investing in practices that encourage the emergence and regular development of innovations.

42.2.3. *How can we manage innovation?*

ISO 56002, entitled "Innovation Management System", emphasizes the importance of referring to eight fundamental principles (Figure 42.1) in order to best manage our innovation management system.

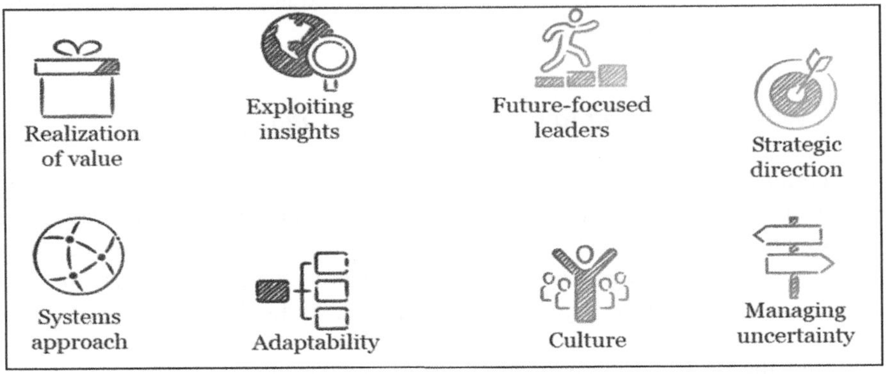

Figure 42.1. *The principles of innovation management (source: Commission de Normalisation en Innovation 2019). For a color version of this figure, see www.iste.co.uk/uzunidis/innovation1.zip*

Thus, in order to develop an organization's innovation dynamic, the standard suggests deploying a management system that goes beyond the simple framework of project development (Figure 42.2) by taking into account the context of the organization, the strategic dimension, all of the resources and skills present and the need to implement an approach of continuous improvement to all practices (Figure 42.3).

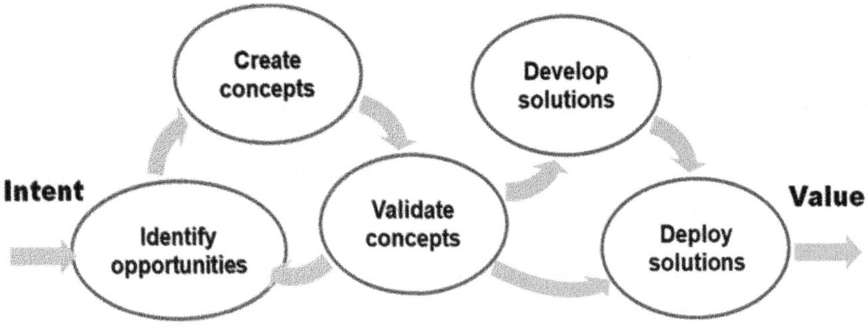

Figure 42.2. *From the project process... (source: ISO 56002)*

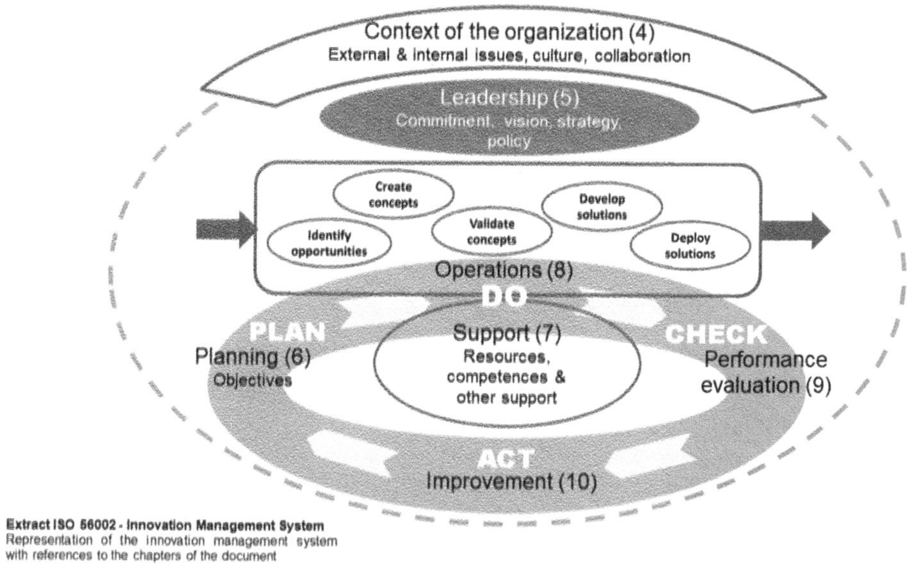

Figure 42.3. *...to the implementation of an innovation management system. (source: ISO 56002). For a color version of this figure, see www.iste.co.uk/uzunidis/innovation1.zip*

Is there not a paradox here between the research conducted on innovation management, which highlights the need for flexibility, adaptability and agility (see the encyclopedia's entry on innovation and creativity), and the desire to standardize, and therefore rationalize, the innovation management system?

42.3. Standards applied to innovation: promoting agility

At first glance, one may be surprised at the fact of wanting to create a standard on innovation. However, a fundamental aspect of the work involved in drafting a standard needs to be clarified here. It can take two forms: a requirements standard or a recommendations standard. The first is the best known, as it is the choice made in particular for quality standards. The clear objective here is to provide an audit framework leading to the possibility of certifying an organization. The second gives rise to a "best practices guide" to be implemented but without any prescription or injunction. So there is no certification at the end of the day. This leads to writing the standard in the following way: "the organization should/could consider..." and not that "the organization must" do something. This nuance is very important because choosing to establish a standard of recommendations for the field of innovation promotes the development of the profession of innovation manager by seeking to avoid the potential shortcomings of certification. Hence, in our opinion, promoting a standard in innovation management on this non-certification basis is not at all in contradiction with the attributes associated, as stated above, with an innovation process.

42.3.1. *Why then have a standard on innovation management?*

It is first and foremost a volunteer-based approach, promoting organizational agility.

The international experts involved in this writing (more than 60 countries, 230 experts from academia, industry or consulting) had the same objectives and values in common, namely:

– Propose a repository of good practices useful to many actors:

- organizations seeking to achieve lasting success by developing their capacity for innovation (innovation can no longer be the result of chance);

- users, clients and other stakeholders seeking to establish and make visible an organization's capacity for innovation;

- organizations and other stakeholders seeking to improve communication through a common understanding of what constitutes an innovation management system;

- training, evaluation or consulting organizations in the field of innovation management;

- policy makers for more effective programs to support innovation and competitiveness of organizations.

– Establish up-to-date and shared definitions:

- within the professional world (companies, consultants, financiers, etc.);

- in international organizations (WIPO, OECD (Oslo manual), WTO, World Bank, etc.).

– Propose proven tools and methods for the part of the process we want to improve

The result is a corpus of recommendation standards (ISO 56000 Series). While ISO 56002 is general, the others specifically develop a key aspect of the management of an innovation process, linking the organization's needs to the content of the standard (Figure 42.4).

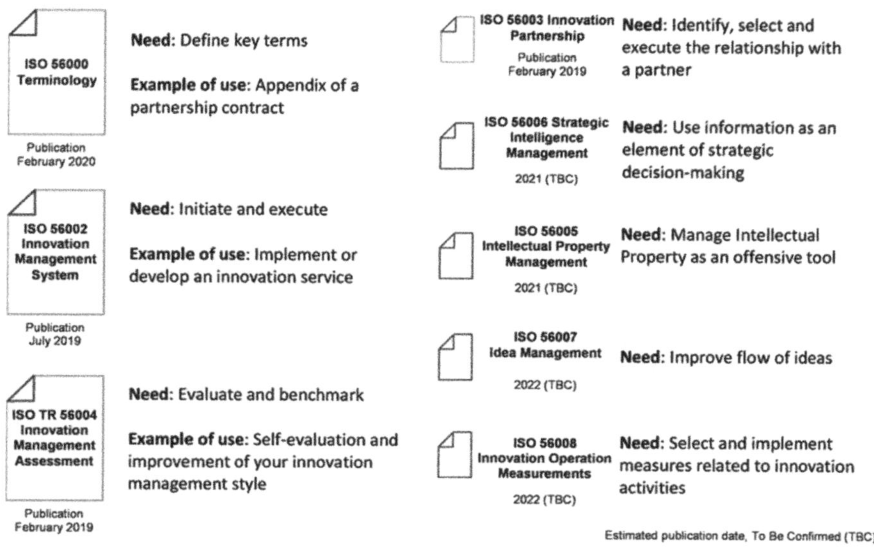

Figure 42.4. *Examples of how to use the guides according to need (source: Commission de Normalisation en Innovation, Afnor 2019)*

As shown in Figure 42.4, we see the main contributions of the standard at three levels:

– a strategic level, because it allows an organization to define its innovation strategy, identify key resources (IP, financing, HR, process, etc.), to gain strength in terms of its innovation approach and balance/diversify its project portfolio by innovating more often;

– a tactical level, because it notably allows an organization to formalize the process, to organize the search for ideas/opportunities, to pilot innovative projects;

– an operational level, because it allows the idea generation phase to be equipped with tools to improve the flow of ideas in terms of quantity and quality and thus access to all forms of innovation.

Thus, the deployment of this series of standards in innovation management has several implications:

– at the level of a company: it encourages the emergence and development of innovation, it contributes to greater autonomy in terms of innovation development, it gives keys to make innovation visible;

– at the level of the national ecosystem: it contributes to the development of the attractiveness of the territories, it encourages exchanges within the innovation support chain, it provides common training reference systems, it can give an advantage in international competition.

42.4. Conclusion

Organizations of all types and sizes have come to realize that innovation is the key to improved performance. The work of the experts for the realization of the international standard in innovation management (ISO 56000 Series) shows that there are eight fundamental principles to be promoted in order to best steer our innovation management system, notably around the notions of value/risk creation, strategic vision, foresight and culture of innovation. They also confirm that managing innovation means investing in practices that are conducive both to the emergence and regular development of innovations and to maintaining a certain organizational agility, which is necessary for setting up a permanent innovation dynamic. Finally, and this is undoubtedly the most important point to be retained from this work, the choice to draft a standard of recommendations and not a certification standard. This implies that, unlike quality management, the certification of organizations will not be possible. On the contrary, the standard will lead to the development of a new profile of innovation manager with an ecosystemic and foresight vision of innovation.

Because chance and luck are no longer enough to innovate!

42.5. References

CEN TS 16555-1 (2013). Innovation Management Systems.

CEN TS 16555-3 (2015). Innovation Thinking.

CN INNOV (2019). Afnor, document officiel de communication sur l'ISO 56000 SERIES Innovation management.

ISO 56000 (2019). Series for Innovation Management.

ISO 56003 (2019). Innovation Management – Tools and Methods for Innovation Partnerships.

ISO 56004 (2019). Innovation Management Assessment.

43

Synchronization – Synchronization and Coordination of Innovation

43.1. Introduction

Faced with a continuously changing environment, reaction speed is crucial. Thus, an organization can no longer act individually and finds itself constrained to belong to a network of partners where collective intelligence exceeds the individual intelligence of each organization. Thus, organizational networks result from the linkages of a central organization with other organizations. More precisely,

> the egocentric network of the organization is composed of the focal organization (called ego), a set of organizations (called alters) that have links with the ego, links between the ego and the alters, and links between the alters. (Wasserman and Faust 1994)

The organizational network is a channel through which an organization can obtain resources and information from the environment. From a collaborative innovation perspective, these networks are places for mutual fertilization and knowledge networking between different organizations (Laperche 2017). This collaborative innovation can only succeed with a management style that fosters the creativity of all employees: innovating with and for the collective. Thus, the partners must reach an agreement concerning the pooling of resources, risk sharing, intellectual property and, in case of success, the distribution of the benefits of the joint innovation project(s). In other words, there must be good coordination between the different economic agents involved. According to Gardet (2009),

---

Chapter written by Sana ELOUAER-MRIZAK.

coordination is the successful orchestration of one of the different organizations that are part of a network. This coordination is complex because of the diversity of the members of a network and their widely divergent objectives.

Modes of coordination are seen as arrangements between economic units that govern the ways in which these units can cooperate to develop the innovation project together (Grandori and Soda 1995). According to Dhanaraj and Parkhe (2006), these modes of coordination reduce uncertainty and opportunistic behavior within innovation networks.

The coordination of the actions of the different actors requires synchronization and coherence to achieve the common objectives of the network. Synchronization, in which individual dynamic units keep pace with one another in a decentralized manner, depends both on the dynamic units and on the properties of the interaction network (Nishikawa and Motter 2010). Although synchronization is an essential part of the coordination process, previous work has focused on the internal functioning of these networks (Dhanaraj and Parkhe 2006; Gardet 2009; Gardet and Mothe 2011), the mechanisms by which these collaborations are formed, the structure of these relationships and their determinants (Soda *et al.* 2019). In this chapter, we try to contribute to this literature by studying the importance of coordination and therefore synchronization between the actions undertaken by the members of innovation networks (section 43.2), the relationship between proximity and coordination (section 43.3) and the importance of these two concepts, namely coordination and synchronization, in ensuring the performance of an innovation project (section 43.4).

43.2. Innovation networks and synchronization

In his book *The Structuring of Organizations*, Mintzberg (1978) defines the structure of an organization as the sum total of the tools used to coordinate its activities. He proposes the following mechanisms for coordinating the entities of an organization: mutual adjustment between agents (coordination of work by simple informal communication), direct supervision, standardization of processes, standardization of objectives, qualifications or skills, and standards. A combination of different modes of coordination will ensure good coordination between teams.

Focusing on innovative firms, Laperche *et al.* (2008) point out that coordination is a fundamental element of these firms, regardless of their size, location or specialization. Effective coordination flows from the standards, rules and procedures that the firm, as part of a network, accepts and implements. These enable the company to manage innovation-related activities, exploit the benefits and regulate the associated risks and costs. In the case of collaborative innovation, companies cooperate with each other or with other organizations resulting in networked structures. Definitions of coordination refer to the skillful and effective interaction of movements and actions, or the regulation of various elements into an integrated and harmonious operation. The act of coordination is intentional and involves getting different people or things to work together for a common purpose or result. The resulting state of coordinated or collaborative action is the cooperation and synchronization of agents' efforts and targeted actions (Barnett 2011).

Inter-company synchronization in product development and innovation is not new. In addition, synchronization can generate performance benefits for companies. However, previous research has largely focused on the relationships between firms rather than on how synchronization emerges in innovation networks or how actors might capture the value of synchronization in different collaborations. Even if synchronization is common in industries where the final product is a combination of complementary products, in other words in industries with very complex products, such as the aerospace industry, where these components are manufactured by several suppliers. Also, companies that produce mobile applications for Apple's iPhone and iPad have developed their own synchronized rhythm. As a result, synchronization can take many forms, and implementation costs vary widely. In addition, keeping part of a company's operations synchronized with those of another organization can present significant control challenges. These challenges are all the more important when it comes to synchronization between several actors in an innovation network. It can therefore be extremely useful to understand what needs to be done to coordinate critical activities among network members, especially in networks involving technology-intensive industries, where innovation is distributed among firms which are strategically interdependent.

Modern industrial ecosystems suggest that the network of relationships between companies (sometimes called the "alliance network") plays a key role in producing synchronization. These relationships can range from intense collaborations (where two or more companies develop products together) to independent alliances (involving less interaction, perhaps just a joint sales and marketing agreement). The type of network determines whether and how synchronization occurs, because it is through these relationships that companies influence each other to speed up or slow down their product development work.

The modes of coordination (Gardet 2009) within these innovation networks make it possible to ensure this synchronization. Among these are the following:

1) the degree of formalism: indeed, formalizing the exchange makes it possible to specify the roles of each of the parties involved. On the one hand, a distinction is made between formal, explicit or even written modes (e.g. standardization of

procedures, technical reports, contracts and confidentiality agreements) and, on the other hand, implicit, verbal or even informal modes (such as the setting up of joint teams (Grandori and Soda 1995), seminars, meetings and transfer of personnel as well as mechanisms for shared decision-making). This mode also allows the parties involved to formally agree to collaborate in a dynamic manner, with the aim of synchronizing their innovation and product development activities on the joint project;

2) inter-organizational trust: this is considered a temporary psychological condition that evolves as the members of the innovation network interact (Gardet 2009). However, between the members of an innovation network, there seems to be a range of situations that can go from mistrust to trust (Gardet 2009). Indeed, mistrust is due to opportunistic behavior by network members focusing on their own interests, contradicting the collective interest. It is possible that some members only pass on part of the information they hold to their partners, either to use it at the right time and thus keep an advantage or thinking that this is what other partners do as well. Good synchronization between members of the innovation network can also limit opportunistic behavior;

3) the distribution of results: a key element of good coordination and therefore successful collaboration is the definition of a rule for sharing results (Vassolo *et al.* 2004). The equitable distribution of results is seen as a mode of coordination that encourages a collective and synchronized effort on the part of project members and stimulates the success of the collaboration;

4) guarantees: a system of guarantees makes it possible to penalize opportunistic behavior or a delay by one of the members of the network;

5) conflict resolution: Gardet (2009) proposes five modes of conflict resolution in the context of relationships within innovation networks:

> joint problem solving (the different parties commit themselves to finding a mutual solution to the problem), persuasion (one of the parties tries to persuade the other members that a given solution is the best way out of the conflict situation), coercion (one, or more, partner(s) force(s) the others to choose the solution they have chosen to resolve the conflict), sanction (the cooperation partner is excluded), calling on a third party (this one carries out an arbitration between the different parties involved (arbitrator or court)).

It is possible that synchronization can be neither planned nor coordinated. It simply results from an appropriate response to the circumstances. Companies respond to signals from other companies and try to harmonize their efforts in order to move the collective project forward.

According to Davis (2013), network structure affects the timing of innovation in two ways. First, it influences the speed at which synchronization develops. Synchronization develops faster and easier in denser networks with a greater number of alliances, such as manufacturing and financial industries. On the other hand, it spreads more slowly in clustered networks where subgroups operate more independently, but with highly interconnected mini-networks. While synchronization can occur quickly within subgroups, it develops more slowly between them. Thus, it may take longer for the differences in timing between subgroups in highly clustered networks to merge into a common timing that synchronizes the entire network and ensures good coordination.

43.3. Coordination and proximity

However, we cannot talk about coordination without mentioning proximity. The latter relates to the distance (geographical, organizational, institutional, cognitive and social) between the actors. Good coordination is synonymous with a certain proximity. Torrès (2001) states that: "proximity modifies the nature of organizational relations and the effectiveness of coordination modes". In other words, organized proximity constitutes the basis for coordination between economic agents. Torrès (2001) even speaks of coordination through proximity. He states that "proximity modifies the nature of organizational relationships and the efficiency of modes of coordination" and proposes two groups of coordination mechanisms. On the one hand, there are the modes of proximity coordination that result from mutual adjustment (a set of more or less formalized interactions between agents) and direct supervision. And on the other, there are modes of remote coordination, which are based on the standardization of skills, work processes and objectives. This standardization guarantees "organizational continuity" between units that can then be geographically dispersed. It is by respecting the same procedures and rules that the different units of an organization are strongly coordinated regardless of their location. But even if this standardization contributes to good coordination, for innovation projects, local coordination is more appropriate. Of course, new information and communication technologies make it possible to guarantee a remote relationship between the different entities, but coordination based on physical proximity is indispensable. Coordination is mainly done through verbal and visual communication. Is there a relationship between the phase of an innovation project and the mode of coordination used (proximity coordination vs. distance coordination)? Indeed, the coordination between the actors operating on an innovation project differs according to whether we are at the level of development, production or marketing. Moreover, depending on the stage of the project's progress, the resources of the members and their skills needed to carry it out change. Therefore, understanding the evolution of the contributions (resources, skills or know-how) made by each member helps to understand the coordination methods that will be put in place to ensure the success of the innovation project.

43.4. Coordination at the heart of innovative performance

Some innovation networks, such as competitiveness clusters or regional innovation systems, involve several economic agents (companies, universities, research centers, public actors) which in turn are part of their own network. Coordination between these different actors must be ensured, on the one hand, between the members of the innovation network and, on the other hand, between each member and its network. Herranz (2010) proposes a strategic coordination framework to ensure the performance of an innovation project involving multisectoral networks. Indeed, a well-defined strategy must generate an implementation process through an adequate structural choice. Nevertheless, it is only through the degree of achievement of strategic objectives that structural effectiveness can be measured. However, the coordination mechanisms between the actors of an innovation project belonging to different networks intervene in this process to finalize the achievement of the strategic objectives because of their complementarity as well as their coherence with the different strategic orientations.

Once the project is completed, the resulting innovation in turn creates coordination problems (Yu 2003) since there will be a change from the initial situation and any change is disruptive. Indeed, the knowledge acquired by the actors is no longer able to solve the new problems posed by the innovation carrier. Knowledge considered as acquired becomes problematic. As a result, coordination fails. In the analysis of a complex and evolving economy, the coordination modes of the system are naturally shaped by its evolutionary nature. Adapting coordination modes is a future challenge for innovation networks that produce change. This coordination will be more complex if the project is driven by several actors simultaneously. Similarly, coordination modes must be rethought in areas where innovation is difficult to protect.

In conclusion, the key to the success of innovation networks is good coordination and synchronization between its actors. Given the heterogeneity of the network members and the fact that the relationships between these partners are governed in a more or less contractual manner, good synchronization will allow the involvement of all partners at the right time and the achievement of the common objective. These partners can be close or distant in terms of, for example, activity and knowledge (cognitive proximity), and in terms of distance (geographical proximity). A certain geographical proximity allows frequent communication between the different network partners and the development of a common language that facilitates coordination, knowledge transfer and the establishment of trusting relationships.

These elements are essential at a time when open innovation is the key to being innovative, when companies of different sizes (large groups and start-ups, for example) are collaborating to innovate.

43.5. References

Barnet, G.A. (2011). *Encyclopedia of Social Networks*. SAGE Publications, Thousand Oaks, CA.

Davis, J.P. (2013). The emergence and coordination of synchrony in organizational ecosystems. In *Collaboration and Competition in Business Ecosystems, Advances in Strategic Management, Volume 30*, Adner, R., Oxley, J.E., Silverman, B.S. (eds). Emerald Group Publishing Limited, Bingley.

Dhanaraj, C. and Parkhe, A. (2006). Orchestrating innovation networks. *Academy of Management Review*, 31(3), 659–662.

Gardet, E. (2009). Modes de coordination instaurés par le pivot d'un réseau d'innovation : le cas d'un porteur de projet TPE. *Management & avenir*, 26, 33–51.

Gardet, E. and Mothe, C. (2011). The dynamics of coordination in innovation networks. *European Management Review*, 8(4), 213–229.

Grandori, A. and Soda, G. (1995). Inter-firm networks: Antecedents, mechanisms and forms. *Organization Studies*, 16(2), 183–214.

Herranz, J. (2010). Network performance and coordination: A theoretical review and framework. *Public Performance & Management Review*, 33(3), 311–341.

Laperche, B. (2017). *Enterprise Knowledge Capital*. ISTE Ltd, London and John Wiley & Sons, New York.

Laperche, B., Munier, F., Hamdouch, A. (2008). The collective innovation process and the need for dynamic coordination: General presentation. *Journal of Innovation Economics & Management*, 2(2), 3–13.

Mintzberg, H. (1982). *Structure et dynamique des organisations*. Editions d'organisation, Paris.

Soda, G., Stea, D., Pedersen, T. (2019). Network structure, collaborative context, and individual creativity. *Journal of Management*, 45(4), 1739–1765.

Torres, O. (2001). Du rôle et de l'importance de la proximité dans la spécificité de gestion des PME. *5ème congrès international francophone PME*, Lille, October.

Vassolo, R.S., Anand, J., Folta, T.B. (2004). Non-additivity in portfolios of exploration activities: A real options-based analysis of equity alliances in biotechnology. *Strategic Management Journal*, 25(11), 1045–1061.

Wasserman, S. and Faust, K. (1994). Structural analysis in the social sciences. *Social Network Analysis: Methods and Applications*. Cambridge University Press, Cambridge.

Yu, T.F.-L. (2003). Innovation and coordination: A schutzian perspective. *Economics of Innovation and New Technology*, 12(5), 397–412.

44

System – National Innovation System: The Primacy of Interactions Between Economic Actors

44.1. Introduction

The national innovation system (NIS) is a concept used as a tool to promote Innovation, Science and Technology policies and as an instrument for disseminating and accessing technological knowledge. More broadly, it enables the objectives of economic growth to be grasped by promoting the effects of innovation and understanding the links with economic development (Lundvall *et al.* 2002). The NIS has been in the limelight in academic and institutional circles since the 1990s, and still is, as an economic policy instrument for comparing national technological performances (OECD). But whatever the debates in this case, revealing the flexibility of the concept according to the field visited, the different authors have unanimously agreed on the theoretical imprints on which the NIS is based.

Indeed, the NIS emerged from a traditional neoclassical vision of innovation, developing in a way that is almost autonomous from the rest of the economic world, under the influence of the progress of a science subject to its own rules. Its functions place it in line with the research of heterodox economists, i.e. the work of the institutionalist and evolutionary approach, which proposes new visions of economic behavior and the process of technological innovation. These latter approaches are complementary, and are based within an economy based on experience, learning and knowledge (Lundvall 1992). Therefore, by rejecting the principle of resource

---

Chapter written by Vanessa CASADELLA.

allocation, the NIS never reaches an optimal stage because of the learning processes that characterize it, which are subject to continual change, undetermined and dependent on development paths (Edquist 1997). The NIS establishes itself as a truly complex dynamic system. From there, a State, like a company, is situated, in their development, on a technological trajectory that largely conditions their capacity to assimilate new technologies. This technological trajectory is determined by the weight of their history, the state of the environment, which is imperfectly known, and the functioning of the market at the present moment.

We will first present the nature of multi-actor interactions before understanding the link between the concept and economic development.

44.2. The NIS and nature of multi-actor interactions

If the NIS exists, it is because it is above all a "system". The numerous formal and informal cooperations between the scientific, industrial, institutional and service producing sectors, formed through the constitution of networks, are all interests that tend to the development of innovations. The links and interactions within and between sectors represent real flows of knowledge and information and are defined as important mechanisms for the transfer of tacit and codified forms of knowledge. These flows, both tangible and intangible, include financial flows between government and private organizations, human flows between universities, firms and government laboratories, regulatory flows from government agencies to organizations, and knowledge flows among these institutions.

Moreover, the NIS remains associated with a national space, and the actors and institutions involved are those whose purpose is to produce knowledge within this space. Lundvall (1992) justifies the national framework with reference to the political, historical, cultural and social importance of the innovation system. Historical evolutions, cultural models, socio-economic structures, political styles, laws, traditions and governance models are all specific and diverse national representations. Nevertheless, and in an internationalized perspective, the NIS is made up of networks of multi-scalar actors and institutional contexts that jointly support (or hinder) the formation and diffusion of an innovation. In some cases, it can be reduced to specific territorial contexts, while in others, it depends on the strategies of actors, networks and institutional dynamics that evolve jointly between different parts of the world. The combination of actors, networks and institutions that support or hinder innovation is very numerous and other systemic structural configurations can lead to similar performance characteristics (Edquist 1997).

In this regard, the NIS places great importance on institutions, and these give rise to differences in behavior and economic performance. Institutions and their interrelationships with technical change are particularly important. They shape the interactions and decisions of economic actors, just as they constitute processes of variety creation and selection related to technical and organizational change. The NIS remains focused on the role of institutions and institutional learning (Johnson 1992).

There are two opposing approaches to defining systemic innovation: a narrow approach related to R&D activities and science and technology (Nelson 1993) and a broad approach related to learning capabilities (Lundvall 1992). For the strict definition, innovation is narrowly defined because the innovative dynamic is only measured in terms of formal activities related to R&D and scientific activities. While innovation may be radical or incremental in nature, it only concerns knowledge creation activities. The narrow conception only takes scientific and technological systems as the object of study. It explicitly considers the determinants and consequences of innovation that are external to its field. The advantage of this restriction is a gain in precision in the analysis. In fact, the literature related to the narrow conception (Nelson 1993) provides detailed studies of the institutional and organizational architecture of the NIS, or studies centered around the firm and its local environment: interactions between suppliers and users, etc. (Nelson 1993).

In contrast to this vision, a broad, cognitive or organic approach has developed with the work of Freeman (1987), Lundvall (1992) or Edquist (1997). The study of the determinants of innovation "naturally" leads to considering influences that are not strictly in the domain of science and technology. The transition to this conceptualization takes place through a logic of proximity of different fields/sectors to be considered, which leaves the door open to relatively extensive interpretations of the system: capacities, skills, culture, customs, national traditions, legislation, etc. Here, innovation, whether radical or incremental, is a continuous cumulative process inherent in the diffusion, absorption and use of knowledge. In this version, the focus is on learning capabilities, which are based on the principle that the competitiveness of individual firms stems from their capacity to learn.

All in all, the NIS appears to be a much-debated concept but always in phase with the proposed approaches. In other words, if the author studies R&D systems, he will use the NIS *stricto sensu*, and if he analyzes the social system in which the research and innovation system develops more globally, he will use the NIS in the "broad" sense. Broad or narrow, the boundaries remain blurred, and the concept of the NIS ultimately takes the form of a "*social technology*" (Sharif 2006) where both technologies (and knowledge) and their environments create a dynamic of diffusion and creation of new knowledge.

44.3. The NIS and economic development

Originally, the NIS was a public policy tool. However, public intervention in innovation policy is not limited to patents, but seeks to promote cooperation and knowledge exchange between different innovation actors. We no longer speak of "innovation policies" in the strictly technological sense, and the performance of an innovation policy is not measured by its effects on R&D but by its real impact on the relations of the system.

Today, the NIS is a "means" and no longer just an instrument of public policy. Moreover, the NIS is just as much a top-down instrument within which the institutional structure and political choices determine the learning trajectory of economic actors, as it is a *bottom-up* instrument where the diversity of corporate decisions and behaviors influences the NIS (Archibugi and Michie 1997). Micro/macro/meso-economic issues are intertwined and the angle of analysis becomes broader.

In this mindset, the effect on development outcomes of inclusion in innovation activities is an emerging research area (Chaminade *et al.* 2018). This topic has so far been largely ignored in studies on systemic innovation and economic development (Cozzens and Sutz 2014). Indeed, most empirical research on inclusion and innovation focuses on microeconomic processes (e.g. frugal innovations), but the importance of institutional structures where the various processes are integrated is largely unknown (Andersen and Johnson 2015). Another focus in a broad approach to NIS is the input of education systems (Lundvall and Christensen 1999) or sustainable development (Chaminade *et al.* 2018). Other focuses include the role of education systems and labor markets, human resource management in organizations, or the use of R&D in public and/or private firms and institutions. The role of universities, on the other hand, was discarded before being more recently brought back into the current debates on the work of the NIS (Albuquerque *et al.* 2015).

All in all, the NIS is a strategic tool for economic development. The overall idea is to understand how learning has enabled a better development of economic actors: individuals, companies, states. Very broad angles of analysis can be used to associate the dynamics of learning with development objectives. Lundvall *et al.* (2002), for example, demonstrated the relevance of the learning/development combination in Denmark. The NIS must be able to respond to the problems of inequality and the fight against poverty. Narayan and Petecsh (2002) have also shown how listening to poor countries is imperative for linking innovation and development in developing countries. It is not a question of listening to the voice of Western countries on the policies to be followed, but rather of bringing up the societal problems of civil society. If this is the case, the emergence of informal innovation systems takes all its legitimacy, as Muller has shown in Tanzania (Muller

2011). In this direction, the system will be registered under the name of a "National System of Innovation and Capacity Building". The focus on skills lies both on the application of knowledge and on their great diversity. The term "construction" refers to innovation *a posteriori* (*ex ante*), so that the analysis of an NIS is based on its conditions of emergence and development and not on components that are *a priori* conditioned by formal processes (Lundvall *et al.* 2002).

44.4. Conclusion

The main contribution of this concept is to consider the relationships between organizations and actors that promote the realization of innovation as significant and determining. The NIS is essential for interpreting the growth and technological competitiveness of the States. It can also be used to solve certain development problems or create new specific knowledge. Broadly defined, the NIS is built between technology and informal learning, domestic and international networks, growth and development, scientific actors and civil society, productive and social capital, top down interests (linked to public policies) and *bottom up* perspectives (created from civil society, such as frugal innovation), as if their structures were perfectly flexible and adapted to the economies observed. All these specificities show the identity of a "new NIS", oriented towards learning capacities, sustainable development, poverty or inequalities, and the construction of skills. In the same way, the NIS is configured or (re)visited from the structuring of an international scale to a national framework. As such, the development of national strategies and foreign cooperations (through alliances, partnerships or even multinational firms) is also proving to be a future challenge for the promotion of the NIS.

44.5. References

Albuquerque, E., Wilson, S., Glenda, K., Keun, L. (2015). *Developing National Systems of Innovation: University-industry Interactions in the Global South*. Edward Elgar Publishing & IDRC, Cheltenham and Ottawa.

Archibugie, D. and Michie, J. (1997). *Technology, Globalization and Economic Performance*. Cambridge University Press, Cambridge.

Chaminade, C., Lundvall, B.A., Haneef, S. (2018). *Advanced Introduction to National Innovation Systems*. Edward Elgar Publishing, Cheltenham.

Cozzens, S. and Sutz, J. (2014). Innovation in informal settings: Reflections and proposals for a research agenda. *Innovation and Development*, 4(1), 5–31.

Edquist, C. (1997). *Systems of Innovation, Technologies, Institutions and Organizations*. Pinter Publishers, London.

Johnson, B. (1992). Institutional learning. In *National Systems of Innovation: Toward a Theory of Innovation and Interactive Learning*, Lundvall, B. (ed.). Pinter Publishers, London.

Johnson, B., Lema, R., Villumsen, G. (2017). Research on innovation and development in the anthropocene. Globelics Working Paper Series, 1, Aalborg University, Department of Business and Management, Denmark.

Lundvall, B.A. (1992). *National Systems of Innovation: Toward a Theory of Innovation and Interactive Learning*. Pinter Publishers, London.

Lundvall, B.A. and Christensen, J.L. (1999). Extending and deepening the analysis of innovation systems – with empirical illustrations from the DISCO project. DRUID Working Paper N 99-12, Aalborg University, Denmark.

Lundvall, B.A., Johnson, B., Andersen, E.S., Dalum, B. (2002). National systems of production, innovation and competence building. *Research Policy*, 31(2), 213–231.

Narayan, N. and Petesch, P. (2002). *Voices of the Poor: From Many Lands*. Oxford University Press, New York.

Sharif, N. (2006). Emergence and development of the national innovation systems concept. *Research Policy*, 35, 745–766

45

Tax – Taxation and Innovation: Incentives, Attractiveness and Innovation Policies

45.1. Introduction

Innovation and its financing raise real questions that are constantly being debated and interpreted or reinterpreted at the present time. While the market naturally encourages innovation, its financing is quite complex and the public authorities have a role to play in this area to define a certain number of levers and incentives. In this sense, taxation is an attractive way to overcome the obstacles related to the costs of innovation (Villemeur 2011). According to the OECD, innovation is the set of scientific, technological, organizational, financial and commercial processes that lead, or are expected to lead, to the realization of technologically new or improved products or processes. It is an important factor in competitiveness, productivity and job creation. With that in mind, governments should seek to provide incentives for firms to invest in research and development (R&D). To this end, the tax system plays an important role in supporting innovation. Between incentives and effectiveness, the aim is to find the right balance between attracting and not discouraging. In this sense, we will present three main axes presenting the link between innovation and taxation: that of incentives, that of attractiveness and finally that of innovation policies.

45.2. Taxation and incentives

Due to exceptions granted in international agreements (e.g. World Trade Organization and European Union), R&D subsidies are one of the few instruments available to governments to help domestic firms strengthen their competitiveness

---

Chapter written by Olivier ESNEU.

without providing direct support (Westmore 2013). Another objective for governments is to support R&D to achieve concrete results in order to stimulate productivity growth, to compensate for the decline in R&D due to various economic crises and to encourage companies engaged in R&D to carry out these activities in the national territory in order to promote economic spin-offs.

Nevertheless, the proliferation and increased generosity of tax incentives for R&D have sometimes had unintended consequences on innovation and the public account balance sheet. The most obvious example is the R&D tax credit. Other tax measures are possible, such as accelerated depreciation schemes for innovation-related equipment or reduced payroll taxes for the employment of scientists and researchers. Another way to stimulate the supply of innovation is to reduce the corporate tax rate on innovation-related profits, particularly in the case of royalties or patent assignments. This is the case in the Netherlands, where profits from innovation are only taxed at a low rate (the "Innovation Box" regime), whereas the general tax rate can be as high as 25%.

Other countries have shown their willingness to promote R&D by implementing tax measures, such as the "patent box" in the United Kingdom, or Canada, which grants a large tax credit for Research & Development. In France, the terms and conditions of government support have been significantly modified between 2000 and 2014. Nevertheless, the research tax credit (*crédit d'impôt recherche*, CIR) is the major support mechanism for innovation, a clear incentive measure created in 1983 (Liu 2013) allowing a tax reduction calculated on the basis of R&D expenses incurred by companies. With its last major reform in 2008, this measure, which is very popular with businesses, has even become the main tax expenditure of the Ministry of Higher Education, Research and Innovation, with a budgetary cost of 6.2 billion euros for 2019. However, in practice, the CIR raises some questions. On the one hand, the question of the real advisability of such a measure can be raised since tax measures in favor of innovation weigh heavily on public finances. On the other hand, there is also the question of its compliance with European rules on State aid. Indeed, the latter are strictly regulated within the European Union due to the risk of a race for tax optimization, particularly concerning the transfer of intellectual property rights in low-tax countries (OECD 2010).

This is why the question arises of adapting the mechanism to the real current economic stakes. In 2013, the innovation tax credit (*crédit d'impôt innovation*, CII), an extension of the research tax credit (*crédit d'impôt recherche*, CIR), was introduced in France. Indeed, SMEs can now benefit from a tax credit, under certain conditions, for certain expenses related to their innovative projects. For this reason, the 2019 French finance budget review is reviewing the taxation of innovation, regarding both the CIR and the special regime applicable to income from patents, in order to make it compatible with European legislation, among others.

45.3. Taxation and attractiveness

To return to the crucial issue of the place of tax incentives in a globalized context, it should also be recalled that research, both fundamental and applied, relies on researchers who are often highly mobile, ready to move to benefit from a good scientific environment or more comfortable incomes. This mobility is also the rule for large multinational companies, which can choose to locate their research and development centers to this or that country depending on their tax attractiveness. The dilemma remains particularly acute at the European level. It therefore appears necessary to better coordinate tax policies: to the many harmful effects already identified from the tax competition that European countries are engaged in, we can now add the harmful effect on innovation and growth in Europe.

There is thus a significant effect of taxes on innovation. These effects are present at the macroeconomic level: for example, an increase in the median or maximum income tax rate in a State leads to a decrease in the number of patents, citations or inventors located in that State. Corporate tax negatively affects the number of patents filed by private companies. However, this observation must be complemented by a more precise study: indeed, taxation may have a greater impact on the location of research between different States than on its total volume. Unfortunately, taxation also affects the research effort of the inventors themselves: an increase in income tax would lead to a decrease in the probability of filing a patent within three years, and to a decrease in the number of citations of these patents, revealing a lower quality of innovation. These effects are particularly strong for researchers employed by private companies, but they remain insignificant when R&D activity takes place in an area dense in innovative companies: this agglomeration effect helps explain why Silicon Valley remains a favorable place for inventions, even though the level of taxes is higher in California than in other American states.

45.4. Taxation and innovation policy

Such analyses require data covering a large number of years because innovation sometimes takes place over a long period of time, making it possible to compare changes in taxation and innovation measures, such as the number of patents filed and the frequency of their citation. In the end, tax measures for innovation can lead to an intensification of innovative activities, particularly R&D activities, but they can also lead to a simple displacement of R&D from one country to another and a subsidization of R&D activities that would have been carried out anyway, even without tax credits.

Public authorities must avoid this risk by also being aware of the administrative burdens created by measures in favor of innovation for companies. In addition, these measures can promote tax optimization, notably by transferring intellectual property rights to low-tax jurisdictions.

It should also be remembered that fiscal measures in favor of innovation are not without cost to public finances. The value of the various R&D tax credits ranges from a very small percentage of total tax revenues (United Kingdom and Norway) to a percentage of around 1% (Canada). This shortfall in revenue generally has to be compensated for, for example, by raising corporate or personal income taxes. This can then have a disastrous effect both on innovation in companies and on economic activity as a whole by discouraging entrepreneurial and innovative activity.

Governments also need to consider whether marginal personal income tax rates are appropriate for highly skilled workers, who can particularly contribute to increased innovation, but are also mobile and often sensitive to tax rates. As a result, it has become difficult to design effective tax policies for innovation in a globalized economy where multinational corporations and intellectual assets are prominent. While each country is unique, new OECD work on tax policy and intellectual capital provides several lessons for policy makers (Westmore 2013). First, tax incentives for R&D should be designed to better meet the needs of young innovative firms, which have very limited opportunities to optimize tax efficiency across borders and thus compete on a level playing field with large multinational enterprises. Secondly, public authorities must consider a better balance between indirect support for corporate R&D (tax incentives) and direct aid (contracts, subsidies, etc.) for innovation. For example, direct support measures would probably stimulate R&D more than previously thought, especially in the case of young companies that do not have the necessary funds to launch an innovative project.

In addition, governments should also ensure the cost-effectiveness of tax incentives by systematically evaluating them to assess the appropriateness of their scope. Finally, the effectiveness of R&D tax incentives depends on the overall regulatory framework and its stability over time. According to OECD data (Westmore 2013), it is thus possible to increase the profitability of investments in intellectual assets by ensuring the proper functioning of the various markets but also by avoiding too many changes in tax policy that may reduce the impact of tax credits.

45.5. Conclusion

Each country, according to its own history, its economy, its structure, its population has developed its own fiscal strategy for innovation. Given the importance of innovation for sustainable growth and development, the public authorities must ask themselves questions on the optimal approach. But optimality is a real balance to be found to attract innovators through judicious incentives without discouraging them through a heavy or complex taxation system. To do this, the goal is not to allow companies to reach out to the State to obtain tax credits or subsidies, but rather to create an environment that is globally favorable to innovation through the development of new companies and products.

45.6. References

France Stratégie (2016). Rapport de la commission nationale d'évaluation des politiques d'innovation. Report, France Stratégie, Paris.

Liu, Z. (2013). Le renforcement des aides fiscales à la R&D industrielle. *Politiques d'innovation et PME en France : une histoire de liens faibles*, L'Harmattan, Paris.

OECD (2010). *Fiscalité, innovation et environnement*. OECD, Paris.

Villemeur, A. (2011). La fiscalité est-elle adaptée à l'effort requis en innovation ? In *Fiscalité et croissance*, Michel, A. (ed.). Presses Universitaires de France, Paris.

Westmore, B. (2013). R&D, patenting and growth: The role of public policy. OECD Economics Department Working Papers, 1047, OECD.

46

Technology – Theoretical Model of Technology for Innovation

46.1. Introduction

This theoretical model for innovation is based on a definition of technology considered as an activity satisfying a human purpose, and technological innovation seen as a new combination of pre-existing technologies exploiting new phenomena discovered by science (Arthur 2009). Actually, new technologies may be generated also by only a combination of pre-existing technologies without direct exploitations of scientific discoveries (Bonomi and Marchisio 2016). These definitions are at the base of a general model for technology and of technology innovation processes.

46.2. Model of technology

The presented theoretical model of technology and technology innovation takes its origin from a discussion held in the 1980s at the Santa Fe Institute between an economist, Brian Arthur, and a theoretical biologist, Stuart Kauffman. These scholars considered that technologies cannot be simply economic goods, but are subjected to explosions of creativity and mass extinctions similarly to biological entities in an ecosystem. That leads to the consideration that there are analogies between the operations existing in the structure of a technology and the action of genes in biology generating new entities, a process for which there was already a mathematical model that it could also be used for technology. The model considers in fact technology as a structure of operations, each characterized by a set of

Chapter written by Angelo BONOMI.

parameters assuming various possible values or choices (Auerswald *et al.* 2000). For example, a heat treatment technology may consist of three operations: heating to a certain temperature, maintaining the temperature for a certain time and a rapid cooling, each operation characterized by parameters of time and temperature. A technological recipe is obtained giving specific values or choices to the parameters of the operations of a technology, and all recipes, which may be obtained by a combinatory calculation, or may be represented as points in a multidimensional discrete space called technological space. A technological landscape may be obtained by associating the value of efficiency with each recipe of the technological space. Learning by doing may be then considered as a search for an optimal recipe in the landscape, and innovation seen as a change in the operational structure of a technology. As the structure of a technology may be represented by a graph and then by its corresponding matrix, it is possible to consider all technologies fulfilling the same purpose in the form of matrices that may be represented by points in a multidimensional discrete space called the space of technologies (Bonomi and Marchisio 2016). The degree of radicality of a new technology, with respect to a pre-existent one, is represented by the respective distance in the space of technologies. The degree of radicality measured in the space of technologies allows a more accurate definition and measure of what is considered a radical (distant) or an incremental (near) technology resulting from an innovation process. The model has a full mathematical description (Bonomi and Marchisio 2016), and its definitions and representations may be used for the explanation of various technological processes that are involved in technology innovation.

46.3. Technological processes

Technological processes may occur in the frame of a single technology or being involved in a set of technologies and may be described using the technological landscape or the space of technologies.

46.3.1. *Externality effect*

Externality of a technology is represented by the influence of external factors, such as changes in raw materials, costs, regulations, failures of equipment, etc. on the efficiency of a technology modifying in this way its technological landscape, leading to the process of searching for new optimal conditions in the modified landscape through learning by doing. In certain cases, the modification of parameters is insufficient to reach an acceptable efficiency and an innovation (change of the structure), generally of incremental type, is necessary. That explains why new technologies may also appear during the use of a technology and not only, for example, through R&D activities.

46.3.2. *Intranality effect*

Intranality of a technology corresponds to the fact that, when operational values of a parameter are changed to improve the efficiency of an operation, such a change may influence the efficiency of other operations and thus the overall efficiency of the technology (Auerswald *et al.* 2000). Optimization of the total efficiency of a technology thus needs a little tuning work among the intranality effects of the various parameter values. An analogous intranality effect also exists for the change of the operational structure of a technology that affects the efficiency of other operations of the technology and that should be considered throughout the whole optimization of the innovation process. Intranality effects may hinder the diffusion of new technologies when some operations of a production are subcontracted to various firms not willing to make the necessary changes to adopt the innovation. This fact has been observed, for example, in the Italian industrial district producing ceramic tiles (Russo 2003).

46.3.3. *Ramification of technologies*

This process is characteristic of an initial radical technology that may generate other technologies constituting a diversification or improvement of the initial technology and that may be represented by a ramification in the space of technologies. Typically, the degree of radicality of the formed technologies decreases with the development of the ramification while the number of ramified technologies increases. This ramification may be shown indirectly by studying the generation of patents starting from that of an initial radical technology as in the example of computerized tomography (Valverde *et al.* 2007). In certain cases, there is the formation of lateral ramifications involving technologies with a different purpose. A good example is the case of ink jet printing that generated additive manufacturing for the production of objects. Printing technology developed further with laser printing, while additive manufacturing used initially for productions with materials at room temperature evolved towards the use of materials necessitating medium or high temperatures. The extension of the ramification process constitutes the bulk of the socio-economic impact of a new technology.

46.3.4. *Velocity of innovation*

The velocity of the formation of new technologies depends on many factors including the speed with which technological changes of operations may be carried out in the development process in search of a good structure suitable for a new technology. Such speeds might be different depending on the technological sector (chemical, mechanical, electronic, etc.) because of physical differences in the time of change of operations during the innovation process. A high velocity of innovation may also be at the origin of effects during the management of projects when implementing a technology where the appearance of an innovation is making the technology chosen for the project obsolete. This phenomenon has been observed, for example, in the case of the Silicon Alley, an area of New York City with a high concentration of firms offering ICT services, and leading to the development of new forms of project management (Girard and Stark 2001).

46.3.5. *The Red Queen regime*

The Red Queen regime is a situation often observed in industrial districts or sectors making the same type of products and it is related to competition among firms in the field of technology innovations. The Red Queen is a character from Lewis Carroll's "Alice's Adventures in Wonderland", who says to Alice "Now, *here*, you see, it takes all the running you can do, to keep in the same place". In these districts or sectors, firms use similar technologies and have similar competences. If a firm introduces an incremental innovation, it gains a technological advantage. However, the other firms have the same competences and new ones may be easily obtained because of the incremental character of the introduced innovation, and possible patent protection might be easily bypassed because of incremental nature and low level of novelty of the patent. Then, the other firms easily react and introduce similar or alternative innovations. In this way, the initial technological advantage of the firm disappears. The multiple repetition of such a situation leads to a continuous technological development of incremental nature without any important economic growth or the appearance of a technological leader firm. Such a situation of technological nature is called the Red Queen regime. In fact, this regime may be disrupted by the appearance of a radical innovation, difficult to be compete with, that makes obsolete previously used technologies putting in danger the existence of firms that cannot counter with the new situation. An historical example of disruption of a Red Queen regime was the entry into the market of digital quartz watches from the Japanese industry that in the 1970s destroyed about 40% of the firms of the Swiss watch district which was based on mechanical technologies (Bonomi and Marchisio 2016).

46.3.6. *Technology transfer and know-how*

For technology transfer, two different technological processes are commonly intended, the first concerning the putting in use of a new technology, and the second the transfer of a technology to another location. A key aspect of technology transfer is the acquisition of know-how to operate the transferred technology. The model of technology may give a description of the nature of know-how consisting of an accumulation of experience by the operator in changing the parameters of a technology to maintain its efficiency following the recurring effects of the externalities and intranalities of the technology. Know-how is a tacit knowledge and it cannot be transferred simply by manuals, but necessitates an effort of imitation and learning by personnel. Transfer of knowledge by putting in use a new technology may be more difficult than transferring to another location because know-how acquired by operating in pilot plants or in the construction of prototypes may be different from that which is necessary to operate the technology at an industrial dimension.

46.4. The process of technology innovation

Beside the previous descriptions of the various technological processes, it is also possible to describe the innovation process in terms of phases or steps starting from the generation of innovative ideas to the use of the new technologies formed. The model considers the five steps reported in Figure 46.1. They start with the generation of the innovative idea, followed by a step in which the feasibility of the idea is demonstrated and then by a phase of development in which the performances are determined and the economy of the new technology is estimated. There follows an industrialization phase and finally the use of the new technology. The difference of this description of the innovation process from that considered in the OECD guide for statistical studies (OECD 2015) should be noted based on three steps: basic research, applied research and experimental development. This description does not take account of the phase of generation of the innovative idea and of the fact that also the use of a technology is a source of technological innovations. Furthermore, the process of technology innovation presented in Figure 46.1 does not take account of scientific research considered in fact only as a source of exploitable phenomena useful for the generation of innovative ideas.

Figure 46.1. *Schematic view of the innovation process*

46.5. Application of the theoretical model

This theoretical model of technology may give suggestions to policies for the promotion of technology innovation. In particular, it emphasizes the importance of the process of generation of innovative ideas that may be boosted, for example, by promoting an entrepreneurial view of results of scientific research and of R&D activity that concern both successful and abandoned projects. The process of ramification of technologies indicates the importance of the intermediate scientific and technical education for an economic growth of a country as the ramification depends mainly on technical activities carried out during the use of a technology. Finally, the model indicates the importance of generation of technologies simply by a combination of previous technologies, and that the innovation process may be boosted by diffusing technology knowledge, for example, through competence centers, hindering in this way the formation of a Red Queen regime in districts or sectors by improving the degree of radicality of innovations, and thus avoiding dangerous disruptions by the appearance of new unexpected radical technologies.

46.6. References

Arthur, B. (2009). *The Nature of Technology*. Free Press, New York.

Auerswald, P., Kauffman, S., Lobo, J., Shell, K. (2000). The production recipe approach to modeling technology innovation: An application to learning by doing. *Journal of Economic Dynamics and Control*, 24, 389–450.

Bonomi, A. and Marchisio, M. (2016). Technology modelling and technology innovation: How a technology model may be useful in studying the innovation process. IRCrES Working Paper, 3.

Girard, M. and Stark, D. (2001). Distributing intelligence and organizing diversity in new media projects. Santa Fe Institute Working Paper, 01(12), 082.

OECD (2015). *Frascati Manual 2015: Guidelines for Collecting and Reporting Data on Research and Experimental Development*. The Measurement of Scientific, Technological and Innovation Activities. OECD Publishing, Paris.

Russo, M. (2003). Innovation Processes in Industrial Districts. ISCOM Project, Venice November 8–10, 2002, revised version 07.02.2003.

Valverde, S., Solé, R., Bedau, M., Packard, N. (2007). Topology and evolution of technology innovation networks. *Physical Review E, Statistical, Nonlinear, and Soft Matter Physics*, 76, 032767.

47

Timing – Timing of Innovation: The Central Position of the Innovative Enterprise

47.1. Introduction

The theory of innovation offers an important place to competitive strategies, but also offers several perspectives on the different stages of the innovation process. In a competitive environment with rapid competitive movements, firms maintain a constant flow of innovations in order to preserve their competitive advantage (Ayerbe and Fonrouge 2005). Thus, the innovation lifecycle sheds light on the innovation process, providing a better understanding of the timing of the stages, the obstacles encountered and the success factors observed from the first attempts at market introduction to its renewal. It is within this framework that the timing or time factor plays an important role in the innovation process, because the profitable investment of a pioneering company often leads to the arrival of a new market entrant (Klingebiel and Joseph 2016).

In order to better understand the notion of the timing of innovation, we first present its origins, with particular emphasis on the characteristics that define it. Then, we justify how the date of introduction of the innovation and the identity of the innovative firm are essential in the theories of the innovation economy. This approach is justified by a more or less coherent analogy of related notions, and also by a rapid evolution of the fields of application, namely, decision theory, real options theory and game theory. Finally, we analyze the extensions of the notion of the timing of innovation through the theoretical foundations.

Chapter written by Babacar NDIAYE.

47.2. Foundations of the timing of innovation

Originally, the timing of innovation was defined identically to the notion of the timing of investment. This analogy stems from the fact that the success of innovation is directly linked to the investment strategy, which is estimated on the basis of a number of evaluation criteria, and that the competitive environment is often neglected (Barzel 1968; Cripps 1997). The definition proposed by Reinganum (1989), in the form of a triptych, to illustrate the concept of timing of innovation seems to be the most complete in economic literature. It is, first, a product or process innovation, a major or minor innovation, an autonomous or systemic innovation taken in isolation or jointly. A product innovation is defined as a significantly improved and higher quality product. A procedure innovation is defined as the creation of new production techniques or methods. These two types of innovation are often concomitant insofar as the introduction of a new product can induce significant changes in the production process (Mairesse and Robin 2011). The concept of the timing of innovation then concerns several sequential innovations and aims to examine the way in which expected benefits – the cost of research and development (R&D) – and interactions between competing firms are combined to determine a pattern of spending between firms and over time. Finally, the timing of innovation concerns the date of introduction of the innovation and the identity of the innovative firm.

From this definition, the most important elements that illustrate the characteristics of the timing of innovation are as follows: the typology of the innovation, the nature of the innovation in relation to the implementation process, the expected profitability, the competitive environment, the innovation lifecycle, the date of introduction on the market and the competitive position of the initiating firm. Among these evaluation criteria, the Net Present Value (NPV) was once the most used criteria to highlight the expected return on investment.

However, with the consideration of option value, i.e. the possibility for the decision-maker to be able to reverse his decision, valuation criteria such as the NPV were often questioned because of the presence of increasing information, mainly due to technological uncertainty and market uncertainty. With the valuation errors resulting from the use of the NPV, particularly the overestimation of irreversible versus reversible projects, it became necessary to construct a new criterion that was considered to be an exact replica of the old one, but included option value.

47.3. Key elements of innovation dating

By considering innovation as a determining factor of competition, the theories of the economy of innovation that were inscribed in the previous definition were, subsequently, oriented towards the two elements that seem more important, namely, the date of introduction of the innovation and the identity of the innovative firm. The first element is analyzed as a deliberate choice between anticipation and postponement. The second element makes it possible to know whether the firm is in the position of first entrant (innovator) or follower (imitator).

Models of innovation and imitation are based on literature that provides a basis for dynamic duopoly or oligopoly game models. In a deterministic environment, in which one firm may engage as an investor and the other as an imitator, each identifies a diffusion equilibrium of innovation in which investments occur sequentially and generally give an advantage to the first firm. Thus, the relationship between firms is analyzed from the point of view of investment capabilities. In the case where firms are symmetrical, competition is formalized as a game from which the date on which the innovation becomes available depends on the investment effort. The question is then whether there is at least one firm that is willing to pay a greater R&D effort than its rival in order to obtain the innovation. This effort, called the "commercial value of innovation" (Reinganum 1989), is an exogenous parameter defined as the maximum bid that a firm is willing to pay to obtain the innovation.

Insofar, as the firms are symmetrical, the firm that acquires the innovation (first mover) strengthens its leadership position over time in relation to the potential entrant (follower). Only the innovative firm benefits from almost all the returns from the innovation because there is an uncooperative equilibrium leading to the dissipation of the innovative firm's income. As a result, the catch-up mechanism is late or non-existent. Otherwise, firms are differentiated by their production efficiency and the incentive to innovate is highlighted by the "replacement effect". This effect is based on the hypothesis that the installed firm has less incentive to innovate than the potential entrant. This weak incentive to innovate is linked to the fact that the installed firm succeeds itself and only benefits from the profit differential resulting from the innovation, whereas the entrant firm benefits from the totality of the profits generated by the innovation. In both situations, it is important to identify the determinants of the positioning strategy.

47.4. The enrichment of the chronological study

The extension of the notion of a timing of innovation in literature is part of the legacy and foundations of the innovation economy. From the legacy of classical economists to the Marshalian school, Schumpeter and Arrow, there are different relationships between innovation, competition, growth, knowledge and the evolution of the economic system (Encaoua and Hollander 2002). Focusing on the Schumpeterian legacy, Antonelli (1999) highlights three concepts that link firms to each other, and also to the competitive environment: creative destruction (this notion concerns the relationship between innovation and growth, i.e. the new innovation replaces the old one), creative reaction (this notion concerns the relationship between innovation and competition, i.e. the form taken by a firm's reaction function determines its competitive strategy) and creative adoption (this notion concerns the relationship between innovation and the evolution of the economic system, i.e. the adoption of an innovation determines its diffusion process). The combination of these three concepts makes it possible to consider that the competitive environment and strategic interactions are the two factors that define the advantages and disadvantages related to the firm's position in the market. It is from this perspective that some authors have proposed a renewed approach to the timing of innovation based on decision theory (Fudenberg and Tirole 1985), real options theory (Chevalier-Roignant and Trigeorgis 2011) and game theory (Azevedo and Paxson 2014).

First, the renewed approach of decision theory is based on stochastic models and concerns the instantaneous probability of innovation discovery, called the rate of chance, which can either be constant with a process that follows a Poisson distribution, or increasing with the simultaneous consideration of the global rate of chance and the number of firms present on the market. Second, the renewed approach of real options theory is based on the combination of call and put options. Thus, the investment option (call) and the disinvestment option (put) are simultaneously taken into account. Finally, the renewed approach of game theory concerns the combination of entry games and investment games. Under the hypothesis of the strong rationality of firms, the link between the strategy resulting from the Nash equilibrium, and the form taken by the reaction function of each firm, determines the investment strategies.

In addition, the extension of the analysis of the timing of innovation through competitive strategies has made it possible to propose a typology for classifying two families of models: patent racing models and auction models. Patent racing is justified by the fact that there is always a mechanism for protecting innovations that favors research activity, i.e. an activity that may or may not succeed, and that may require more time and expense than expected. Conversely, auction models are explained by the fact that the result of R&D depends not only on the investment effort that favors the development activity, but also on the absence of technological uncertainty. Research and development activities are the main factors in the realization of an innovation.

47.5. Conclusion

The upheaval of the industrial economy and the tools for analyzing investment strategies help explain the changes in the study of the timing of innovation. The notion of the timing of innovation is a theme that is quite developed in literature, but its different applications lead to multiple interpretations. In spite of the very diverse economic analyses on the timing of innovation, the common feature of its foundation remains R&D. The consideration of competitive strategies *vis-à-vis* the analysis of this approach can be explained, on one hand, from the point of view of the tools used to estimate the return on investment. On the other hand, the evolution of the timing of innovation concerns the consideration of competitive strategies in the analysis of a new approach, based on different fields of application. Thus, the diversity of the fields of application of the timing of innovation provides a basis for analyzing it from different angles, leading to results that are not necessarily identical. Moreover, this is the reason why renewals and evolutions of the theory give rise to advantages and disadvantages, depending on the position of the firm in the market (choice between an innovative firm or an imitative firm). Consequently, the characteristics of analytical models (deterministic or stochastic) generally determine the specificity of the behavior of economic agents.

47.6. References

Antonelli, C. (1999). *The Microdynamics of Technological Change*. Routledge, London.

Ayerbe, C. and Fonrouge, C. (2005). Les transitions entre innovations : études de cas et proposition d'une grille d'interprétation. *Finance contrôle et strategie*, 8(2), 39–64.

Azevedo, A. and Paxson, D. (2014). Developing real option game models. *European Journal of Operational Research*, 237(3), 909–920.

Barzel, Y. (1968). Optimal timing of innovations. *The Review of Economics and Statistics*, 50(3), 348–355.

Chevalier-Roignant, B. and Trigeorgis, L. (2011). *Competitive Strategy: Options and Games*. MIT Press, Cambridge.

Cripps, M.W. (1997). Bargaining and the timing of investment. International. *Economic Review*, 38, 527–546.

Encaoua, D. and Hollander, A. (2002). Competition policy and innovation. *Oxford Review of Economic Policy*, 18(1), 63–79.

Feldman, M.-P. and Audretsch, D.-B. (1999). Innovation in cities: Science-based diversity, specialization and localized competition. *European Economic Review*, 43(2), 409–429.

Fudenberg, D. and Irole, J. (1985). Preemption and rent equalization in the adoption of new technology. *Review of Economic Studies*, 52(3), 383–401.

Klingebiel, R. and Joseph, J. (2016). Entry timing and innovation strategy in feature phones. *Strategic Management Journal*, 37(6), 1002–1020.

Mairesse, J. and Robin, S. (2011). Productivité et innovations de procédé et de produit dans les entreprises industrielles et de services. *Économie & prévision*, 1–2 (197–198), 21–44.

Reinganum, J.-F. (1989). The timing of innovation: Research, development, and diffusion. In *Handbook of Industrial Organization*, Schmalensee, R.R. (ed). 1, 849–908.

48

Trajectory – Innovation Trajectories and Dynamic Capabilities

48.1. Introduction

The notion of trajectory became popular in the economics of innovation and organizations in the context of the development of evolutionary analysis (Nelson and Winter 1982), which focuses on the question of change and the behavior of economic agents and in particular organizations, considered as economic systems. The question of the intensity and direction of technological change is at the heart of the analyses. G. Dosi (1982) analyzes technological paradigms and trajectories in analogy with Kuhn's (1962) study of scientific paradigms. The trajectory is also studied in the case of the firm, although the authors refer more to the notion of the "evolutionary path". This path is dependent on skills and accumulated organizational routines, which define the coherence of the firm, while favoring the emergence of sources of inertia and lock-in. The current challenge for companies is to develop the dynamic capabilities that will enable them to accumulate the organizational routines that are specific to the control and direction of technological change. The constant enrichment of "knowledge capital" (Laperche 2017), all the scientific and technical information and knowledge produced, acquired and systematized by one or more companies with a productive objective and, more broadly, a value production process, is for us the essential pillar.

We first return to the definition of the concepts of paradigms and technological trajectories. Then, the trajectory is studied in the context of the evolution of the company. A reflection follows, both on the role of dynamic capabilities and knowledge capital in the formation of trajectories and on the consequences of their collective formation.

Chapter written by Blandine LAPERCHE.

48.2. Paradigms and technological trajectories: theoretical and empirical approaches

Seeking to understand the determinants and directions of technological change, and not satisfied with the explanations provided by analyses based on the "Demand Pull" and "Technology Push" supply-side pressure, G. Dosi (1982) proposed an interpretation of the innovation process in terms of technological paradigms and trajectories. A technological paradigm is thus defined as a set of procedures, the definition of its relevant problems and the specific knowledge related to their solution (p. 148) or a "model" of the solution of selected technological problems, based on selected principles derived from the natural sciences and on selected material technologies. The paradigm derives from the state of the information base, knowledge base and available capabilities (Nelson and Winter 1982). Each paradigm defines its own conception of progress based on specific economic and technological trade-offs. Within this paradigm, just as "normal science" is seen by Kuhn as a realization of the promises of the scientific paradigm, the technological trajectory is defined as the "normal" activity model of problem solving (i.e. progress) within a technological paradigm (Dosi 1982, p. 152).

The question of choice, of the selection of the technological problems to be studied, is fundamental since it determines the dominant technological paradigm at a given period and the associated technological trajectory(ies). This selection is neither the result of chance nor of market forces alone, but rather the result of the influence of a set of economic, social and institutional factors, each of which will play a specific role in the process of the genesis of technological innovation. The analysis of technical change in terms of paradigm and trajectory makes it possible to explain discontinuities (radical innovations associated with new paradigms) and continuities ("normal" technical progress, associated with minor, cumulative innovations along trajectories) as well as their interactions. Along the trajectories, actors identify opportunities and solve problems by reusing and adapting solutions already used in the past. However, this dependence on the past can be a source of inertia and a brake on innovation.

Empirical work on technological paradigms and trajectories has focused on macro-/meso-scales, such as the study of technological revolutions and techno-economic paradigms by C. Perez (2002), and meso-/micro-scales, i.e. on sectoral dynamics as well as on the trajectories followed by firms in several sectors. This is the case within the manufacturing sector, following the taxonomy proposed by Pavitt (1984) (who defines four technological trajectories: Science Based Industries, Specialized Suppliers Industries, Scale Intensive Industries, Supplier Dominated Industries), as well as in services or in combined industry and services. These different trajectories are explained by "technological regimes" (Winter 1984) reflecting different sectoral dynamics, characterized by a particular combination of technological opportunities, conditions of appropriability, cumulativity of technological advances and properties of the knowledge base (Breschi *et al.* 2000).

48.3. The company's trajectory or the evolution path

The notion of trajectory is associated with the theoretical analysis of the firm, its boundaries and its specialization, although the term "evolutionary path" is generally preferred for its study. In evolutionary analyses of the firm, as in the resource-based theory, the firm is seen as a collection of resources to be managed. Here, the main questions concern the coherence of the firm (degree of proximity between the activities of a large modern firm) and its evolution (change of portfolio of activities or main activity), and therefore its mastery of technical progress (Dosi *et al.* 1990). Firms' developments and objectives are defined in the course of learning and coordination processes, according to trial and error (search) procedures that must lead to satisfactory results. The adoption of the hypothesis of limited rationality is explained by the importance of the uncertainty in which organizations act and interact.

The learning process is a process by which repetition and experimentation mean that, over time, tasks are performed better and faster, and new opportunities in operating procedures are constantly experienced. This cumulative process results in the production of knowledge that materializes in organizational routines defined as patterns of interactions that constitute effective solutions to particular problems. They form an "organizational memory", resulting from the replication of actions, a stock of knowledge produced by learning and mobilized by the company in its activity. They are integrated in the skills of employees, and also in the company's documents, archives and artifacts. These routines, which are tacit, constitute "specific assets" for the company that are difficult to transfer.

Recent work on routines emphasizes their "internal dynamics" (Feldman *et al.* 2016). Routines form repetitive and recognizable patterns of independent actions by multiple actors within an organization. Feldman *et al.* (2016) show how routines are implemented in specific times and spaces (i.e. they are situated), how they are patterns of action (i.e. these patterns are related to the tasks performed by the organization as part of a routine, such as hiring, budgeting and pricing) and how they interact (i.e. how routines influence each other and how they work together to support stability and change).

The company evolves by following a path determined by the skills accumulated through learning. Specific assets therefore determine the evolution path or trajectory of the company. It is the secondary or complementary assets to the main asset that, present along the value chain, can allow the company to change direction.

Evolutionary theory of the firm thus makes it possible to understand the endogenous transformation of the firm over time (Dosi *et al.* 1990).

While accumulated skills can differentiate companies and can strengthen their competitive advantage, they can also be a kind of trap. Routines are thus also seen as a source of inertia, locking the organization into a precise trajectory and slowing down its evolution. Path dependency precisely expresses this "forced" evolution of the firm, constrained by past investments. Mired in their routines, companies can neglect new technological opportunities or changes in the economic environment. In the context of technological change, lock-in situations can be explained by increasing returns on adoption and by institutional and strategic inertia. The same reasoning can be applied to the firm.

48.4. Trajectory formation: dynamic capabilities and knowledge capital

The work of resource-based approaches, where researchers focus on skills, dynamic capabilities and absorptive capacities, allows us to understand how trajectories are formed within firms, and also how new combinations result from the development of these capacities outside the paradigm. According to Teece *et al.* (1997), dynamic capabilities refer to the firm's ability to integrate, build and reconfigure internal and external competencies to respond rapidly to changes in the environment. The perception of the opportunities and threats of the environment and the selection of problems to be solved are therefore carried out within the company through the implementation of these dynamic capabilities. Among these dynamic capabilities, the absorption capacity is central. Absorptive capacity was first defined by Cohen and Levinthal (1990) as the firm's capacity to recognize the value of new information, transform it into knowledge, assimilate it and apply it for business purposes. Four dimensions of absorptive capacity are generally identified: acquisition, assimilation, transformation and exploitation (Zahra and George 2002).

The production and constant enrichment of "knowledge capital" (Laperche 2017) by the firm illustrates these dynamic capabilities, capable of producing new organizational routines, drawing technological trajectories within existing paradigms and eventually provoking the emergence of new paradigms and trajectories.

48.5. The collective dimension of trajectories and its consequences

The study of how knowledge capital is built up shows that it is not only the result of internal investments by companies (in R&D, human resources, equipment and technical devices, and also in intangible resources), but also increasingly of multiple cooperations with different types of organizations (complementary or competing companies of the same size, innovative start-ups, universities and research laboratories, communities). In this current context of open innovation (Chesbrough 2003), knowledge capital is not produced in a vacuum, but within innovation networks. The organizational routines of the actors confront and interact within innovation systems. The study of trajectories is thus deepened, insofar as they are collectively shaped. It is true that the empirical works previously cited strongly emphasized the collective dimension and the vertical links between producers, suppliers and users of technologies. This trend towards cooperation is intensified by the concomitant evolution of technologies (e.g. connected "objects" or "services" that induce the use of ICTs in any type of product or service) and management standards (which bet on openness and cooperation).

What are the potential effects of such a "socialization" of technological trajectories? On the one hand, the pooling of resources, made necessary by the imperative of permanent innovation combined with the imperative of return on investment, can contribute to accelerating the pace of innovation (and therefore technical progress). But learning to work together requires an alignment of organizational routines, and can lead to a certain amount of mimicry and thus to the multiplication of sources of inertia. This can be detrimental to technical progress itself (the emphasis would be more on minor innovations, within the same trajectory, than on radical innovations). Could networks and other eco(systems) of innovation, the cradles of trajectories, thus be a new source of "bureaucratization" of technical progress?

48.6. Conclusion

The notion of trajectory has taken different paths in economics and innovation management, mainly driven by evolutionary theories and resource-based approaches. Initially focused on the analysis of major technological developments, their periodization, their continuities and discontinuities and their determinants (in the analysis of paradigms and technological trajectories), it is also used to study the firm, its evolutionary path and its innovation strategy. The formation of trajectories is based on organizational routines, dynamic capabilities and thus the knowledge capital that the firm manages to accumulate over time. These different works converge on a vision of the collective formation of trajectories, within sectors linked by forms of cooperation and competition, essential to the permanent innovation imposed by the globalized competitive race. This raises the question of the benefits, which have been widely studied, and the limits (less well understood by the current literature) of the collective formation of technological or innovation trajectories. The constraints of financial results with which firms are also confronted are also a determining factor in the evolution of trajectories (Laperche 2020); these are all avenues for future work.

48.7. References

Breschi, S., Malerba, F., Orsenigo, L. (2000). Technological regimes and Schumpetarian patterns of innovation. *The Economic Journal*, 388–410.

Chesbrough, H. (2003). *Open Innovation: The New Imperative for Creating and Profiting from Technology*. Harvard Business School Press, Boston.

Cohen, W.S. and Levinthal, D.A. (1990). Absorptive capacity: A new perspective on learning and innovation. *Administrative Science Quarterly*, 35, 128–152.

Dosi, G. (1982). Technological paradigms and technological routines. A suggested interpretation of the determinants and directions of technical change. *Research Policy*, 11, 147–162.

Dosi, G., Teece, D.J., Winter, S.G. (1990). Les frontières de l'entreprise : vers une théorie de la cohérence de la grande entreprise. *Revue d'économie industrielle*, 51, 238–254.

Feldman, M.S., Pentland, B.T., D'adderio, L., Lazaric, N. (2016). Beyond routines as things: Introduction to the special issue on routine dynamics. *Organization Science*, 27(3), 505–513.

Kuhn, T. (1962). *The Structure of Scientific Revolutions*. Chicago University Press, Chicago.

Laperche, B. (2017). *Enterprise Knowledge Capital*. ISTE Ltd, London and John Wiley & Sons, New York.

Laperche, B. (2020). Mutation des trajectoires des entreprises et innovation : capital savoir et opportunités financières. *Marché et organisations*, 39, 91–110.

Nelson, R.R. and Winter, G. (1982). *An Evolutionary Theory of Economic Change*. Harvard University Press, Cambridge.

Pavitt, K. (1984). Sectoral patterns of technical change: Towards a taxonomy and a theory. *Research Policy*, 13, 343–373.

Perez, C. (2002). *Technological Revolutions and Financial Capital: The Dynamics of Bubbles and Golden Ages*. E. Elgar, Cheltenham.

Teece, D.J., Pisano, G., Shuen, A. (1997). Dynamic capabilities and strategic management. *Strategic Management Journal*, 18(7), 509–533.

Winter, G. (1984). Schumpeterian competition in alternative technological regimes. *Journal of Economic Behavior and Organization*, 5, 287–320.

Zahra, S.A. and George, G. (2002). Absorptive capacity: A review, reconceptualization, and extension. *Academy of Management Review*, 27, 185–203.

49

User – User Innovation: Interactions Between Users and Firms in Innovation Processes

49.1. Introduction

Both end-users (the final consumers of goods) and intermediate users (firms) hold a creative power that often leads to novel solutions to their daily problems. Users have the potential to revise and re-innovate existing products launched by manufacturing firms. They can also invent completely new products from scratch. When one of these two situations takes place, the output of their creative process is called a user innovation, “an innovation driven or created by those who will benefit from using it” (Franke 2013). Famous examples of (commercial or industrial) user-generated innovations that rapidly became mass market products are the umbrella, the vacuum cleaner and the dishwasher. A complementary phenomenon is user entrepreneurship, which refers to “the commercialization of a new product and/or service by an individual or group of individuals who are also users of that product and/or service” (Shah and Tripsas 2007, p. 124). User innovation can be generated by means of the individual action of a single user or the collective action of groups of more users. Referring to the first case, a single user innovator is a “single firm or individual that creates an innovation in order to use it” (Baldwin and von Hippel 2011, p. 1402). In the second case, user innovators can collaborate and form an ad hoc community in order to achieve their innovation purposes (Bogers *et al.* 2010). Individuals, persons or firms and communities of end-users develop such innovations alone or with the complementary contribution of established firms implementing open innovation strategies (Bogers and West 2012). After the introduction, we present the main motivations pushing users to develop innovation

---

Chapter written by Francesco SCHIAVONE.

by themselves. Then, the main approaches by which users are integrated in the innovation processes of firms are reported. Finally, the symbiosis between user innovation and paradigm innovation is illustrated.

49.2. Motivations for user innovation

Literature in innovation has quite outdated articles that refer to it. Spontaneous innovation by users, for instance, appears in research because of Adam Smith (1776). He was the first scholar that detected such orientation in the innovation of technology users. This type of active orientation was and is still present in many ways, but literature did not follow its development. It is only the past 40 years that research on it has re-emerged (Rothwell and Gardiner 1985; von Hippel 2005). With the world developing in hand with technology at such a fast pace, it is no surprise that innovations are also on the rise.

Users innovate for many reasons. However, Bogers *et al.* (2010) reported the two main motivations that push users to innovate. First, they refer to the low costs of innovation, in which many factors take part. Second, they refer to the stickiness of information factor held by users, which refers to "the incremental expenditure needed to transfer that unit from one place to another in a way that can be accessed by any information seeker" (Franke and Piller 2004). It is important to note that while information always flows from users to manufacturers, this does not always occur in the best way. The harder it is to transfer information from users to manufacturers, the more expensive the manufacturer-driven innovation process will become. The new approach should make users more interested in becoming part of the market and developing new solutions for common needs. Users who have previous training, specific backgrounds and even technical abilities should always be considered and encouraged to innovate. It is always a plus when an innovator has specific training, as this can help minimize the costs of consultancies and the development of the innovation in its first stages. Among the other benefits of having the user develop an innovation by themselves is the elimination of agency costs between customers (the principal) and firms (the agent). Customers will look for new solutions that can help satisfy their specific needs as best as possible, while firms are primarily interested in developing innovations at low cost without taking the customer's needs into account.

Another key motivation for user innovators when developing a new idea, and by consequence a new product or service, is the benefits they can gain from their innovations. According to von Hippel (2017), user innovators decide to innovate not only because of personal needs, but also because of their willingness to help people, for profit goals, for fun and even to learn. Each one of these general categories has a wide and heterogeneous variety of needs and purposes that drive user innovation. Users can decide to innovate old declining technology because they want to keep it in the market for one reason or another. By using their technical or theoretical knowledge and their interest or passion about it, they help to improve it and keep it in the market. A great example of this is found in the radio-amateurs community, in which some lead-users developed some multimedia software and then freely distributed it via the Internet, to connect old ham radios to the novel and have a better performing VOIP technology (Schiavone 2012).

49.3. The role of users in innovation processes

Although all user innovators have the interest to develop an innovation, not all of them have the same qualities, skills and characteristics. Some users decide to take a more managerial role, conducting and managing the user innovation process rather than taking an active role in the actual development of the innovation. These types of innovators are known as lead users. They display two main characteristics: "They face needs that will be a general need in the marketplace in the future, but they face them months or even years before the bulk of that marketplace encounters them. They also have significant benefits by obtaining a solution to those needs" (von Hippel 1986). Lead users are the first to perceive a need within the market and therefore, given the lack of options, decide to arrange and coordinate the innovation process necessary to fill in this gap. They recollect and hold relevant consumer knowledge, use their previous experience and are ailed by their innovative personalities (Schreier and Prügl 2008). Firms can benefit from the introduction of lead users in their companies as well. By doing so, they get an outside view of the needs of the market in the real time and help decrease costs directed to market research. A great example of the introduction of lead users into industry is Hilti AG, who are focused on the construction market. They decided to reach out to 12 client firms and interview them, in order to innovate pipe-hangers and use their creative ideas as a motivation to innovate (Herstatt and von Hippel 1992).

49.4. The symbiosis between user innovation and manufacturer innovation

User innovation, in fact, complements manufacturer innovation (Gambardella *et al.* 2017). Although this may seem contradictory, the mutual exchange makes the collaboration more impactful and the bilateral feedback enriches the process. User innovators provide innovative ideas and designs to the manufacturers and also wake up an interest in them that may have been missed. By doing so, this gap in innovation that was lacking can be filled and further developed. Producers can now not only support, but also help develop, improve and evaluate and redesign innovations in collaboration with the user innovators. It is through this symbiosis that proper and effective products or services can emerge.

An example of such complementarity comes from the so-called frugal innovation, which refers to "reducing the complexity of existing goods and therefore having cost advantages in comparison with existing solutions" (Zeschky *et al.* 2011, p. 39). Under this concept, products are to become more practical and unnecessary components are taken out to have a product that better adapts to the masses and is accessible in cost and practicality. Budget constraints can limit the proper development of innovations, which actually makes innovators more creative and adaptive to what is available, and for the collaboration by users. When this happens, low-tech innovations are created, and although they may be rudimentary in some aspects, they can easily adapt and satisfy the market needs. This type of innovation can be produced by the innovator with more liquidity availability in partnership with other interested parties (such as users), or with a manufacturer that decides to take part in their innovation process.

Commercialization of user-generated innovations can be complex and sometimes they end up in a corner due to a lack of knowledge on how to share and sell it to the world. This can be because of poor market reach, because the diffusion did not take place in the proper way or with the right channels, or even because of a lack of interest from the market. User innovators do not tend to innovate with profit in mind; they usually do so because they see the need and cannot find anything in the market that fits it. This can in a way be counterproductive because good ideas can go to waste and not fulfill needs in a general way. Innovations can also fall short in proper development due to a lack of knowledge, products or guidance; this can also have a negative impact on the way a product is delivered to the masses. Everything that was previously mentioned can make it harder for the innovator to properly commercialize and diffuse their innovation. More attention needs to be paid to innovators; in order to take full advantage of their innovations, more scrutiny is needed. Once an innovator is detected, they should have the communities' backup so that their innovations do not go to waste and can fulfill other people's needs.

Throughout time, firms have played the big role in innovation and have practically controlled the industry, leaving little room for smaller entities to take part. Players such as customers, stakeholders and others have played a marginal player role, but this is now changing. This shift is now permitting the marginalized to have a voice and take part in the innovation process. According to Baldwin and von Hippel (2011), in recent years, producer innovation is now moving towards a collaborative innovation with users. This collaboration gives more power to the user and also allows their voice to be heard. Firms are now smarter and see the benefits of such a collaboration. Users have let them know, either directly or indirectly, that, although they are needed, they are not indispensable. Having a need makes everybody creative and it is a matter of the survival of the fittest. This empowerment of the user gives us all an opportunity to one day form part of such an evolutionary process. Together, greater innovations can be available in the market and needs that were not being heard will now be covered effectively and efficiently.

49.5. Conclusion

In conclusion, after more than 40 years of empirical research, user innovation can be considered an established and alive domain of study within innovation theory. Over the last decade, the spread of information and communication technology and technical digital knowledge across users was boosted and is likely to further increase in the next years. The diffusion of this phenomenon will be in several household industries. The current centrality of such a phenomenon in many relevant industries is likely to offer user innovators various opportunities and better context conditions for ameliorating their value creation and value-sharing processes in the near future. Several governments around the world should set up specific policies and ad hoc programs to support entrepreneurial activities for this special type of innovator in some years. These policy-making actions would make the weak links between user innovation and user entrepreneurship stronger. They are still poorly analyzed and understood by scholars and practitioners. Therefore, user innovation is complementary to a number of other instances of innovation, such as open innovation, digital platforms, crowdsourcing and crowdfunding and 3D printing. The intersections of user innovation theory with these subjects are promising avenues of exploration for future research. Such intersections could provide new evidence and shed light on novel methods of integration of the user paradigm and the manufacturer paradigm. Moreover, another interesting line of research about user innovation should be the search by scholars, of cases and evidence of this paradigm in other industries, outside the well-known box of the so-called household sectors.

49.6. References

Baldwin, C. and von Hippel, E. (2011). Modeling a paradigm shift: From producer innovation to user and open collaborative innovation. *Organization Science*, 22(6), 1399–1417.

Boer, H. and Gertsen, F. (2003). From continuous improvement to continuous innovation: A (retro)(per) spective. *International Journal of Technology Management*, 26(8), 805–827.

Bogers, M., Afuah, A., Bastian, B. (2010). Users as innovators: A review, critique, and future research directions. *Journal of Management*, 36(4), 857–875.

Franke, N. (2013). User-driven innovation. In *Oxford Handbook of Innovation Management*, Dodgson, M., Gann, D.M., Phillips, N. (eds). Oxford University Press, Oxford.

Herstatt, C. and von Hippel, E. (1992). From experience: Developing new product concepts via the lead user method: A case study in a "low-tech" field. *Journal of Product Innovation Management*, 9(3), 213–221.

von Hippel, E. (1986). Lead users: A source of novel product concepts, *Management Science*, 32(7), 791–805.

von Hippel, E. (2005). *Democratizing Innovation.* MIT Press, Cambridge, MA.

von Hippel, E. (2017). *Free Innovation.* MIT Press, Cambridge, MA.

Lettl, C., Herstatt, C., Gemuenden, H.G. (2006). Users' contributions to radical innovation: Evidence from four cases in the field of medical equipment technology. *R&D Management*, 36(3), 251–272.

Shah, S.K. and Tripsas, M. (2007). The accidental entrepreneur: The emergent and collective process of user entrepreneurship. *Strategic Entrepreneurship Journal*, 1(1–2), 123–140.

Tran, V.T. and Ravaud, P. (2016). Frugal innovation in medicine for low resource settings. *BMC Medicine*, 14(1), 102.

Zeschky, M., Widenmayer, B., Gassmann, O. (2011). Frugal innovation in emerging markets. *Research-Technology Management*, 54(4), 38–45.

50

Value – The Value of Innovations: Specificity and Evaluation Methods of Innovation

50.1. Introduction

The end of the 20th century was marked by the emergence of a new business model, that of the "fabless company", i.e. a company that no longer manufactures products itself, but creates value through the sale of innovations developed through its own R&D. The development of fabless companies has only been possible through the recognition of innovation as an asset and the establishment of an "innovation market". This movement was based on a specific institutional framework in which intellectual property (particularly patents) took on new functions. Furthermore, unlike many other goods and services, innovations are generally indivisible and, above all, singular. They are indivisible in the sense that we cannot often exploit just a fraction of an innovation. They are singular in the sense that each innovation is inherently different from previous ones. As a result, we cannot simply infer the value of an innovation by observing recurrent transactions in a market. The evaluation of innovations therefore requires prior detailed examination of the sources of their value. This calls for specific methods for estimating their private value and to a discrepancy between the value thus estimated and their book value. However, the value of innovations is not limited to their private value. It also has a social dimension, the recognition of which partly shapes the institutional frameworks at the origin of the valuation of innovations, notably the patent system.

Chapter written by Marc BAUDRY.

In this chapter, we first discuss the source and specificity of the value of innovations before looking, respectively, at the methods for evaluating their private and social value.

50.2. Where does the value of innovations come from?

Innovations are inventions that have entered the industrialization and commercialization phase. A characteristic of this commercialization is that it is accepted and empirically validated (as detailed below) that it generates excess value in relation to the remuneration of factors at their marginal productivity. This excess value comes from friction in the acquisition and disposal of the resources mobilized to generate innovations. The identification of this friction is essential in order to develop an effective strategy for valuing innovations, on one hand, and to evaluate them, on the other. The mechanism, detailed in Baudry and Dumont (2017), can be summarized as follows. First, there is friction in the acquisition of resources. This is particularly true of human resources. It takes time and effort to process knowledge and successfully convert it into innovations.

The recruitment of engineers or researchers may not be sufficient if the company's organizational structures do not allow for a good deployment of their knowledge. Firms that have succeeded in mobilizing the required resources can thus have a period of time during which they are protected from competition and can either exercise market power in the commercialization of their innovations (not only for product innovation, but also process innovation that would not be only be used internally) or benefit from cost advantages (for process innovation).

In both cases, for the innovative firm, the marginal product of the resource will exceed its acquisition cost. However, difficulties can also arise in the transfer of resources. They are of two types. The first lies in the specificity of the mobilized assets. The second is asymmetry of information. Combined, they make it very difficult for a firm to transfer the product of its R&D to another firm or to develop an open innovation strategy. Indeed, the acquiring firm needs to know in detail what it plans to buy in order to identify how much it is willing to pay for it. However, once they have this knowledge, the firm no longer needs to pay for it.

In the absence of a corrective mechanism, this would drastically limit the possibilities of transferring inventions from a firm with the resources to develop them, but not to industrialize and commercialize them (typically a start-up) to a firm with fewer resources or agility to innovate, but more resources to industrialize and commercialize (typically a large firm). Intellectual property, and more specifically patents in the case of industrial inventions, solves the problem of difficulties both in the transfer of knowledge and its acquisition. The valuing of innovation thus often goes hand in hand with patents.

The issue of asymmetry of information in the transaction of an innovation can be resolved by the obligation to disclose the technical content of the invention in exchange for the exclusive right to the latter conferred by the patent. It is thus possible to make the innovation known to others, while protecting oneself from the risks of imitation. From this point of view, a patent offers a major advantage over other strategies for protecting innovation, such as secrecy. By favoring a "market of innovations", it allows the specialization of certain drivers of innovation. Similarly, it encourages the adoption of an open innovation strategy in which partners often need to know the contribution of others before committing themselves. Moreover, by conferring an exclusive right, even if only temporary, to the development of the patented invention, the patent secures income for its holder. Hence, in addition to the attention paid to estimating excess remuneration over marginal productivity of factors attributable to R&D efforts, work on the evaluation of innovations has often also sought to identify an "excess over excess" attributable to patents or to attribute the total effect to patents.

50.3. Methods for assessing the private value of innovations

By applying the macroeconomic analysis of the Solow residual to sectoral or microeconomic data, a long series of research has sought to estimate and then explain Total Factor Productivity (TFP) growth. The reader will find a fairly representative illustration in Griliches (1980). These works are generally based on a Cobb–Douglas specification of production function, which has the advantage that, in its log-linearized form, the coefficients of capital and labor correspond directly to the share of the added value, considering these factors under the assumption of remuneration at their marginal productivity. These shares are either set at their observed level or estimated in order to isolate the part of the growth rate of value added that is not explained by the growth of these two factors. This residual growth, referred to as the TFP growth rate, is then explained by the cumulative R&D expenditures used as a proxy for the stock of knowledge.

As detailed by Griliches (1988), among others, it is possible to infer from the latter relationship the rate of return on R&D investment. More precisely, since expenditures on researchers' salaries and laboratory equipment are already included in the measurement of labor and capital, what is thus estimated is the additional return on investment attributable to R&D activity. Griliches (1980) highlights considerable variations in this excess return, depending on the sector, ranging from 2% to 25% or more. His results are nevertheless in line with those of Mansfield *et al.*

(1977), one of the few surveys carried out to directly assess the value of the rate of return on investment in R&D.

An alternative approach to TFP analysis has been proposed. Known as Tobin's Q approach, it addresses the issue from a financial perspective rather than one of production function. According to this approach, the difficulties mentioned above in the mobilization of resources to generate innovation mean that the market value of an innovative firm will exceed its book value assimilated to its liquidation value. The difference in value is interpreted, here again, as the value of innovations. It is all the more marked because, as detailed by Baudry and Dumont (2017), accounting rules rarely allow R&D and patents to be capitalized on.

Tobin's Q approach, however, focuses on the ratio of the two values rather than on the difference between them and focuses on marginal rather than average values. Hall *et al.* (2005) present one of the most successful examples of Tobin's Q approach. Specifically, they introduce patent citations to take into account qualitative aspects in the measurement of the stock of knowledge. Moreover, Bloom & van Reenen (2002) compared the results obtained with Tobin's Q approach and those obtained with the TFP approach on the same data panel. They find that R&D expenditures and patents contribute more to explaining the higher value with Tobin's Q approach than with TFP. They explain this by showing that much of this excess is in fact an option value, i.e. the value of the opportunity acquired by the firm to exploit innovations in the future, rather than immediately. However, it is to Abel *et al.* (1996) that we owe the formalization of the link between this concept of option value and Tobin's Q theory.

The aforementioned work systematically confronts the difficulty of calculating the stock of knowledge as a major resource in the innovation process. The method generally used, both when the stock is approximated from the flow of R&D expenditure and when the flow of patents filed and/or granted is used for this approximation, is the so-called perpetual inventory method. However, its implementation requires knowledge of the rate of depreciation to be applied to these flows. Pakes & Schankerman (1984) and a series of subsequent works by these authors have provided an original answer to the measurement of this rate. They rely on the fact that, for most patent offices, a patent remains in force only if its holder pays renewal fees at certain time intervals. For many patents, however, these fees are no longer paid well before the maximum 20-year renewal term. Pakes & Schankerman (1984) showed how to calculate a rate of decline in patent income from renewal data. This rate of decline is then equated with the rate of depreciation of knowledge. Another advantage of Pakes & Schankerman's (1984) model is that it makes it possible to infer the value placed on patents by their holders from renewal behavior. However, this value is that of the legal protection conferred, but not necessarily of the patented invention in its entirety.

	Private value	Social value
Parametric approach to TFP	Excess value created compared to the pure and perfect competition framework	Excess value created compared to the pure and perfect competition framework + Value created by knowledge externalities or destroyed by crowding out effects
Non-parametric approach to TFP	Increase in value over time at given quantities of production factors (no reference to the competitive framework)	Increase in value over time at given quantities of production factors (no reference to the competitive framework) + Value created by knowledge externalities or destroyed by crowding out effects
Financial approach (Tobin's Q)	Excess value realized compared to the pure and perfect competition framework + Option value associated with future opportunities	

Table 50.1. *Summary of the different value concepts and valuation methods*

50.4. The social value of innovations

The evaluation of innovations cannot be reduced to their private value alone for two reasons. The first reason is that the gains from one innovation may come at the expense of another. An innovative firm takes market shares from its competitors, who thus see the value they create reduced. Based on their survey data, Mansfield *et al.* (1977) sought to take this effect into account. These same authors also corrected their evaluation of the social return on investment in R&D. The correction takes into account the fact that, without this investment, innovations would sometimes still have appeared, albeit later. The second reason is that there are positive externalities to the accumulation of knowledge. By moving from one employer to another, an engineer also transfers some of the tacit knowledge in which their original employer had invested. The return on investment thus goes beyond the firm's boundaries. The patent system also implies a diffusion of knowledge between firms through the necessity of disclosing patented content. The positive externalities thus implied could be evaluated by taking advantage of the networks of citations between patents and the technological proximity of the patenting firms (Jaffe 1986). They imply that governments must find the right balance in patenting between, on one hand, granting a large number of patents to ensure a wide dissemination of knowledge and, on the other, restricting the number of patents granted in order to limit the market power exercised to the detriment of users of the patented technology. This arbitration is not without consequences for the private value of innovations, which, as we have seen above, can be increased by obtaining a patent.

The social value of innovations is typically addressed by the TFP method, using macroeconomic data to assess the net effect of innovations by firms in the same country. The most recent developments improve the method in two respects: first, by considering more flexible representations of the macroeconomic production function, and second, by taking into account the fact that the dynamics of the TFP can result from the reduction of technical inefficiencies (which is achieved through parametric or non-parametric estimation of a production frontier). It is in this spirit that Färe *et al.* (1994) first evaluated the evolution of the TFP in several industrialized countries using a non-parametric approach to their production frontier. As summarized in Table 50.1, these techniques can also be applied at the microeconomic level.

50.5. Conclusion

The private value of an innovation results from the capacity it offers the innovator to extract themselves from the competitive pressure of the market and from the ability of institutional frameworks to secure the exchanges relating to this innovation, for example by using patents. The common denominator of the methods used to evaluate this value is therefore that they associate it with an excess of remuneration in relation to the competitive framework, whether this excess comes from immediate gains or the potential for future ones. Similarly, the increase in Total Factor Productivity at the macroeconomic level is largely associated with the social value of innovations. The latter is, however, characterized by the fact that it is exempt from negative crowding out effects induced by innovations and the positive effects of knowledge externalities among economic stakeholders. Whatever the approach, the social value of innovations depends closely on the approximation made of the stock of knowledge and its depreciation, an approximation for which relevant research has provided some original solutions.

50.6. References

Abel, A.B., Dixit, A.K., Eberly, J.C., Pindyck, R.S. (1996). Options, the value of capital, and investment. *Quarterly Journal of Economics*, 111(3), 753–777.

Baudry, M. and Dumont, B. (2017). *Patents: Prompting or Restricting Innovation?* ISTE Ltd, London and John Wiley & Sons, New York.

Bloom, N. and van Reenen, J. (2002). Patents, real options and firm performance. *Economic Journal*, 112, C97–C116.

Färe, R., Grosskopf, S., Norris, M., Zhang, Z. (1994). Productivity growth, technical progress, and efficiency change in industrialized countries. *American Economic Review*, 84(1), 66–83.

Griliches, Z. (1980). Returns to research and development expenditures in the private sector. In *New Developments in Productivity Analysis*, Kendrick, J.W. and Vaccara, N. (eds). University of Chicago Press, Chicago.

Griliches, Z. (1988). Productivity puzzles and R&D: Another nonexplanation. *Journal of Economic Perspectives*, 2(4), 9–21.

Hall, B.H., Jaffe, A., Trajtenberg, M. (2005). Market value and patent citations. *RAND Journal of Economics*, 36(1), 16–38.

Jaffe, A.B. (1986). Technological opportunity and spillovers of R&D: Evidence from firms' patent, profits, and market value. *American Economic Review*, 76(5), 984–1001.

Mansfield, E., Rapoport, J., Romeo, A., Wagner, S., Beardsley, G. (1977). Social and private rates of return from industrial innovations. *Quarterly Journal of Economics*, 91(2), 221–240.

Pakes, A. and Schankerman, M. (1984). The rate of obsolescence of patents, research gestation lags, and the private rate of return to research resources. In *R&D, Patents, and Productivity*, Griliches, Z. (ed.). University of Chicago Press, Chicago.

51

Work – Innovative Behavior at Work

51.1. Introduction

The aim of this chapter is to provide a state-of-the-art review of the work carried out on the concept of innovative behavior at work by an employee, i.e. at the individual level. To do this, we first define the concept of innovative behavior at work and indicate how it is measured. In a second step, we summarize the results of the main research conducted on this concept, i.e. on the determinants of innovative behavior at work. Finally, we conclude by identifying avenues for future research. At the individual level, these address the positive and negative consequences of innovative work behavior. At the collective level, they invite work on the concept of innovative behavior in a team.

51.2. Organizational innovation and work behavior

Organizational innovation is essential for organizational growth and sustainability (Janssen 2000). However, organizational innovation is not a "black box" but the result of the work of the people who make up the organization. The concept of individual innovation was initially seen as a characteristic of personality, then as the result of the high level of perceived discretion of people in skilled jobs. Today, individual innovation reflects behavior (Kanter 1988) in that it corresponds to a way of acting and reacting in a work situation. Innovation is translated into action: observable creative actions and actions relating to the implementation of an idea.

Chapter written by Audrey BECUWE.

Researchers in management and organizational behavior then proposed a concept at the individual level, namely the innovative behavior of the employee (Scott and Bruce 1994). Management researchers interested in innovative behavior at work have focused their attention on human behavior and processes rather than on the technical aspect of innovation. This attention to the human aspect of the process has led researchers to mobilize theories borrowed from psychology and sociology, to understand the factors that influence innovative work behavior at the individual level.

The employee who adopts an innovative behavior can be qualified as an innovator. It is a form of deviance known as positive deviance, with a desire for social transformation. Although Alter (2002) distinguishes several types of innovators (central innovators, specialized innovators, relay innovators, follower innovators), the archetype of the organizational innovator is nevertheless found in the figure of the intrapreneur. Among their distinctive qualities are an ability to identify problems and provide a response to them by combining heterogeneous elements, i.e. to "tinker", acting as a smuggler by transporting ideas from one world to another, and an ability to position oneself within networks (Guichard and Servel 2009). Beyond this figure of the innovator, employees are likely to be called upon to innovate by participating in creative communities within an organization. They do not necessarily possess the above-mentioned qualities, but will gradually adopt an innovative behavior from the collective and when the context – particularly emotional – is favorable.

According to Janssen, employees' innovative behavior at work is "the intentional creation, introduction and application of new ideas within a work role, group, or organization to benefit role performance, the group, or the organization" (2000, p. 288). According to Battistelli and Picci (2008), this behavior can pursue two types of objectives: work-related outcomes and personal outcomes. Work-related outcomes refer to performance of one's role, i.e. an improvement in the quantity or quality of individual performance, while personal outcomes refer to role adaptation, i.e. any positive emotional and/or cognitive evaluation related to oneself and resulting from work, such as self-esteem. From this perspective, Farr and Ford's (1990) motivational model of individual innovation emphasizes that in implementing a new initiative within their role, individuals take into account not only the results related to the task but also more personal results such as self-esteem (Battistelli and Picci 2008).

Innovative behavior by employees is not always a formal requirement of organizations and is not the subject of an explicit contract between employer and employee, which is why it is often described as discretionary or extra-role behavior.

In fact, these behaviors are often not valued by the organization's reward system (Janssen 2000).

Innovative behavior at work is a process that can be broken down into three stages: the production, promotion and realization of innovative ideas (Kanter 1988; Scott and Bruce 1994; Janssen 2000). The production of innovative ideas arises from the perception of work-related problems (Scott and Bruce 1994) as well as incongruities, discontinuities and emerging trends within the organization (Janssen 2000). Idea generation is linked to employee creativity. In this sense, creativity corresponds to a phase of innovative behavior. The second stage involves the promotion of these ideas to potential allies in the organization, through networking or coalition building with colleagues who support the innovative idea (Scott and Bruce 1994). The third stage, the realization of innovative ideas, consists of producing "a prototype or model of innovation that can be experimented with or applied by the employee in his or her work role, within a group or in a given organization" (Janssen 2000, p. 288). This third stage corresponds to the concept of intrapreneurship proposed by Pinchot in the 1970s. Intrapreneurship is a process that allows an employee to adopt entrepreneurial behaviors within his or her organization in order to develop new services, products, processes, etc. (Janssen 2000).

An employee's innovative behavior is therefore part of a social process that starts with the creativity of an individual or a group. What is more, these behaviors can be carried out in a discontinuous manner; the process is not linear (Scott and Bruce 1994) but can be described as iterative, disjunctive and cyclical. In other words, employees may contribute to distinct stages of the process and some back and forth between the different phases is possible.

The first scale for measuring innovative behavior of employees was proposed by Scott and Bruce (1994). The instrument is unidimensional and includes the three dimensions mentioned above: an employee's innovative behavior is assessed by his or her supervisor. It was not until the work of Janssen (2000) that a multidimensional scale based on the one proposed by Scott and Bruce (1994) was developed: the behavior is evaluated by the supervisor as well as self-evaluated by the employee. More recently, De Jong and Den Hartog (2010) developed four dimensions of innovative behavior. They distinguish between idea exploration and idea generation. Idea exploration corresponds to taking advantage of the appearance of an opportunity or a problem in order to suggest solutions or alternatives to improve products, processes or services. Idea generation results from combining and reorganizing existing information and concepts to solve problems or improve performance. The multidimensional nature of the scale seems relevant to De Jong and Den Hartog (2010) in that it better reflects the practice of innovative behavior in which each of the stages of this behavior is distinct from the others, and likely to have diverse determinants.

While there is no consensus in the scientific community on the number of steps involved in innovative behavior, work in social psychology as well as workplace psychology and in management has been developing for about 30 years. The latter have mainly focused on the determinants of innovative behavior at work and have been based within several theoretical frameworks.

51.3. Theoretical perspectives on work behavior

In their paper, Anderson *et al.* (2014) identify three main theoretical perspectives that have been mobilized by researchers on innovative work behavior:

– The component theory of creativity and innovation. The theory proposes an interactionist model of organizational creativity that describes the creative process and identifies the social and psychological components that allow an individual to be creative and, ultimately, an organization to innovate.

– Climate theory for innovation, or the four-factor model. The theory proposes four major factors for innovating within a team: perceived support for innovation, task orientation, participatory safety, and vision.

– Ambidextrous theory of innovation. According to this theory, the organization reconciles activities of exploration (the organization's ability to innovate) and exploitation of innovation (development and marketing of innovation) in order to manage contradictory demands for innovation at different levels of the organization.

Beyond the conceptual framework, researchers have recently turned their attention to the history and consequences of innovative behaviors at work (Anderson *et al.* 2014), calling for the design of new, more holistic research models. In this perspective, contextual and individual explanatory factors of innovative workplace behavior have been highlighted by researchers, as has the impact of innovative workplace behavior on employee performance.

Hammond *et al.* (2011) conducted a meta-analysis on the history behind innovative behavior at the individual level. The individual factors associated with innovative behavior are personality traits (openness to experience, proactivity), intrinsic motivation, self-efficacy (belief in one's ability to perform a particular task), organizational justice and job characteristics (role perceptions, autonomy and job complexity).

The impact of individual factors on innovative work behavior also depends on the work context. The work context includes factors related to the work team as well as those related to the organization. Contextual factors related to the work team include the structure and composition of the group (diversity of members), participation in decision-making, or the work climate. At organizational level, the determinants of innovative behavior at work include strategy, innovation climate and internal culture, as well as the external environment (uncertainty of the environment).

Research on the consequences of innovative behavior at work is becoming scarcer. Studies have highlighted the idea that innovative behavior at work is likely to generate conflict with co-workers who are more resistant to change. Moreover, innovative work behavior is associated with employees' stress reactions. It should be noted that the consequences of innovative work behavior have been only partially researched. However, as Battistelli and Picci (2008) point out, employees who innovate may fear losing control and are aware that they are likely to face disappointment from their colleagues and collaborators. In fact, studying and understanding the consequences of innovative behavior at work is a priority.

51.4. Conclusion

In summary, innovative behavior at work is a behavior desired by organizations but not always required or recognized. In this respect, it is an extra-role behavior, beyond the prescribed role. This behavior is a social process. Indeed, it is through interaction with colleagues at work that a person is likely to come up with an idea and it is often through support from colleagues that implementation of an idea is made possible.

In terms of methodology, studies of innovation behavior at the individual level have often identified three main stages in the innovation process. The first stage refers to the concept of creativity, the second has a political dimension in that it requires the identification of "allies", while the last refers to the concept of intrapreneurship. Researchers are currently mobilizing multidimensional scales. The measurement of innovative behavior at work can be objectivized by taking into account the evaluation of an employee's innovative behavior by other actors in a 360-degree evaluation perspective (e.g. by colleagues, customers and suppliers, etc.) to be completed by factual and numerical elements.

Much research on innovative workplace behavior has focused on the determinants of behavior. Two broad families of factors impact innovative workplace behavior: individual and contextual factors. The consequences of innovative workplace behavior have received little research attention. Whether they are positive consequences (such as task performance, employee well-being and meaningful work) or negative consequences (i.e. conflicts, stress, etc.), the consequences of innovative behavior at work have not been investigated. Future research would benefit from integrating innovative behavior at work, not only as a dependent variable but also as an independent variable.

Moreover, the social nature of the innovation process has not been sufficiently taken into account. The contributions of several employees, i.e. of a work collective, have been neglected for a long time. This is how the concept of innovative behavior at work, at team level, emerged and it requires further development.

51.5. References

Alter, N. (2002). *Entreprise : les innovateurs au quotidien*. Futuribles, Paris.

Anderson, N., Potocnik, K., Zhou, J. (2014). Innovation and creativity in organizations: A state-of-the-science review and prospective commentary. *Journal of Management*, 40(5), 1297–1333.

Battistelli, A. and Picci, P. (2008). Implication au travail, sentiment de compétence et engagement affectif ont-ils une influence négative sur le comportement d'innovation ? *AIPTFL* [Online]. Available at: https://www.coursum3.org/lufr-5-sciences-du-sujet-et-de-la-societe/?wpdf_download_file=/home/ichigo1vs/www8/wp-content/uploads/cours/UFR5/D%C3%A9partement%20de%20Psychologie/M2/2011-2012/Cours%20second%20semestre/PTO/Battistelli%20e%20Picci_C_0197%20(deleted%2048c56f0c-67a76-5be3f7dd).pdf.

De Jong, J.P.J. and Den Hartog, D.N. (2010). Measuring innovative work behaviour. *Creativity and Innovation Management*, 19(1), 23–36.

Farr, J.L. and Ford, C.M. (1990). Individual innovation. In *Innovation and Creativity at Work: Psychological and Organizational Strategies*, West, M.A. and Farr, J.L. (eds). John Wiley & Sons, Chichester.

Guichard, R. and Servel, L. (2006). Qui sont les innovateurs ? *Sociétal*, 3, 26–31.

Hammond, M.M., Neff, N.L., Farr, J.L., Schwall, A.R., Zhao, X. (2011). Predictors of individual level innovation at work: A meta-analysis. *Psychology of Aesthetics, Creativity, and the Arts*, 5(1), 90–105.

Janssen, O. (2000). Job demands, perceptions of effort-reward fairness and innovative behavior. *Journal of Occupational and Organizational Psychology*, 73, 287–302.

Kanter, R.M. (1988). When a thousand flowers bloom: Structural, collective, and social conditions for innovation in organization. *Research in Organizational Behavior*, 10, 169.

Scott, S.G. and Bruce, R.A. (1994). Determinants of innovative behavior: A path model of individual innovation in the workplace. *Academy of Management Journal*, 38, 1442–1465.

52

X-Innovation – The Polymorphism of Innovation

52.1. Introduction

In recent years, innovation has come to be known by many different qualifiers. According to Benoît Godin, who uses the term "X-Innovation", this multiplication of terms tends to call the hegemony of "technological innovation" into question (Godin 2020; Laperche 2020). In spite of the different forms of innovation already put forward by Schumpeter at the beginning of the 20th century, technological innovation has indeed been established as a symbol of progress and growth. According to Godin, the multiplication of terms reflects a phenomenon of appropriation of innovation in different circles, at the service of their own economic, political and social interests, as much as the anguish of novelty in academic disciplines, symbolized by "publish or perish" and the increase of the h-index. In any case, this Prévert-style glossary, whose main entries used in *Innovation Studies* are presented here, underlines the diversity of innovation, invites reflection on its processes and questions its impacts.

The terms used in this glossary highlight the current importance of *organizational forms* of innovation, which are the basis for the effectiveness of organizations in developing new services and products adapted to the needs of consumers, with the following qualifiers: agile, managerial, open, participatory, digital.

They highlight the potentially harmful impacts of technological innovation, introducing qualifiers to insist on the need to integrate the *objectives of sustainable development* in the reflection on innovation, both as a process and as a result: environmental (eco-innovation), responsible, social.

Chapter written by Blandine LAPERCHE.

They continue and refine long-standing reflections on the *competitive impact* of innovation, at the level of the firm's boundaries, sectors and product lifecycle. The older qualifiers are minor and radical, as well as disruptive, strategic, systemic and dual.

Finally, they make innovation a *global phenomenon*, not only initiated by and in industrial countries, but also in emerging and developing countries, and reveal the complexity of international transfer and exchange networks. Frugal (and jugaad) innovation and reverse innovation are classified here.

Innovation in all its meanings falls into the category of "cultural goods", analyzed by Fernand Braudel (Braudel 1995), marked by phenomena of assimilation and reinterpretation between civilizations, each of which "resembles a station of merchandise, which constantly receives and dispatches heterogeneous baggage". This diversity confirms the role of innovation, appreciated in a long historical dynamic, as a driver of change.

52.2. Terms

Agile innovation

Agility can be defined as an organization's ability to immerse itself within its ecosystem and involve all the entities that make up this technological, economic, societal and cultural environment. Agility consists of integrating flexibility in all the services of an organization and in its relations with the outside world. It concerns all the stages of the production process, from the design to the distribution of new goods and services. The objective is to adapt to the changing needs of demand and to respond to them specifically, by involving all stakeholders in this process. Agile innovation is deployed in an organization (small or large, private or public) and infiltrates all of its organs; it is thus reliant on interactions. It is a new state of mind, a new ability to adapt, innovate and interact in the shortest, most flexible and proactive way, because change cannot be improvised, and agility is built by taking the context, culture and understanding of one's community into account.

Digital innovation

Digital innovation refers to the digital transformation of companies, due to changes in the design, production and distribution of goods and services generated by digital advances: big data, open data, Internet of Things, digital learning, digital marketing, artificial intelligence, etc. The digital transition is infiltrating personal and professional daily life. New digital technologies are giving rise to new uses, innovative ways of communicating, working together and doing business. By reducing spatio-temporal barriers, companies are now rethinking their processes, operating methods and managerial practices. When digital technology is mastered, it enables them to respond effectively to needs while reducing development cycles. Opting for digital innovation is often the first episode of a digital transformation of the current state of affairs, through the development of a new product, service, process or business model, which allows the company to gain in connectivity, intelligence and agility while opening up to new areas of growth.

Dual innovation

Dual innovation is generated by industrial research or experimental development work focused on military, as well as civil applications. Some specific technologies find applications in both of these fields, due to their characteristics. This raises the question of the mechanisms of technology transfer from civilian to defense (spin-in), and from defense to civilian (spin-off). However, given that technology can be defined through all of the knowledge it is composed of, studying dual innovations means studying the diffusion of knowledge produced in the field of defense, and the similarities that may exist between this knowledge and that produced in the civilian sphere. Dual innovation does not only come from technology transfer; it is essentially due to the co-design of knowledge between civilian and military companies and institutions. The proximities in technological production between the civil and defense spheres play an essential role in the structuring of a dual innovation. Dual innovations are particularly observable in large product–services systems.

Environmental innovation (or eco-innovation)

Paraphrasing the OECD, this can be defined in the same way as an innovation, i.e. the implementation of a new or substantially improved product (good or service) or process, new marketing method or new organizational method in company practices, workplace organization or external relations. But two dimensions are added: it aims at reducing environmental impacts, and it also integrates the institutional and social structures that are indispensable for its implementation, in order to achieve this environmental objective. Environmental innovation is seen as the main tool of green growth, which could initiate a new cycle of activities, wealth and job creation. It can be implemented by a company (eco-design, eco-management, eco-products) and can be the driving force behind a territorial transformation, bringing together a community of actors around a circular economy project, for example. However, it comes up against possible rebound effects (shifting environmental impacts from one stage of the production process to another) and the effects of decoying, summarized by the term "greenwashing", which emphasizes the apparent strategies of innovation for environmental purposes, while hiding less virtuous practices.

Frugal innovation (and Jugaad)

These types of innovation have a reflection aimed at doing better with fewer resources in common; they are part of "resource-constrained" innovations. They most often rely on processes based on resourcefulness and do-it-yourself thinking and aim to develop simple, less expensive products, thus making them more accessible to low-income consumers. Originally developed in emerging countries, particularly in India where the term "Jugaad" originated, and also comparable to the D system of "Do It Yourself", these forms of resource-constrained innovation are also cultivated by multinational companies in their *reverse innovation* strategies. In this case, frugal innovation is analyzed as an engineering process that reduces the complexity and cost of a product without degrading its quality or image. When it is developed in industrial countries, frugal innovation is imbued with the objectives of sustainable development. It is also sometimes associated with *disruptive innovation*, particularly when the resulting, often low-cost products, challenge established barriers to market entry.

Managerial innovation

Managerial innovation is generally defined as a non-technological innovation, which involves the design and implementation of new practices, structures, processes and management techniques aimed at increasing the efficiency of the organization. It requires a transformation of behaviors and can lead to questioning the hierarchical relationships within the organization or redefining the roles of the actors, generally in favor of greater flexibility and collaboration. It can concern all the functions of the company (accounting and management control, marketing, human resources, design and production of goods and services, information systems, etc.). It gives a human and collective dimension to organizational innovation, by placing management and the acquisition of individual and collective skills at the heart of organizational transformation. For example, the implementation of *open innovation* in an organization requires new structures and new practices aimed at managing cooperation in the best possible way. It therefore requires and drives managerial innovations that unify teams around new projects developed by companies.

Minor (or incremental) innovation

As opposed to *radical innovation*, minor innovation is an enhancement of existing innovations. It is based on continuous improvement processes, and the term incremental is often used to describe it. Minor innovation makes it possible to extend the lifecycle of products whose fundamental characteristics remain the same, while at the same time encouraging the renewal of the product through new features. Minor innovation may concern technology (improvement of technical capabilities), as well as the addition of functionalities/services to an existing product, or a change in appearance (color, packaging, etc.). It can be used to enhance the attractiveness of a product, to reach new niches or market segments because of new features added or the new image given to the product or service, and to introduce technological advances to an existing product to improve its performance and durability. Minor innovation can be a tool to reduce the company's production costs and increase its profits.

Open innovation

Open innovation or collaborative innovation is an organizational practice that emphasizes the need for the company to build its knowledge capital by relying on both internal investments and collaborations with a diverse set of players (other competing companies, suppliers, start-ups, research labs, communities, the crowd). External information and knowledge is thus integrated into the internal knowledge stock through learning processes (outside-in). It also means that the valorization of this knowledge capital is not only carried out by the company itself in its own value creation process, but also through collaborations with other companies, for example through licensing agreements (inside-out). Both processes can be combined. Sometimes presented as the opposite of and successor to a closed model (rarely observed in reality), it has become a managerial norm, to accelerate the innovation process, while mutualizing costs and risks. However, its implementation can encounter difficulties, which result in transaction costs and risks regarding appropriation of intellectual assets. It also requires the alignment of partners' organizational routines and the creation of new collective routines.

Participatory innovation

Participatory innovation involves, as its name implies, the participation of employees, regardless of their function, in the technological, organizational and commercial innovation process of the company. As employees become transmitters of ideas, or even project leaders, participatory innovation decompartmentalizes innovation, not reserved for engineers and marketing managers, with the aim of reinforcing the agility of the organization. As a management approach, it requires the implementation of tools for listening and dialogue. These are digital platforms, internal challenges (hackathons), creative spaces such as fab-labs or coworking spaces. They lead to the recognition and enhancement of ideas from employees, whether they are individuals or organized internal communities.

Radical (and disruptive) innovation

When we talk about radical innovation, as well as about disruptive innovation, we are referring to the impacts caused by innovation. Reference is immediately made to the phenomenon of creative destruction, in which the old foundations of the economy are called into question in favor of new ones. At the sectoral level, radical innovation, as well as disruptive innovation, proposed by new market entrants, breaks down barriers to entry and calls established equilibriums into question. However, radical innovation and disruptive innovation are not synonymous. Indeed, historically, radical innovation has been associated with technological innovation, which primarily targets affluent consumers, capable of acquiring new and expensive technologies. As these technologies mature and are mass-produced, they become affordable and spread to all consumers. On the other hand, disruptive innovation, which is more simply designed and inexpensive – so much so that it is closer to *frugal innovation* – is primarily aimed at lower-income consumers, then moves up the range and challenges the power of established players, who have remained focused on the most demanding consumers.

Responsible innovation

Responsible innovation relates to how innovation is designed and carried out. In this sense, it implies that the impacts of innovation (social and environmental, the way in which it responds to major societal challenges such as the fight against climate change, food security, the development of inclusive societies, the maintenance of health and well-being) depend largely on the process by which it is generated. To be responsible, innovation must therefore involve stakeholders (researchers, innovators and wider society) who must interact and collaborate to ensure the ethical acceptability, sustainability and societal relevance of the innovation.

Reverse innovation

Reverse innovation challenges the traditional product design–production–distribution cycle, as defined in the 1960s. According to the latter, innovations designed in industrial countries are first diffused in those countries and then in other industrial countries. As they mature and imitation phenomena inevitably occur, their production is relocated to developed and then developing countries, which then become exporters. Reverse innovation thus reverses this process. It is an innovation first conceived in an emerging or developing country, to satisfy these markets characterized by growing demand, which is then disseminated and possibly improved in industrialized countries. Products designed in emerging countries may be developed by local companies (such as Tata's Nano in India), as well as by multinational companies attracted by markets and growth, the existence of technological capabilities and lower production costs (such as Renault's Kwid or General Electric's medical equipment). The resulting innovations fall into the category of resource-constrained innovations, just like *frugal innovation*, for example.

Social innovation

Social innovation is all the new responses to pressing social needs that are often unsatisfied or poorly met. It is based on interaction and cooperation between all the actors concerned, based in the public and private sectors and civil society. The reduction of unemployment, human development, social cohesion, reduction of inequalities, etc. are all issues that fuel social innovation and motivate its actors to promote more inclusive and sustainable growth. Often driven by social and solidarity economy actors, socially innovative projects aim to strengthen the well-being of a given population and a given territory, and may concern areas such as education, social action, health, culture or employment.

Strategic innovation

Strategic innovation is the core business of a company. The specific assets it contains (in terms of knowledge and know-how, in the fields of technology, organization or marketing) help define the boundaries of the company. The specific assets that make up the strategic innovation are indeed very often subject to strong protection and are internalized by the firm, unlike other less specific assets (or assets which have not yet become so), which can be the subject of *open innovation* strategies. Strategic innovation also determines the hierarchy within innovation networks. Its owners protect it individually or collectively (in the latter case through cross-licensing) and it allows the erection of barriers to entry that protect markets from potential new entrants. The latter then have no choice but to develop *radical* or *disruptive innovation* strategies if they wish to challenge established hierarchies.

Systemic innovation

Systemic innovation is born and spreads from a breakthrough innovation that stems from the sociotechnical system of innovation, which is itself “naturally” unstable. This innovation, by multiplying itself, through the interplay of actors, thanks to incremental intra- and inter-sectoral innovations, and also thanks to disruptive subsidiary, ancillary and related innovations, leads to the creation of new combinations of innovations, known as “systemic innovations” (product, process, organization, management or commercial innovations). In turn, systemic innovations (sets of innovations coming from new combinations made possible by the diffusion/adaptation of the disruptive innovation) again disrupt the sociotechnical system, whose robustness depends on the solidity of the routines it generates. Systemic innovation is largely due to the fact that the firm tends to make greater use of the resources of its environment (education, environment, health, finance, needs and aspirations, etc.) than to invest in all the phases of achieving the combination of knowledge, skills, ideas, technologies, capital, etc.; this can be explained by the fact that investments in the acquisition of production resources are less costly than those devoted to the production of these resources. The innovation networks that emerge in this way create routines that (a) place the socio-technical system on a “path of dependency” and (b) predefine the evolutionary trajectories of future systemic innovations.

52.3. References

Braudel, F. (1995). *A History of Civilizations*. Penguin, London.

Godin, B. (2020). *The Invention of Technological Innovation. Languages, Discourses and Ideology in Historical Perspectives*. Edward Elgar Publishing, Cheltenham.

Laperche, B. (2020). Technological innovation education and labor. *Journal of Innovation Economics & Management*, 33(3), 235–239.

List of Authors

Laurent ADATTO
CNAM
Paris
France

Camille AOUINAÏT
Production fruitière en région alpine
Agroscope
Switzerland

Raphaël BARY
ERPI Laboratory
University of Lorraine
France

Marc BAUDRY
EconomiX UMR 7235
and Climate Economics Chair
University of Paris Nanterre
France

Audrey BECUWE
CREOP EA-4332, CeReS
University of Limoges
France

Angelo BONOMI
IRCrES – Istituto di Ricerca sulla
Crescita Economica Sostenibile
Consiglio Nazionale delle Ricerche
Moncalieri
Italy

Sophie BOUTILLIER
ISI Laboratory RII
University of the Littoral Opal Coast
Dunkirk
France

Thierry BURGER-HELMCHEN
BETA–CNRS–INRAE
University of Strasbourg
France

Vanessa CASADELLA
CRIISEA Amiens
University of Picardie Jules Verne
France

Patrick COHENDET
Mosaic
HEC Montreal
Canada

Dominique DESJEUX
CEPED
University of Paris, Sorbonne SHS
France

Béatrice DUMONT
CEPN–CNRS and
Climate Economics Chair
Louis Bachelier Institute
University Sorbonne Paris Nord
France
and
The College of Europe
Bruges
Belgium

Sana ELOUAER-MRIZAK
ISI Laboratory RII
University of the Littoral Opal Coast
Dunkirk
France

Olivier ESNEU
University of Picardie Jules Verne
France

Joëlle FOREST
Chaire Saint Gobain
"Ingénieurs Ingénieux"
INSA Lyon
France

Delphine GALLAUD
CESAER
Agrosup Dijon
France

Stéphane GORIA
Centre de recherche sur les
médiations (CREM)
University of Lorraine
France

Pierre-Benoit JOLY
LISIS – Laboratoire Interdisciplinaire
Sciences Innovations Sociétés
Université Paris-Est Marne-la-Vallée
France

Fedoua KASMI
ERPI Laboratory
University of Lorraine
France

Sana KHAN
EDES Institute of Sustainable
Business and Organizations
ESDES Lyon Business School
The Catholic University of Lyon
France

Blandine LAPERCHE
ISI Laboratory RII
University of the Littoral Opal Coast
Dunkirk
France

Michael E. LAVIOLETTE
TBS Research Centre
TBS Business School
Federal University of Toulouse
France

Christian LE BAS
EDES Institute of Sustainable
Business and Organizations
ESDES Lyon Business School
The Catholic University of Lyon
France

Marcos LIMA
Skema Business School
Université Côte D'Azur
Nice
France

Céline MERLIN-BROGNIART
CLERSE
University of Lille
France

Thomas MICHAUD
Independent researcher
France

Laure MOREL
ERPI Laboratory
University of Lorraine
France

Paul MULLER
Bureau d'économie théorique
et appliquée
CNRS
University of Lorraine/University
of Strasbourg
France

Babacar NDIAYE
Laboratory of Applied Economics
and Modeling
Amadou Mahtar Mbow University
of Dakar
Senegal

Florin PAUN
Agilising Innovation
France

Cédric PERRIN
IDHE.S-Evry
University of Évry-Val d'Essonne
France

Elisa SALVADOR
ESSCA School of Management
Paris
France

Francesco SCHIAVONE
DISAQ
Università degli Studi di Napoli
Parthenope
Naples
Italy

Béatrice SIADOU-MARTIN
CEREFIGE – Centre Européen de
Recherche en Economie Financière et
en Gestion des Entreprises
University of Lorraine
France

Bérangère L. SZOSTAK
Bureau d'économie théorique
et appliquée
CNRS
University of Lorraine
France

Damien TALBOT
CleRMa
IAE Clermont Auvergne
University of Clermont Auvergne
Clermont-Ferrand
France

Ludovic TEMPLE
INNOVATION, CIRAD, INRAE,
Institut Agro
University of Montpellier
France

Leïla TEMRI
UMR MOISA
Institut Agro – Montpellier SupAgro
France

Slim THABET
CRIISEA Amiens
University of Picardie Jules Verne
France

Cheikh Abdou Lahad THIAW
GREDEG CNRS
University of Nice Sophia Antipolis
Nice
France
and
École supérieure polytechnique
Cheikh Anta Diop University
Dakar
Senegal

Dimitri UZUNIDIS
ISI Laboratory RII
University of the Littoral Opal Coast
Dunkirk
France
and
Technical University of Crete
Greece

Michel VIGEZZI
University of Grenoble-Alpes
France

Giovanni ZAZZERINI
INSME – The International Network
for SMEs
Rome
Italy

Index

D, E, F

G, H, I

K, L, M

N, O, P

R, S

T, V

Summary of Volume 2

Other titles from

iSTE

in

Innovation, Entrepreneurship and Management

2021

BOBILLIER CHAUMON Marc-Eric
Digital Transformations in the Challenge of Activity and Work: Understanding and Supporting Technological Changes
(Technological Changes and Human Resources Set – Volume 3)

2020

ACH Yves-Alain, RMADI-SAÏD Sandra
Financial Information and Brand Value: Reflections, Challenges and Limitations

ANDREOSSO-O'CALLAGHAN Bernadette, DZEVER Sam, JAUSSAUD Jacques, TAYLOR Robert
Sustainable Development and Energy Transition in Europe and Asia
(Innovation and Technology Set – Volume 9)

BEN SLIMANE Sonia, M'HENNI Hatem
Entrepreneurship and Development: Realities and Future Prospects
(Smart Innovation Set – Volume 30)

CHOUTEAU Marianne, FOREST Joëlle, NGUYEN Céline
Innovation for Society: The P.S.I. Approach
(Smart Innovation Set – Volume 28)

CORON Clotilde
Quantifying Human Resources: Uses and Analysis
(Technological Changes and Human Resources Set – Volume 2)

CORON Clotilde, GILBERT Patrick
Technological Change
(Technological Changes and Human Resources Set – Volume 1)

CERDIN Jean-Luc, PERETTI Jean-Marie
The Success of Apprenticeships: Views of Stakeholders on Training and Learning
(Human Resources Management Set – Volume 3)

DELCHET-COCHET Karen
Circular Economy: From Waste Reduction to Value Creation
(Economic Growth Set – Volume 2)

DIDAY Edwin, GUAN Rong, SAPORTA Gilbert, WANG Huiwen
Advances in Data Science
(Big Data, Artificial Intelligence and Data Analysis Set – Volume 4)

DOS SANTOS PAULINO Victor
Innovation Trends in the Space Industry
(Smart Innovation Set – Volume 25)

GASMI Nacer
Corporate Innovation Strategies: Corporate Social Responsibility and Shared Value Creation
(Smart Innovation Set – Volume 33)

GOGLIN Christian
Emotions and Values in Equity Crowdfunding Investment Choices 1: Transdisciplinary Theoretical Approach

GUILHON Bernard
Venture Capital and the Financing of Innovation
(Innovation Between Risk and Reward Set – Volume 6)

LATOUCHE Pascal
Open Innovation: Human Set-up
(Innovation and Technology Set – Volume 10)

LIMA Marcos
Entrepreneurship and Innovation Education: Frameworks and Tools
(Smart Innovation Set – Volume 32)

MACHADO Carolina, DAVIM J. Paulo
Sustainable Management for Managers and Engineers

MAKRIDES Andreas, KARAGRIGORIOU Alex, SKIADAS Christos H.
Data Analysis and Applications 3: Computational, Classification, Financial, Statistical and Stochastic Methods
(Big Data, Artificial Intelligence and Data Analysis Set – Volume 5)
Data Analysis and Applications 4: Financial Data Analysis and Methods
(Big Data, Artificial Intelligence and Data Analysis Set – Volume 6)

MASSOTTE Pierre, CORSI Patrick
Complex Decision-Making in Economy and Finance

MEUNIER François-Xavier
Dual Innovation Systems: Concepts, Tools and Methods
(Smart Innovation Set – Volume 31)

MICHAUD Thomas
Science Fiction and Innovation Design (Innovation in Engineering and Technology Set – Volume 6)

MONINO Jean-Louis
Data Control: Major Challenge for the Digital Society
(Smart Innovation Set – Volume 29)

MORLAT Clément
Sustainable Productive System: Eco-development versus Sustainable Development
(Smart Innovation Set – Volume 26)

SAULAIS Pierre, ERMINE Jean-Louis
Knowledge Management in Innovative Companies 2: Understanding and Deploying a KM Plan within a Learning Organization
(Smart Innovation Set – Volume 27)

2019

AMENDOLA Mario, GAFFARD Jean-Luc
Disorder and Public Concern Around Globalization

BARBAROUX Pierre
Disruptive Technology and Defence Innovation Ecosystems
(Innovation in Engineering and Technology Set – Volume 5)

DOU Henri, JUILLET Alain, CLERC Philippe
Strategic Intelligence for the Future 1: A New Strategic and Operational Approach
Strategic Intelligence for the Future 2: A New Information Function Approach

FRIKHA Azza
Measurement in Marketing: Operationalization of Latent Constructs

FRIMOUSSE Soufyane
Innovation and Agility in the Digital Age
(Human Resources Management Set – Volume 2)

GAY Claudine, SZOSTAK Bérangère L.
Innovation and Creativity in SMEs: Challenges, Evolutions and Prospects
(Smart Innovation Set – Volume 21)

GORIA Stéphane, HUMBERT Pierre, ROUSSEL Benoît
Information, Knowledge and Agile Creativity
(Smart Innovation Set – Volume 22)

HELLER David
Investment Decision-making Using Optional Models
(Economic Growth Set – Volume 2)

HELLER David, DE CHADIRAC Sylvain, HALAOUI Lana, JOUVET Camille
The Emergence of Start-ups
(Economic Growth Set – Volume 1)

HÉRAUD Jean-Alain, KERR Fiona, BURGER-HELMCHEN Thierry
Creative Management of Complex Systems
(Smart Innovation Set – Volume 19)

LATOUCHE Pascal
Open Innovation: Corporate Incubator
(Innovation and Technology Set – Volume 7)

LEHMANN Paul-Jacques
The Future of the Euro Currency

LEIGNEL Jean-Louis, MÉNAGER Emmanuel, YABLONSKY Serge
Sustainable Enterprise Performance: A Comprehensive Evaluation Method

LIÈVRE Pascal, AUBRY Monique, GAREL Gilles
Management of Extreme Situations: From Polar Expeditions to Exploration-Oriented Organizations

MILLOT Michel
Embarrassment of Product Choices 2: Towards a Society of Well-being

N'GOALA Gilles, PEZ-PÉRARD Virginie, PRIM-ALLAZ Isabelle
Augmented Customer Strategy: CRM in the Digital Age

NIKOLOVA Blagovesta
The RRI Challenge: Responsibilization in a State of Tension with Market Regulation
(Innovation and Responsibility Set – Volume 3)

PELLEGRIN-BOUCHER Estelle, ROY Pierre
Innovation in the Cultural and Creative Industries
(Innovation and Technology Set – Volume 8)

PRIOLON Joël
Financial Markets for Commodities

QUINIOU Matthieu
Blockchain: The Advent of Disintermediation

RAVIX Joël-Thomas, DESCHAMPS Marc
Innovation and Industrial Policies
(Innovation between Risk and Reward Set – Volume 5)

ROGER Alain, VINOT Didier
Skills Management: New Applications, New Questions
(Human Resources Management Set – Volume 1)

SAULAIS Pierre, ERMINE Jean-Louis
Knowledge Management in Innovative Companies 1: Understanding and Deploying a KM Plan within a Learning Organization
(Smart Innovation Set – Volume 23)

SERVAJEAN-HILST Romaric
Co-innovation Dynamics: The Management of Client-Supplier Interactions for Open Innovation
(Smart Innovation Set – Volume 20)

SKIADAS Christos H., BOZEMAN James R.
Data Analysis and Applications 1: Clustering and Regression, Modeling-estimating, Forecasting and Data Mining
(Big Data, Artificial Intelligence and Data Analysis Set – Volume 2)
Data Analysis and Applications 2: Utilization of Results in Europe and Other Topics
(Big Data, Artificial Intelligence and Data Analysis Set – Volume 3)

UZUNIDIS Dimitri
Systemic Innovation: Entrepreneurial Strategies and Market Dynamics

VIGEZZI Michel
World Industrialization: Shared Inventions, Competitive Innovations and Social Dynamics
(Smart Innovation Set – Volume 24)

2018

BURKHARDT Kirsten
Private Equity Firms: Their Role in the Formation of Strategic Alliances

CALLENS Stéphane
Creative Globalization
(Smart Innovation Set – Volume 16)

CASADELLA Vanessa
Innovation Systems in Emerging Economies: MINT – Mexico, Indonesia, Nigeria, Turkey
(Smart Innovation Set – Volume 18)

CHOUTEAU Marianne, FOREST Joëlle, NGUYEN Céline
Science, Technology and Innovation Culture
(Innovation in Engineering and Technology Set – Volume 3)

CORLOSQUET-HABART Marine, JANSSEN Jacques
Big Data for Insurance Companies
(Big Data, Artificial Intelligence and Data Analysis Set – Volume 1)

CROS Françoise
Innovation and Society
(Smart Innovation Set – Volume 15)

DEBREF Romain
Environmental Innovation and Ecodesign: Certainties and Controversies
(Smart Innovation Set – Volume 17)

DOMINGUEZ Noémie
SME Internationalization Strategies: Innovation to Conquer New Markets

ERMINE Jean-Louis
Knowledge Management: The Creative Loop
(Innovation and Technology Set – Volume 5)

GILBERT Patrick, BOBADILLA Natalia, GASTALDI Lise,
LE BOULAIRE Martine, LELEBINA Olga
Innovation, Research and Development Management

IBRAHIMI Mohammed
Mergers & Acquisitions: Theory, Strategy, Finance

LEMAÎTRE Denis
Training Engineers for Innovation

LÉVY Aldo, BEN BOUHENI Faten, AMMI Chantal
Financial Management: USGAAP and IFRS Standards
(Innovation and Technology Set – Volume 6)

MILLOT Michel
Embarrassment of Product Choices 1: How to Consume Differently

PANSERA Mario, OWEN Richard
Innovation and Development: The Politics at the Bottom of the Pyramid
(Innovation and Responsibility Set – Volume 2)

RICHEZ Yves
Corporate Talent Detection and Development

SACHETTI Philippe, ZUPPINGER Thibaud
New Technologies and Branding
(Innovation and Technology Set – Volume 4)

SAMIER Henri
Intuition, Creativity, Innovation

TEMPLE Ludovic, COMPAORÉ SAWADOGO Eveline M.F.W.
Innovation Processes in Agro-Ecological Transitions in Developing Countries
(Innovation in Engineering and Technology Set – Volume 2)

UZUNIDIS Dimitri
Collective Innovation Processes: Principles and Practices
(Innovation in Engineering and Technology Set – Volume 4)

VAN HOOREBEKE Delphine
The Management of Living Beings or Emo-management

2017

AÏT-EL-HADJ Smaïl
The Ongoing Technological System
(Smart Innovation Set – Volume 11)

BAUDRY Marc, DUMONT Béatrice
Patents: Prompting or Restricting Innovation?
(Smart Innovation Set – Volume 12)

BÉRARD Céline, TEYSSIER Christine
Risk Management: Lever for SME Development and Stakeholder Value Creation

CHALENÇON Ludivine
Location Strategies and Value Creation of International Mergers and Acquisitions

CHAUVEL Danièle, BORZILLO Stefano
The Innovative Company: An Ill-defined Object
(Innovation between Risk and Reward Set – Volume 1)

CORSI Patrick
Going Past Limits To Growth

D'ANDRIA Aude, GABARRET Inés
Building 21st Century Entrepreneurship
(Innovation and Technology Set – Volume 2)

DAIDJ Nabyla
Cooperation, Coopetition and Innovation
(Innovation and Technology Set – Volume 3)

FERNEZ-WALCH Sandrine
The Multiple Facets of Innovation Project Management
(Innovation between Risk and Reward Set – Volume 4)

FOREST Joëlle
Creative Rationality and Innovation
(Smart Innovation Set – Volume 14)

GUILHON Bernard
Innovation and Production Ecosystems
(Innovation between Risk and Reward Set – Volume 2)

HAMMOUDI Abdelhakim, DAIDJ Nabyla
Game Theory Approach to Managerial Strategies and Value Creation
(Diverse and Global Perspectives on Value Creation Set – Volume 3)

LALLEMENT Rémi
Intellectual Property and Innovation Protection: New Practices and New Policy Issues
(Innovation between Risk and Reward Set – Volume 3)

LAPERCHE Blandine
Enterprise Knowledge Capital
(Smart Innovation Set – Volume 13)

LEBERT Didier, EL YOUNSI Hafida
International Specialization Dynamics
(Smart Innovation Set – Volume 9)

MAESSCHALCK Marc
Reflexive Governance for Research and Innovative Knowledge
(Responsible Research and Innovation Set – Volume 6)

MASSOTTE Pierre
Ethics in Social Networking and Business 1: Theory, Practice and Current Recommendations
Ethics in Social Networking and Business 2: The Future and Changing Paradigms

MASSOTTE Pierre, CORSI Patrick
Smart Decisions in Complex Systems

MEDINA Mercedes, HERRERO Mónica, URGELLÉS Alicia
Current and Emerging Issues in the Audiovisual Industry
(Diverse and Global Perspectives on Value Creation Set – Volume 1)

MICHAUD Thomas
Innovation, Between Science and Science Fiction
(Smart Innovation Set – Volume 10)

PELLÉ Sophie
Business, Innovation and Responsibility
(Responsible Research and Innovation Set – Volume 7)

SAVIGNAC Emmanuelle
The Gamification of Work: The Use of Games in the Workplace

SUGAHARA Satoshi, DAIDJ Nabyla, USHIO Sumitaka
Value Creation in Management Accounting and Strategic Management: An Integrated Approach
(Diverse and Global Perspectives on Value Creation Set –Volume 2)

UZUNIDIS Dimitri, SAULAIS Pierre
Innovation Engines: Entrepreneurs and Enterprises in a Turbulent World
(Innovation in Engineering and Technology Set – Volume 1)

2016

BARBAROUX Pierre, ATTOUR Amel, SCHENK Eric
Knowledge Management and Innovation
(Smart Innovation Set – Volume 6)

BEN BOUHENI Faten, AMMI Chantal, LEVY Aldo
Banking Governance, Performance And Risk-Taking: Conventional Banks Vs Islamic Banks

BOUTILLIER Sophie, CARRÉ Denis, LEVRATTO Nadine
Entrepreneurial Ecosystems (Smart Innovation Set – Volume 2)

BOUTILLIER Sophie, UZUNIDIS Dimitri
The Entrepreneur (Smart Innovation Set – Volume 8)

BOUVARD Patricia, SUZANNE Hervé
Collective Intelligence Development in Business

GALLAUD Delphine, LAPERCHE Blandine
Circular Economy, Industrial Ecology and Short Supply Chains
(Smart Innovation Set – Volume 4)

GUERRIER Claudine
Security and Privacy in the Digital Era
(Innovation and Technology Set – Volume 1)

MEGHOUAR Hicham
Corporate Takeover Targets

MONINO Jean-Louis, SEDKAOUI Soraya
Big Data, Open Data and Data Development
(Smart Innovation Set – Volume 3)

MOREL Laure, LE ROUX Serge
Fab Labs: Innovative User
(Smart Innovation Set – Volume 5)

PICARD Fabienne, TANGUY Corinne
Innovations and Techno-ecological Transition
(Smart Innovation Set – Volume 7)

2015

CASADELLA Vanessa, LIU Zeting, DIMITRI Uzunidis
Innovation Capabilities and Economic Development in Open Economies
(Smart Innovation Set – Volume 1)

CORSI Patrick, MORIN Dominique
Sequencing Apple's DNA

CORSI Patrick, NEAU Erwan
Innovation Capability Maturity Model

FAIVRE-TAVIGNOT Bénédicte
Social Business and Base of the Pyramid

GODÉ Cécile
Team Coordination in Extreme Environments

MAILLARD Pierre
Competitive Quality and Innovation

MASSOTTE Pierre, CORSI Patrick
Operationalizing Sustainability

MASSOTTE Pierre, CORSI Patrick
Sustainability Calling

2014

DUBÉ Jean, LEGROS Diègo
Spatial Econometrics Using Microdata

LESCA Humbert, LESCA Nicolas
Strategic Decisions and Weak Signals

2013

HABART-CORLOSQUET Marine, JANSSEN Jacques, MANCA Raimondo
VaR Methodology for Non-Gaussian Finance

2012

DAL PONT Jean-Pierre
Process Engineering and Industrial Management

MAILLARD Pierre
Competitive Quality Strategies

POMEROL Jean-Charles
Decision-Making and Action

SZYLAR Christian
UCITS Handbook

2011

LESCA Nicolas
Environmental Scanning and Sustainable Development

LESCA Nicolas, LESCA Humbert
Weak Signals for Strategic Intelligence: Anticipation Tool for Managers

MERCIER-LAURENT Eunika
Innovation Ecosystems

2010

SZYLAR Christian
Risk Management under UCITS III/IV

2009

COHEN Corine
Business Intelligence

ZANINETTI Jean-Marc
Sustainable Development in the USA

2008

CORSI Patrick, DULIEU Mike
The Marketing of Technology Intensive Products and Services

DZEVER Sam, JAUSSAUD Jacques, ANDREOSSO Bernadette
Evolving Corporate Structures and Cultures in Asia: Impact of Globalization

2007

AMMI Chantal
Global Consumer Behavior

2006

BOUGHZALA Imed, ERMINE Jean-Louis
Trends in Enterprise Knowledge Management

CORSI Patrick *et al.*
Innovation Engineering: the Power of Intangible Networks